AT THE BOTTOM OF
THE GARDEN

DIANE PURKISS

AT THE BOTTOM OF THE GARDEN

A Dark History of Fairies, Hobgoblins, and Other
Troublesome Things

NEW YORK UNIVERSITY PRESS
Washington Square, New York

First published in Great Britain by
Allen Lane The Penguin Press 2000
First published in the U.S.A. in 2001 by
New York University Press
Washington Square
New York, NY 10003

Set in 10.5/14 pt Postscript Linotype Sabon
Typeset by Rowland Phototypesetting Ltd, Bury St Edmunds, Suffolk
Printed and bound in Great Britain by The Bath Press Ltd, Bath
Cover repro and printing by Concise Cover Printers

CIP data available from the Library of Congress

ISBN 0-8147-6683-8

For Michael and Hermione,
and for Tessa, whom we never had a chance to know

Contents

List of Illustrations

Photographic acknowledgements
are given in parentheses

1. Athene with snakes, shield, swastikas and gorgon's head. Attic red-figure amphora by the Andokides painter, *c.* 525 BC. Antikensammlung, Berlin. (Photo: BPK/Staatliche Museen zu Berlin Preußischer Kulturbesitz)

2. Nereid on Ketos. Relief from the lid of a silver pyxis found at Canosa di Puglia, *c.* 130 BC. Museo Nazionale, Taranto. (Photo: Bridgeman Art Library)

3. Lilith (Inanna-Ishtar). Terracotta relief from Mesopotamia, Larsa period, *c.* 2000 BC. (Photo: The Art Archive/Christie's/Eileen Tweedy)

4. Odysseus and the Sirens. Athenian red-figure stamnos vase by the Siren Painter, *c.* 490 BC. British Museum, London. (Photo: Bridgeman Art Library)

5. 'How Melusine escaped by flying out of the window in the form of a serpent.' Woodcut from *Melusine* by Jean d'Arras, Lyon, *c.* 1500. (Photo: Mary Evans Picture Library)

6. 'How Melusine returned to Lusignan every night to meet her two children.' Woodcut from *Melusine* by Jean d'Arras, Lyon, *c.* 1500. (Photo: Mary Evans Picture Library)

7. The Lady of the Lake Meeting Guinevere. Illumination on vellum from *The Story of Sir Lancelot*, French School, fourteenth century [Ms Fr. 120]. Bibliothèque Nationale, Paris. (Photo: Bridgeman Art Library)

8. Fairy-witches dancing in a ring. Woodcut from an undated English chapbook. (Photo: Fortean Picture Library)

9. Fairy ring. Woodcut from *Historia de Gentibus Septentrionalibus* by Olaus Magnus, Antwerp, 1558. (Photo: Fortean Picture Library)

10. Ann Jeffries with the fairies who helped her to perform healing cures in 1645. Illustration from *Legends and Miracles and Other Curious Stories of Human Nature* by J. E. Smith, 1837. (Photo: Mary Evans Picture Library)

11. *Robin Goodfellow.* Woodcut by English School, sixteenth century. Private Collection. (Photo: Bridgeman Art Library/Fotomas Index)

Acknowledgements

This book is an imperfect and limping creature. Some fairies will be very offended at not finding their names here, but I can only plead weakly that fairyland became so overcrowded that it was simply not possible to mention them all. I do not pretend to include all, so no exclusions should seem hurtful. Likewise these acknowledgements, which none the less register as fully as I can the truth that this book would never have materialized at all if it had not been for the efforts of a lot of people, most of whom fairy glamour may cause me to forget. If I have failed to invite anyone to the christening of this book, I hope they will not be too offended.

When I made it known that I was working on fairies, pictures, references and good spells began arriving by almost every post. More good things flew on the invisible wings of e-mail from people in Australia to the Rocky Mountains. Sparkling wands of expertise were waved over my first stumbling attempts at storytelling by attentive audiences in New Zealand, Oxford, Reading, Swansea, Washington, Hull and San Francisco.

Among the Beerbohm Treeish throngs of helpers, I must nevertheless single out the following, who provided prodding questions, crucial information and equally crucial kindnesses: Robin Briggs, Julia Briggs, Miranda Chaytor, Marion Gibson, the late and very sadly missed Gareth Roberts, Annabel Gregory, Kate McLuskie, Ralph Hanna, Kellie Matthews-Simon, Dianora, Nicola Bown, Juliette Wood, Carolyn Oates, Angelique Richardson, Margot Louis, Elizabeth Heale, David Wootton, Mary Phillips, Stuart Clark, Elizabeth Clarke, Danielle Clarke, Gail Kern Paster, Pippa Berry, Carolyne Larrington, everyone at girlsown, Sharon Achinstein and David Norbrook, Frances

xi

Boyle and her children Clare and Leo Hennessy, Clare Brant and Ewen Green, and my parents Phillip and Fay Purkiss. My agent Caroline Davidson and her assistants, my editor at Penguin Margaret Bluman and my copy-editor Monica Schmoller disproved any lingering notion that fairies and the forces of commerce should have nothing to do with each other, by their sensitive attention to what I was trying to do. The British Academy (now the Arts and Humanities Research Council) and the University of Exeter showered some fairy gold on this project in the form of paid research leave. Cecilia Mackay found beautiful images. My husband Ivan Dowling, as usual, did everything possible to help: no fairy he, but perhaps an angel. My son Michael lent me fairy books, accompanied me to performances of *Peter Pan*, and he and his baby sister Hermione daily reminded me of the joyful gulf between living children and story children. This book is dedicated to them, and to Tessa, the daughter we never had the chance to know.

And I'm not going to thank a single one of them, in case they take the thanks and go away and I never see any of them again.

Introduction: Fear of Fairies

It was almost dark on a winter evening in Oxford when I first caught the fascination of fairies. I had always thought of fairies as dull, too pretty to be interesting. But suddenly I found myself reading about a fairy that wasn't pretty at all. He was Yallery Brown, a sprite from the Fen Country of Eastern England, and he was inexorably, mindlessly cruel. He was found by a farmhand who heard a soft weeping sound, like a child crying. The man was a kindly soul, and he searched for the child, to comfort it. What he found, when he overturned a rock, was a little withered thing with bright dark eyes and a cloud of long yellow hair. The little thing made him a promise: to stay with him for ever and to help him with his work, as long as he was never thanked. So far, not so bad. But Yallery Brown's help turned out to be no help at all. Everyone avoided the farmhand because they could see his work being done for him by invisible hands. Things went from bad to worse, until one day the poor farmhand thanked his helper in a despairing effort to get rid of him. From then on Yallery Brown spoiled everything he did, and haunted him day and night, crying out, 'Loss and mischance and Yallery Brown/ You've let out yourself from under a stone.' The farmhand died friendless and destitute, with that voice ringing in his ears.

As I stared out into the gathering darkness, I tried to think about why what I had just read seemed so shocking. The misery of the story seemed to rise from the dark wood of the oak desk in front of me; it smelt of the past, a past when little lights strove in vain to pierce the great fetid darkness of the Fens. The farmhand had been kind and helpful; in fairy tales, that is supposed to be rewarded. Instead, he was brutally punished. And fairies were supposed to grant wishes, weren't they? My own mother had told me that she had once read a story of a wishing fairy who appeared whenever you pulled up a bluebell; she had gone around denuding the landscape of bluebells ever afterwards. Yet Yallery Brown had granted a wish cruelly, like some local incarnation of Delphic Apollo, making you wish you had never wished, taking from you your dearest things under the guise of giving you what you wanted. Above all, Yallery Brown was almost believable, unlike the pretty fairies I thought I knew. I felt a shiver down my spine, proof of a kind of authenticity.

As I walked home that night, Oxford's spires were a cold fairy forest, its minarets those of an elven palace. It was as if the city had been built for someone other than the leaden mortals inhabiting it. I thought about courtly fairies, the fairies of romance who could talk to kings, the fairies with whom Elizabeth I had been compared, that cold Queen of England looking in the glass. I thought, too, about Hans Christian Andersen's Snow Queen, the cruel enchantress who loves Little Kay because he has a splinter of ice at his heart. Those dreaming spires were the icicles of her arctic palace, where no mortal could live in the terrible cold unless his heart became a lump of ice. In that black frost, Little Kay sits desperately working on mathematical formulae, unable to feel anything except the abstract beauty of numbers. It was hard to avoid the idea that Oxford was the Snow Queen's palace sprung to life. And yet, was this all illusion, paranoid fantasy even? Who could believe in a fairy city? In artificial light, Oxford has a pasteboard quality. It looks like a painted flat, a stage-set for an exotic and archaic pantomime. I thought of panto fairies, transformation scenes, glittering troupes of dancing fairies, just little girls wearing sequins and makeup, yes, but dancing out a common dream. Even the plain commonsense Co-op Supermarket was full of fairies that night, crude images of plump, winged figures on bottles of Fairy Liquid and tubs of Fairy Margarine. What kind of concept could embrace my mother's Good Fairy Bluebell and Yallery Brown, Elizabeth I and Fairy Margarine? What kind of people could believe in any or all of them, and why? Why do we need fairies so badly?

In trying to answer these questions, I read hundreds of stories about fairies, and I unearthed a rich and exciting seam of story that ranged from the nursery terrors of ancient Athens to accounts of alien abductions. I was bewildered by the sheer variety of human imaginings, and fascinated by the longevity of the preoccupation with fairies. Yet hardly anyone seemed to believe in them, not even me. As a child I once disgraced myself at a performance of James Barrie's play *Peter Pan*. There is a point in the play where the fairy Tinker Bell is dying, having saved Peter by drinking poison meant for him. Peter, frantic to save her, invites all the children in the audience to comfort her by clapping their hands to show they believe in fairies. I refused to clap, feeling uneasy and coerced, and wanting to be the kind of super-cool child for whom fairies were invariably stupid and silly, the kind of daughter my mother wanted me to be.

Yet part of me yearned secretly for frills, pink tulle, lace, wings and a wand. At times, fairies seemed to stand for a luxuriant, seductive ultra-pink feminine power to which my mother meanly denied me access. No one ever let me have a fairy costume; they were vulgar, low. Today one sees middle-class mothers and children in toy stores, tussling over frilly fairy skirts. Surprisingly, it is often the daughter who wants to wear the fairy costume and the post-feminist mother who would be more comfortable with a tomboy in pirate costume. These changeling daughters want to inhabit the fairy vision of pure, unadulterated femininity, recognizing its power to fascinate. When we say we don't believe in fairies, we are sometimes saying that we don't believe little girls are – girly. Even the most grossly commercial fairy is an aspiration, a wish breathed out. A wish that may turn out to be the wrong one.

Given how incredible fairies seem to most of us, where do fairy beliefs come from in the first place? Human nature seems to abhor a blank space on a map. Where there are no human habitations, no towns, where villages dwindle into farms and farms into woods, mapping stops. Then the imagination rushes to fill the woods with something other than blank darkness: nymphs, satyrs, elves, gnomes, pixies, fairies. Now that we have mapped every inch of our own planet, our remaining blank spaces lie among the stars. Unable, like our forebears to tolerate space uninhabited, we have made with our minds a new legion of bright and shining beings to fill the gaps left by our ignorances. Aliens are our fairies, and they behave just like the fairies of our ancestors. In this sense, fairies are not part of a dead-and-gone past. We need to understand them in order to understand ourselves.

Why, though? Why do people prefer fairies to nothingness? And why fill these gaps with *fairies*; why not angels or hydras? As I read more and more, I began slowly to see some patterns emerging in the stories of fairy encounters. A fairy is someone who appears at and governs one of the big crises of mortal life: birth, childhood and its transitions, adolescence, sexual awakening, pregnancy and childbirth, old age, death. She presides over the borders of our lives, the seams between one phase of life and another. She attends christenings and stages funerals, organizes first party-dresses and lays dead kings to rest. (Note that I say 'she'. Although male fairies can do these things, in mortal realms these tasks are women's work.) She is the one who says, 'You shall go to the ball'; she is also the one who says, 'You shall prick your finger on a spindle and die.' In lesser ways, she controls the borders of the household, decides what is to count as clean, and what dirty.

She is a gatekeeper, and she guards the entrance to a new realm. Like all gatekeepers, she is Janus-faced, ambiguous: she has a lovely face, a face of promise, and a hideous face, a face of fear. That is how Yallery Brown and the Bluebell Fairy can share the same name. Like all change, she offers the dual promise of bliss and terror. People who seek change seek her out: adventurers, knights-errant, Romantic poets and artists. Yet she also comes to those who do not seek her.

So when we meet what might be a fairy, we can decide whether she is one by thinking about what fairies do. In symbolizing transformation and its borders, fairies themselves take a thousand forms and tell a million stories. The demons of the Sumerian nursery and the little winged creatures of Peter Pan's Kensington Gardens seem wildly different, but they fulfil common cultural purposes.

Fairies can represent cultural as well as personal transitions: changes of reign, of epoch. Recently, fairies were pressed into service – not too successfully – at the coronation of the current queen and at the funeral of the late Princess of Wales. Buried on an island, Diana – always markedly fairylike – becomes Our Lady of the Lake. Diana's spectral returns on a Buckingham Palace portrait of her cruel Bad Baron husband's most luckless ancestor, Charles I, suggest the vengeful fairy who was once a mortal spurned by her lover. The fairy is millennial: it is no coincidence that the current interest in fairies came at the end

4

of a century, the end of one era and the beginning of another. We stand on a tremendous borderline, between the old world we know and the new one we are to bring to birth. Beside us on this momentous chronological fault-line stands the fairy, just where she has always stood: on the edges, on the fringes, on the cracks. It is time we went to meet her, got to know her, learned her many resonant names. For in her we get to know ourselves and our desires.

Before we begin to get to know fairies, we may have to do some unknowing, for fairy stories swarm about the origin and nature of these beings. Some such stories are beautiful, but they are beautiful lies, or at any rate beautiful half-truths; they make sense to us emotionally, mythically, rather than in terms of evidence and reason. This is just, for no one would link fairies with reason, and it is not surprising that those who searched for the single meaning of fairies should have been benighted, indeed pixy-led into some odd wastelands. Resorting to prosaic numbers and lists might help to clear away the clouds of marsh-gas.

Fairies are a race-memory of pygmy ancient Britons

This is an old theory, whose best-known exponent was perhaps the Egyptologist Margaret Murray, but it has been given a new lease of life by neopaganism and by Marion Bradley's fantasy novels about King Arthur, the Avalon series. Basically, the theory is that fairies are the ancient Britons, who were driven into the hills by the Celts/the Saxons/the Christians (choose your own bogey) and took to living in caves, shooting at animals and enemies with poison darts. For its proponents, this theory explains why fairies cannot bear cold iron: the ancient Britons were primitive and pre-Iron Age, and iron to them was the symbol of the people who had conquered them. It also explains fairies' small stature (the ancient Britons were small because of their poor diet) and their affinity with nature (as hunter-gatherers).

This is a gorgeous idea; for one thing, it gives fairies breath and life, rescues them from story, turns them into people, and our favourite kind of people too – oppressed, indigenous people. Then the idea of a people with no visible memorial, but with a kind of wrong-headed, bowdlerized memorial in story alone, is very seductive.

However, there are problems. Dull problems, doubtless, but problems all the same.

There is, for instance, a complete lack of supporting evidence. There is not a jot or scintilla of evidence that the ancient Britons ever lived in the hills, or that they ever abhorred iron. They were inconsiderate enough to leave no written record of their practices whatsoever. Admittedly, this leaves everyone free to believe as they may, but it does mean that this particular fairy story is short on material support. Secondly, and more disturbingly, the plausibility of the theory hinges on its assumptions about the relative sizes of conquerors and conquered. In actuality, neolithic people were considerably shorter than hunter-gatherers because of their poor diet of grain compared with the richly varied meat and vegetation diet of their predecessors. And in any case, the notion that fairies are small comes far more from literary culture than from popular folklore, as we shall see.

As if this were not enough, there is a marked incompatibility between the theory and fairy beliefs. In England, fairies do not live solely in the hills, but also in vast underground caverns; perhaps the ancient Britons also hollowed out the ground, but it seems unlikely. Just why fairies should be seen as repositories of incredible wealth when they were really the primitive Britons is also hard to explain. It's also unclear why fairies should be linked with the dead if they are really the ancient Britons. A tendency among some to regard all such inconsistencies as the result of later corruption of pure traditions does not add to the plausibility of the whole, since it smacks of special pleading.

Finally, this 'explanation' really explains nothing. Why should oral culture assiduously maintain the memory of a conquest that took place hundreds of years previously? Why should people claim to meet ancient Britons who had died out as a culture before their great-grandparents were born? To say that fairies 'were' ancient Britons does not address why or how people continued to believe in them, why they were still important.

Nevertheless, like most stories that seduce, this one contains a grain of truth. It is true that all British Isles cultures, and some European cultures, associated fairies with neolithic sites, including barrow tombs and stone circles. This does not mean that they identified fairies with the real people who had built such tombs. What it means is that they had no idea who the builders were, but were intelligent enough to see that they must have been very different from themselves. Fairies fitted this description perfectly, with one huge added qualification: their links with the dead meant that they could be and often were equated with ancestors, including remote or important ancestors who had achieved legendary feats. This interpretation, common in Celtic places, was however foreign to England, where fairies' links to neolithic sites prompted not dreams about ancestors but a passion for the buried grave-goods found in tombs.

Fairies are pagan gods, reduced in stature

This used to be a very popular way of understanding fairies. Because they were linked to nature – sometimes, and more often in literature than in folklore – it was possible to see in them reduced, tamed, Christianized forms of important deities. The fairy queen, for instance, who as we will see is linked with sexuality, with death and with the testing of warriors, was often assumed to be a form of the Celtic goddess Morrigu or Morrigan. The Green Knight, whom we shall meet in due course, is often seen as a pagan god, the Green Man. (The fact that the Green Man is himself a twelfth-century and entirely Christian invention somewhat blunts the force of such an argument.) But the main problem with them is their lack of attention to cultural specificity. An analogy: my mother's generation watched the film *Casablanca*. So did mine. But we watched for such different reasons and saw such different things in it that we might more accurately have been said to be watching different movies. It is not helpful to argue that fairies used to be pagan gods if that is no longer what they were by the eleventh century, and they were not. To say that fairies were once gods is helpful in the sense that it is helpful to say that cars were once ox-carts; such a statement would be of limited value if what we wanted was to understand why cars were so important to people.

Which may simply be a long way of saying that this book is not interested in where fairies began, but in how they work. The question of how they began working can be left for others.

All fairies are benign goody-goodies

My students invariably stare at me sceptically if I suggest that Gawain's Green Knight is a fairy, because they think they know that fairies are tiresome little wingy thingies who are always good. The belief in the goodness of fairies has even sneaked into the hazily neopagan explanations above; fairies are used to give paganism a good name. Actually, as we shall see, fairies are an invention that almost wholly lacks moral engagement. In stories about fairies, there are exceedingly strict rules of behaviour, but these apply not to the fairies but to human beings, and they exist for reasons of self-preservation, not morality. Fairies later acquire moral connotations in Victorian England, but even this is short-lived and equivocal. Rather than good or bad, fairies are more simply and plainly *dangerous*.

There are hundreds of different types of fairy

Thanks to the vivid and entertaining taxonomies of the folklorist Katherine Briggs, many people have formed the impression that there are hundreds of different types of fairy. This idea is at the opposite end of the scale from the notion that all fairies represent a dying people or religion. Too much synthesis is replaced by too much fragmentation. What there are is hundreds of different fairy names, and thousands of different fairy stories, but only a few really significant types of fairy in popular culture:
1. Brownies, hobs and familiars; live in one house or serve one person, and overlap with
2. Fairy guides; often dead; conduct a person to fairies and/or teach them fairy lore.
3. Fairy societies; seen in fairy world or on ride; include king and queen.
4. Poltergeist/demon fairies, eventually melt down into tricksters; overlap with 1.

Even these basic types can be reduced still further. There are fairies with their own household – who might entertain you or take you as a servant – and fairies who live in yours, and who might act as your servants. Sometimes, as we shall see, the roles are blurry. But both these roles are analogous to human social structures; early modern people knew what it was to be a guest, to be an apprentice in a larger household, to be a servant and to have a servant. Fairy beliefs are filtered through the commonsense of everyday social relationships. Perhaps now a royal fairy would be a corporate boss; a household fairy might be a nanny or a cleaner.

Once upon a time there was a pure, austere oral culture involving fairies, that was taken away by print-the church-schools-radio-Walt Disney-television (make your own choice of villain)

Actually, popular culture has always been a mixture of high and low. People take stories from various places and retell them. Take print: it is often read or even sung aloud, which is probably why a humble Scottish magician whom we shall meet later has heard of the literary Thomas the Rhymer. When sung or read or retold, print passes into oral culture, and circulates in that form. You can see the process in any school playground, where a mix of film, television and print culture is daily transformed into the violent and fierce oral fantasies of children's games. Or take the person with three or four chapbooks on which their imagination works eagerly, expanding, filling in. Or take the way a whole strand of oral culture can form around particular figures – Oscar Wilde, Elvis – and create a kind of cultural firestorm which pulls in and transforms other kinds of stories and beliefs. High culture does not trickle down, but flows. And trash also dribbles steadily out of the bins in which some seek to confine it.

Shakespeare knew this, and that is how he came to give us – for better or worse – our fairies. He works on the stories he knows. Shakespeare was not knowledgeable about popular fairy culture, but he had read the indefatigable Reginald Scot, and he put his fairies together with classical myths, willy-nilly. Just so does an unknown Scottish witch named Alesoun Peirsoun put fairies together with

Hermes Trismegistus; just so do Andro Man and Bessie Dunlop put the dead of their own families together with major battles in Scottish history.

None the less, one can legitimately express an aesthetic preference for Elspeth Reoch or the Gawain-poet over Shakespeare or Herrick, and I do. This preference, however, which is entirely a product of my own all-too-predictable moulding by post-Romantic aesthetics which admire roughness, violence and misery over prettiness, should not become the basis for a theory. One of the recurring problems with fairies is that hard bony thought constantly melts into a jelly of aesthetics. Which is part of the fairy's bag of tricks, tricks which let her vanish whenever she likes.

In trying to get a fix on such a coy and protean creature, I am taking many kinds of risk. And I do not only mean the kind of risk of credibility involved in writing about something that constantly shifts and shudders into new forms. Perhaps more worryingly, to catch a fairy is anyway unlucky. Even to say the word 'fairy' costs the sayer a year of life. So, dear reader, be careful. Do not read this book aloud. You never know.

I

Ancient Worlds

Take my advice, if you meet anything that's going to be human and isn't yet, or used to be human once and isn't now, or ought to be human and isn't, you keep your eyes on it and feel for your hatchet.
(C. S. Lewis, *The Lion, the Witch and the Wardrobe*)

Maps of the world in older times used to fill in the blanks of exploration with an array of fantastic creatures, dragons, sea monsters, fierce winged beasts. It appears that the human mind cannot bear very much blankness – where we do not know, we invent, and what we invent reflects our fear of what we do not know.

Fairies are born of that fear. The blank spaces on the village map, too, need to be filled; faced with woods and mountains, seas and streams that could never be fully charted, human beings saw blanks, blanks they hastened to fill with a variety of beings all given different names, yet all recognizable as fairies. Our fairies have become utterly benign only now, when electric light and motorways and mobile phones have banished the terror of the lonely countryside.

Used as we are to benign fairies, it is very hard for us to understand the fairies of the past. We think of fairies as bringers of light, enchantment, wonder. Encountering a fairy in a beechwood in 1500, we would be suicidally incautious, making such critical errors as speaking to him or even inviting him across the threshold. We need to recover the fear of fairies in order to understand their importance to pre-industrial people. Oddly, we can do that far more easily on foreign ground. Standing on the shores of the ancient Mediterranean world, we can forget our preconceptions of fairies, and encounter their truly alien quality for the first time.

Thus equipped with a sense of distance and alienation, we will be able to appreciate our own native fairies rather better.

The ancient Mediterranean world was thronged with demons, diverse demons with different meanings. We will meet a number of the demonic host in this chapter, because to understand these mysterious beings, long lost to history, is to understand the fears and preoccupations later fairies represent. Child-killing demons and nymphs are the joint ancestors of medieval fairies, who in turn are the ancestors of our own fairies. And yet you will find none of these demons in any dictionary of fairies, and you will not find an entry on fairies in any classical dictionary. In fact, if you take a casual look in any dictionary of folklore you will probably find the assertion that fairies are a part of Celtic mythology, though exactly what part is often left tactfully unexplored. However, the more I worked on materials from the ancient world, the more I felt convinced that the origin of fairies lies not in Northern Europe, but in the Mediterranean civilizations of Mesopotamia, Egypt, Greece and Rome. None of these civilizations used the word fairy, of course, but all had beings that behaved exactly as fairies behaved in Northern Europe during the Middle Ages: babysnatchers, man-snatchers, seductresses with a piece missing, givers of fortune with one hand and misery with the other.

In journeying into the fairy past we are going back from safety to terror. Into the dark. Where do fairies come from? From the dark. To find the origins of fairies, we must go back to the dark – dark of our own past, dark of the world's past.

Darknesses

You are five years old. It is a hot night, and the darkness is thick. You can hear the soft breathing of your nurse. She is asleep, and you are alone, terribly alone with your thoughts. Your thoughts make you clutch your amulet, an amulet, made you are told, of a hyena's tooth. Above your bed hangs a terrible grinning face; it too is your ally against whatever is out there.

On a table stands the nightlight, giving off a faint, warm glow of flame, dispelling a little of the heavy darkness. If you were to get up and go to the window you would see other pinpricks of light: torches, perhaps, lighting ways home, and other soft olive-oil flames in other nurseries. Beyond these lovely bright points of light, those lights that are the city, lies your father's farm, the olive grove tossing in the night wind. Beyond that, nothing. Only the endless woods, mountains, stretching on and on in unbroken darkness, alive with the soft rustles of small nameless creatures, large fierce ones, boars, leopards, even lions. The wild dark, so much larger than you are, so much larger than the city your fathers made. The tiny circle of the nightlight keeps back the dark, but does not banish it. The dark is in the room, stronger, larger than you are, than man is.

You are an Athenian child. You are the child of a citizen, part of the greatest civilization Europe has yet known. Yet civilization does not quite extend to your nursery; it is there in the nightlight, but beyond the light is darkness. And you are haunted by demons of the dark no different from those that made your remote ancestors cling to each other in their cave dwellings. Demons of the dark, demons that mark the limitations of civilization. What do you see in the blackness? The mind of man, child or adult, abhors a vacuum. Darkness is blank, and must be peopled, must be filled with terrible *things* that symbolize its fearful power.

Let us begin then, in darkness. Descriptions of hauntings, ghosts and demons as smoke, clouds, dream-shapes and shadows are familiar throughout Greek and Latin literature; scenes of terror are often set to flickering light, like the shifting flame of a candle. Or a nightlight. Talking of dreams, Aristotle writes that 'in some young people, even if their eyes are wide open and it is dark, many moving shapes appear, so that they often cover their heads in fright'. The Greek fear of the dark and equation of darkness with death can be seen in the coloration of ghosts. The ghost of one of Odysseus' sailors, who raped a local girl and was stoned to death by the villagers, is *deinos melas*, scary black. The demon who appears in the New Testament Apocrypha *Acts of Peter* is 'a woman exceeding foul . . . black and filthy, clothed in rags, and with an iron collar about her neck and chains upon her hands and feet, dancing'. The underworld is itself a place where everything is black.[1]

The image of a man with a dark face is the simplest of all terrors. The Greek god Hermes impersonates a bogey, a chimney-demon, blackening his face to frighten children:

when any of the girls does disobedience to her mother, the mother calls the Cyclopes to her child, and from within the house comes Hermes, stained with burnt ashes. And straightway he plays bogey to the child and she runs to her mother's lap, with her hands over her eyes.[2]

Why is the child scared? Here is another child, thousands of years later:

'Could I be left there?' he asked.
  'Left where?'
  'There.' He pointed to the coal-yard.
  'Don't point!' said nurse.
  'What is that place?'
  'The place where coal comes from.'
  'Could I be left there?' he persisted.
  'Not unless one of the coalmen came over the wall and carried you off and left you there, which he will do unless you're a good boy.'
  Michael caught his breath.
  'Can coalmen climb?' he asked, choking at the thought.
  'Climb like kittens,' said Nurse.[3]

Pure terror. The coalman is black, which means he is alien. He will take the child to somewhere dark, dirty. And there the child will be lost, lost for ever behind the darkness, the blackness. Can children be recognized with their faces daubed with coal-dust? Can their parents ever find them again?

Thousands of years apart, these chimney-demons are both rebukes to the child. Both stories are called forth by the child's naughtiness, by an assertion of autonomy, individuality, difference. Wilfulness is identity, and often it is a way of testing the parent, to see if his or her love can survive the ordeal of disobedience, a way of testing the limits of the self, to see if the self can survive separation. What these stories do is tell the child that it can't. Can't survive. Can't be loved. That disobedience will mean the utter loss of the self in swirling blackness. The dissolution of identity. We fear the dark both because we cannot see in it and because we cannot be seen in it, cannot be known, recognized. Just as coal-dust and chimney-dust disguise, so the darkness obliterates who we are. This, we shall see, is what the child can fear from demons. But demons also provide a story of how the incompleteness of the childhood self can be transcended.

Child-demons

These creatures come from the same marginal place as the children who are their prey: from unlife. From death, yes; like European fairies, as we shall see, demons are often the dead. Egyptian texts mention 'dead men and women' who come to attack the child in its bed.[4] Many demons are straightforwardly the unborn, the stillborn. The ancient Mesopotamian demon Kubu is called 'the little one who never saw the sun', 'the little one who never suckled his mother's milk', 'the little one who never knew his own name'.[5] Lacking these rituals of recognition, identity, love, lacking a mother's welcome into life, Kubu is forever trapped between death and life. As desperate recompense, he degenerates into a killer of other babies by disease. His motivation is not part of the story; we are not told whether he kills for company or for vengeance, and it does not matter. He kills because of what he is, anomalous, trapped between states of being; he reproduces himself in killing, trapping others as he is trapped.

Foetuses and newborn babies were thought to have a special relationship with the underworld which allowed them to control, or to act as, powerful demons through the performance of magical rituals. In AD 371 a Roman tribune named Numerius confessed to ripping open a live pregnant woman and using her offspring to stir up malevolent spirits in order to learn about the end of the empire.[6] Even in twentieth-century Iraq, the stillborn were buried separately from adults, often in the doorway of the house or by the door of the mother's room. The stillborn in Sumeria had a special place in the underworld; in one of the sources for *The Epic of Gilgamesh* a mother asks, ' "In your visit to the underworld, did you see my little stillborn children who never knew existence?" "I saw them." "How do they fare?" "They play at a table of gold and silver, laden with ghee and honey." [7] This generously consolatory notion also testifies to the power of the unborn among the dead, over death. Kubu and other stillborn demons are consolatory, too; though threatening, they give shape and name to what never had shape or name, and allow it to be remembered.

Like menstrual blood, like the placenta, also very powerful in magic, babies issue from the womb. Like demons, they come in from the dark. As well as being locked in struggle, babies and demons are also bound together in fundamental likeness. What could be more unknown, yet more carefully and desperately imagined, more passionately *felt*, than the baby in the womb? The womb, like the tomb, is the place where a crossing from death to life is made. It is a blank space on the map, too; it produces no stories, evokes no memories. Perhaps it is *the* blank space on the map, the one we always seek to fill with stories.

Though it is usual at this point to relate such stories to the high rates of stillbirth and neonatal death in the ancient world, I suspect these additional terrors merely worsened the eternally complex relations between the pregnant woman and the foetus she carries. A pregnant woman is herself an anomaly, a problem of identity: neither one nor two, as the French psychoanalyst Julia Kristeva points out, and curiously suspended between life and death; if pregnant with a son, she may also be suspended awkwardly between sexes.[8] She herself therefore takes on some of the mixture of characteristics which typify the demon. Within her is someone unknown, who every day takes over more of her body, becomes less easy to ignore. Like any takeover, this can feel hostile.

But it is also the mother's job to protect the baby, which can also seem exquisitely small and vulnerable; vulnerable, perhaps above all, to her own rage. When I was pregnant, I was often amazed by the hardness of the baby I carried. I had expected a squidgy Cabbage Patch doll, and what was inside me felt much more like an animated frozen chicken, hard and knobbly. Perhaps this was why I used to dream every night that I was giving birth through a great wound in my stomach to a creature covered in green scales, with fierce teeth. As it looked savagely about from the gaping cavity in my abdomen, my heart would go out to it in a rush of passionate tenderness. 'Poor baby,' I would croon. 'Life will be hard for you because you are so ugly. But I love you, and I always will.' This dream is about fear, but it also about love. In linking pregnancies and their loss with demons, the mothers of the ancient world set up the same complex relations between fear and love.

Such feelings seem universal, but are also intensely social, orchestrated by the needs of societies. Vase-paintings depict the goddess Athene doffing her helmet or wearing the *aegis*, the emblem with the fearsome face of the gorgon, back to front to avoid alarming the baby Erichthonius, the future king of Athens. Being a Greek child, Erichthonius is a scaredy-cat. And what he fears in the *aegis* is an infant bogey, Gorgo, who is a gorgon, but one who patrols the nursery. From child-bogey to mother-bogey: the pendulum of fear swings between the passionate parts of this, the most intense of all one-to-one relationships.

Pure fear: the gorgon

She is a symbol of pure fear. Gorgo means fright. Some terrible noise was the originating force behind the gorgon, a guttural animal-like howl that issued from the throat and required a huge, distended mouth.[9] The inhuman shrill cry of the gorgon is the same one uttered by the dead. The familiar, paralysing image of the gorgon's head, with its gaping mouth and snaky hair, is a symbol of the fear that turns the onlooker to stone, a freezing fear that prevents action. The gorgon is also like a warrior at the moment of attack: the blazing brilliance of arms, the unbearable radiation from head and eyes, the long streaming hair. She is like Achilles in the ditch, giving his war-cry to signal his return to the battle, perhaps the most terrifying moment in the *Iliad*, a moment when an almost supernatural force of war is unleashed on the Trojans. She is also the violent cry of those killed, the death-grin, the gnashing teeth, head thrown back, howling at the sky. Warriors had to stand firm when confronted with such spectacles; only children were allowed the luxury of terror. By experiencing the menace of grinning death in the nursery, the fear of such menace could, the

Greeks hoped, be put away with other childish things. Warriors who ran away could be likened to children running from demons.

Children, the Greeks believed, were naturally cowardly. Their cowardice was the main thing that made them different from adults. Children's fearfulness was everywhere attested. In Plato's *Phaedo*, fears in the adult have their roots in childhood. 'Within us there is a child frightened by hobgoblins', says Socrates, 'that is why we fear death.'[10] Plato's contemporary, the Athenian historian Xenophon, describes a group of fleeing warriors as 'like children fearing demons'.[11] To be a warrior is to be someone willing to stare down the gorgon of fear, someone who has transcended the space of childhood. Demons are a sign of what has been left behind in the women's rooms, what must be left behind if the child is to become a man.

A Greek warrior, then, was above all a man who could deal with nursery terrors. For Greek men, the hero Perseus set an example of how to deal with these terrible creatures: having killed the gorgon Medusa, Perseus used her head as a weapon. With the help of the gods, demons can be destroyed and their power seized.[12] The power to slay the child-killing demon marks out the hero's own childhood. Heracles, prodigious slayer of monsters, was sent two poisonous snakes to kill him in his cradle by Hera. Heracles at once proved his unchildlike prowess and courage by killing the snakes with his bare hands.

Hera's snakes were on a murder mission: child-killing demons come from the land of death, the undiscovered country, the ultimate impenetrable darkness. They bring death with them. As Socrates shows, to see them is to see death; to stop fearing them is to stop fearing death. Child-demons are about the process of leaving childhood behind. They are what the boy-child must leave behind in order to be a man.

There is another way to think about the way manhood needs demons: Kubu is a Greek Peter Pan, or rather, Peter Pan is a nursery demon. Kubu is the boy who couldn't grow up; Peter Pan, it will be remembered, is the boy who wouldn't grow up. In his early incarnation, *Peter Pan in Kensington Gardens*, Peter Pan was a boy who could never grow up, never be named or fed by his mother, because he had flown away to avoid growing up. He chooses this fate. Later, tragically, he makes the decision to return, but makes it too late. Reaching the nursery he sees that his mother has barred the window and replaced him with another boy. From then on, Peter is trapped, however insouciant he is about it. In later stories, Peter is joined by boys who have fallen out of their perambulators, their suspiciously womblike perambulators (is this a mere bowdlerization of miscarriage – mis*carriage* – or stillbirth?). Peter has become trapped in an endless babyhood. He is called a Betwixt-and-Between, a being caught between unlife and life.[13] Like Kubu, he takes to stealing children, as he was 'stolen'. In all his incarnations, Peter Pan is a nursery demon feared by mothers, who kidnaps children and steals them away, as he steals Maimie from the daylight park, the Darling children from the safety of nightlights and Nana. And in all his incarnations, Peter is akin to and in league with the fairies. Barrie may have happened by the sheer instinct of his genius on one of the oldest of all fairytales, and this may explain Peter Pan's continuing and haunting resonances for each new generation.

However, Barrie inverts the values embodied in the story of Kubu and similar Greek demons. In ancient Greece, everyone wants and needs to grow up; growing up is good, and to remain a child is to be forever consigned to the helpless panics of the nursery. In Barrie, *growing up* rather than perpetual childhood is the thing to be feared as a loss of identity, an idea very lavishly reinforced by Steven Spielberg's film of the story, *Hook*. When the Lost Boys leave the Neverland, they are lost indeed. 'The bearded man who doesn't know any story to tell his children was once John.' Like Kubu, John has lost his name and has no identity. Heroism in *Peter Pan* is not confined to adults who have left childhood behind, but confined to children who still revel in childishness; only children can defeat monsters like Captain Hook. All adults can do is be judges, and boring things like that. 'You see that judge in a wig coming out at the iron door? That used to be Tootles.' The Lost Boys are never more thoroughly lost than when they agree to grow up; it is *then* that they lose their names and become the tragic ghosts of their former boisterous selves.[14]

Girls who never grew up

So far this has been a story about men growing up; what about little girls? Odd as it may seem, the only figure comparable to the male hero and his glorious triumph on the battlefield is the woman in labour.[15] This too involves a conquest of fear, even now; how much more so before anaesthesia, instruments, hospitals. Pregnancy and childbirth, like the battlefield, were places where Gorgo roamed. There is a physical likeness between the Gorgon-like rictus of the dying warrior, screaming as his guts are pierced, and the agonized grin of the woman giving birth. An ancient Egyptian statue shows a woman crouching, muscles corded in her neck, every nerve straining; she looks as fierce as Medusa.[16] Both warrior and woman's bodies are opened, and the open body is open to death. Both bleed; both are wounded. And both are giving their woundedness, giving their body to something other than themselves. Both are likely to die, prematurely, before their allotted time; both deaths are violent, cutting off a young life. As we shall see throughout this book, the restless and envious dead, those most likely to return as fairies, are those who die by violence, cut off before their time. It is the analogy between the woman in childbirth and the dying warrior that explains why the dead may come to claim her. For she looks like (and to some extent is) one of the dead.

But whereas heroes were uniquely equipped to defeat demons, including Gorgo, pregnant and labouring women were uniquely vulnerable to them. Heroes transcend childhood; pregnant women, psychically and socially, often return to it. The mark of the hero's transcendence of childhood is his removal from the women's rooms to which pregnancy and motherhood confine the woman. Pregnant, parturient and lactating women take on the vulnerability of the child to terrors as long as their bodies are one with the body of that child. All demons preyed particularly on childbearing women and their infants. And yet childbirth and the successful rearing of the child to maturity represented a triumph over death as great as any enacted on the plains of Troy by the greatest heroes. Like the warrior, the labouring woman and her child were constantly exposed to death.

So if giving birth was the adult female equivalent of the male warrior's confrontation with death, it is not surprising that a female demon who is also a lost child should be one who has never managed to marry or have children. The Sumerian *ardat-lili* demons are girls who died before they married or bore children; this engendered their thirst for other children's blood, and also for a husband to replace the blank in their own lives.[17] Gello is an ogre on the island of Lesbos, who was the tormented soul of a girl who had died young, and who keeps returning to earth to steal children. Because she died prematurely, the people of the island of Lesbos said that her ghost haunted little children, and they attributed premature deaths to her. She is herself specifically called 'untimely dead' by the classical writers Zenobius and Hesychius, one who has died before completing her life on earth. At the time of her death, she had not experienced those things that defined her as a woman: parturition and nurture. She herself was incomplete; because of her death she would never be complete, would always be outside the category 'woman'. She ought to be a woman but is not.

Incomplete women are exiled not only from the world of the living but also from the world of the dead, wandering, as the *Odyssey* has it, between the upper world and the underworld. This category of dead was called the *aoroi*, and they were crucial in magic rituals because they were not securely locked into death, but could be summoned by the living. Anxiety about them was not confined to Greece; an Egyptian charm tells of a nameless ghost who longed to kiss a child or take it in her arms. Such beings were also acutely vulnerable; unprotected by the walls of the underworld, they were at the mercy of any magician able to summon them.[18]

Gello was long remembered in Byzantium and is still feared by Greek peasants. 'I claw at the eyes of small children and I strangle infants,' she declares unabashedly.[19] Her image has been Christianized, but in a manner which retains the theme of incompleteness; Gello now preys especially on the unbaptized, searching for 'an open door after midnight at houses where there are unbaptized children'. She is most often seen by those whose baptism was botched by a priest who incompetently leaves out a few key words of the ritual.[20] Like Gello, such children are caught between one phase of life and another; forever incomplete, not properly named, they resemble that which threatens them, just as Gello's ancient victims did.

Perhaps this is why Gello seems to long to complete herself by becoming a mother, a perverse and murderous mother, though. Toni Morrison's terrifying Beloved is a kind of Gello, and she appears in the novel that bears her name.[21] Beloved is the ghost-daughter of Sethe, a former slave. When they come from the plantation to take Sethe and her family back into slavery, Sethe cuts Beloved's throat because it is her only way of stopping them. The spiteful baby-ghost never has a name; only Beloved. A vengeful child-demon, she gradually takes over her mother's life, feeding on her, loving her lover, eventually swelling with a bizarre pregnancy which represents her absorption of her mother's place and role. Morrison is drawing on African and West Indian legends of the vengeful child-demon; in Nigeria, miscarried children are spirit-children who keep returning mischievously to the womb and then refusing to be born.[22] They are child-killers because they prevent the birth of other children. Yet Morrison's novel also echoes meticulously the terror of the child who has never been named, a terror which resonates deeply because it is so ancient.

Like Beloved's, Gello's feeding is an expression of inner hunger. A Byzantine legend makes this clear: in it Gello longs to suckle babies, but when she puts an infant to her breast, the breast drains the infant's blood instead of nourishing it. Hunted down by three Byzantine saints, she makes a remarkable suggestion: 'If you can return in the hollow of your hand the milk which you have sucked from your mother's breast, I will return the children of Melitena.' The saints comply; 'lifting up their eyes [they] spoke to the Lord, and they vomited at once into the hollows of their hands something like mother's milk'. Gello returns the dead children at once.[23]

These stories of child-demons are very complex. They are about the parent's simple fear that the child will die young, but also about more tangled fears of loss of identity in the darkness of death, of being forgotten, being absolutely lost in the sense of never having been known. They are about the parent's fear of the child that comes in from the formless dark and invades the home. This fear can be assuaged by the processes on which Kubu and Gello miss out: by naming rites, the passage of time, the acquisition of language, the familiarity of daily conversation, the transition to adulthood. What does it mean to love someone who is not known? Any mother of the pre-verbal child might attempt an answer. Yet the psychoanalyst Adam Phillips also calls this pre-verbal child 'the beast in the nursery', a lost and inaccessible self that is truly and perhaps blissfully nameless.[24] Whether we long for that noblest of all savages, or long to surpass it and acquire names and language, it continues to haunt the nurseries of our imagination. Threatening to draw us back into the dark, the child without a name is our other self. As the Greeks knew, it is the self we must not be if we are to grow up.

Mother-demons

You are what the child in the nursery fears, what roams beyond the circle of his nightlight.

You are lost for ever in the dark. For you there is no light; there can never be light. Once, a long time ago, you knew what light was; once there was day, and the broad fields of the sky were reflected in your eyes. Now you no longer remember. You do not know where you begin or end. You do not know your own story. You do not know yourself. It is you who are the darkness. And you are alone, utterly alone in the dark. You cannot feel any more, you cannot smell, taste, touch.

But if there was another? Someone to share the darkness with you? Someone on whose warm blood floats light? If . . . if there was a baby, perhaps. Or a mother. Someone whose blood is rich with love. You could drink the love, with the blood, and the love would fill you, fill you utterly, until you are flowing with love. Until you have some love to give back. Feelings of your own. Breasts flowing with love, with milk, hurting with love. Now your breasts are empty, dangling, as your womb is empty, aching. Now is nothing. And you are nothing. Unless . . . unless . . . unless another comes to be in the dark with you and to fill it with light, to teach you the ways of the day.

It will not be like the last time. Of course it will not. The last time, where you drank too deeply of the feelings, the blood, the light, and the little life swam away from you, leaving you lonely in the darkness again. Leaving you without a memory of what you had felt.

It will not be like the last time. It will never be like the last time. Never again.

Not all nursery terrors were children. There were also mothers, mothers who had failed. The one who most closely resembles the wicked fairies of Western Europe is Lamia. According to the ancient historian Diodorus Siculus, Lamia was a young girl of Libyan origin. Zeus loved her and had an affair with her, but every time she gave birth to a child, Zeus' wife Hera, out of jealousy, arranged for it to die. Ashamed and miserable, Lamia hid herself in a solitary cave. In her despair she became a monster jealous of mothers more fortunate than herself, and she seized and devoured their children.[25]

The story of Lamia is about the value of children to women in a culture where having children is vital to social identity. Lamia does not steal children in order to rear them. If she cannot have them, no one will, and she can *never* have them because to be loved by her is to die, as her own children died. She is a rampaging, dangerous metaphor for childlessness; in her, the ache of longing has turned to bitter poison. The always extreme Greek competitiveness has eaten her away, and to make herself level with those whose children live she must reduce them to the same miserable status as herself.

In this, Lamia is very like Medea, the ultimate bad mother, and perhaps the ultimate nursery bogey too. In Euripides' tragedy, Medea, the wife of Jason, kills her children – and his – to punish Jason for leaving her for another woman. Her contest with Jason is so intense that her children are reduced to pawns, and yet she loves them, talks about them with love, longs to hold them. What is shocking about her is that she incarnates the murderous impulses which motherhood must suppress if it is to succeed. Euripides' murderous mother may derive from the nursery bogeys that haunted the dark. Euripides is the first ancient author to make Medea the murderer of her children. He may have got the idea from nursery demons like Lamia, spectral murderous mothers. There was a shrine to Lamia in Corinth, where Medea lived; this may have inspired Euripides.

Lamia and Medea might be the kind of bogeys that exist to guard a boundary between acceptable and unacceptable behaviour. Medea and Lamia mark the spot which says: thou shalt not kill thy children, however much you hate them. This says something to children, too:

there are bad people Out There. Stay inside, near the warm lovely glow of the lamp. Don't wander in the dark.

There is another oddity about Lamia: in order to punish her still more, Hera made her unable to sleep, which explains her nocturnal wanderings, but had another, more alarming result. To compensate her, Zeus gave her the power to take out her eyes and replace them when she wished with other people's. To do this, Lamia prowls the world, taking out the eyes of others, especially children, to replace her own tired, red-rimmed eyes. Her battening on youth to remedy her own defects is truly vampiric, and it is not surprising that female spirits who attached themselves to children and sucked their blood were also called lamiae. These creatures rise to the light from underground lairs, like the later fairies of Western European tradition, such as the fairy host of the Scottish borders.

In a culture which values youth and finds age repulsive, like that of ancient Greece (or like our own culture), Lamia's predatory abduction of youth might signify the way children and parents are divided by age. I remember as a child finding my mother's wrinkles worrying, even horrifying, and now as a mother I sometimes feel the same way about myself when I look at my own face next to the fresh face of my five-year-old son. Yet the idea that mothers steal youth from children inverts what really seems to happen; children 'steal' youth from their mothers. Lamia is invariably depicted marked by the terrible stigmata of the childbearing woman. A fifth-century Athenian vase shows her as a naked woman tied to a palm tree, and tortured by satyrs. She has a sagging belly and pendulous breasts, signs of *ageing*, and in particular, of the ageing that follows childbearing.[26] The result of being taken over by that demonic child inside is to become an object of fright *to* the very child who has stolen your youth. In trying to rob children of their youth to restore her own, Lamia is a picture of the tangled feelings of the mother whose own youth has been absorbed, eaten, by the child she bears.

Such marks of ageing are also, of course, objects of straightforward horror in a culture like that of ancient Athens. Old women are automatically hilarious, disgusting and somehow more sexual than one would suppose – which adds to the disgust. Depictions of Lamia emphasize the lower bodily strata: the belly, the anus, the vulva. The

Athenian comic dramatist Aristophanes describes Lamia farting in public; she also has huge and filthy testicles. As well as testicles, an anonymous ancient scholar credits her with a 'staff', slang for penis. These attributes seem to have less to do with hermaphrodism than with an unseemly display of the body and its sexuality.[27] The modern Greek Lamia has monstrously large breasts, or sometimes one monstrously large breast. The psychoanalyst Melanie Klein claimed that all infants long to devour the breast; they project those feelings on to the breast, suspecting it of longing to eat them up.[28] This is exactly the threat embodied by Gello, with her deadly suckling; her breasts are truly devouring. If Lamia is a kind of monstrous walking mammary gland, like the runaway giant breast in Woody Allen's film *Everything You've Always Wanted to Know About Sex*, then her terror is explained.

As well as wanting babies, Lamia is lustful. In this role, she is the forerunner of the seductive queen of the fairies who dazzled and deceived medieval knights (we shall meet her later). For instance, there was once a beautiful lady who appeared mysteriously in Corinth, apparently equipped with fabulous riches and a beautiful wardrobe. She was a great success at every party, and attracted many proposals of marriage from the local youth. However, on her wedding day to a young man of Corinth she was exposed as a lamia by Apollonius of Tyana, the now-forgotten holy man who was one of Jesus Christ's chief competitors for the title of messiah to the Roman Empire. This lamia's riches are mere illusion, as is her human form. When this is pointed out to her, she weeps, and vanishes in an instant. Philostratus, who tells the story, links her to the nursery demon: 'She was accustomed', he writes, 'to feed on beautiful and young bodies, since their blood is the purest.' The lamia uses her allure to catch her prey: 'Now these desire indeed the pleasures of love, but yet more do they desire human flesh, and use the pleasures of love to decoy those on whom they will feast.'[29] Oddly, Philostratus' lamia finds herself a faint cultural echo in the Australian Aboriginal Bagini, whose siren loveliness entices men into their caves. The Bagini have sharp teeth, however, and devour their lovers. Lamiae can be difficult when slighted; Apuleius tells the story of two lamiae who, in vengeance for one young man's rejection, tore out his heart before the face of his companion.[30] This leaves young men courted by a lamia with a difficult choice: saying yes is fatal, but so is saying no.

Lamia is both a nursery ogress and a sexual temptation. Baubo, too, has two sides. She is both a nocturnal spectre, a kind of ogress who lives in a dark underground cavern, and also a term for the female sexual organs. Figurines of Baubo show her head in her crotch. *Baubo* means vulva. She is also an old woman, and it is her cheerful jokes and vulgar gestures that cheer the Greek fertility goddess Demeter when she is mourning the disappearance of her daughter Persephone, stolen by Hades, Lord of the Dead.[31]

And yet Baubo also draws attention to something else about the Greek nursery demon, something easy to miss: its comic, playful potential. Fear provokes laughter as easily as screams. Children often laugh when they are frightened. Both fear and laughter depend on surprise, the rupture of expectations. Many demons found their way into the repertoire of comic masks. Aristophanes uses the word for hobgoblin to mean both demon and a comic mask.[32] In an exactly similar way, the Romans hung masks called *oscilla* (literally, 'little faces') in trees to frighten away ghosts, yet the masks could be called by the same names as the demons they were supposed to frighten. Like the masks in a Greek satyr play, these *oscilla* are connected with the development of early Roman comic drama and the rough, abusive bantering that preceded it; it is no coincidence that the evidence for the Roman nursery demons Larva and Mania mostly comes from the comedies of the Roman dramatist Plautus.[33] We will see that play (meaning both theatre and games) is central to demons. Terror, when acted out, is displaced, managed, controlled. By playing a game of demon and victim, mothers and children can manage their fear of each other.

Games were played between mother and child in the ancient world too, as the story of the demon Mormo illustrates. Mormo is somehow vague; she seems to have begun as a mask of the god Hermes, daubed with ashes to frighten children. This is a 'chimney-demon', one of the demons of darkness with which we began this story.[34] One anonymous writer speaks of Mormo as a name whose utterance frightens children, but also tells a story about her; 'they say that she was a Corinthian woman who, one evening, purposefully ate her own children and then flew away. Forever thereafter, whenever mothers want to scare their children, they invoke Mormo.'[35] The story is noticeably similar to that of Lamia in that Mormo bears children but then fails to nurture them successfully, and the story may have been invented to bring her into line with other, similar demons. However, there is also a subtle and horrifying difference which does suggest that more is happening there than copying; no other story speaks of mother-demons *eating* their children. Destroying them, yes, but not eating them. So if a mother threatens her children with Mormo, is she implying, almost unbelievably, that she herself will eat them? If so, what can this mean?

To the modern reader, it is reminiscent of Maurice Sendak's account of how he came to write his compelling children's picture book *Where the Wild Things Are*. The Wild Things are modern nursery demons who metaphorically come into Max's nursery; in a kind of dream-narrative, Max sails to their country. Once there, the Wild Things declare their intention of eating Max, whom they also love and worship; when he finally goes home, they announce, 'We'll eat you up, we love you so', to prevent his departure. Sendak claims the Wild Things are really his aunts in Brooklyn, who would lean over him 'with their bad teeth and hairy noses' and announce: 'Oh, you're so cute I could eat you up!' The young Sendak thought they might really do it if his mother didn't hurry up with the cooking.[36] The pleasure taken by adults in the dimpled, delicious body of a child can feel very dangerous to the child. His mother is always armed with this fatal knowledge: he was inside her once, and he could be again.

Yet children love such stories and clamour for them, casting now themselves, now the parents in the role of devourer: it's a game, and games are a child's way of managing threats. That Mormo was part of a game can be seen in a fascinating vignette of domestic life in Hellenistic Alexandria by the poet Theocritus. Two friends are on their way to a festival. One, Praxinoa, has a child who clutches at her skirts and cries to go with her. To persuade him to be good, the mother cries, 'I shan't take you, baby. Mormo! Horse bites. Cry as much as you like, but I can't have you lamed.'[37] Then she hands the infant to the nanny-slave.

Male classicists who gloss this passage interpret Mormo as a terror, and paraphrase the passage as a mother's attempt to frighten her child into silence with threats of being bitten on the leg by a horse-demon. And it is possible that Praxinoa is reminding the baby that she is going out into the dark, the abode of demons; if he goes out with her, he may be lamed by Mormo.[38] However, if a child is crying, you don't frighten it: that makes it cry more. You *distract* it with a game. When Praxinoa says goodbye to her child, she plays a little game with the baby, a game very like peek-a-boo. 'Boo!', for example, is a word we use to frighten children and also one we use to play with them: hiding our faces, slowly revealing them to howls of laughter, or pouncing comically on them from behind the door. They learn to use the word on us, and on each other. Praxinoa says 'Mormo!' to her baby where we might say 'Boo!'. Perhaps the 'Mormo-bite' was acted out, with a little nip, a ticklish nip to the leg? Marina Warner has recently and persuasively argued that there is real fear in such games, fear of *eating the wrong thing*, fear of being eaten.[39] But there is also reassurance. The Mormo-bite reassures the baby because it testifies to Praxinoa's desire for the baby, her interest in him. Like a kiss, it suggests that Mother's desires are still bent towards the imperious infant, even if she is at that moment giving proof of a life beyond the nursery.

A frustratingly fragmentary lament for a dead friend by Erinna, the Greek woman poet, so good that she was compared to Homer and Sappho, also relates Mormo to a game, but a deadly one. The poem, known in antiquity as the *Distaff*, begins by recalling two little girls playing a children's game called the tortoise. In this game, one girl, the tortoise, sits in the middle of a circle responding to the other children's questions. When they ask her what she is doing, she replies 'weaving', and then she is asked how her child died. 'From white horses he leapt to the sea,' she replies. At this answer the tortoise girl leaps to her feet and chases the others; the one she catches becomes the next tortoise. Erinna remembers being chased by her friend Baukis as the new tortoise.[40]

It already sounds as if this game has some links with nursery demons. The tortoise is a bereaved mother, and she becomes a child-snatcher after this has been enacted. The children are playing with death and fear, just as children now do in 'What's the time, Mr Wolf?'.[41] Perhaps this is why the game seems appropriate in a lament for a friend who died young, perhaps in childbirth; a friend who herself has become a kind of demon to Erinna, reminding her of death, catching her up in the pain of loss. Confirmation of the relation between demons and the loss the poem describes comes when Erinna refers to Mormo:

> For little ones . . . the Mormo brought fear
> . . . she wandered about on four feet,
> shape-shifting from one thing to [another].

The fear of Mormo, limited to children, is like the tortoise-game: a fear put away. Yet it also predicts Baukis's untimely death, for Mormo is a nursery demon, presider over lives which are cut off before their due time.

Another incomplete Greek demon is Empousa, who shifts shape like Erinna's Mormo. When Empousa appears to Xanthias and Dionysos in Aristophanes' play *Frogs*, she has a phosphorescent face, and transforms herself from a bull to a mule to a beautiful young girl, then to a dog. She makes her appearance in the underworld, the land of the dead, linking her with the other demons of death. She also resembles the other demons in that she uses seductive powers to attract men; when she manifests herself as a beautiful young girl, Dionysos cries, 'Let me get to her!' He is only deterred when she turns hurriedly into a dog. They then notice that she has one brass leg, and the other is made of shit. Unsurprisingly, their enthusiasm for intercourse with her ebbs sharply.

Yet ancient Greek prostitutes may have adopted the names of female Greek demons; a humorous catalogue of prostitute-names includes Chimaera, Scylla, Harpies and Sirens. The orator Demosthenes, who is trying to blacken the name of his rival Aeschines, calls his mother 'Empousa', perhaps in this spirit. No one can be sure what this means, but most Greek prostitutes had nicknames. It is possible that such names advertised a particular erotic service, just as a modern client visiting Miss Whiplash would know just what he was likely to get. On the other hand, they may have been mere satire, suggesting the notorious rapacity of whores, or perhaps their supposed liquorishness. Or perhaps Demosthenes just meant that Aeschines' mother was old and ugly, and perhaps demon-names signified prostitutes who were similarly hideous; the lecherous old woman of Aristophanes' *Parlia-*

ment of Women is also called an empousa, suggesting again that like Lamia this demon signified the horror of the ageing female body. To be a female demon is to be particularly embodied and incarnate, to be both sexual and repulsive.[42]

Beyond Greece: Lamia, Lilith, Lamashtu

Your womb contracts one last, wrenching time. The baby's head crowns tearingly, and he slithers out into the midwife's hands. Blood, agony, terror – all wiped away by the giant actuality of this tiny piece of flesh who lies screaming in your arms. He is a blank sheet, but with his own face. The love rushes in, and with it comes a new and terrible fear. You have staked happiness on something mortal. And you know how dangerous that is, because you live in the world of ancient Sumeria, and you have seen death creep into every house in your village.

One night your child will not stop screaming. You touch him and his skin is scarlet, raging, hot. You offer the breast, the only surcease; he will not drink. And the next night it goes on. And the next. You will not say the words your heart knows; if this goes on . . . no more nights. Endless night.

No. No, no. What to do? What to do? Your mind patters anxiously, rehearsing stories you have heard, stories that give names to the fear that engulfs you. You try this and you try that. Nothing works.

There is a final sobbing breath. The little body becomes still, then cold. This hard little corpse is not your baby; it is a carapace, a stiff skin shed by a summer cicada going into winter. Where is your baby? If only you could fold him back into your body, where he was safe. If only he had never come out of the darkness inside you. If only he could be inside you for ever so you would not have to feel so empty. But life has stolen him from you. As you stroke his cold hair one last time, you whisper the name of the cruel darkness that took him from you. You whisper, with hatred and fear and daring: Lamashtu.

Demons were by no means unique to ancient Greece. The female child-killing demon can be found in different forms all over the vast melting-pot of the Mediterranean basin in ancient times. Lamia could well derive from an even older Sumerian demon, Lamashtu.[43] In the picture on the vase mentioned earlier, Lamia's facial features and hair follow the conventions antiquity used to represent black people: thick lips, black skin, squashed nose. She is tied to a palm tree, which also suggests an African setting. Lamia is elsewhere called the daughter of Belos, meaning Baal; that is foreign. All this may be because Lamia is really Sumerian Lamashtu; but Lamashtu is also called a 'foreigner' and is said to live in the swamps or mountains. Egyptian child-killers, too, are said to come from Asia. In exactly the same spirit, Napoleon became a nursery bogey in nineteenth-century England; nurses menaced their charges by saying, 'Boney will get you!'[44] Wherever the centre is, the demon comes from the periphery. Rather than preserving the origins of each individual figure, this kind of reference might show us the way all antiquity thought about its demons. They are from elsewhere, not one of us, not from around here. They are the ladies from outside, which is what Sicilians call fairies.[45]

Lamashtu is a Mesopotamian demon feared by pregnant women, women giving birth and mothers. She can steal children, perhaps even from their mothers' bodies.[46] She is usually depicted naked, with a lion's head, dangling breasts like Lamia's, and the feet of a bird of prey, and in some depictions she allows a pig and a dog to suckle her breasts: another sign of pollution and the lower body, for pigs are unclean, associated with greed and stench.[47] Like Lamia, Lamashtu kills unborn children in the womb, as well as the newborn. 'Great is Anu's daughter', says a somewhat tremulous incantation, 'who torments the little ones, her hands are a snare-net . . . she sweeps the innards of pregnant women, violently she tears the child out of the pregnant [womb]'.[48] Infants bothered by Lamashtu found it hard to settle to feeding; 'if the infant is continually frightened at its mother's breast . . . the daughter of Anu has chosen him'. Lamashtu longs to suckle babies, like Gello. 'Bring me your children', she begs, 'that I may suckle them; let me put the breast in the mouths of your daughters.' Lamashtu's suckling killed the infants, and her eagerness for the little mouth at her breast was such that she forced children out of the womb before their time, in miscarriages or premature births, so that she could put them to her deadly breasts. The child-killing ogress Putana, of Indian mythology, also longs passionately to suckle and kills with the breast: 'Then the horrible one, taking him on her lap, gave the baby her breast, which had been smeared with a virulent poison. But Krishna, pressing her breast hard with his baby hands, angrily drank out her life's breath with her milk and killed her instead.'[49]

Lamashtu may also be among the origins for the Hebrew Lilith, a winged female demon who strangled children. Lilith is first known from a chilling inscription dating from the 7th-8th century BCE: 'To her that flies in rooms of darkness – pass quickly, quickly, Lilith.' One story illustrates Lilith's dark and malevolent power: the prophet Elijah meets Lilith, and says, 'O wicked Lilith, where are you going with your foul unclean host?' Lilith's reply freezes the marrow with its frankness: 'My Lord Elijah, I am going to that woman who has given birth to a child, to give her the sleep of death, to take her newborn child, to drink its blood, to suck the marrow of its bones, but to leave its flesh untouched.' Elijah tells her that if she does this she will be turned into a speechless stone by the will of God. Lilith, duly daunted, gives way: 'My Lord, for God's sake remove the excommunication, that I may be able to flee, and I swear by the name of God that I will avoid the roads that lead to a woman with a newborn child, and whenever I see or hear my names I will depart.' And she tells him the names.[50] Lilith brings an unnatural way of death to the child; it is a hidden death, a death that leaves no clear outward sign. Lilith works in the dark; by leaving the child's flesh untouched, by refraining from abducting it, she adds mystery to her crimes. The story, however, is about laying Lilith bare; Elijah prises from her both the nature of her malevolence and her secret names, and thus gains the upper hand.

It is appropriate, then, that the story should appear on the amulets worn by Hebrew women in childbirth.[51] Of course the story includes Lilith's names, which themselves have power over her, but the story itself is another way of naming her; the whole tale says: 'Darkness is dispelled. We know you, Lilith, and so there is no darkness here, no secrecy, no silence.' Amulets were fixed over childbeds and sometimes on all four walls for protection. In other places, a circle was drawn around the lying-in bed, and the names 'Sanvi, Sansanvi, Semangelaf, Adam and Eve, Barring Lilith' were chalked upon the walls or the door. The circle and its names of power created an enclosed space around the opened body of the labouring woman, protecting her from Lilith, who might otherwise exploit that opening.[52]

Like Lamia and Lamashtu, Lilith has a problematically leaky and excessive body, a body which signifies her evil nature by its openness. At the solstices and equinoxes, some Hebrew stories say, it is dangerous to fetch fresh water from the wells because they are polluted by blood. A Kabbalistic interpretation of this event understands the blood as Lilith's menstruation, falling from the sky as she flies overhead on her deadly errands. Does that menstruation signify Lilith's own failure (at that moment, at least) to produce children, so that her murderousness (like Lamia's and Mormo's) is about the jealousy of the inadequate mother? One story implies that Lilith eats her own children, making her like Lamia and Medea in failing to achieve completion by rearing her children to adulthood. But she is also a demon who makes sure that mothers keep the rules: 'Do not leave an infant alone in the house by day or night, nor pass the night alone in any abode. For thus does Lilith seize man and child in her fatal embrace,' urges one ancient Hebrew saying. Popping out to gossip with friends on the step while the baby snoozes is transformed from a mild transgression into a deadly risk by this night-demon.[53]

In Hebrew legend, Lilith is often replaced by other demons: the evil eye, the star Margalya, the demon Maimon the black, so like the Mammone, the children's bugbear of early nineteenth-century Southern Italy.[54] Still other Hebrew demons include Shibbeta, who eats people after strangling them, and especially strangles children who eat food touched by unwashed hands; this is another demon who enforces the rules of housework and childcare. There is also the Keteb Meriri: the Talmud says it is most powerful at noon, especially during the hot summer months. One horrifying story of its power over children survives, without rhyme or reason: Sefer Hasidim reports that a group of children on their way to school one noon were suddenly confronted by the Keteb. All but two of the children died. This supernatural version of the Dunblane killer is unique in attacking children in a group, in a public place.[55]

Lilith and Lamashtu and Lamia remain active for hundreds of years. Here is a familiar story with an unfamiliar twist: a demon called Avezuha, the wing of Satan, rashly assails the Virgin Mary and the infant Christ. She looks very like Lamia, with 'the hair of her head hanging down to the ground, eyes like stars, hands of iron, the nails of her hands and feet like sickles'. She is even franker than Lilith; when she meets St Michael the Archangel, she declares: 'I am going to Bethlehem in Judea, for I have heard that Jesus Christ is going to be born of His Virgin Mother Maria, and I am going to hurt her.' 'Whereupon the Archangel Michael took hold of the hair of her head, fastened an iron chain round her, stuck his sword into her side, and began to beat her terribly in order to make her tell all her secret arts.' She began, and said, 'I change myself into a dog, a cat, a fly, a spider, a raven, an evil-looking girl, and thus enter into the houses of the people and hurt the women and bring trouble upon the children, and I bring changelings, and I have nineteen names.' And the Archangel Michael said to her, 'I tell thee, and I conjure thee, that thou shalt have neither the power to approach the house of X the servant of the Lord, nor to hurt his property, his flocks, nor anything else that belongs to him. Thou shalt go to the desolate mountains where no one lives, and there shalt thou abide.' This story was collected in about 1900, in Romania. It shows how the child-killing demon remained constant, though it acquired new adversaries, saints and angels. Caught up in Christianity rather than abolished by it, this early fairy remained herself and retained her traditional functions.[56]

Thinking hate

We can begin to put together what we know about child-killing demons now: they are incomplete; they have failed to pass from a transitional phase to a phase of completion. Sometimes they are simply and straightforwardly dead; sometimes they are never born. They seek hopelessly to complete themselves through the ingestion of others (devouring, sex) but their appetites can never be satisfied because what they truly desire is no longer available: a full lifetime. Their incompleteness is shown by their bodies, which are grotesque, provisional and open to change.

Child-killing demons sometimes disguise themselves oddly; an Egyptian incantation of the New Kingdom remarks simply: 'Perish, you who come in from the dark! You who creep in with your nose reversed and your face turned back, and who forgets what he came for. Did you come to kiss this child? I will not allow you to kiss this child.'[57] The mixture of love and hate in the demon's desire to deliver a fatal kiss is also typical. Adam Phillips has a patient, a little girl, who uses spiders to think hate with. Whenever this child wanted to hate, she conjured dream-spiders for herself, spiders she feared, but also needed.[58] The ancient world used demons to think the child's hate for the mother, the mother's hate for the child, the child's love for the mother, the mother's love for the child. The undiscovered country from which demons come turns out to be the human heart after all.

Feet

A final word: about feet. Child-killing demons ancient and modern are united by podal oddity. There is an ass-legged demon who appears to Solomon in the *Testament*; she has a beautiful female body to the knees, while the Romanian demon Avezuha has 'the nails of her hands and feet like sickles'. Lucian's parody of the *Odyssey* involves men meeting a party of beautiful ass-footed demons who want to devour them while they sleep off sex. Empousa, in the *Frogs*, has one leg of brass and the other of shit.[59] Roman *striges*, monstrous nocturnal birds of prey, have feet turned backwards. Modern Greek demons look normal on top, but have defective legs; modern lamiae are beautiful women with the legs or feet of an ass, or sometimes of a goat or cow, or else have feet that do not match. Sometimes a lamia has three or more feet, and of different sorts. One may be of copper, another a donkey's, another a cow's or a goat's or human or whatever else. The little, mischievous modern Greek demons known as *kallikantzaroi* are also marked by odd feet; some are one-footed, some club-footed. Furthermore, podal abnormality is a cultural constant when it comes to demons: the Australian Aboriginal Bagini, for example, have the feet of cockatoos – claws which allow them to hold down their human prey while they tear at his flesh with their hands.

What can all this possibly mean? How do odd feet tie in with the bizarre status of these demons, caught between one stage of life and another? Their nature is symbolized by their bodies; just as these demons are caught – neither unborn nor born, neither mothers nor not-mothers, neither girls nor women – so their bodies are divided: between organic flesh and metal, between life and waste, between human and animal. A leg made of dung or brass looks prosthetic, too, and the same might be said of animal legs. It is as if a bit has dropped off these demons and has been hastily replaced with something near to hand; a dung leg sounds particularly like a bodge job. Odd feet are a sign of incompleteness, the incompleteness which is these demons' very being. We could go even further and see such legs as signs of terrible damage, perhaps even castration?

As *signs* above all; for all this leg-lore is designed to allow the listener to recognize demons when in disguise, a need borne out by the stories of their changeability and deceptiveness. (Perhaps the footless demon who most resembles these is Stevenson's Long John Silver. His missing leg is so memorable that it has become part of the standard portrayal of a pirate, down to the figures who man the Playmobil pirate ship.[60]) Yes, but why *feet*? Bodily anomaly could as well be signified by a vegetable nose. There are two possibilities. First, odd or anomalous feet produce an odd or anomalous gait, and an odd gait is often a sign of dealings with the underworld.[61] Heroes, too, often have odd feet (Oedipus, Achilles, Jason) and we have seen that in the ancient world demons are what heroes defeat, and also that demons are defeated by what is like them; like turns away like. So odd feet suggest that one is either trapped in the twilight between death and life, or that one can come and go between death and life. Secondly, feet and legs are polluted or dirty because they are close to the ground. The feet are where the body ends and the ground begins. They are part of the lower body, the belly, the genitals, the anus, and associated with all three. This is one reason why feet and legs are eroticized in many cultures. Such bodily lowness is also symbolized by the fact that many of the odd feet of demons are animal feet; classical mythology abounds with creatures whose lower bodies are animal and their upper bodies human: satyrs, centaurs, fauns, silenoi, and the god Pan, are all associated with sexual licence.

This second meaning of deformed or abnormal feet is especially relevant to a second group of beings, beings who resemble medieval fairies even more closely than do child-killing demons. This group of beings, the nymphs, or as modern Greeks would say, nereids, also have deformed feet, sometimes the feet of goats or asses.[62] And as we shall see, nymphs are exquisitely sexual, in the eye of the beholder at least. To find nymphs, though, we must come out of the darkness and into the blazing, raging light of noon. Nymphs come from the blank spaces on the map, too, but from spaces made blank by dazzle and glare. Into the light.

Bright light burning: nymphs

You are nineteen, and you are a young man, a beautiful young man. It could be any time: the ancient world, the modern world; on these Grecian hillsides, the sheep and goats graze just as they have always done. It is midday, the time of day when the sun arcs down like a bright-edged sword. Your eyes are as blind as midnight because of the brilliance of the light, the shimmer of heat. You are all alone in this white, dazzling world of pure light. You have taken refuge from the heat under a tree, a tree by a stream. The water imparts some coolness to the air. The tree bends lovingly over the water. In the shade, you begin to relax, to feel sleepy. The soft sliding of the water over stones is soothing. Gradually, though, you begin to hear another noise mixed in with it, the sound of bubbling laughter, soft sighs.

Suddenly, every hair on your head stands stiff with fear. You can feel a soft, cool hand caressing your thigh.

For an instant, a breath, the world stands still. Then you run and run and don't stop until you reach the village, lungs bursting, mouth full of white dust.

You will tell this story for the rest of your life, tell it with fear and longing.

You will always wonder if you were right to run.

What was it that touched your thigh? Better not to say it, even think it. The modern Greek peasants have many names for them: 'the ladies', 'our maidens', 'our good queens', 'the kind-hearted ones', 'the ladies to whom we wish joy', 'our good ladies'.[63] The ancients called them nymphs. Now, there are things we all think we know about nymphs.

They are female divinities perceived as dazzlingly beautiful young women; they inhabit and express differentiated nature: water (rivers, springs, the sea), mountains, trees. They are ubiquitous in popular imagination, folklore and art. They are either immortal or endowed with superhuman longevity. They are constantly getting into love-trouble, at least according to Ovid, whose *Metamorphoses* might have been subtitled 'Nymphs and their Ways'. They sound benign, bland and boring in their predictability; in Ovid, the only question is which feature of the landscape they will ultimately become. But these repetitive stories of nymphs on the run are not representative of the nature of nymphs.

Nymphs are caught between the world of gods and the world of men; they eat ambrosia, the food of the gods, but their lives, though long, are destined one day to end. Hence they are not goddesses, and like mortals they can suffer from familiarity with the gods.[64] Their anomalousness is like that of the child-killing demons, both dead and undead, both mothers and not-mothers. Nymphs are anomalous in other ways, too. The Greek word for nymphs is *numphae*, and it is a word with many interlaced meanings. The word *numphe* means a young woman at the moment of her transition from maiden to wife or woman; a *numphe* is trembling on the brink of change, waiting through long hot days for . . . she knows not what. A *numphe* is a mixture of ignorance and desire, for desire must feed on knowledge. *Numphe* also means clitoris, and refers to the barely opened buds of roses, themselves vulval in shape and tenderness. Nymphs' gardens, wedding songs and eroticism are all linked; a nymph is both a girl waiting for sexual fulfilment and the site of that fulfilment.[65] Though they do not sound very much like the demons, nymphs resemble them in that they are 'stuck' in a particular phase of life. Whereas child-killing demons are 'stuck' in foetal expectation, or in pre-maternity, nymphs are 'stuck' at another life-transition, the change from girl to woman.

Until one realizes this, the silence around nymphs is baffling. Unlike the child-killers, they have no point of view of their own, but enter into the stories of others, sometimes briefly, sometimes for a long time. People see them out late, dancing in the fields. Why are they there? We never find out. A nymph looks after a foundling, but what is told is the baby's story, not the nymph's. What does she feel when it grows up? We never learn. Like illuminations, nymphs brighten the edges of stories without reaching the middle. Why this terrible blankness? Because all nymphs are young girls to whom nothing has happened yet, nothing that needs to be told. To be more exact, all nymphs have only the beginning of a story, a genealogy; just as a baby might. But they go no further. Suspended between birth and maturity for ever, nymphs are *girls* who cannot grow up. Their whole story is to have no story. They are forever young, forever on the brink of love, marriage, commitment. But not there yet, and so nowhere.

Or so Odysseus found. Odysseus is the first recorded victim of nympholepsy, theft-by-nymph, a phenomenon recorded from the very earliest epics until the present day. Every now and then, nymphs feel an overwhelming desire for some mortal, and abduct him. Usually he stays with them for a period of time (seven years is common, and eternity always possible). He may disappear for ever, like Heracles' lover Hylas, or he may be released to rejoin his family. But he is not unchanged by his sojourn in the nymph's arms. Often he is gifted with prophetic or shamanistic powers; even more often he becomes the creator or embellisher of a cult place, person or special inspiration. He makes a shrine to his lover in a cave or grotto. The nympholept was part of a tradition of holy men, men who were lifted to a higher plane of being.[66] Odysseus' story begins with the hero held prisoner by a beautiful nymph, Calypso. The story is so important and so revealing that it deserves detailed treatment. Calypso seems to offer him everything: beauty, home, love, even immortality if he will only promise to stay. Yet he longs to leave, to return to scrubby Ithaca; every day he sits on Calypso's perfect beach and cries, like some stranded tourist in Barbados, dreaming of the grey streets of Luton. He's in Paradise, and he's miserable. Is the man an idiot? The answer is no. To live in the paradise of the nymphs is a great sacrifice, one too great for Odysseus to bear.

Is he held prisoner by his own helplessness, or is Calypso exercising a kind of magic power over him, similar to the kind used by fairy queens to restrain their lovers? To understand who Calypso is, we have to understand where she is first; we have to understand her island, Ogygia. She lives in a grotto of great and lyrical natural beauty that is also somehow well-tended – Sissinghurst coupled with a Mediterranean beach:

A great fire
blazed on the hearth and the smell of cedar
cleanly split and sweetwood burning bright
wafted a cloud of fragrance down the island.
Deep inside she sang, the goddess Calypso, lifting
her breathtaking voice as she glided back and forth
before her loom, her golden shuttle weaving.
Thick, luxuriant woods grew round the cave,
alders and black poplars, pungent cypress too,
and there birds roosted, folding their long wings,
owls and hawks and the spread-beaked ravens of the sea,
black skimmers who make their living off the waves.
And round the mouth of the cavern trailed a vine
laden with clusters, bursting with ripe grapes.
Four springs in a row, bubbling clear and cold,
running side-by-side, took channels left and right.
Soft meadows spreading round were starred with violets,
lush with beds of parsley. Why, even a deathless god
who came upon that place would gaze in wonder,
heart entranced with pleasure. Hermes the guide,
the mighty giant-killer, stood there, spellbound . . .[67]

Or is it natural? This is not natural beauty, but civilized beauty. The description begins with a fire, a fire in which the natural scent of fragrant woods is harnessed by a knowledgeable housewife to bring perfume to the home. A fire is a sign of culture; and not only culture, but the female sphere, the hearth, the very sphere that Penelope is guarding for Odysseus in Ithaca. The next thing we see is Calypso singing as she weaves, like any country housewife, making cloth, turning raw materials into civilized ones. And the vine is not wild, but domestic, tame; here we have all the ingredients for a man's country estate; not a wilderness, but a park is before us.

This is no great surprise, because even modern Greeks believe that nymphs are connected not with the untamed natural wilderness, but with the housewifery that turns nature into culture. 'She keeps house like a Nymph' is a stately compliment. Like fairies, who become more and more obsessed with neatness as early modern society does,

Calypso's weaving is less a sign that she is a slave to domestic obligation than a sign of her gender: that is what women do, wherever they are, whoever they are. But Calypso is also *not* a woman, and her home is not Ithaca, though it *looks* like Ithaca. In the *Odyssey* it is called *leimones malakoi*, the soft meadows. Sounds wonderful? Yes, but the sirens' killing-ground is called *leimon anthemoesis*, a meadow in bloom.[68] A sinister association indeed, since the first time we see Calypso she is singing. *Leimon* can also mean female genitalia; these female seductresses live on islands that are like their bodies, that express their bodies' desires and beauties. Ogygia is the navel of the sea, and a navel can be a figure for the vagina. Ogygia is a 'sort of marginal space as a place apart, far from the gods and far from humans',[69] a place whose smiling blank façade conceals – something. What?

Death, I think, and the land of death. Calypso lives in a cave. Many nymphs are troglodytes. They lie with Silenus and Hermes in caves in the *Homeric Hymn to Aphrodite* (263); the nymph Maia conceived Hermes in a cave, and like Calypso's cave, hers is a place of conceal-ment for tricksters; Hermes hides there after he has stolen the cattle of Apollo. Caves are places where gods and heroes live, suspended between life and death, yes, but dead to the world of action, the world of heroism. But caves also have another meaning; they are places where men live, true, but they are also places uncannily close to graves. They are holes in the earth; structurally they resemble tombs and tombs resemble them. Caves can be gateways to the underworld, and hence often oracles of the dead. Calypso's home is like a Greek household, and she herself like Penelope, but there is also something deathly about it all.[70] Ogygia is too close to the underworld for comfort, too *like* death in function.

Or so it proves for Odysseus. Calypso's name means 'concealer'; Calypso conceals Odysseus on her island. As long as he is with her he is lost, he is not himself, not able to function as Odysseus. All he does is sit weeping and staring at the sea, filled with longing for home. Calypso is not merely the hidden one but 'the one who hides'; she enchants and bewitches Odysseus so that he might forget Ithaca. As long as he is with Calypso, Odysseus is cut off from his family; they cannot be with him, and they cannot give him his grave and remember him. On Ogygia he is neither alive nor dead: although still alive he is already, and ahead of time, like someone blotted out from human memory. Having disappeared, he no longer has fame; he is *akleios*, without glory.[71] He is in a prison with transparent walls thousands of miles thick and they muffle his name.

What does Calypso offer, then? First, escape from the challenges of the return. But most importantly, immortality: never to grow old or sick or die. But to be immortal with Calypso exacts a terrible price, one too high for Odysseus to pay; he must renounce his career as epic hero. What Calypso offers is an obscure, anonymous immortality, as anonymous as the deaths of those many humans who could not take on a heroic fate and form, and are in the underworld as an indistinct mass of the nameless, the *nonumnoi*.[72] To be 'among the nymphs' can be a euphemism for death, but if so it is this silent kind of death, not the speaking heroic death which leaves an everlasting fame.[73] Calypso appears to offer an escape from death, but actually offers an end to the only means by which men can beat death: everlasting fame. Wrapped in the thick scented smoke of Ogygia, Odysseus' fame is lost for ever. After seven years of this, Odysseus longs to resolve the anomalies of his situation by really dying.

Karl Reinhardt says 'there is no story at all that can be told about Calypso'.[74] This storylessness, this silence, is because she is a nymph. Nymphs are always girls, and nothing has yet happened to girls (which is why girl groups are still bland, for all their maenad shrieks of GirlPower). In the ancient world, they do what Calypso does: they weave, they sing, they keep house. The only things that can happen to them have not happened yet: marriage, children. Calypso keeps a tidy cave; that is the most that can be said about her. In being with her, Odysseus is relegated to the blank silence of the girl's world, a terrible fate for a hero. It is as if Achilles had never shed his women's clothes. But once he escapes, his story can begin again, a story that tells of adventure and that culminates in his restoration to his own household, a household that will perpetuate his name. It is proverbial that once an exploit has been accomplished, it must not remain hidden (*kalypsoi*) in silence but must be celebrated in praise poetry. Odysseus' decision to leave Calypso is the reason the *Odyssey* can exist, for there can never be an epic about a girl.[75]

Of course, that leaves Calypso surrounded by her own white silence. We know she does not want Odysseus to go, but we don't know what she does when he leaves at last. Such is the fate of nymphs. They give stories to men, but have no stories of their own. Prophetic, oracular and other verbal powers were often the result of nympholepsy; the cave of the nymphs on the peak of Cithaeron once contained an oracle, and many of the natives were possessed of the oracular power, and these were called *nympholeptoi*, 'nymph-possessed'.

Being taken by a nymph leads to all kinds of magical or powerful speech. In *Phaedrus*, Socrates ventures outside the city walls at noon, and remarks,

Does it seem to you as it does to me that something supernatural is happening to me? Hear me then in silence, for I really believe there is something supernatural about the place. So if as the speech goes on I become nympholept, do not be surprised, for I am already not far from speaking in dithyrambs . . . Do you not see that I will soon be possessed by the nymphs to whom you deliberately exposed me?[76]

Socrates is sitting by water, the river Ilissos; that makes it worse, for nymphs love water and shade. It is midday. But he is also playing, teasing as he always does; serious fear and joking are intertwined.

Nymphs also inspired Longus to write his novel *Daphnis and Chloe*; the entire story is a description of a painting which the author came upon one day in a sacred grove of the nymphs on the island of Lesbos, and which so charmed him with its beauty that he was filled with intense longing to rival it in a narrative.

Chloe was herself reared by nymphs, after being exposed. Like demons, and like fairies, nymphs have a special affinity with children, especially those left exposed, improperly safeguarded. However, nymphs are the benign face of child-stealing; they may abduct children, but they do not devour them. Instead, they rear them. They are particularly drawn to children abandoned by their mothers, bastards, children who are the result of rape.[77] A child conceived out of wedlock in the *Homeric Hymn to Aphrodite* is cared for by the nymphs:

As for the child, as soon as he sees the light of the sun, the deep-breasted mountain nymphs who live in the great and holy mountain shall bring him up ... these nymphs shall keep my son and rear him, and as soon as he is come to lovely boyhood, the goddesses will bring him here and show you your child.[78]

These nymphs are not a frightening but a consoling fantasy; they let a mother tell herself that she is not *really* killing her child by abandoning it, but leaving it to a better fate. Just so do the tragic girls who leave their babies in public lavatories console themselves with the thought that the child may be adopted by someone very rich and nice.

Modern nymphs

In modern Greece the nymphs are no longer so benign. They do not only rear the children they are given; they *take* children that do not belong to them. One story reveals their difference from classical nymphs, and their even closer likeness to fairies. A man heard the nymphs singing and dancing in the forest, and this is what they sang: 'The marathos and the apiganos [rue] and one more herb which – if your mother only knew it – she would never lose a child.' But the nymphs never said what the name of the third herb was.[79] Children may be stolen by nymphs, and are sometimes replaced by a weak nymph changeling. Sometimes they die and are afterwards seen dancing with the nymphs.[80] Other children disappear, after a period of worrying 'abstraction'; one little girl who liked to walk by herself in the woods and fields was soon taken. Not all children are stolen away; sometimes the nymphs attack them. One woman told the story of a family whose child 'was beaten by the nymphs during his sleep. At that time he was a baby and when he awakened in the morning his face was black and swollen.'[81] Whether such children die, or disappear, or lose some faculties, 'seized' is the word applied.

Nymphs are especially dangerous during marriage and childbirth, but their behaviour is different from that of the child-killing demons; they kill the mother, but preserve the child and even give it extra beauty and wealth. Like medieval fairies, they can be appeased by the sharing of household food. Foods containing honey are put out for the nymphs for forty days after the birth: 'a white cloth is spread upon the spot, and on it is put a plate with bread, honey and other sweets, a bottle of good wine, a knife, a fork, an empty glass, an unburnt candle and a censer'. Sometimes an old woman says, 'Good day to you, good queens, eat the little cakes and heal my child.'[82] Though not as desperate as invocations to the child-killing demons of the ancient world, there is a family resemblance to them. Somehow, nymphs have got themselves mixed up with nursery terrors.

Why have nymphs become so much more hostile in modern Greece than they were in ancient times? The usual explanation for belief in child-killing beings is a high rate of infant mortality and birth defects, but it seems unlikely that Greek villagers are worse off now than in classical times. What seems more plausible as an explanation is the declining rate of infant abandonment and exposure. Stories about nymphs' love for children originally express and manage women's feelings of guilt and anxiety about the fate of the children the father decides not to rear. Having set such stories in motion, they take on a life of their own; the countryside became full of nymphs who love children. But in the post-Christian era, they are not given any. What more natural than that they should take to stealing them?

Young men

Nymphs always did steal young men; somehow classical culture could tolerate the idea of a youth abducted by a woman. Not so modern Greece; the boot is now on the other foot and it is nymphs who are 'abducted' by men. A range of stories tell of village youths who fall in love with a nymph and manage to abduct her by stealing her headscarf. As long as the man keeps the headscarf, he also keeps the nymph. Such stories very closely parallel the better-known stories of Scottish mermaids or seal-women who marry mortals, and, like those stories, these are tales of ancestry; their purpose is to figure a family's relationship to a particular part of the country, their 'wedding' to their land or craft.

One man who loved a nymph discovered the secret of keeping her from a cunning woman: he seized her headscarf, and the results were spectacular: she 'at once began to transform herself . . . first she became a lion . . . then a snake, and then fire, but he would not let go. Then at last she returned to her proper form, and went home with him, and was his wife and bore him a son, but he kept the kerchief hidden from her, lest she become a nymph again.'[83] The mother of Achilles, the sea-nymph Thetis, likewise transforms herself into a number of shapes to escape the clasp of her human suitor Peleus. The nymph is like the medieval fairy-lovers of ballads. She sets her beloved a love-test: can he hold her as she shifts shape? Can he find the true nymph among all her transformations? If he can, then he can take her girlhood, her always-the-sameness, and make it different.

Such encounters are not safe, as another story reveals. It was winter, and a shepherd was staying outside to be near his flocks. In the night a woman he thought was his wife came and slept with him. In the morning when he saw his wife he said, relishingly, 'Not even as newlyweds was it so good.' His wife was amazed; she didn't know what he was talking about. The dreadful realization steals over them both: it must have been a nymph. Of course he falls ill at once: his penis swells up and turns black, and after some futile recourses to modern medicine, he tries the magical remedy of sprinkling holy water at the spot where he made love with the nymph. But the sprinkling should have been done *before* he went to the doctor; he dies for his lack of faith.[84] (I know what you're thinking: you're thinking that this nymph story is a great excuse for a one-night stand and a venereal disease. It's a little more complicated than that; the point is, why does *this* culture have *this* excuse? Different cultures, different plausibilities. Next time you go out on the tiles, try telling your own partner that . . . no, don't. Fall back on 'working late', which shows quite clearly what gods we believe in here in England.)

The shepherd's mistake is to *tell*, to reveal his encounter with the nymph. Speaking of fairy encounters is invariably a serious mistake. This probably enforces a norm. Peter Walcot, writing about Odysseus' cunning in the *Odyssey*, argues that Greek peasants practise a systematic policy of misdirection in matters great and small, in order to protect themselves in a social environment full of enemies and charged with unremitting suspicion. People lie not only to conceal faults, but to cover up trivial facts, since any information which gets out gives power to an enemy. Even children are taught to be constantly vigilant against innocent-sounding questions.[85] Revelation is danger. The closed mouth is a safe mouth. Any opening of the body is fatal. Talk is fatal. Don't ask, don't tell, don't make yourself cheap. Nymph stories enforce a cultural norm crucial to village society: don't give yourself away. And it's no coincidence that this phrase has a sexual as well as a verbal meaning.

Ancient fairies

What have we learned about fairies if both child-killing demons and nymphs are fairies? Many things.

Fairies come from outside, from outside the community, civilization, even when they seem to share its values.

Fairies were either once people or are like people who have become trapped at a certain indeterminate phase of life.

Fairies have links with the dead, and some *are* the dead.

Young men, women in childbirth, and babies and children are particularly vulnerable to fairies.

Fairies are compelled to repeat their own circumstances in the lives of others; if they die prematurely, they cause the premature deaths of others; if they are trapped in eternal, storyless youth, they try to trap others in it too.

Fairies have bodies which reflect their anomalousness, subtly or directly.

Fairies are also particularized to the local situation, as the changing role of nymphs indicates.

Fairies are common to peasant cultures, cultures where the centre of life is the village and the space around it.

All this time, I have been sedulously ignoring a vital question: why on earth are these beings fairies? Everybody knows – or at least everybody thinks they know – that fairies are Celtic, and here I am insisting that fairies' origins lie in the ancient cultures of the Mediterranean. Yet the more stories about ancient demons I read, the more I was struck by their extraordinary similarity to medieval and early modern fairies. I can't yet convince you of the similarities because I have still to tell you about Northern European fairies. The similarities are there, however. Take them on trust for the moment; the proof will arrive in due course. I promise.

There are three possible explanations for why these beings recur in the cultures of the ancient Mediterranean and also in Celtic cultures and their later by-products. I again resort to the brisk administrative clarity of a list.

Firstly, common humanity: these are universal cultural archetypes produced by common psychic pressures in every culture.

Secondly, common structures: in societies with similar social structures, similar social solutions will be produced; so, for instance, all village societies will produce taciturnity as a norm, and will therefore develop a corpus of folk-beliefs about the disastrous results of loquacity.

Thirdly, direct transmission: the Celts learned these stories from their contacts with the Mediterranean peoples, just as the Mediterranean peoples learned these stories from each other.

The problem with the first explanation is that it makes it difficult to understand the relative decline of such beliefs in the post-war era in the West. Note that I say *relative*; some do survive, in partial, flattened forms which will be discussed in due course. Nevertheless, the question remains: if fear of demons is central to human nature, why do we no longer share it? We do not habitually attribute the deaths of young babies to the malfeasance of their stillborn siblings, nor would we reach for the holy water if suffering from the grim symptoms which plague the shepherd in the story of the nymph told above. I suppose we could go the self-abasing Jungian route of arguing that we have somehow ceased to be human, but short of that I think we must abandon universality as an explanation.

The second explanation is far more seductive, and has the doubtful merit of being acutely fashionable with recent folklorists, not as an explanation for fairy beliefs, but as an explanation for anything at all. Embarrassed by the drastic cultural conflations of their predecessors, modern mythographers are eager to prove that they are not George Eliot's Mr Casaubon, writing the useless Key To All Mythologies. To do this, they insist on the specificity of every story, so that stories with folk motifs dating back to antiquity must be explained via the practices of such-and-such a village in drawing its well-water from a site between the church and the tavern. This approach has often been valuable, and there is no doubt that local factors invariably play a part in shaping the precise characteristics of a particular story. For instance, many nymph stories (and, as we shall see, fairy stories) specify a particular location for nympholepsy, often a tree. This is a common feature, but it is still worth finding out for each local story what significance the tree had; is it one in the village? outside it? with edible products? poisonous? associated with particular deities, saints or heroes? The results are not always interesting, but they often are.

What we can see at such moments, however, is not the birth of entirely new stories, but the ceaseless reshaping of old stories to fit new contexts. Sometimes this involves simple changes of geography, sometimes changes in point of view, sometimes more drastic changes in narrative. But in every case, the result is a blend of continuity and change. We have asked about change; we need to ask about continuity now, and about the plausibility of the third explanation I offered. What if fairies – contrary to every common assumption – actually originated in the ancient world of the Mediterranean and not in the Celtic darknesses of Northern Europe? Is this possible?

The answer is yes. The Celts had a lot more early contact with the Greeks than most people imagine, encountering them regularly as foes and trading partners from the sixth century BCE onwards. During the period of the Roman Empire, Greek ideas and culture were diffused – in Romanized forms – throughout the Celtic world. The Celts picked up and 'Celticized' large slices of Roman religion, political culture and military know-how. Before and through the Empire, Celts were in constant contact with Greek culture for hundreds of years.[86] To assume that they kept to their own folkways without any outside influences during this period is like assuming that no one in modern Britain is at all influenced by French culture today, despite the frequency of cross-channel ferry sailings. Another reason for the idea that fairies drift on the wings of empire from the Mediterranean to the Celtic regions is that attempts to explain the origin of fairy beliefs with reference to Celtic culture only have failed. No one now believes that the fairies are dethroned Celtic gods, or memories of vanishing ancient

Britons.[87] If they cannot be explained through Celtic culture alone, then it seems at least worth trying to explain them as a product of the cosmopolitanism of empire rather than the parochialism of Northern Europe.

Cosmopolitan fairies? I wish I could tell you that I'm certain of it. But as with all else in fairyland, this theory may be a glittering deception. Folktales slide across the surface of men's minds, often leaving no trace of their passage. They may fly from mouth to mouth around a village and stop at its borders, or make a slow, sneaking journey to the ends of the earth, disguising themselves as everything from queens to beggars. Either way, they often leave few readable marks of their passage in the book-culture which is all that is left to us of the world that made the first fairies. In this sense, we always end with fairies where we began – in the dark. But at least we know which part of the dark to look at.

2

Medieval Dreams

You are about to meet beings called fairies at last, and yet these beings are familiar; we have already met them. They are not the pagan gods, and the behaviours they inspire in people are not half-forgotten pagan rites offered to the Olympian or chthonic pantheons. Rather, people in classical times lived their lives and practised their religions alongside other beings, beings not hostile but different from us and dangerous to us. We have met those beings. And those beings, who are not simpler than Artemis, but who attract less official attention, survived her demise. They went on unchanged to lie comfortably alongside Christianity, as they had lain alongside the Delphic oracle; well, perhaps not quite as comfortably, but without spleen.

Why did they survive when so much died with the coming of the One True Faith? Because they were not official; they did not attract attention. They did not have big, visible shrines and priests and holy texts of their own. They were oral, popular. And there was another reason. The people of the villages still found them useful, in all the old ways. Soon, they were mingling promiscuously with the new, Christian-speaking dead, the saints, the angels, and creating new stories and meanings.

'Birth, and copulation, and death./ That's all the facts when you come to brass tacks:/ Birth, and copulation, and death', wrote T. S. Eliot with elegant languor. These three abide, and all three are the fairies' domain. In the middle ages, fairies were the ones who presided over birth, and copulation, and death, and the ones who made all three go wrong. Therefore they are the ones who enforce the rules, but they are also the ones who articulate the unspoken, silent desires that lie within all three events, the desires that go beyond what society can accept.

The story of fairies, the story I tell, is not a continuous story, but fragments of story, pieces, woven into the fabric of lives. It's like walking through a forest, getting occasional glimpses of – something, somethings – moving through the trees beside you. Yet each glimpse shows something different – a faun, a green man, a nicely dressed lady. There is never a cohesive whole, only figures lost in a forest. We are going into that forest now. What you see depends on what you are. If we follow medieval minds into their fairy forest, we will see that women and men take separate paths. Let us go with women first, and see, again, fairies whose flickering lights mirror babies, children, mothers.

St Guinefort and the lost children

It is the year of Our Lord, 1312, and you are on a pilgrimage. You reach the place towards which you have been journeying. It is a wood in France, a wood which has grown up where there was once a village or a proud tower. You can still feel the stones underfoot, shaped stones, fallen now, smothered by the tall trees. It is dark and cool in the wood, yet you know that there is danger. There are wolves. There are also what you call fauns – small beings, on whose account you have come. A river runs through the wood, and by the river is the tomb of a saint, the oddest saint in the old Catholic pantheon, a saint who is also a dog. St Guinefort the Greyhound Dog, protector of children. Many years ago, more years than you can count, a dog called Guinefort saved a child who was drowning in this very river. Now you need his help for your own child. To this wood come mothers, mothers carrying children, children who are sick and weak, thin.

Your own child is squalling in your arms. No matter how often you feed him, it is never enough; he is always hungry, never satisfied, never happy or sleepy. Never anything but crying, angry. Yesterday he bit you, bit your breast in passionate hunger. You shift his weight from one hip to another.

You look at him, at the angry face, and you know he is not yours.

The rite begins. The mothers offer salt, which fairies are known to hate; good mothers will carry salt in their pockets until the baby is christened.[1] They hang the children's swaddling clothes, their baby things, on bushes. This is a common way to cure a child's illness; the illness passes from the child to the clothes to the plant. In this case, though, these are not just any clothes, but the baby's first clothes, treasured, but also guarded, containing perhaps some essence of the baby's self, some essence that will call him home to your arms. For the purpose of the rite is to compel the fauns who live in the forest. The fauns must come because the sick children the mothers have brought are not really their own children. Their real children, their own fat and comely babies, have been taken by the fauns. You hold the thin angry child in your arms. In your mind there is a picture, a clear picture, a baby, plump, rosy, smiling up at you. Your heart turns over; this is what the fauns have taken from you, the joy of loving, of being loved, of getting it right, this business of motherhood. The next part of the ritual begins. The mothers pass one child nine times between them, backwards and forwards. While they do this, they beg the fauns to return their baby. It is your turn. After the passing, you place the screaming, thin baby you have brought at the foot of the tree by Guinefort's tomb. He is naked, as he was at birth.

Then you turn, quickly; you will not listen to his cries, to his screams of pain and rage. You must not look back if you are to win your own child from the fauns, from the underworld that lies beneath the forest. You must stay away from him, stay where you cannot see him or hear him, until the candle you hold has burnt out.

You wait, in an agony of suspense. You know this: sometimes the child dies in this rite. Sometimes a wolf comes from the forest and devours the child. Sometimes the fauns come and take back their own; sometimes, sometimes, they bring the stolen human child with them. And you too are alone, with only the guttering light of the candle to protect you from the vast imperial darkness of the forest. Can you hear? Hear wolves? Hear the terrible footsteps of the fauns? St Guinefort, St Guinefort, bring back my child!

At last the candle droops, darkens. You run back to the tree. And there is your own true child. You smile. He smiles shakily at you, his tears drying as you scoop him up, weeping now, both of you, weeping with love and relief. Now he must be dipped, dipped nine times in the ice-cold river to cleanse him. But he is your own baby, your own little love, once again. The fauns have relented.[2]

It is the Middle Ages. And in the woods are still beings who are a danger to children. The same beings, in fact, who were in them in classical times. The only difference is that children have now acquired a protector they did not have before – St Guinefort.

What is happening here? Love, or hate? A misguided superstitious attempt to save a child sick with some disorder that medieval medicine did not acknowledge? Or an excuse for infanticide? Love, or violence? It might be both. The story of the changeling, in all its manifestations, involves an extraordinary mixture of love and hate: love for the stolen baby, the perfect baby, hate for its replacement, its replacement that cries all day. Nowadays, there is no way that mothers can acknowledge that every mother sometimes hates her child, sometimes wishes him dead. Hate and love criss-cross in the passion of the mother–child bond. The medieval culture of the village and field was wiser; it gave women an outlet for their feelings. Women could say, 'It is not my own child I hate, of course not. I love my own darling child. It is this other, this thing, this alien who does not love me back. That is what I hate. How can he be mine when he cannot be satisfied with me? I want my dream-baby back.' The fauns, who both love the child and harm it, carry the mother's feelings, and they give her a chance to prove the depth of her love to herself by being willing to sacrifice the child in order to have him back.

We know the Guinefort ceremony is partly about love because it could have a happy outcome. One of two things could happen. The child could be found dead, in which case the mother had rid herself of an impossibly demanding baby in a manner more-or-less sanctioned by her culture, if not by the Church. Or the child could pass through death, through the woods, the dark woods, the realm of the fauns, which is death, and live, be born again. Naked it could return to death, return to the struggle between life and death that is birth. The child waited for its mother, in the dark, in danger, so the mother waited for the child, waited in pain, in danger, just as once before, the child waited in the dark of the womb to see his mother's face. In the Guinefort ritual, both labour again for a birth. And by that labour, the child could be born again. A clean slate, with a new face on. A new leaf. As death, a ritual death, the fauns could offer to start life over again for the mother and her baby.

This barely Christian ritual appears to involve Guinefort not just as protector of children, but as an animal who has been tamed. The wood is full of animals who have not been tamed (wolves) and half-animal beings who cannot be tamed, but only resisted (fauns). As a tame animal, Guinefort is on the side of humans against the old, uncanny forces of the wood. But as an animal he can speak to the animal; he is a bridge between the human world and the world to which the babies have been taken. If you actually went into such a wood in the Middle Ages, it would probably be to hunt, and you would of course take dogs with you, for protection and use. This makes it natural for medieval people, even those not in the hunting classes, to think of taking a dog to look for lost children. From that, we can learn a little about the beings who took the children. No one speaks to them; no one speaks of them. The less we all know about them, the better. Only our surrogates know them, our Guineforts. Writing about fairies in the Middle Ages is, as we shall see, writing about nearly nothing. Talking about fairies is so fatal that very few people are willing to do it. That is why we are left with glimpses. No one wants to conjure a whole.

Changelings

Practices like the Guinefort ritual were not uncommon. In Germany, the child had to be taken to Cyriac's Mead and left lying there, fed only on water from Cyriac's Well; after nine days it would either die or recover. In other places, the parents had to approach the fairy's hillside dwelling and ask for their child to be returned. Bishop Burchard of Worms at the beginning of the eleventh century imposed a year's penance on mothers who put their children 'on the roof or in a hole' in the hope of curing their illnesses. A way to get rid of a changeling is to leave it somewhere, a crossroads, a border between districts. Suicides are also buried at crossroads to prevent their ghosts from finding their way home, and because a suicide's ghost is anomalous. To place someone at a crossroads is to divest oneself of them, to declare that they have no home among us. The child must be placed there, and the mother must go away. She must not speak a word; the refusal of speech is always an important element in countermagic. Peasants don't trust speech; they don't have our liking for it. To speak is to give something of yourself away, and there are powers eager to make use of what you have. To speak is also to open the body. Just as one must not eat the fairy food, so one must close one's mouth on words. She must keep walking, without turning, until she hears the child cry. Then she can run back and embrace her own dear baby, returned by the fairies.

Another way to get rid of it is cruelty. One woman, who consulted her minister, was instructed to beat the child, then hide out of sight and sound for a quarter of an hour. When she came out, her baby was black-and-blue, but it was her own baby again.[3] In Ireland, hot iron was often advised. Another method was to do something peculiar – boiling water in an eggshell – and this would provoke the changeling into giving himself away in speech. Often this becomes a comic folk-story; one changeling tells his babysitter where his parents keep the whisky, and suggest they both pour themselves a drink.[4] This sounds jolly, but other remedies were deadly, and people did try them; as late as the 1890s, a woman in Cork was set on fire by her husband in the belief that the fairies had changed her. There was a case in the early 1980s of a baby who wasn't growing. The mother believed it was not her child, that it had been changed with another child, her own, after the birth. It was hospitalized, and began to gain weight at the normal rate. This child may have been starved because his mother blamed him for the disappearance of her 'own' child.[5]

Otherwise, the baby changeling would be left in some of the places where mothers characteristically abandoned the bodies of their mur-dered children. Infanticide was much more common than now, with no social security for unmarried mothers and plenty of social opprobrium. Forced to give birth in privies, and in out-of-the-way places, by the dung-heap, roadsides, woods, the mothers simply left their unwanted infants in them. Changelings too, though, similarly unwanted, were left in privies, on the dung-hill, by the side of the road. The places may mark the longing to kill. It is even possible that some desperate women laid claim to a belief in changelings as a way of explaining how they came to bury their dead infants in the local rubbish heap. Yet the beliefs were so close that no lie might have been involved. The women who left their children in the privy were pretending their children were mere bodily wastes; it is a short step from this to the belief that one's child is not a real child. In folktales, changelings are most often the children of single parents.

Fighting for a baby

If the changeling sometimes showed the mother at her darkest, though, it also gave her a heroic role. She could fight passionately for her baby against the most dangerous beings in her world. A Gaelic song, which may be older than Guinefort, records a sung battle between a mother and the fairy who desires her child. The fairy begins with dismay at his own child's weakness and ugliness, the mother with her pleasure in the sensuous beauty of her baby:

> FAIRY He is my ungraceful child,
> Withered, bald and light-headed,
> Weak-shouldered, and weak in his equipments,
> That have never been put to use.

> MOTHER He is my ruddy child, plump and praiseworthy;
> My yew-tree, my rush, raised to women;
> My bird and my eggs, since you have taken my time with thee,
> My watchful care, my calved-cows, and my heroes with thee;
> Last year you were under my girdle,
> You are this year neatly gathered
> Continually upon my shoulder
> Through the town.[6]

It is as if the mother's voice has been bisected into good and bad. All mothers have moments when their babies seem hideous, even deformed; all mothers also have moments when they believe their own child is the most beautiful in the history of the world. The song gives the bad voice expression while allowing the mother to disavow it; it is not me who feels these things about my baby; it is not my baby that is ugly, but someone else's baby. What the mother praises is also interesting. She urges the baby to stay with her, not only by tenderness, but by promising that the end of her tenderness will be to make a warrior. She sees the man inside the child. She promises manhood, and this promise is what wins the child. The fairy, by contrast, though struggling to imitate her, her passion, her shaping power, can only offer a life on the hillside:

> MOTHER This is a MacLeod by heredity
> In his coat of mail; . . .
> Pother, pother I'll do about thee,
> Narrow plaids I'll make about thee,
> O pother I'll make about thee, thou soft warrior,
> O tender one, thou art mine, thou soft soldier,
> The fruit of my womb, thou soft, tender warrior,
> My breast that you took, you soft champion,
> Reared upon my knees, thou tender champion, since you are mine.

> FAIRY I'd prefer to see thy cattle-fold,
> High, high on the shoulder of the mountain,
> A white coat, ruffled green,
> About thy white shoulders, and a shirt.

It is taken for granted here that a baby wants to be a man. No attempt is made to appeal to the baby; he is choosing his future, not his present, in deciding whom to go with. A child is simply and solely the father of the man he will become. The fairy, who offers a kind of way out of warrior masculinity, is quite simply to be despised, however rich in cattle he may be. It is interesting too that the baby is a MacLeod. The MacLeods have a special link to fairies, and at Dunvegan Castle to this day you are shown a banner given to a MacLeod by the fairies, a banner that will gather an army to them if it is used sparingly. But the saying of the clan name seems to be less an evocation of the MacLeods' supernatural associations than an attempt to remind the baby of his real identity so that he does not lose it in the fairy's song. It is before baptism, before naming, that the baby is vulnerable to the fairies, just as he would have been in ancient Athens or Sumeria. The mother wins this battle; her final, triumphant cry, 'You are mine!', silences the fairy.

What was a changeling? For some, a changeling was a baby who failed to thrive; the baby was so thirsty for milk that it fed all day, exhausting one wet-nurse after another, and never seemed to get better. By the fifteenth century, to call someone a changeling was in France a terrible insult. In *Table Talk*, Martin Luther said that changelings, or *Wechselbalge*, were spirits of water or of the wood. He also saw them as demons; from fairly early in the Middle Ages, fairies were equated with demons by the learned of the Church, on the principle that whatever is not with us is against us, in the same way that the pagan gods were seen as demons.[7] Many saints, including St Lawrence and St Bartholomew, were stolen from their mothers as babies and replaced by ever-hungry demons. St Stephen, too, is abducted by the devil as a baby. The devil leaves an *idolum*, a statuette, in his place. These saints knew about death, knew about worlds other than this one. Their abduction made them special, or marked them as special already, but also marked them as the demons' foe.

Why did fairies want babies? No one knows. The short, modern answer is that fairies reflect a mother's love, just as the fairy in the Gaelic song reflects her words. Babies, especially boy-babies, are wanted because everyone wants a baby – or is supposed to. But why do the fairies want human babies? This is not the right question: the point is that babies are, in certain crucial ways, like fairies. We have seen that fairy beings in the ancient world are liminal, borderers; so medieval fairies remain. They wander between the dead and the living. Later on, we will meet a fairy who was once a man, a man who died in a battle, died at the moment when the sun was sinking, when it was neither dark nor light, neither night nor day. Medieval folklore was much attracted to such liminal states, often expressed in terms of sharp paradoxical riddles: cherries without stones, being neither clothed nor naked. For the living, sunset is a moment. For this man, it became his entire reality; he could not move on, but became stuck. Fairy is the name the Middle Ages gives to such 'stuck' beings, and they seek unbaptized babies in order to make them stuck too. Until the baby takes on the family's name, the name the family choose, it is not yet part of that human community. So it must be part of some other community, a community that is not the dead, but the liminal. The notion is then extended from babies to adults. At any time in our lives, at any moment when we are between one part of the day and the next, like midday and midnight, one part of the year and the next, like the Twelve Days of Christmas, one part of our lives and the next, like marriage, between life and death, like after childbirth or battle, at any of these moments that other community of shadows stands ready to claim us.

Milk and bodies

Adults could be taken by fairies too. Sometimes death was reinterpreted as being fairy-taken. A woman called Katherine Fordyce of Unst was thought to have died at the birth of her first child, but a neighbour's wife dreamed that Katherine came to her in a dream; Katherine told the woman she had taken the milk of her cow, the milk she could not get. But it would all be made up to her, she promised, if the woman would give Katherine 'that which you will know about soon'. The woman refused, and it was as well, because Katherine was talking about her unborn child. However, the woman Katherine visited was wise and kind; she called her baby Katherine Fordyce, and Trow-bound Katherine, as the villagers called her, reappeared after the birth and promised that the household would prosper as long as the child Katherine was in it. Katherine the child grew however, and eventually was to be married; that night, there was a terrible storm, and from then on everything went amiss with her parents. The trowies' blessing had been lifted. We can understand this peculiar story by beginning with a simple question: Why did Katherine take the milk? Probably to try to avoid eating fairy food. Commensality, a willingness to eat together, is a powerful social glue in pre-industrial societies. To accept food is to make oneself part of a community. In a poignant Irish lullaby, a young woman refuses to eat the food of the fairies, declaring: 'I have eaten no bite nor supped no drink of theirs/ But cold mashed potatoes on my father's dresser!'[8] This fairy-taken woman desperately revisits her home to eat their leftovers, and the food she eats symbolizes her status as an outsider with nothing of her own. The song is a lullaby, and of course lullabies are often about terrible threats to the child, cradles crashing to the ground, mothers tiring of crying children. Lullabies soothe by acknowledging dangers, and also repelling them by soft rhythmicity. A baby too is an outsider, as is the woman having the baby. Just as Guinefort's votaries have to repeat birth to get their babies back, so every lullaby imagines the child in danger and so safeguards him. The story, too, is a story of mingled fear and consolation; Katherine is gone, but she is also reinvented as the blessed daughter whom she cannot claim for the fairies. Symbolically, this is a story about the way children go on after death. Or at least, go on for a while; both the Katherine Fordyces lose their identity in marriage. One of the things the fairies can symbolize is the experience of going from the birth-home to the marital home, often already ruled by another woman, the husband's mother. Irish folklore expert Angela Bourke suggests that refusal to eat could be a woman's only weapon in this situation of loneliness and outsider status. Like an anorexic, the trapped wife might well begin eating antisocially, eating only leftovers or milk from one particular cow rather than accept her place at her husband's side. If so, then again the fairies allow women to express feelings and to behave in ways that would never normally be permitted.

The Green Children

Sometimes fairies brought babies instead of taking them. Ralph of Coggeshall tells the story of the Green Children. In Suffolk, at St Mary's of the Wolfpits, a boy and a girl were found near the mouth of a pit. They looked human, but their skin was startling; it was green, green all over. They could speak, but no one could understand their language. A knight called Sir Richard de Caine took them in. They could not stop crying. They would not touch bread, meat, cheese. At last some fresh, raw beans were brought in, and the children fell on them desperately, ate and ate. The boy still cried all the time, and soon he languished and died. The girl gradually got used to human food, bread and meat, and as she did so her green colour faded. She entered the household of the knight who had rescued her; she was a good servant, though 'rather loose in her conduct', says Ralph disapprovingly. She said she had come from a place where everyone was green, where everyone lived under ground, where they saw no sun, but lived in a light like that after sunset. In another telling of the same story, the girl said her country was called St Martin's Land, and St Martin was known to them and worshipped. There were churches, but no sun. They could see a beautiful bright land across a broad river, but they could never reach it.[9]

The best thing to do with this beautiful oddity is to leave it alone in its Borgesian glory, but I am not going to be quite as sensible as this. There are two very striking things here; one is the twilight fairy country from which the children come. There is no sun; it is under the earth, but lit with its own light, its own liminal light. This fairyland is permanently in the state of the down-going of the sun. Similarly, it is St Martin's land. St Martin's Summer is a common term for a little burst of summer weather just at the onset of winter. St Martin's day, or Martinmas, an important feast day in the medieval church, marks the beginning of true winter. The fairies are again poised between two states. Like Tennyson's Lotos Eaters, living in a land where it is always afternoon, they are frozen on a temporal threshold, unmoving. For them, time has stopped. Fairyland is a little timewarp. Secondly, the children's experience might be a way of telling in reverse-angle shot what it might be like for a human child to visit fairyland. The children cannot eat human food, just as we must never eat fairy food. They are lonely, heartbroken, crying. They are frightened by difference. Above all, they have to move into time. The power of the story comes in the end from our pity for these ultimate strangers in a strange land, these small, vulnerable ETs.

Green

As well, the children are green, and it is this, taken together with the land in which they live, that links them with fairies. For fairies are always linked with green. Never, never, says Somerset folk wisdom, never dress your child in green until after the christening. In the ballad 'The Wee, Wee Man', the ladies of the King of the Fairies, who are so beautiful that they outshine the Queen of Scotland, are wearing green.[10] Green is often a sign that fairies are present. In a culture where the word 'fairy' cannot be pronounced without risk, green clothing is often a covert sign to the knowing that fairies are what is being discussed.

And yet the best, and the best-known instance of green in medieval literature belongs to one who is not unequivocally a fairy. This is the Green Knight, Gawain's opponent and friend in the greatest medieval romance of them all, *Sir Gawain and the Green Knight*. The poem begins with Arthur's court enjoying a sumptuous Christmas feast, a good party. Suddenly, an unexpected guest arrives, a man, gigantic, carrying a holly branch, the tree which is green when all others are bare, and a huge axe. He has red eyes, and he is bright green all over. The stunned Round Table knights wonder if he is real, or a phantom or fairy. He suggests a Christmas game. He will receive a blow from any knight, if the knight will promise to receive the same from him in a year's time. Gawain leaps up and volunteers, and cunningly strikes off the knight's head. But the knight is quite unworried; he picks up his head, which invites Gawain to find him at the Green Chapel in a year's time. Gawain sets out, but accepts hospitality on the way at the castle of a knight called Sir Bertilak, who tests him by leaving him at home with his beautiful, seductive wife while he goes hunting.[11]

There are many things that link the Green Knight with fairies, though at no point is he called one for sure, and the poem seems to want to keep its listeners guessing about the ferocious creature's identity. He wears green; he is related to Morgan le Fay, who he says is his aunt; he has also another identity as a courteous knight; and we shall see that fairies often have a beautiful and a horrible face. His wife may also be an aspect of Morgan le Fay, in which case she too has a lovely and a hideous aspect. In his incarnation as Green Knight, the knight lives at the Green Chapel, which is not a chapel at all but a barrow or mound, of precisely the kind fairies inhabit. He also seems like the incarnation of winter and spring together; he embodies the terrifying chill of the winter landscape, and he has power over that landscape, hunting on it with confidence and skill in a series of passages which make hunting look like a rite of mystical communion with the land. And yet he gives life, though he threatens death; he and his chapel are the only green things amid the winter snow. It has thus been suggested that he is Christlike, but he is also reminiscent of the perpetual St Martin's Summer of the country of the Green Children. None the less, the Green Knight does not behave like a fairy, or perhaps, more accurately, he behaves like a fairy who has been changed out of all recognition by moralization. There is a faint, very faint trace of fairy behaviour in that his plan will allow him to capture a knight and bring the knight to his house, but his plans are altogether different. He does not want Gawain, or even Arthur, in any capacity; he merely wants to test them, to find out if they are truly virtuous. Again, the test does involve resisting first sensuous temptation and then a gift, and one must also resist the gifts of the fairies. However, the test occurs in the world of knightly courtesy and convention; Gawain is not supposed to refuse the gift because it would be fatal to take it, but because he has given his word to share anything he gets with his host. Gawain takes the gift, but he is not thereby bound to the fairy world for ever. The knight releases him; no fairy would. The Green Knight is a reformed fairy, one improved by the moral reflexes of Christianity.

Saints and fairies

Other attempts to reform the fairies were less successful. When Jeanne D'Arc was accused of witchcraft, her interrogators were especially eager to know about a fairy tree she had frequented. Jeanne told them that yes, she knew the tree; it was, she said, known locally as the Tree of the Mistresses, or sometimes the Tree of the Fairies. As always, the fairies are located in a remote past: Jeanne reports that the old people say that long ago the fairies were at the tree, and that girls used to hang bunches of flowers on the tree; Jeanne herself also made wreaths there for the picture of Our Lady of Domrémy. It is as if Jeanne is not making a very strong distinction between the Good Ladies and God's Lady; both the standard terms of the fairies ('white ladies', 'good ladies') and those for the Virgin ('Our Lady') share a respectful reluctance to name the person. As Wolfgang Behringer notes, Jeanne's use of prophecy and healing as her claim that such powers derive from 'good' apparitions in any case line her up with local cunning folk.[12]

There is one interesting element of Jeanne's account which has deep later resonances. Near the fairy tree, she says, was a spring, where sick people would scoop up the water to drink; the water healed them. Jeanne did not have much luck conflating the Virgin Mary with the good ladies, but her much later sister in vision and prophecy,

Bernadette Soubirous, was to be more fortunate. Like Jeanne, Bernadette frequented a site linked with the fairies, and like Jeanne, she saw visions of a beautiful lady there. Like Jeanne, Bernadette associated the sight with a healing spring, a spring in which the sick could shed their illnesses. Like Jeanne, Bernadette chose a term redolent of fairy lore to describe what she saw, saying that her lady was *uo petito damizela*, a little lady; Pyrenean fairies were often dwarfish.[13] This lady was not a fairy – she bore a golden rosary – but one has to ask how meaningful the distinction was to Bernadette, as it may not have been meaningful to Jeanne. Fairies, like saints, were capricious, powerful; they could blast or reward. Like saints, too, fairies are the dead, and a category of the dead who are still active, still alive; like fairies, they can be talked to, visited. Like fairies, they like gifts; they like, need, to be propitiated. To the peasants of Orleans and Lourdes, the Virgin – and the Fairy Queen – were not goody-goodies, but tough disciplinarians; the Fairy Queen's caprices were reflected in the Virgin's often harsh punishment of those who flouted her authority. At first, some in the Lourdes community did suggest that Bernadette had seen not the Virgin, but a pious neighbour who had passed on much more recently. Unlike Jeanne, her visions were accepted, and her healing spring became the fountain of Lourdes. Of course, nothing was said about the fairies by the Church, but the influence of Pyrenean fairy stories is evident at Lourdes. Saints and fairies: when not opposed by doctrine, it can be seen that these are natural allies, and that each makes sense of the other.

The poachers and the Fairy Queen

But when men go into forest spaces, they see otherwise: they see as adventurers, conquerors, warriors, fighters – in terms of male identity. Nowadays we think of fairies as about women, and as long as we see fairies as mainly a threat to the nursery this image is subtly perpetuated. But medieval fairies were also important in men's lives, as a different kind of fairy story shows. A band of Kentish protesters stole deer from the deer park of the Duke of Buckingham at Penshurst. Stealing deer was not just a crime committed by the hungry. It was a kind of protest, a little like the looting of yuppie shops after the Poll Tax Riots in 1989. It said: here we are. We're hungry and we don't trust the rich. These poacher-protesters were a diverse group, containing some yeomen, husbandmen, various tradesmen including the local butcher, and some labourers. They were indicted on 29 June 1451, at Tonbridge, and it was said that they:

> with others unknown to the number of one hundred men, in riotous manner and arrayed for war, viz. with jakkes, salades, brygantes, breastplates, hauberks, cuirasses, lances, bows and arrows, and covered with long beards and painted on their faces with black charcoal, calling themselves servants of the queen of the fairies, intending that their names should not be known . . . broke into a park of Humphrey Duke of Buckingham called Redleff [Redleaf] at Penshurst and chased, killed and took away from the said park 10 bucks, 12 soses [possibly 'sowres', juvenile bucks] and 80 does belonging to the said duke, against the king's peace.[14]

The name 'servants of the queen of the fairies' had been used in January 1450 by the leader of another conspiracy, and the later servants of the queen were in turn carrying on from the rising of April 1451, which may have been caused by the threat of further repressive measures in the wake of Cade's rising.[15]

Why would a burly bunch of rebels eager to show themselves as hungry and oppressed, call themselves the servants of the queen of the fairies? What did it mean? We can only guess. Drag? Protesters were sometimes led by men dressed as women; it meant that the world was upside-down, was not unfolding as it should. Occult knowledge? Jack Cade was supposed to have raised the Devil and used magical books to bring about his rebellion only a few years earlier.[16] Subjects of another monarch, hence protesters against the existing order? Does allegiance to the queen of the fairies signify being outside; outside the law, for instance? Does 'servant of the queen of the fairies' mean 'no-man', nonexistent, catch-me-if-you-can? Does it mean 'yah boo sucks, guv'? Almost certainly all these rebels gave the answer in response to a question about whom they served; the queen of the fairies is another form of disguise, of face-blacking. Does the queen of the fairies confer on her followers the power to disappear? Or does the

Fairy Queen stand simply for undeserved wealth, a kind of early modern answer to the National Lottery, and hence for poaching, for rebellion, for social inversion? We probably cannot know the answers, but the possibilities are suggestive, as we shall see.

The stolen toyboys

But the commonest of all fairies met by men in the greenwood is a story which becomes part of a genre – chivalric romance. It begins as one of the generic markers of the romance of adventure, one of the defining stories of knighthood and chivalry. The story is clear and simple in the ballads 'Thomas the Rhymer' and 'Tam Lin'.[17] A young man is alone in the countryside, taking his ease, when he sees a beautiful lady. He does not know it, but she is the queen of the fairies. He speaks to her, and somehow speaking to her is a mistake; it traps him. He finds himself her prisoner, and he must go to fairyland with her to 'serve' her for seven years. Fairyland is dangerous, the antithesis of the queen's smooth, courtly exterior. Tam Lin is in danger of being sacrificed to hell, part of a tithe that the fairies pay to the devil as their feudal overlord, while the fairies of 'Thomas the Rhymer' are explicitly associated with death and violence:

> It was mirk, mirk night and there was nae stern light
> And they waded through red blude to the knee:
> For a' the blude that's shed on earth
> Runs thro the springs of that countrie.

The blackness and the blood; formlessness, terror, entrapment. And yet blood and darkness are also associated with sexuality, bodily hunger. Fairyland is hungry for human blood, vampiric, and this hunger for blood symbolizes a hunger for blood products, for male seed, male flesh. This passion for blood links fairies to ancestors, to the dead. Ancestors, if neglected and not fed carefully, are vengeful, and are apt to drink the blood of the living members of the family. A Highland legend says that you must bring water into the house at night so the fairies don't quench their thirst with your blood. Women seem particularly hungry for blood: an old woman given shelter for the night in the Highlands was surprised drinking the blood of her hosts.[18] In Ireland, according to Lady Wilde, the peasants sensibly refused the common medical procedure of bleeding patients, because being bled would make the good people angry.[19] Fairies are also said to have dried bodies, hard, wrinkled, bony; they need blood. They need new blood.

Fairyland – or the way to it, at least – is a kind of womb as imagined by a terrified male, a maternal body which does not nurture but destroys. To enter fairyland is to be born again, to go through birth as an adult, an adult who is conscious of the dreadful process.[20] When fairyland finally releases the escaping man, he receives a gift, the gift of prophecy, or of power, sometimes even kingship. To be born *again* is to free oneself from the biological mother, the birth mother. This is what women resist when the fairies try to seize their male babies, promising them that even though born of woman, they can still be warriors, still be lords of wide lands. But motherlessness, or freedom from the mother, has always been the mark of the hero. And the heroes of medieval romance are freed from their mothers by the fairies. This is especially apparent in the ballad 'Alison Gross', where an ugly witch transforms a young man into a hideous serpent because he refuses to be her lover. He is rescued by the caresses of the Fairy Queen:

> But as it fell out on last Halloween
> When the seely-court was riding by,
> They queen lighted down on a gowany bank,
> Not far from the tree where I used to lie.
> She took me up in her milk-white hand,
> And she's stroked me three times o'er her knee;
> She chang'd me again to my own proper shape,
> An I no more toddle about the tree.[21]

The queen strokes the serpent-man over her knee, a gesture which suggests both a euphemistic depiction of sex, and a mother soothing a fretful infant. In doing so, she gives him back what another woman took from him. In these stories about the Fairy Queen, men are satisfyingly often on the receiving end of magic, transformation and imprisonment. It is as if the Fairy Queen allows men to risk the kind of dramatic physical change usually reserved for women. Masculinity may still be defined by stability, but the Fairy Queen's reassuring, soothing presence allows it to experiment with being protean – at least in fantasy.

Masculinity and death

There are bases for this idea of empowerment through fairy abduction: simply, the fairies represent the dead, the dead ancestors who give all heroes, all knights, their identity. Male identity comes from the father; in the Celtic regions, all identity comes from one single all-powerful ancestor. The odd formulation of the chiefs' titles – *the* MacLeod, *the* MacDonald – implies that the individual is nothing; his meaning comes from descent. All over the British Isles there are burial mounds, mounds that were once the barrow-tombs of neolithic kings or heroes, places where such figures could continue to impart their power of fertility to the soil. In the Celtic areas, the clan system preserved intact the idea of a powerful, though dead, male ancestor who gives a name and an identity to everyone in the clan. His fertility is crucial; everyone descends from him. A memory was also preserved of the mounds as places of the dead, places where the powerful dead might impart virtue to the surrounding countryside, long after the names of their original inhabitants were forgotten. Wayland's Smithy, on the Ridgeway in Oxfordshire, is an excellent example of this process; it is a barrow tomb of a neolithic king, but it is now associated with a Norse hero, Wayland Smith, a blacksmith of cunning and moral ambiguity, who helps travellers by shoeing their horses if they leave him a piece of silver. Successive inhabitants of the area retained the idea of the barrow as a place of the helpful dead, but substituted one of their own heroes for the original inhabitant. Just in this way, the fairies, and particularly those fairies who are in any case recently dead male heroes, end up inhabiting the mounds – also ambiguous, also able to help.

Another Celtic legend also involved acquiring heroic stature from an alternative mother, an alternative birth. Encountering the female body through sex, returning to the vagina from which you emerged in all its terrible difference, could also free a man from the bonds of birth, and make him fully masculine. The figure I am referring to is the *Cailleach bheara*, the hag of Beara. The original *cailleach* of Beara is described in a well-known eighth-century poem. *Cailleach* means both hag and nun, and also means 'veil'. This *cailleach*, who speaks the poem of lament and regret, is a childless former concubine, once seductive, now broken, her beauty lost, her hair thin and dull, and her rich robes thinned and shredded to rags. She had enjoyed kings and warriors, but not as their wife; she is among other things an unloved penitent with nowhere to go, nothing to own, and no one to care for her. She mourns for herself and also for the country which has abandoned her. Her childlessness is significant; we have seen that in other cultures, Mediterranean cultures, childless women often become unhappy, immortal hags. Their childlessness means that they live for ever, instead of living through their children. But they prey on the children of other people. And so does the *cailleach*, in a way. She is often a hostile ogress who devours those she meets; she also injures children, and she is the reason babies cannot walk after birth. The marks of her fingers can be seen on their backs; her willingness to prey on small babies does recall fairies.[22] But she is also the old woman who becomes young again when married to the true heir.

In the best-known version of the story, an eleventh-century story about the sons of Eochaid Muigmedon, three brothers who are hunting in the forest are stopped by a hag who will only allow them to drink at the well if they are willing to kiss her. Not only is she ugly, but diseased also; her middle is spotted with pustules and her green teeth reach to her ear. Only the true heir is brave enough not only to kiss her, but to lie with her, whereupon she becomes beautiful. This story, though spectacular, is not an ancient story of a legendary goddess, but a political myth designed to advance the claims of a particular family to the high kingship. Nevertheless, folklorists want to see the territorial goddess in it, the goddess whose body is Ireland. The hag often boasts of a knowledge of the landscape lost to humans; that she has seen the land when a mountain was a plain or when a lake covered what is now fields. She is also the author of mysterious features of the landscape, like the round towers of Sligo. She has knowledge of the land and how to use it; she knows the best grazing and so forth. Again a memory trace.

Other legends present her as a wealthy farmer, also in touch with the land.[23]

Cailleach and enchantress: the woman of his dreams

She is not quite a fairy, but like the Green Knight she has some fairy characteristics and she imparts some of her own traits to English fairies of romance. The fifteenth-century romance *Thomas of Ercledoune* is an inversion of the *cailleach* myth; when Thomas of Ercledoune has had sex with his fairy lady, she loses her beauty:

> Thomas stondeth in that stead,
> And beheld that lady gay,
> Her hire that hung upon her head,
> Her eyen seemed out that were so grey;
> And all her clothes were away,
> That here before saw in that stead,
> The to shank was black, the other grey,
> The body blue as beaten lead![24]

For Thomas of Ercledoune, desire breeds a monster where once there was beauty, or rather, lays bare the aged truth which lies behind feminine deceit. Thomas's eyes, which were the part of him that previously desired, are now the part that is punished with the sight of anxiety that is the ageing female body:

> In faith, this is a doleful sight
> That thou art so faded in the face,
> That before shone as sun bright!

And yet that spectacle is part of Thomas's imprisonment, for when the now-loathly Fairy Queen speaks, she does so as one who can now claim a year's service from him. The equation of the sight of the queen's ugliness with Thomas's imprisonment occurs along a sight-line; the lady tells him, 'this middle-earth thou shalt not se'. Loss of sight mirrors his original failing; unable to see through the Fairy Queen's scheming, he now cannot see what he wishes to see, and will himself go unseen. Like Thomas the Rhymer, this unseeing is replaced by supernaturally enhanced sight once Thomas emerges. The Fairy Queen gives her lovers prophetic sight or speech as payment in kind for what they have been forced to renounce.

The best-known and best-loved appearance of the fairies in medieval literature owes a lot to the myth of the *cailleach*, though the borrowings may be unconscious. On the journey of the Canterbury pilgrims, no character is more memorable than the Wife of Bath, the five-times-married and sexually indefatigable widow on the lookout for Number Six. Even though recent scholarship is inclined to see her as an untidy anthology of misogynist truisms, she manages to be much more interesting than her male opponents. She is not a Riot Grrrl, nor a realistic portrayal of a medieval woman, but a literary creation symbolizing the bodily aspects of woman: sexuality, appetite, gusto. The tale she tells is appropriate for a woman, because it is a romance, and romances, even in the Middle Ages, were associated with women readers, women who had the leisure to read and who wanted to be entertained by what they read.

The Wife begins her story by linking what she has to say to the fairy realm. In the old days of King Arthur, she says, 'Al was this land fulfild of fayerye.' The Elf-Queen, with her jolly company, was always dancing in green meadows. But she speaks of many hundreds of years ago; no one sees the elves any more, because now the great holiness of the friars has filled the country. They are thicker than motes of grass in a sunbeam, and their diligence in blessing everything is responsible for the absence of the fairies; for where once the elves walked, now the friars walk. Now, she says, women may travel safely, because the friar is the only remaining incubus. The note of irony is clear. The Wife is making a pun on the similarity of the words fairy and friar, and she is implying that the friars are like the fairies, a menace, and particularly a menace to women's chastity.[25]

This startling idea of fairies as rapists may derive from a Middle English romance called *Sir Degare*, in which a princess, lost in a forest, is raped by a fairy knight, or it may derive from ballad versions of the same essential story.[26] In the ballad 'Lady Isabel and the Elf-Knight',

Lady Isabel is the victim of imprudent speech, as Thomas the Rhymer is. She hears an elf-knight blowing his horn, and she says, aloud, 'If only I had that horn, and that knight to sleep in my bosom.' In a second, the knight leaps in at her window. Her own words have enchanted her, and she goes with him to the greenwood. He orders her to get down from her horse, so he can kill her. She begs him to spare her. He says that she is the seventh king's daughter he has slain here, portraying himself as a kind of fairy serial-killer. She manages to persuade him to lie with his head in her lap (a common euphemism for sex) and he falls into a charmed sleep. Then she binds him and stabs him with his own dagger, crying: 'If seven kings' daughters here ye have slain, / Lye here, a husband to them a'.'[27] This is one of many ballads which point to the sexual menace of the fairies and their votaries.

And it is sexual menace which seems to link the fairies and Gawain. The Wife of Bath's story begins with a rape. Gawain is riding through the wood, and he meets a lady; like the sexual encounters in fairy romance and ballad, this one takes place in a forest. He sees the lady, and despite her demurrals, 'By verray force, he rafte hire maydenhed'. The queen is so angry that she wants to have him executed, but she agrees to spare him if he can answer a riddle; what does a woman want? Obviously the riddle is an exact punishment; having ignored the desires of his victim, Gawain must now rectify things by finding out what women's desires are. Of course he can't do it; it's a gorgeous revenge. This was the question which notoriously baffled Freud, and Gawain seems less well-equipped than he to find out the answer. He goes from house to house, desperately accumulating answers; it's rather like reading six feminist polemics in a weekend. All the answers are different. And soon the year is almost up, and Gawain the Rapist is about to go home to face death, when in a forest he suddenly sees four-and-twenty ladies dancing. He goes towards them, quickly, hoping they can help him, and they vanish. But left on the green is a woman, a hideous woman.

Now, these twenty-four dancers must be fairies, the fairies the Wife mentions at the beginning of her tale, the ones that used to dance on the green before the friars came. Which strongly implies that the woman they leave behind has something to do with the fairies too, and so does her strong resemblance to the *cailleach bheara* and to the unmasked Fairy Queen of Thomas of Ercledoune. She further resembles the *cailleach* and the Fairy Queen in that she offers to help Gawain to the answer to his riddle, something that plainly can't be got without supernatural assistance, and also in the price she puts on her help. Gawain must promise to marry her. The answer, famously, is that women love their wills; that women want the mastery, and it is the right answer. From then on, it's the Frog Prince story; Gawain tries to get out of his promise, and the court makes him marry the hideous dame, which he does with much audible groaning. Especially, he dreads the wedding night, and again tries to dodge his duty. But again she compels him. Chaucer, however, stops short of the blunt Irish myth in which sovereignty involves sexual intercourse with age and ugliness, with the poor, with death itself. The lady offers Gawain a choice; she can be ugly and true, or beautiful and perhaps unfaithful. By now Gawain has learnt his lesson; he gives her the mastery, and she becomes beautiful and promises to be true as well.

This is not a Deep Myth about Winter Turning to Spring, I think. Rather, the story seems to be offered as a kind of cure for the extremes of the stories it rewrites: the rape, the *cailleach*, the deceiving Fairy Queen. The rape is a story of a male sexuality that is not merely out of control, but actively seeks blood. It is not explained; it *is*. The hag is a story of magical power coming from a powerful meeting of opposites: youth and power accept age and death as their mates in mortal life. The deceiving queen is the same story in reverse: looking wilfully for beauty is a way to find death. In Chaucer's story, the sharp edges of folklore are softened; there is an answer to the riddle of our own desires, an answer that brings perfect satisfaction. With Chaucer, we can see the long process of the domestication of the fairies beginning. Both the dancing maidens and the Loathly Lady are helpful; both of them mean well; the Loathly Lady's desires turn out to be quite legitimate, however frightening to the more timid men in the audience, since she is a suitable partner for Gawain after all. And yet . . . The Wife adds firmly that she hopes Jesus Christ will send us all husbands meek, young and 'fresh abed'. Nothing could be cannier or more down-to-earth. Nothing could be more like the Fairy Queen's own desire, her desire for men, for their blood, for their seed. Nothing could be scarier.

Now, why would a woman tell such a story? I think what made Chaucer put it into the mouth of the Wife of Bath is not the Loathly Lady story, but what triggers it – the story of the rape. A woman who became pregnant in the Middle Ages often had to explain herself – to her family, certainly, but also to other interested parties – the priest, the local church court, the parish who would have to support her. We might dismiss stories of young girls who meet exciting, erotic, violent fairy princes and lords in the woods as the best excuse since the Virgin Mary said the Holy Spirit had done it. However, there might easily have been a horrible, bitter grain of truth in such tales; perhaps rapists said 'I'm the Fairy King' much as the poacher-protesters said 'We're servants of the queen of the fairies'. Perhaps the women too were saying, 'king of the fairies', and meaning 'shan't tell'. In the romance of Sir Degare, a fairy knight rapes a woman, and instructs her to bring the child of the rape back to the forest so that he can be claimed and acknowledged by his fairy sire. Is that what women thought they were doing when they left a child in the woods 'for the fairies'? Given that illegitimacy was a probable cause of infanticidal behaviour, it may be that such practices were a way of explaining paternity. In agony, in shame, a woman might feel that she had indeed wandered from what she knew into an unknown country, a wasteland in which they waded in red blood to the knee.

The ones who go below before their time

There's another meaning for all these aged fairy hags, too. Old age also means death. The association of the Fairy Queen in particular with death is evident in medieval romances; in Chaucer's *Merchant's Tale*, and in *Sir Orfeo*, for instance, she is equated with the queen of the underworld, Proserpine.[28] *The Merchant's Tale*, itself dark and deadly, invokes the trope of Proserpine the Fairy Queen as part of a description of a garden of love: 'Ful ofte tyme he Pluto and his queene,/ Proserpina, and al hire fayerye,/ Disporten hem and maken melodye'.[29] This is the court of death at play, and a reminder of the irreducible otherness of death at the heart of what seems most familiar and homelike.

In *Sir Orfeo*, Heurodis is asleep on the grass beneath an 'ympe-tree' when she first encounters the king of the fairies; hers is essentially the same story of encounter and erotic abduction as the ballad and ravishment romances. *Sir Orfeo* contrasts the dark *abysme* character-istic of fairylands with the noonday brightness of the Fairy King, whose crown is made 'of a precious stone/ As bright as the sun it shone' (151–2). His apotropaic power is of brightness rather than darkness. His underworld is not a place of darkness, but of unnatural light, light that comes from overwhelming wealth:

> All that land was ever light,
> For when it should be dark and night
> The rich stones light gone
> As bright as doth at noon the sun. (345–8)

Perhaps a male kidnapper does not set in motion ideas of darkness and blood as his landscape, his estate, coextensive with himself. An astonishing and horrible spectacle awaits Orfeo. The wall of the under-world is made of mutilated bodies, the bodies of those who have died before their time:

> Of folk that were thither y-brought,
> And thought dead and never nought
> Some stood without a head
> And some no arms nade,
> And sum through the body hadde wounde. (365–9)

The other categories of wounded mentioned are those shrivelled in fire, the drowned, the mad and women in childbed. This is a collective spectacle of horror, but it is also a portrait of those whose deaths have come about through a violent assault on the body's integrity, whether from within or without, by another. These are people lost before their time, invaded by violence, symbolically raped. They are like Heurodis, and she is like them. Such persons – those who died in the middle of things – become unfinished, testaments to unfinished lives. They have left-over energy, energy that in pre-industrial folklore nearly always goes into malice and anger with the living. Such beings become remnants or wraiths, troublemakers.[30] Here they are the kind of dead who live in fairyland. For the Fairy King is the one who cuts off Heurodis in similar fashion.

The castrating wound, amputation, endless bleeding, is doubly limiting to warrior masculinity, for it actually prevents full participation in those activities which define masculine power, and its display is a deterrent to entry to the king's domain. It threatens to halt Orfeo's story, to turn him away. Yet perhaps because he has been living outside the law as a wild man, a madman, Orfeo's own power is sovereign. It is revealed not as power of the arm, but as power of the tongue; unlike Thomas and Lanval, his tongue remains his own, so that he is able to sing his way out of fairyland. Whereas other stories show masculinity defeated by the feminine, Orfeo manages to win a duel between himself and the king, prefiguring the serene (or supremely anxious) mastery of Malory's Lancelot.

The figuration of the fairies as the dead of the community in *Orfeo* is partly a way of staging a dialogue between the living and the dead in that romance. Such dialogues occur in epic, in the *Odyssey* and the *Aeneid*, and in medieval tales like the legend of the Three Living and the Three Dead. But it may also glance at the ambiguous relations between death and festival in medieval and early modern cultural rituals surrounding death. Medieval graveyards were sacred spaces, rigorously policed, and laboriously reconsecrated if blood or semen were spilt in them. And yet the very need to express such rules points to their violation; the thirteenth-century council of Rouen forbade dancing in cemeteries, and the cemetery of the Innocents in Paris was reputed to be the haunt of prostitutes.[31] To see the untimely dead as reanimate in the world of fairy offers a grotesque understanding of festival in death, a *danse macabre* which reminds the living of their frailty while offering a backhanded consolation to them.

Fairies make knights

The association between fairies and an underground world, first elaborated by Giraldus Cambrensis, links the Fairy Queen with the dead.[32] Even more clearly, the kidnapping water-fays like the Lady of the Lake and the lake nymphs of Froissart's *Meliador* imprison their male lovers or protégés at the bottom of a dark lake, another kind of underworld. There, the knights can *dream* of adventure or love, can make up or tell stories, but can only live stories by leaving the feminized space of the deep water behind them. In order to leave, the knight has to express a desire for wholeness, for adventure, for a trial of masculinity in action, and he is then granted powers which characteristically, though not invariably, enable him to surmount his trials. And yet those powers signify the Fairy Queen's ongoing and threatening control of him, as well as his liberation from it.

What might inspire the telling and retelling of this story? Interest in – investment in – fairies is investment in what can come from a space that is outside history: knowledge, money, disability, ability. Moving outside history allows the self to be reinvented; it is almost a rebirth. And yet in that rebirth, women are still half-workers; the Fairy Queen is more in control of the shaping of identity than any mother. One way for us to understand the re-citation of this story is by looking at Malory's omission of it in its usual forms and his substitution of another, different story for it. The omission occurs at the beginning of the story of Lancelot, where the traditional tale of Lancelot's background and the Lady of the Lake's role as his protector and patron are simply dropped. His arrival at court is described, but not his childhood or youth. Instead, Lancelot is simply presented to the reader as the one who 'passed all other knyghtes', 'the fyrste knyght that the Frey[n]sh booke makyth men[c]ion of aftir kynge Arthure com from Rome.'[33] Fathered by a book rather than mothered by a lady, the child of his own reputation, Lancelot's sudden blazing appearance is the perfect masculine autotelic birth.[34] All traces of the real or fairy mother have been removed, and, as we shall soon see, all traces of desire for her too. When Lancelot encounters Malory's ambivalent Fairy Queen, Morgan le Fay, the situation at first looks familiar from the Thomas romance and ballads, and from *Lanval*. Just as Thomas was lying 'on Huntlie banke', so Lancelot is sleeping under an apple tree; just as the lady in the English *Launfal* wears green cloth, so the horses of the queen's knights 'bare a cloth of grene sylke on four sperys betwyxte hem and the sonne'.[35]

But Lancelot does not waken to desire; he does not even *see* the

Fairy Queen. Instead, his sleep is prolonged by enchantment so that he can be carried off against his will to the Castle Chariot. This prolonged sleep is what allows Lancelot to avoid sight, avoid the entrapping spectacles of beauty and wealth.[36] When offered the chance to be the lover of one of the ladies, the suggestion is less a seduction than a threat; Lancelot must choose one, 'or else to dye in this prison'. So there is no seduction, no veiling of the monstrous truth of fairy femininity, which is presented as simply entrapping and destructive.

The superplus of machismo that Malory adds to the story of knight and supernatural lover might be inspired by the terrors produced by the long defeat in the Hundred Years War, the experience of warfare, the political crisis of the Wars of the Roses, by special anxieties about the growing coterie of courtiers who were not soldiers, by an early and self-conscious attempt to reconstruct the romance hero as masculine.[37] In any case, his rewriting of the story seems a perfect illustration of the repression of the feminine which Cathy La Farge notes as characteristic of the *Morte Darthur*.[38] Lancelot finds a way to invent and reinvent himself without recourse to uncomfortable feminine spaces, whether transcended or not: prowess in arms, prowess in perception, both autotelic. The story of Sir Lancelot and the four queens, and the story of Sir Lancelot's encounters with other not-very-deceptive women suggest all these, in that all are dominated by questions of masculinity; what it is and what it ought to be. The refusal of the supernatural spectacles of unstable femininity, however, suggests an anxious inability not only to confront the feminine, but to confront war and its potentially diminishing effects.

Prior to Malory's intervention in them, these stories show that femininity does not lie in apotropaic spectacle, but in the ability of that horror to mask itself, and in the complex interplay between mask and identity. There is no sense that the queen of the fairies is *really* old, or bloody, or the author of castration and deformity. Rather, both beauty and deformity turn out to be appearances. Femininity is the instability of these appearances, their shimmering refusal to resolve themselves into a single stable object of desire.[39] For Malory, masculinity is the ability to resolve oscillation into a solidity which can be grasped and rejected. This is done through not seeing, but also through not speaking first, through refusing the gift of the tongue made by the

Fairy Queen's other victims.[40] The closed, continent body, symbolized by the closed mouth, is for Malory the masculine body. Yet Thomas the Rhymer does not intend to speak to the queen of the fairies; he mistakenly believes her to be the Virgin Mary. This mistake leads him to address her in language fraught with the rhetoric of courtly and amorous submission:

> True Thomas he took off his hat
> And bowed him low down till his knee:
> 'All hail, thou mighty Queen of Heaven
> For your peer on earth I never did see.'[41]

The Fairy Queen's power over the young man depends on masquerade, on misrecognition of the uncanny as canny, on wavering alterity.

The story of the young man and the Fairy Queen is told again in *Lanval*, attributed to Marie de France. Like the Thomases – both Erceldoune and Rhymer – Lanval is taking his ease in a natural setting, a river-meadow, when he is approached by a beautiful and well-dressed lady. He agrees to become her lover, and she makes him promise not to tell anyone. Her initial gift, the result of union with her, is bottomless wealth and prowess. Pressed by Guinevere to become her lover, Lanval refuses, and blurts out his secret, losing all the wealth he has been given and also losing the lady's love. Accused of assaulting Guinevere, he is about to be executed when the lady appears and rescues him. There is some debate about whether the lady is truly a fairy, but she may have influenced later fairies whether or not Marie saw her as one. The early fifteenth-century English verse romance *Sir Launfal* describes the lady as the daughter of the 'King of Fairie' (280), and significantly alters the colour of her attendants' gowns from purple to green (235). In both versions, the threat she poses is indirect; rather than herself revealing an ugly underside of blood and darkness, she is twinned with a Guinevere who exemplifies the terrors of the feminine: devouring passion, the will to obliterate, destroy, the direct threat of death. Like True Thomas, Lanval is constrained in his tongue, symbolically castrated; whereas Thomas cannot lie, Lanval cannot tell the truth. His linguistic potency is the price he must pay for sexual pleasure and social advancement. The sacrifice becomes intolerable only when

Lanval's mastery is threatened from another direction by another dominant woman's desires, desires which may be enacted without his consent. Although rescued from this bad woman's longing to murder him in order to exact her price from his body in one way or another, the rescue itself implies a refusal of potency which condemns Lanval to the ranks of effeminate courtier-knights. Marie's purpose may have been to deflate machismo, or to satirize effeminacy.[42] Lanval, unlike the other knights discussed here, returns to the world and then has to be rescued from it – in a manner which plainly emasculates him, however swooningly happy the ending – by the lady, who takes him to Avalon.

The most recent folktale version of this story has removed all trace of empowerment. A young man, who longs for a local girl, makes a fairy cake, and he sits and waits. The door opens, and a dark fairy comes in, and stretches out her hand for the cake. 'Not for thee,' he said, but he shouldn't have spoken. Then a fairy comes and stretches out her hand. He taps her on the wrist and says, 'Not for thee.' But he shouldn't have touched her. Then comes a most beautiful lady in green, and she says, 'For me,' and she eats the cake. After that she was always with him, and he told her his wishes, and she granted them, but somehow they always went wrong. He married a cruel old woman for money; his pretty sweetheart died of the plague and he prayed to die too. But at length the fairy wore him down and he died. As he lay in his coffin, a dark cloudy shadow came down over it, and out of the darkness a voice said, very cold and clear, 'For me.'[43]

EARLY MODERN FAIRIES

3

Birth and Death:
Fairies in Scottish
Witch-trials

You do not want to be the main character in the stories I am about to tell. Not even in imagination. And I will not make you live these stories, even in imagination. For one of the ideas that emerges now is that stories about fairies are so powerful as to be positively dangerous.

Women's stories of fairies

In the stories that follow, stories told by a group of Scottish witches between 1550 and 1670, fairies are the fantasies of the dispossessed. They do not come from wealth and privilege. They come from the deeps of misery. People whose lives are a perpetual struggle to survive are suddenly faced with one burden too many, an extra burden. One storyteller can stand poverty, but not being too ill to work. Another can stand childbirth, but not the death of the longed-for child. One can bear up under the scorn of neighbours, but not under their discovery of one's shameful incest. A fairy story is a story about reaching rock bottom – in that sense, a story about dying – but it is also a story about finding a way out, if only in story.

And yet we must not be sentimental about these stories. Most of those who have written about them have succumbed to this temptation. Fairies, for them, are part of a great rich oral culture of closeness to the soil and to nature, a culture lost to us through print/radio/cinema/television – select the villain of your choice. The stories you are about to hear are certainly rich, complex, often elliptical because to their teller their meaning is very plain, because they were always inner stories; others are full of the elegant flourishes of the talented public storyteller. But they are not stories of a kind, acceptant, pastoral world, but brutal, violent, often plain *mean* stories of mean lives, stories not of warm closeness to a benign earth, but of too much closeness to an earth that cannot give enough food, stories not of community sharing, but of villages hostile and towns unfriendly. They come from hurt.

These stories are told by particular, named individuals. However, they are probably based on what are often called folktales, that is, stories told as a pastime, for fun, for a giggle, for instruction, for warnings. Individuals might seize on some of these stories, love them, adapt them, make them their own.

What we must remember is that tellers frequently knew – as well as we do – that they were telling stories. The early modern populace did not 'believe' in fairies and they did not disbelieve. Fairies both are and are not; they exceed the terms of what is likely or acceptable or sayable in the everyday. They are encountered on boundaries either in space – between town and wilderness – or in time – at midday, at midnight, at the change of the year, on the eve of a feast, on Hallowe'en or May Eve, in a festive space marked out from normal life, like Yule, or 'the reathes of the year'. Yuletide (the twelve days from Christmas to 6th January, Twelfth Night) was especially important for apparitions of various kinds, perhaps because it was the boundary of the year. They could also be encountered at moments of social or physical transition: birth, copulation and death, adolescence, betrothal, defloration, and of course death and burial.

The way fairies hover between belief and disbelief is what makes them natural symbols for other things that cannot be said, or cannot be acknowledged, or cannot be believed. Fairies also share many of the characteristics of the dead; in some stories they *are* the dead, or the dead are with them, in others it is difficult for teller and reader alike to tell the difference between a ghost or revenant and a fairy.[1] This also means they can symbolize other losses; loss of self particularly. But the link between fairies and the returned dead is not a confusion; like the dead who come back to feast in their homes, the dead for whom many Scottish families put out food at key times of the year, the fairies are both a society separate from human society and crucially intertwined with it. Like the dead, they are foreign and familiar; like the dead they need gifts from the living, and give gifts back; like the dead, they can be angered. Like the dead, they are both present and absent.

We think of witch-trials as cruel, about terrible duress. All perfectly true, and perhaps especially true of these Scottish trials, the products of religious and political upheaval, conducted by the Scottish judicial system, which unlike the English system routinely used torture to interrogate suspects and strangled, then burned, those found guilty.[2] Our mental picture of witch-trials is of meaningless hysteria, waves of unreason in which no sane person can find reason, of people going mad together. This picture is never true, but it is actually a very little truer of Scotland than it is for most of Europe; Scottish witch-trials do occur in bursts, especially in the years 1591–7, and 1628–30.[3] And yet the two women whose confessions I am focusing on here were tried outside these bursts of activity: Bessie Dunlop was tried in 1576 and Elspeth Reoch in 1616. They were not accused simply because everyone was making accusations. Almost certainly, both came to be accused for local reasons, rather than because of large political or religious ideologies put suddenly into innocent heads. Both were magic users, cunning women. Most likely this was enough.

So our prejudices about witch-hunts do not mean we should discount as rubbish what accused women said to their interrogators. Miranda Chaytor, historian of witchcraft, has pointed out that the flow of confession is important in deciding its origins. Long detailed paragraphs generally come from the accused; a series of sentence-long items of confession come from the interrogator. It was when women got their teeth into their own stories that they ensured the preservation of those stories for us.[4]

Why should we use Scottish witch-trial materials for a way into understanding the layers of popular fairy belief that lie completely hidden from view beneath the surface of better-known Renaissance fairy texts like *A Midsummer Night's Dream*? For one thing, these materials are unusually rich as a source for fairy stories. Scottish élite views of witchcraft created a unique opportunity for these fairy stories to be told. The Scottish élite believed that witchcraft consisted of a deal, or compact, between a witch and a devil. This led the Scottish interrogators to question women closely about supernatural encounters with beings from other planes, much more closely than did English interrogators. When you are being asked questions by a man who has the power of life and death over you, and who may well be holding an instrument of torture – unlike in England, Scottish witches were then tortured – you are probably going to try to say *something*. But people cannot talk about what they don't know, but only about what they know. If asked to produce a story under pressure, people will draw on stories they have heard, stories they have read, stories they have already told, stories they think others will believe. (A citizen of modern Britain, asked to explain his speeding, will give an answer from what he hopes is the shared repertoire of stories – he will say his wife is ill, or that he has a train to catch. He will not say that he is on his way to meet the ambassador from the planet Plooph.) The predominance of fairy stories in Scottish witch-trial material is proof that the accused women thought that such stories were believable, and therefore proof that they were part of the storytelling currency of the day – which is not the same as saying that such stories were fully believed. Scrabbling frantically for an answer, women probably told their interrogators stories that they had heard, changed to the first person, and stories that they had told as pastimes, not meaning to be believed. They also told stories that they had told to others to illustrate their own supernatural powers. Though I shall be writing about these stories as if they were autobiographies, any writer will tell you that the genre involves fiction as well as truth.

As if things were not already too complicated, we also have to bear in mind the way in which these stories were written down, as well as the circumstances in which they were told. Court reporters took down only what seemed to them relevant. Some wrote in detail, apparently taking down every word. Others left a lot of scornful *et ceteras* to mark their passage. We shall never know how accused witch Isobel Gowdie described the king and queen of the fairies, because the record breaks off with a weary '*& c*' as she is halfway through her story. There is a sharp break in Elspeth Reoch's story where the father of her child might have been mentioned. Sometimes one could travel back in time just to wring the clerk's neck. We do not know what else might be omitted. What is more, these women did not simply say what witch-hunters were hoping to hear. They said things from which most members of the élite would have been struggling to wring meaning.

A common story

And yet, ironically, these stories were recorded for posterity because that struggle led to a mistake about their meaning. When these women talked about fairies, interrogators thought they were hearing about a pact with the devil, as we can see from one of the commonest Scottish witch stories, one that recurs in dozens of cases. The following is just one version of it:

The second time the devil appeared to her at the foot of her own yard about five years after in the likeness of a man in green clothes, and that he desired her to become his servant . . . and that she promised to become his servant. Whereupon he desired her to renounce her baptism and Jesus Christ, which she did . . . but cannot presently remember whether he had carnal dealings with her at that time or not, but remembers perfectly that afterward he did lie with her.[5]

In all these confessions, and there are dozens, a woman meets a man, who may be wearing black or green, or may have a specific name. He asks her to be his servant, or he offers her something. She may refuse at first, but eventually agrees. He then has sex with her. The woman often confesses to renouncing baptism at his request, or to receiving a mark from him, plainly under prompting from her interrogator; these are the stock items which identify a story of pact witchcraft, and we can disregard them. Is this, by any chance, a fairy story? We cannot be sure (though the green clothing is suggestive). Whatever the nature of the being involved, he is always otherworldly. The experience is of a change of identity through sexual intercourse, a female experience that happens every day through marriage. Sex is a way of saying something, confirming something; a magical act, creating a relationship of dependency and bondage. It is not a story about liberation or choice.

The story of Elspeth Reoch

One woman told just such a story, but also told us far more. On 12
March 1616, in Kirkwall, Orkney, a woman called Elspeth Reoch was
charged with witchcraft. This is her story.[6]

Elspeth confessed that when she was a young girl of twelve, she was
staying with her aunt who lived in a loch, when one day, having been
out of the loch in the countryside and waiting at the lochside for a
boat, she had a strange encounter, a fairy encounter. Two men come
to Elspeth. One is clad in black, and the other has a green tartan plaid.
The fairies of Scotland often wear green, and also wear plaids.[7] The
man with the plaid pays her a compliment: he says she is a 'pretty'.
Their interaction is sexualized by this overture. He then offers her a
courtship gift, the gift of knowledge: 'he would learn [teach] her to
know and see any thing she would desire'. The other man is not
enthusiastic, claiming that Elspeth will not keep the source of her
knowledge to herself. It is basic to fairy folklore in all cultures that the
source of a fairy gift has to remain a secret, or else it is lost. But the
man in green presses on, and here Elspeth asks an eager question. She
asks how she could know that? What must she do, to know so much?
His advice is also about boundaries and changing states: 'And he said
Take an egg and roast it. And take the sweat of it three Sundays. And
with unwashed hands wash her eyes wherby she should see and know
any thing she desired.' The man in green sends her to her family, where
she uncovers a secret. Elspeth goes to another aunt's house, where
there is a widow, perhaps a lodger, that has with her a granddaughter,
perhaps visiting her relative as Elspeth is visiting her aunt. This girl is
an image of Elspeth in age and circumstances. But this girl is pregnant,
pregnant with a child whose father is the husband of another woman.
No one in the family knows this yet, but the man in green tells Elspeth,
and tells her what to do. She 'should look in her face', a shaming,
challenging gesture, and tell her 'she is with bairne [child] to an other
wifes husband'.

At first the girl denies Elspeth's words. But soon she realizes that
Elspeth is a source of knowledge. This girl has been shamed; her
pregnancy and its origins have been revealed. It is as if Elspeth has

abruptly brought the infant to birth. And this premature birth suggests the idea of abortion. The girl asks Elspeth if she can give 'some cure at her that she might part with bairne'. The baby can be silenced in death, returned to the unspeakable. Elspeth urges the girl to consult someone else, Allan McKeldow, who refuses to procure an abortion for the girl. Immediately the narrative continues: 'within two years she [Elspeth herself] bore her first bairne which was gotten by one James Mitchell at the kirk of Murthilie upon Spey within Balveny'. Elspeth follows her adolescent encounter with another even more extraordinary meeting with the fairy after childbirth. She has her baby in her sister's house, within the bosom of her birth family. And yet the house proves to be as liminal as the lakeside by virtue of her own parturient presence in it, for she sees again

the black man . . . that first came to hir at Lochquhaber And called him self a fairy man who was sometime her kinsman called John Stewart who was slain by McKy at the down going of the sun. And therefore neither dead nor living but would ever go between the heaven and the earth.

He 'deals with' Elspeth for two nights, and he is relentless. He will never let her sleep, 'persuading her to let him lie with her':

And upon the third night that he came to her she being asleep and laid his hand upon hir breast and woke her. And thereafter seemed to lie with her.

Such childbed encounters with apparitions of many kinds are reasonably common in Scottish and even English witchcraft cases, though no other confession that I know of mentions sex.

Women often come back from encounters with the fairies damaged. In Elspeth's case the price for the opening of her body is the closing of her mouth:

And to be dumb for having teached her to see and know any thing she desired He said that if she spoke gentlemen would trouble her and gar [make] her give reasons for her doings. Whereupon she might be challenged and hurt . . . And upon the morrow she had no power of her tongue nor could not speak.

The setting for Elspeth's first encounter with the fairies is significant. Elspeth is on a visit within the family, but outside the parental home; she is also outside this foster or substitute home, outside the loch, but also on the side of the loch, on its margins. She is suspended between home and the strange world, just as her adolescence suspends her between her birth family and the family she will enter at marriage. Throughout most of Europe, fairies are linked to features of the known landscape, especially to dangerous, marginal or conspicuous places; Elspeth's encounter by a loch is evidently part of the Scottish idea of the otherworld. In Scotland, lochs are inhabited by water-spirits who drag the unwary down to their abode; the Loch Ness monster is a last trace of these kelpies. (This belief has a social function; it is a way of saying that lochs – any water – can be death to the unwary.) But lochs are also often property boundaries, and sometimes clan and hence identity boundaries, spaces between one name and another. Women, who remain outsiders in their husbands' clans, even in their fathers', are metaphorically on the lochside all their lives. Spaces like the one in which Elspeth has her first fairy encounter are not women's spaces, in the sense that (say) the kitchen or the birthing room are. Rather, they are spaces of femininity, marginal as women are, places out of place, times out of time.[8] Such silent places can become occasions for talking about what is also marginal, what cannot be said.

The spell offered to Elspeth also reflects the theme of the female body. An egg is a common ingredient in fairy magic and countermagic; it symbolizes birth, hidden life, the pregnant belly, food. The spell – for that is what it is – is also about renunciation; Elspeth is not to eat the egg, but only its sweat, the moisture of its boiling, just as folktales warn against eating the fairy food, a particularly hard prohibition for a hungry islander for whom eggs may have been a luxury. The refusal of fairy food is in folktales always a test, a test of greed and self-control. Elspeth must close some parts of herself in order to open others. In folklore, a simple act of refusal – food refusal or refusal of rituals which make the individual acculturated, fit for the household, fit for the family – is responsible for fairy abduction, and this is probably what lies behind the later associations between fairies and enforced cleanliness, so eagerly taken up by élite bossyboots like Ben Jonson and Robert Herrick. In one Irish story, a girl is abducted because she and her sister refuse to wash their shoeless feet in the warm water that has been saved for the purpose after potatoes have been cooked in it; the next day she is found black all over, 'black as the hob'. So Elspeth's egg is renounced. The egg remains untouched, unbroken; it is what it exudes, the sweat or steam of its boiling, which Elspeth must take and use. This becomes the fairy ointment, a staple of folktales, which confers magic sight on the eyes on which it is rubbed. There are English cases involving the fairy ointment; it confers the ability to see not only the fairies, but stolen and lost goods and buried treasure; in other words, it is the foundation of a cunning woman's business credentials.[9] Elspeth must not wash her hands before touching the ointment. Such gestures mark a renunciation of a place within human society for a place outside it. To refuse food, or water for washing, is to refuse the household that offers them, Elspeth's family household.

What kind of knowledge does Elspeth want more than food? Knowledge of the female body. Elspeth's correct divination of her kinswoman's pregnancy and the baby's father shows that she now knows about the interior of the female body, about secrets, about the family's secrets, sexual secrets. To be cunning is to know. There is something spiteful about the knowledge, too, and something more than spiteful about Elspeth's use of it. And this is not the story of happy, carefree sexuality, endorsed by fairies, for which some may have been hoping.

Perhaps this is an older woman recalling the unbelievable oddity of adult sexuality as seen by a maturing child. Perhaps this is a secret hugged in the embrace of a miserable teenager. But it is also about the specific discovery that sex can be the ruin of women and their reputations. More deeply, it is about the discovery that not all babies are wanted, that not all babies are part of kinship structures which are authorized, which make sense. Like women in Scotland, the baby is always already marginal to kinship groups. The baby and the girl who carries it are silences, silences Elspeth has breached.

And yet Elspeth too is breached; she too has a child born outside marriage. Elspeth has learnt her lesson of knowledge all too well. The result of sexual and familial knowledge is that Elspeth has become the mirror of the disgraced granddaughter. One outsider begets another. Or – to put it another way – Elspeth's story of the pregnant girl who is desperate to get rid of her baby is a self-portrait. Unwanted babies in early modern Scotland were occasionally left 'for the fairies', a euphemism for child abandonment. The frustratingly elliptical record of the case of Jonet Drever shows this: 'the said Jonet Drever . . . To be convicted and guilty of the fostering of a bairne in the hill of Westray to the fairy folk called of hir our good neighbours.'[10] Where other neighbours shun the mother of a bastard, the fairies can be good neighbours indeed.

Elspeth's story is one of emergence into an unruly womanhood, not sanctioned but no doubt exploited by her society. But her story does not end there. Elspeth's encounters with the fairies occur at the two most common life moments for such encounters: the threshold of womanhood and the aftermath of childbirth. The moments in life when a fairy encounter is most likely are infancy, puberty and childbirth for women. And in childbed, Elspeth's fairy returns, and this time what he wants is clear. He wants the female body she now knows.

Sex from the dead? This makes sense – though it is wildly aberrant – in the system of Scottish ancestry, where everyone descended from a single heroic ancestor.[11] Identity is imparted to the clan by the dead through sex and reproduction. What happens to Elspeth is close to a perverse drama of clan identity. But Elspeth is a woman, and she seems to get her identity from the dead in another, more indirect fantasy, a fantasy about birth and the birth process. The baby is born, the illicit baby, and it brings with it a fairy kinsman to have sex with her, sex that is trebly illicit: after childbirth, with a kinsman, with the dead.

Youngish girls are often taken by the fairies or by fairy lovers. This is frequently dramatized in popular culture, in stories and ballads about fairy or demon lovers. In one Irish story, 'The Orphan and the Fairy', the girl is, like Elspeth, an outsider; as an orphan, she lives with her grandmother, and 'there's always some extra work for her more than any other child'. She has no male kin who can protect her. On the beach, she meets and befriends a fairy boy, who appears to be her ally and companion, her friend in her lonely, family-imposed tasks; he may even symbolize her rebellion against working for a family that does not really include her. So far, so idyllic, or so the romantics among us moderns would have thought. But for a hardscrabble, subsistence culture, there is no surcease for loneliness like this. The storyteller bluntly says that the girl 'had no sense'. When she gets home on the second evening, her grandmother is alert to her pallor and illness, but the girl will not tell what has happened. Finally she goes again and delouses the boy and rearranges his hair for him, fatal acts that offer to mother him, creating a kinship relationship between them which threatens to replace her shaky ties to other mortals. On her return that third night she finally tells her grandmother about these meetings. Her grandmother cunningly tells her to ask for a cure for a sick calf, then applies the same cure to the girl. She is to shake it on the young man. 'He rose up in a single ball of fire and disappeared off into the ocean.' This is, in the terms of the kind of culture Elspeth Reoch inhabited, a happy ending.[12]

But why is Elspeth silenced? What makes her dumb? With her lower body breached by birth and by the fairy man, the only opening left to Elspeth's control is her mouth. Her silence seals her upper body. It mirrors her restraint with the egg, when her mouth closed against the temptation of food, and it is from this her 'sight' comes. Ritual silence is important for magic in some folktales; in the Brothers' Grimm story 'The Seven Crows', the girl has to remain silent for seven years – one for each brother – to transform them. Yet, like hers, Elspeth's silence is not really her own. It is a sign of her fairy lover's care for her, but also his power over her. He has sealed her body against others, made it his. The fairies normally require silence from those they help. In breaking his seal, breaking silence, Elspeth appears to take control, but in reality simply puts herself under the control of yet another set of men, her interrogators. Talking about them is clearly Elspeth's way of saying something about herself, something about herself so important that she would rather die than stop saying it. And yet to talk is to lose everything, including her one protector. For in fairy legends those who talk about the fairies incur their wrath. Interrogator and fairy man, apparently opposed, are united in wishing to punish Elspeth for what she says.

Other punishment came Elspeth's way, too; whatever the interrogators thought, her brother took her silence as a terrible sign of her fairy dealings, and as an affront, too:

wherethrough her brother dang [hit] her with a branks [bridle] until she bled because she would not speak and put a bow string about her head to gar [make] her speak And thereafter took her three several [separate] times Sundays to the kirk and prayed for her From the which time she still continued dumb.

This is the terrifying violence we have also seen directed at changelings, remedies for the fairy-taken. Elspeth's brother strikes her with a brank, a bridle, because it has an iron bit, and iron was inimical to fairies. Perhaps he also uses a brank because it is an instrument for taming animals, and also for taming women, scolds? Speaking too much, speaking too little; both might seem equally a defiance of male authority. At this point, he may actually believe that Elspeth is a fairy, that his sister has been replaced by a fairy image or changeling. Hitting her with the bridle is a test as well as a cure; by making the fairy-image suffer, he may hope to get his own, loving, compliant sister back. Putting a bowstring about her head may be sympathetic magic, making a tight circle around a body that is itself too enclosed in order to open it. It may also be an attempt to bind a fairy, and it may link up with a Highland fairy character whom we shall meet in due course, a character called 'the bowman' by his votaries. As part of these attempts, Elspeth's brother also gives Jesus a chance to show what he is made of; he goes to the kirk to pray, taking Elspeth with him – by force. The violence displayed by Elspeth's brother has affinities with the kind of violence to which women who refused to conform in matters of religion were subject, and also with violence whose overt aim was the control of unruly women, and of course Elspeth is sexually unruly, somehow, perhaps more so than her brother knows. Or does he know best of all? Elspeth's brother behaves like her senior legitimate male relative. This may just be because her father has died and she has no husband. Or there may be another, deeper reason. What exactly does it mean to Elspeth's brother that she has closed her body, her mouth? And what does it mean to Elspeth that she tells a story of incest with a dead kinsman? This is speculation – we cannot know the truth – but it may be that in this drama of fairies and force is enacted a story of brother–sister incest that cannot be told.

Janet Weir: fairies and incest

One reason this seems possible is because another seventeenth-century Scottish woman talked about fairies in relation to incest with her brother. Janet Weir is the sister of Major Weir, a Cromwell supporter, a covenanter, whose many enemies finally cornered him with a series of charges of sexual deviance, bestiality and incest with his sister:

Margaret Weir, the wife of Alexander Weir, Bookseller in Edinburgh, testified, that when she was of the Age of 27 years, or thereabouts, she found the Major her brother and her sister Jane[t], lying together in the Barn at Wickes-shaw, and that they were both naked in the bed together, and that she was above him, and that the Bed did shake, and that she heard some scandalous Language between them in particular, that her sister said, she was confident she should prove with Child.[13]

In this story, what Janet does is a violation of many norms: the incest taboo, yes, but as well she is on top, and she is talking eagerly about having a child who will be the offspring of incest. And yet Janet, when asked about incest, talks about fairies, telling a story which seems to have little to do with this story, a story about fairies. Why? Why might both Elspeth and Janet talk fairy when they think incest?

First, incest puts you outside the law and gives you magical powers. If you survive this huge apocalyptic transgression of the oldest and strongest of all taboos – if the house does not fall on you, and the lightning bolts remain in the sky – then you are, you must be, special, magical. The gods of Egypt and Greece, and some royal families, are allowed to commit acts of incest that would destroy ordinary mortals; this shows how special they are. Oedipus himself eventually becomes magical. The outsider status conferred by incest can be desolation, or a source of terrible power, because from outside, the wounded subject can strike at the healthy. Incest is a symbol of magic and a reason for it. Writing about modern incest survivors, recovered-memory guru Judith Herman reluctantly admits that some women embraced their crime with defiance and pride. As initiates into forbidden sexual knowledge, they felt they possessed magical powers. One woman described herself as a 'bad witch' and expressed the fear that she could cause others to sicken with her thoughts.[14] Loathing herself, this woman has nevertheless turned self-loathing to some account. Such stories also hint at the possibility, unthinkable till recently, that incest might be a pleasurable fantasy for some women. Having survived the transgression of this taboo, what can she fear? She is invulnerable. Incest is surviving outside the normal. Perhaps that is what Janet and Elspeth are talking about. Women are outsiders in the Scottish kin system anyway. If they divest themselves of their position within that kin system as receptacles for male identity, male seed, what other kind of identity can they have? Or what kind of identity can women have that is not Other? Fairies, of course, are a kind of ultimate symbol of otherness, and perhaps also an alternative, unauthorized kinship structure; if you are outside human kin relations, perhaps you can be inside something else, something more glamorous.

There is another point of connection between incest and fairies: incest is analogous to death, because it places you outside the community's laws. Fairies are associated with the dead, sometimes they are the dead or are captives of the dead. Elspeth's black man is dead. Bessie Dunlop's fairy guide was also dead: 'Thome Reid, who died at Pinkye, as he himself affirmed; what would tell her, when ever she asked.'[15] Like Elspeth's fairy helper, Thom Reid has died young, by violence. To gain knowledge and identity from the dead is to gain it from ancestors. But what if that knowledge is somehow of the wrong kind, as it is in Elspeth's case? What if it places you not inside the clan or kinship structure, but outside it? Incest is about kinship bonds. Compact witchcraft involves a change of kinship, with or without an explicit disavowal of previous ties. Sex with a person is a way of compact with them, a means of becoming someone different. For women, this is most aptly symbolized in marriage. Yet marriage is never inclusive in Scotland; kinship is agnatic rather than cognatic, carried through the male. Married women remain marginal to their husband's clan; that is why Scottish women keep their maiden names after marriage. They are conduits for their husbands' seed, names. Fairies are a clan, and women can join them without being included. The outsider status of the incest victim symbolizes this fragility of identity, this permanent exclusion. Covenanting, which as everyone knows has to do with Scottish notions of kinship, is a religious kinship structure in which women could be included. This is especially relevant to Janet Weir. Weir died accusing the men and women who saw her die of breaking faith with the Protestant covenant.[16] The charge of incest of which she was accused mirrored their lack of fidelity.

Something much more basic is at work here too: the pleasure of making up or confessing to crimes one has not committed, the pleasures of the kind of supernatural Munchhausen's syndrome in claiming to be fairy-taken. Both a confession of incest and a story of being taken cast the woman as culpable victim, someone who falls into evil and does not try hard enough to escape. Perhaps something really spectacular had to happen to women to allow them to be seen and to see themselves as suffering victims. There is also the pleasure of invention. Inventing horrors leads to invented displacement from those horrors, a double displacement, as this testimony from an alleged Satanic abuse survivor and multiple personality disorder victim shows. The speaker is a woman called Angela:

It started to get into ritual abuse memories, I've had memories of being in a cage with wild, hungry cats and snakes, naked and cold and hungry and terrified. They poked something real hot, like a red-hot poker, in the cage. Then when I was five, I was tied upside down and lowered over a fire until it started to singe my hair.[17]

Angela has created a truly dramatic trauma, one which places her outside the law and gives her the power to tell stories and be heard. Perhaps appearing with Oprah or Rikki Lake today offers the perilous thrills which used to be offered by the early modern courtroom; you will be heard, but also condemned. Now, Jasmine, one of Angela's 'alters', a 'personality' allegedly created by the abuse, takes over the story:

I have a red light to keep me safe, like blood, when I go to the woods . . . I go to the Blue Land, where the wind blows a lot, and bells make sounds, and people teach you things without saying a word.[18]

Angela has made a trauma, and she has also created her own refuge from it, the Blue Land, an infantile space with affinities not with early modern Scottish fairies, but with post-Romantic fairies, little jingly thingies representing ideal childhood. Like Angela, Janet Weir invests both in trauma and in its recuperation through supernatural refuge, though the refuges are very different. Janet's equivalent of the Blue Land is a story about spinning, which is told in several different ways in different reports on her trial:

That when she kept a school at Dalkeith, and teached children, a tall woman came to [her] house when the children were there; and that she had, as appeared to her, a child upon her back, and one or two at her foot; and that the said woman desired that [she] should employ her to speak for her to the Queen of Fairy, and strike and battle in her behalf with the said queen (which was her own words); and that the next day a little woman came to [her], and did give her a piece of a tree, or the root of some herb or tree, as she thought, and told her that as long as she had the same, she would be able to do what she should desire; and then the said woman did lay a cloth upon the floor near the door, and caused the declarant set her foot upon the same, and her hand upon the crown of her own head, and caused the declarant repeated these words thrice, viz. 'All my cross and troubles go to the door with the' which accordingly she did; and that she gave the woman all the silver she had, being some few turners, and some meal; and that after the said woman went away, the declarant did spin a very short time, and that she did find more yarn upon her pin, and good yarn, nor she thought could be spun in so short a time; which did so affright [her], that she did set by her while, and did shut the door, and did stay within her house for the space of twenty days or thereby, and was exceedingly troubled, and weeped because she thought what she had done in manner forsaid was in effect the renouncing of her baptism.[19]

A woman is accused of incest and of abetting her brother's sorcery, and she at once comes out with a long rigmarole about a cunning woman, a fairy lady and spinning. We might begin to unravel the meaning of this apparent *non sequitur* by starting small. Why spinning? First, names. The Scottish folktale 'Whuppity Stoorie' is a version of *Rumpelstiltskin*, but in Scotland it is a woman who helps another mortal woman with her spinning; the woman must either find her helper's name, be 'taken' herself or give her her child.[20] Giving up your baby in exchange for your own power or security is the ultimate crime in agnatic kinship. There is a hint that the cunning woman who offers Janet her services may be about to do just this, since she carries her child with her. The name is also honour or reputation, so the entire story may be a screen, an attempt at self-exculpation of the loss of name and kinship structure implied in the charge of incest. The second idea is that the central motif in Janet's story is the same as that in the folktales: being able to spin with help from the fairies is about gaining an undeserved reputation for industry when you are actually a lazy girl. It is deceit, pretending to be someone other than who you are.

Thirdly, the woman who helps with Janet's spinning may have a deeper meaning. Very often in fairy stories, fairies are the only allies a woman has. A fairy may be someone who will take your side when everyone else has abandoned you. Children commonly fantasize a rescuing hero when in difficulty – even quite everyday difficulties – at school or at home. Abused children engage in what is called Positive Projective Anticipation, the belief that a future friend or spouse will some day help undo the effects of the current situation.[21] So, of course, do children who are not abused; such fantasies surface in folktales like *Cinderella*, where inadequate parental care is supplemented by the care of a dead mother who sometimes returns as herself, sometimes as a fairy.[22] For Janet Weir, positive projective anticipation might have ceased to take the form of orthodox Christianity and come to take the form of a fairy who gained her a reputation for spinning and industry, perhaps even offered to gain her a few extra pennies. She knows this is a rebellion, an alliance with someone outside the Kirk, which is why she feels so miserable, so guilty.

The intertwining of memory and desire, speech and silence, in these stories mimics uncannily the dilemmas of our own day, our own anxieties about recovered memories and whether they can be deemed a syndrome. As psychologist Janice Haaken observes, both sides in the current recovered-memory debate seem eager to argue that violent sexuality and violent desire always comes from outside the woman – from the perpetrator, from the therapist.[23] But in these cases, violent desires seem intrinsic to the stories these women are telling, stories which are not part of the usual script of pact witchcraft, though they can be forced roughly into its shape. Not only do these stories undo our assumption that fairies are small gauzy wingy thingies, they also undo the assumptions about the true nature of femininity which tend to accompany the gauzy wingy beings. And that is only one part of their supreme relevance to our own preoccupations. In these witchcraft cases, we can actually witness the process by which story turns into memory. What happens here is that cultural materials in general circulation are appropriated by individuals. We think of memory as individual, but one of the commonest forms of forgetting is what is termed source amnesia, forgetting the source of acquired information. A story originally heard as about another can slowly come to feel as if it is our own story. In describing two Scottish women's telling of fairy stories, we may be dealing with just such a phenomenon. If so, we need to ask what it was about the standard stories of fairy encounter that made it possible for Elspeth Reoch and Janet Weir to claim those stories for themselves, to make them their own. It may be that these stories in circulation always did represent a specific world of female desires and anxieties, that they were always a way of saying the unsayable. If so, they could easily become what Haaken calls 'transformative memories', memories, whether authentic or not, that make sense of a life, that turn its disorder and fragmentation into meaning.[24] If so, they may also be transformative of us in looking at the complex, tangled otherness of the past.

Fairies and the dead

These are two detailed stories of meeting with fairies. In hearing them, we must keep reminding ourselves that fairies are the dead, and especially dead kin. Accused witch Alesoun Peirsoun's fairy guide, for example, is 'one Mr William Sympsoune, her cousin and mother-brothers-son, who she affirmed was a great scholar and doctor of medicine, that healed her of her disease in Lothian, within the town of Edinburgh, where she repaired to him'. William is a lost child 'who was taken away from his father by a man of Egypt, a giant, being but a bairne [child], who had him away to Egypt with him, where he remained to the space of twelve years or he come home again'. This supernatural entity is not parochial. Alesoun is talking about a child kidnapped by gypsies, again a common subject of folklore, but one also taken back to Egypt, in High Renaissance culture already recognized as the home of serious and learned magic.[25]

This is another instance of the overlap between what might be termed 'oral' culture and writing; it is not a question of learning corrupting the pure orality of folklore, as of Alesoun's imagination eagerly seizing on diverse materials from different cultural layers. If William Simpson really did disappear as a child, one of those materials must have been family stories about him, as well as more general oral and written stories, oral stories that come from books. Alesoun, however, did not merely encounter the fairy-dead in her own home, as Elspeth and Jonet did. Alesoun was for a long time 'away'.

She could not say readily how long she was with them; and that she had friends in that court which [who] was of her own blood, who had good acquaintance of the queen of Elphane, which might have helped her: but she was whiles well and whiles ill, and a while with them and an other while away; and that she would be in her bed healthy and fair, and would not wit [know] where she would be on the morn: And that she saw not the Queen there seven year.

Alesoun keeps talking about her good friends at court because these alone explain how she manages to come and go to the fairy realm. 'And that she had many good friends in that court, but were all away now: And that she was seven year well handled [treated] in the Court of Elfane and had kind friends there, but had no will to visit them after the end.' Alesoun's 'friends', the dead and the revenant that go alike to the Court of Elfame, are her community; her identity depends on them; she keeps repeating the fact that she has friends, desperately, like a child accused of being unpopular. For her, these friends – these dead friends – give her meaning and status. For the courts, they were all devils. What to Alesoun made her an insider, to the courts made her very much an outsider.

Another kind of Scottish fairy gets its links with the dead not from clan structures, but from the Vikings. An Orkney woman, Katherine Jonesdochter, is steeped in Norse folktales. Her indictment says that she is accused of haunting and seeing the trowis [trowies] rise out of the kirkyard of Hildiswick and Holiecrosse Kirk of Eschenes and that she saw them on the hill called Greenfall at many sundry times and that they come to any house where there was feasting or great merriness, and specially at Yule.[26]

These are plainly Yuletide demons, like the Greek *kallikantzaroi* and the Norse elves, the *jolarsveinar*, but they are also the restless dead. Both mischief spirits and the dead are attracted by merrymaking, festivity and feasting; like the forlorn ghosts of Homer's *Odyssey*, they come in the hope that an excess of vital spirit will restore them. However, the mischief-spirits have vital energies of their own, and the dead, as ever, have identity to impart. For in Norse folklore, as in Scotland, the elves have been widely regarded as the spirits of ancestors, male and female.[27] In Katherine's story, then, many myths are amalgamated; though their behaviour is like the alfar – the Norse elves – the trowies are also like Norse trolls because they live underground, under boulders, in mounds, under the sand, in a sea cave below a house.[28] Here, though, underground has become, sensibly, the dwelling-place of the dead, and a Norse myth is being diluted by Scottish fairy lore.

For in Norse myth trowies are not the dead, but only the keepers of the dead; various stories mention a midwife or a fiddler seeing people, generally women, who were believed to be dead in a fairy dwelling. This may be due to the related belief that the fairies take people (especially women who died in childbirth) and leave wooden images in their place, which would be buried as their corpses. Or they may leave living images; this may be what Elspeth's brother thinks has happened to her. Of course, fairies too can be seen in this light. In 'The Three Yells', a dead Shetlander summons back his neighbour in a dream to meet him at a place called the Hole of Cudda, 'famous for trows', at midnight. The dead man tells the other his wife is unfaithful, it has been 'a job to get back to this world again', and the other must go home before he hears the third of the three loud yells of the title. He manages to be just inside the door when the third yell sounds, but his mare's hindquarters are still outside, and she drops dead.[29]

How to recognize a fairy

The Scottish fairies that Elspeth and Jonet met were not tiny, not wee, not twee. They looked like people – up to a point.

One of the best-known – though least analysed – stories of fairies told by an accused witch is that told by Bessie Dunlop, charged with witchcraft in 1576, at Lyne.[30] Bessie's story is not a coherent chronological narrative like Elspeth's; she rambles, perhaps because her interrogators, like us, are prodding, unknowing, at a kind of story they no longer understand. It is right that we should meet her first in glimpses too, for those glimpses convey how difficult it is for us to grasp the whole of her from the pieces left to us. Each fragment needs careful reading as much of its significance for her is buried in details that we can easily miss because we have lost touch with the mentality that produced it. It needs to be interwoven with the stories of others, supplemented, bulked out, in order to make sense to us.

When Bessie Dunlop was asked what kind of man her fairy guide Thom Reid was, she said he was

an honest well [very] elderly man, gray bearded, and had a gray coat with Lumbart [Lombard] sleeves of the old fashion; a pair of gray breeks [trousers] and white schanks [stockings], gartered about the knee; a black bonnet on his head, close behind and plain before, with silken laces drawn through the lips thereof; and a white wand [staff] in his hand.

Thom's clothes are noticeably old-fashioned, but to us at the millennium turn this might conjure up visions not of fairies, but of ghosts, who routinely advertise their status as such by failing to keep up with the Conrans. And Thom is a ghost of sorts – one of the dead, one who died by violence, by premature separation from the world, in battle. His clothing is frozen at the moment of his death. In a different way, William Simpson also represents the past. He has some links with Catholicism; he is the revenant of a man who also died before his time, 'for opening of a priest book and looking upon it'.[31] Andro Man, a village magician whom we shall meet later, shares this sense that fairies represent an historical or legendary past: '[he] kens sundry dead men in their company, and that the king that died in Floddon and Thomas Rymour is there'. Is it because they are the untimely dead that fairies often wear old-fashioned clothes, and become associated with a vanishing past – of Catholicism, of monarchy, or rural contentment? Perhaps. If so, it is significant that these things are linked with the fairies most often by those who mourn their passing. 'It were a good world when the fairies danced and the priest prayed.'[32] Perhaps the message is that Catholicism, monarchy, rural life, were also dead by violence. At the same time, it is odd to think that all that cosy, queasy nostalgia, so loved by the élites of the eighteenth and nineteenth centuries, derives from the stark fact that fairies are the dead.

Birth and childbirth

As the dead, fairies are concerned with birth and childcare. Like elderly grandmothers, whose involvement with their family and wisdom about the bodies it contains are symbolized by their longevity, the fairies of Scotland are a resource in birth and child-rearing – of a kind. For they can be killers, and, as fantasies, can stand in for the murderous longings of reluctant mothers. Jonet Drever left an elliptical fragment of such a fairy story: 'the said Jonet Drever be convict[ed] and guilty of the fostering of ane bairne in the hill of Westray to the fairy folk called of her our good neighbours'.[33] Reading – perhaps guessing – between the lines, it seems clear that Jonet has had a baby, a bastard, and like the women of ancient Greece, she has abandoned it to the care of the fairies. Which may be a way of saying that the baby is left for the dead, for dead. Babies regarded as changelings were often ill-treated, but here there is a hint that Jonet was not thinking of changelings, but of paternity. She had a fairy lover, it seems, and she may have left him his baby, as women did leave babies in their rich, mortal, fathers' care. 'Take your son, Sir!'

Or Jonet may simply have been thinking of the fairies as experts on mortal babies. Fairies, like other 'good neighbours', did call on women in childbed. Birth was a time of especial vulnerability in early modern culture. The woman's body was shielded from the world by a series of elaborate rituals; for ten days, the room in which she lay was closed to the outside world, even the windows closed by heavy drapes. With the labouring mother were all the important women from the village, called gossips, assembled to drink a kind of hot eggnog called caudle, to talk about local affairs, and to help the midwife and the labouring woman. It was like giving birth at a WI meeting, or a hen-night; the last, faint trace of this custom is the baby shower, now happily separate from the event it portends. The period after childbirth, called lying-in, which lasted for up to a month, saw the mother still confined to the birthing room, and for the first ten days the sheets could not even be changed. The gossips would continue to call on the mother, but no men were admitted, not even the father. Lying-in was a common time for suspicions of bewitchment to arise; it was a time when the unclean mother and the unnamed baby were only insecurely anchored to the things of this world. Elspeth sees her fairy ancestor again after childbirth. Bessie Dunlop, too, is visited by Thom Reid, who like a modern labour coach says that she will be fine, nothing to worry about.

We have met Bessie Dunlop a few times in this chapter, but now is the time to retell the kernel of her story, its black and terrible heart.

While still in her childbed lair, Bessie has another visitor, a visitor who from her behaviour could be one of the gossips of the village. Bessie's new visitor is a stout woman. She sits down beside Bessie; she asks for some caudle. But then the woman suddenly says that Bessie's baby will die. This is close to ill words, of the sort that a witch might say. Visitors to women after childbed had to choose their words with great care: too much praise, or gloomy predictions, could actually bring about the death of the vulnerable, unbaptized baby. At first, Bessie has no idea of the woman's identity, but when speaking to Thom, he explains that the woman is the queen of the fairies Elfame, the woman who has asked Thom himself to look after Bessie. In retrospect, it is clear that the queen of Elfame has come for Bessie's baby. Bessie is trying to say that the fairies attend her in exchange for the baby. Women in this culture do not have much to bargain with: only their bodies and their babies, neither of which really belongs to them.

Bessie meets Thom Reid, her personal fairy, just a few days later, and her luck turns. Bessie is driving her cows along the way to pasture, and talking to herself. She is crying, because a cow has died, because her husband and child lie sick, and because she herself has just risen from childbed. She must have been tired, in pain, perhaps in the throes of the terrible hormone crash that follows delivery. Thom says hello, and proceeds to give her a lecture on acceptance of misfortune: '*Sancta marie*', said he, 'Bessie, why do you make such great dole [sadness] and cry so much for any worldly thing?' This is a fairytale encounter; often in folktales, the unlucky son or daughter is in tears, when a kind voice asks what the problem is; the best-known example is Cinderella and her fairy godmother. After the problem is explained, the kind being helps to solve it. So Bessie answered, 'Alas! have I not great cause to make great dole? For our goods have dwindled away, and my husband is on the point of death, and a babe of my own will not live; and myself at a weak point; have I not good cause then to have a sore heart?' After a rebuke to Bessie for blaming God for her troubles, and for asking him for something she should not have asked for, Thom tells her that she will lose more livestock, and that her baby will indeed die, which confirms the queen's words, but that (in exchange?) her husband will recover. Then Thom disappears 'in through the yard of Monkcastell; and I thought he went in at a narrow hole of the dyke that no earthly man could have gone through; and so I was afraid'. As well she might be, for by his disappearance into the earth she knew Thom Reid was a fairy, one of the dead of the mounds. He comes from where her baby will go.

Other children were 'taken'. John Ferguson brings what the Scots call a 'sharg bairn' to a fairy witch called Jonet Andirson. Jonet shows that she knows fairies are involved by crossing the child with a knife, and she then tells John that 'what is away is away'. 'Away' is a common euphemism for being with the fairies. Jonet is saying that she cannot get the baby back for John, but she has some good news: as long as he looks after the 'sharg bairn', the sickly child-changeling, he will not want. The implication is that if he looks after a fairy, then the fairies will look after him.[34]

James Chrystie is ordering a cradle made for his new baby, for his wife is near her time. Isabel Haldane, who traffics with the fairies, comes past and tells him not to bother, because he does not need it. For one thing, his wife will not be lighter until some five weeks have passed, and for another, the baby will never even suckle his mother;

he will 'die and be tane [taken] away'.[35] So it all turns out. Yet Isabel's telling phrase, 'die and be tane away', suggests that James's baby does not *simply* die. Her knowledge of his imminent demise comes from the fairies, themselves the dead; do they know who willed it because they are the ones who take the dead? We have seen before that fairies are particularly associated with those who die before their time – in battle, in childbirth – and the death of an infant is certainly premature; this may even explain fairies' particular fondness for babies and children as victims. Yet the fairies and the dead could also be invoked to protect babies. The cunning woman Katherine Grant invoked the dead to cure a child she was herself suspected of infecting: reaching the child's home, she asked for a cup of water, with a knife, and she moved the knife in the water, and said:

> The dead upraise
> To the cradle she get
> To mend the bairne
> That bitten was,
> In name of the father, the son and the Holy Ghost.[36]

Like Jonet, Katherine uses a knife, which the fairies were supposed to hate. Yet fairies *are* the rising dead, and she invokes them.

In all near-subsistence cultures, the lives of children are always at risk. Fairies were a way of thinking and talking about child health and child illness, and the powerful feelings of ownership, love and fear that such ill children could cause. Basic to all these stories is the idea that a sick child is somehow 'taken', somehow no longer owned by the mother who bore it, but by some other woman. Similar fantasies clustered around the figure of the witch, but here there is an added twist; while the witch was hated, satisfyingly, unequivocally, in these stories the fairies bring benefits to the parents of the sick child, bring something in exchange for taking the child away. They are too powerful to fight – like some kind of local nobility who come and take food, people, children as they please – and this luckily justifies the parents in taking what they are sent and resigning themselves to the loss of a child. Luckily, because otherwise it might seem that the parents in these stories have sold their children.

Fairies and adolescence

But fairies had other meanings, too, meanings to do with adolescence. For most of these people, a story about a first encounter with a fairy was a good time to try to describe what a fairy *was* and what it could do. Take Katherine Jonesdochter, for example. Katherine's fairy was mysteriously called 'the bowman', which may have nothing to do with arrows. The bowman may be the living man, from Norse *bua*, to live. Norse spirits often live in (natural) hills; Katherine's lives in Hiliswick and Bechenes, and Katherine is from Orkney, where the debts to Scandinavian culture are especially clear.[37] The bowman comes to her in her mother's house, before she is a woman, and he is interested in sex. He lies with her then, this adolescent girl; it is almost as if he *is* her awakening sexuality. And he continues to lie with her for forty years, especially at Hallowe'en and Holy Cross Day. So this is an Elspeth-type story, a story of an adolescent girl whose first sexual encounter becomes an encounter with knowledge. In exchange for sex, the fairy man gives Katherine knowledge, and knowledge is power. He gives her magical weapons which allow her to cure her cows, and do anything else she wishes.[38] Another Jonesdochter, a relative of Katherine, also sees a sign of the bowman. One day her own children are playing, and she notices among them a little creature, a small child-sized man, a man whom she calls the bowman's bairn.[39] In this enigmatic little story, the sexuality of the bowman is folded back into the story of one child who is 'different' from all the others.

Isabel Haldane's experience of being swept away is similarly astounding. She is lying in bed when she is suddenly taken, by God or the Devil, to a hillside. The hill opens, and she goes in, staying from Thursday till Sunday at midnight, the full Sabbath. There she meets a man with a grey beard, a dead relative, and it is through his help that she is released. As Angela Bourke shows, being swept into the air may be a metaphor for the experience of childbirth. Robert Kirk, the Scottish clergyman, is called in to interpret the case of a woman who, after having a child, lies 'like an unextinguished lamp', silent, unable to laugh, unable to eat; she wanders the fields at night, conversing with 'a people she knew not'.[40] Abstracted from her usual circumstances, this woman is lost in a world of death.

Meeting fairies

For Elspeth, for Bessie and for Katherine, meeting the fairies is anxious, but there are rewards. For others, the fairies are simply hostile. Like Bessie Dunlop, Janet Trall is visited by the fairies after childbirth, but unlike Bessie's experience, her encounter is pure pain and madness: 'when I was lying in child bed lair I was drawn forth from my bed to a dub [puddle] near my house door in dunning [her village?] and was there puddled and troubled . . .'[41] This sounds like the jolly tricks played by seasonal demons like the trowies. But Janet's tone is more serious; if all this was a joke, it was not one she found funny. What happens to her also recalls the ritual humiliation sometimes inflicted by villagers on unruly women; ducking in a puddle is not unlike ducking in a pond. Are the fairies symbolic of Janet's hostile community? A metaphor for her terror of – something? Something in herself? Something They would blame her for if They knew? When the fairy folk come again, during harvest, things seem worse. The fairy man appears to want only to help Janet, and yet she refuses to have anything to do with him. Somehow the result is: 'They drave me down and then I was beside myself and would have eaten the very earth beside me.' Janet's absolute despair, her deep mourning – for eating dirt is a universal sign of mourning and also of extreme self-abasement – are well in excess of anything the fairies do; it is as if the fairies are a symbol of whatever pushes her into a pit of despair. Is it childbirth and motherhood, then, that so affects Janet? I hesitate to begin the process of pathologization, but her extreme feelings are reminiscent of what is called post-partum psychosis today, and this is often accompanied by visions or hallucinations. Feelings of passionate love and protectiveness mingle with feelings of acute estrangement from the baby, from all people. And from oneself; to be beside oneself, as Janet is, is also to be outside oneself.

Eating earth can have another meaning, however. A revenant can be laid by eating the earth from its grave. The action 'grounds' the revenant, prevents the dead from roaming. Janet may be 'earthing' her fairy oppressor. Or – more simply – she may be 'earthing' herself, ingesting her home ground to keep herself from being swept 'away'. Or – a final possibility – eating the dirt may just be the ritual act that will join her to the fairies for ever, a way of allying herself with the dead, with death itself. Stopping the mouth with earth is a way of speaking of one silenced in death. Whatever the truth, this powerful and suggestive act points to the links between fairies, darkness and death.

Bessie returns the fairies' visit; she goes inside the hill. Thom takes her up to the door, and at the door he forbids her to speak, no matter what she hears or sees. Like eating the fairy food, speaking opens the mouth and allows change to become permanent; once the boundaries of the body have been breached, magic can be done. And when they have gone forward a little way, Bessie sees twelve people: eight women and four men, and the men are dressed like gentlemen, and the women have plaids around them. She does not recognize anyone except Thom; this is not one of the fairy hills inhabited by the dead of the community, and nor is it a fairy ride in which the fairies' entourage is made up of selected members of the living community. And yet Bessie herself is invited to join the group. Adjured to keep silent by Thom, she does not reply, and the fairies are carried away by an ugly wind, leaving Bessie lying sick on the ground. Women were usually sick on returning from fairyland. Only Thom's return cures her. She then asks Thom who the people were; they are 'the good wights', the good people or good neighbours that live in the Court of Elfame. She does not want to go with them until she knows the reason for doing so. Thom suggests that they would give her money, clothes, the appearance of gentlefolk. Bessie stoutly resists these efforts at embourgeoisement: she says she lives with her own family, and could never leave them. Thom gets very angry, and he says huffily that if that's how she thinks, she won't get any good of him. Here we learn that there is more to the bargain with the fairies than Bessie had imagined. Her child is not enough; she must also join the fairies, throw in her lot with them, in order to benefit from them. Not so much fairies as *famiglia*, these fairies believe that those who are not with us are against us. Walking between the worlds is a short-term arrangement at best.

Isobel Gowdie has a simpler, more nourishing encounter: 'I was in the Deunie-Hills, and got meat from the Queen of Fairie, more then I could eat.'[42] The queen of the fairies nourished her, giving her meat. Given Gowdie's stress on the queen's fine clothes, and the king's, we might see this as a fantasy of dining with the great, or perhaps as a traditional piece of hospitality extended to a poor woman by a rich family.[43] This would not be incompatible with seeing the story as a fantasy version of such hospitality, in which the social barriers of class are broken by the anomalousness of the supernatural, so that Gowdie can dine with the fairy king and queen almost as their friend as well as their dependant; certainly, her attempt to describe their accoutrements in detail implies an identification with their elevated social station. It is suggestive that the fairies give Gowdie meat, for meat suggests upper-class and celebratory meals. The fact that the fairy court is surrounded by 'elfbulls' is especially significant, for in the Scottish Highlands cattle were a sign of wealth, as well as a source of meat; bulls mean a lord's house. However, Gowdie may simply be using the term as a synonym for food in general. If so, this is indeed a fairytale, for English folklore is full of stories about peasants who gain advancement in great or little ways by association with the fairies. And yet these fairies are also menacing, for Isobel sees them preparing their elf-shot with which they can make mortals sicken. If the meat is what Isobel wants, a fantasy projection by a woman who is chronically hungry, are the arrows also a projection of power by a woman who is chronically powerless, but perhaps angry? All such signs of ambiguity are missing from James I's characteristically inattentive and careless summary of fairy visits: 'they have been transported with the Phairie to such a hill, which opening, they went in, and there saw a fair Queene, who gave them a stone which had sundry vertues, which at sundry times hath been produced in judgement'.[44] But what is intriguing is that just like the populace to whom he cannot be bothered to listen, James seems here to be projecting his own desires on to the fairies. No one mentions that the queen is pretty, though some do say that she is neatly dressed.

Why all this emphasis on what fairies were wearing? One might be inclined to assume that it arises from a need to provide evidence that these were fairies, and yet the descriptions seem hopeless as a means of identification: some fairies wear green, but others wear white, or grey, or no specific colour but a particular kind of clothing. Is it an effort to pin down social status? But again the descriptions are not always helpful in this respect. One suspects that the descriptions simply add verisimilitude to an otherwise unconvincing narrative, rather in the way Philip Larkin says we believe Hugo Drax will blow up London because he wears a Patek Philippe watch. Umberto Eco calls this 'the wandering gaze', and it is essential to commercial popular narratives like Mills and Boon and Ian Fleming. Like pulp fictions, too, the fairies offer a fantasy of social advancement, sometimes on a very grand scale.[45]

Making money from fairies

The fairies are particularly the friends of the very poor, sometimes their only friends. Jonet Rendall is a beggar, who meets a fairy. Like Bessie and the others, she is miserable when he appears; someone has just refused her appeal for charity. His name is Walliman. Walliman is a name analogous to others given to brownie-hob spirits; another from Westray is called Wilkie, and exists to frighten children.[46] Like the hobs, Walliman offers Jonet help with her main occupation, which is not housework, but begging. Is this a fairytale? Yes and no. She does not become rich, but Walliman can make her a more successful beggar, offering a kind of protection racket. He does offer to show her how to heal people in order to get alms from them – for a moment, we glimpse a world of alternative medicine sold by door-to-door mendicants – but more usefully, he promises that whoever gives her alms will be the better for it by land or sea. And, of course, those who do not will not be healed, and will suffer whatever fate Jonet wishes for them. This enforces what until the Reformation was a moral norm – the giving of alms – but does so in a way that no established church can ever approve. *Maleficium*, ill-wishing, often enforces social norms, such as universal invitations to large events like christenings – as in Sleeping Beauty – and here it ensures the same tradition of uncritical open-handedness on which the poor relied. Other fairies simply offer a stupendously simple fantasy of social elevation: 'thou art a poor woman and a beggar among a company of harlots, go with me and I'll make thee a Lady and put thee in a brave castle where thou shalt want nothing and I will free thee of all the poverties and troubles thou art in', offers one fairy guide.[47] Other fairies offered money by indirect means; as we shall see in due course, a career as a cunning man or woman was a way out of absolute rock-bottom poverty for some, while others were offered the opportunity to look for treasure that would make them rich. Though this was more important in English fairy beliefs, it does happen in Scotland too; Walter Ronaldson was visited every year, twice a year for twenty-seven years by a spirit, a spirit who awoke him from sleep by calling him by a pet name, almost a childhood name: 'Wattie! Wattie!' He saw it sitting on his chest near his bed 'like a child, with a shaven head, clad in white like a shirt', Then it gives him some advice; it tells him to go to Weathman's house in Stanivoid, because there he will find both silver and gold, and goods. Walter digs diligently with three other men, but the search proves fruitless. Nevertheless, he still believes what he has been told; the gold can be found if well sought. Hope springs eternal from the human breast; even in the dock, Walter cannot let go of his dream.[48] And dreams of gold, as we shall see, were what led people to search for the fairies in England, too.

4

Desire of Gold
and the Good Neighbours:
The Uses of Fairies

Anything as dangerous as fairies must have its uses, for otherwise no one would desire danger. Danger can itself be the use, of course: the quick pulse of blood, the sense of being singled out, heroic. And the fear of fairies is, as we have seen, a way of talking about other, unnameable fears – and desires. But for the practical English, fairies had a very particular use, a sunny upside that made any danger worth braving. They were the possessors of solid cash.

The story of Susan Swapper

In the salt sea-marshes of Southern England, a woman dreaming of fairies was also dreaming of gold. A witchcraft trial in Rye – a setup where the political enemies of one of the accused women's husbands managed to corner his godly wife (though not for long) – yields a fairy story of unparalleled richness in the English archives. The story begins with a woman who is terrified of being taken 'away'. She is expecting a child, and in her mind, this makes her a target. The fairies are gathering.

Susan Swapper the wife of Roger Swapper of Rye aforesaid Sawyer sayeth that about Mid Lent last past she being in the Chamber where she did lie with her husband in bed in the night time about the hours of Twelve and one of the clock there appeared to her four spirit[s in] Likeness of two men and two women.[1]

This is a deposition from the Rye witchcraft trial, brilliantly discussed by Annabel Gregory some years ago. It is a case where some hard facts have been uncovered, but where the specificity of the fictions that are spun around them also deserves attention. For whereas many of the Scottish cases involve a single fiction, albeit one woven from diverse tales, this case is one of overlapping and contradictory fictions, tangled into a single narrative that bobs and weaves, changing direction several times. Susan meticulously describes the spirits, and plainly finds it relevant to say that one is wearing green. When they reappear the second night, Susan is terrified:

then the next night after they appeared again to her, and the woman in the green petticoat called [her]: 'Sue, come and go with me or else I will carry thee', whereupon she . . . being afeard with that vision and the calling of her by her name, called to her husband and waked him, and willed him to hold her, And he awakening turned unto her and answered her: 'Wherefore should I hold thee?', and she replied unto him again and said 'Here is a thing that will carry me away', and he said again unto her I see nothing and so turned about from her, and then the said vision which she so did see de[parted] from her.

She begs her husband to protect her. He does not, but his voice drives back the dark, and they do not take her this time. This is a story of someone who is not-quite-taken, who manages to resist for just long enough. We can return to this story that does not get told in due course, but it is the same one told by many Scottish women, including Janet Trall. What is curious is that this fairy story is swept aside by another, a story which dominates English fairy material. This new story is about cold hard cash. Susan is given a healing spell by her spectral fairy visitors, but she mysteriously interprets it as a treasure spell:

And the woman in the green petticoat said unto her I would have you go unto young Anne Bennett and Call her and go into her garden with her and dig and set sage and then you should be well. Whereupon in the morning this examinate sent unto Mistress Tayler to come unto her w[hi]ch accordingly she did and then she told her what the woman had said unto her. And in the afternoon after dinner Mistress Tayler did pull open two pales of her garden and sent for [Susan] and so they went both together into the garden and this examinate did dig in the garden with Mistress Tayler.

A healing spell, and yet both women at once begin a search for buried treasure. Why? First, the very idea of digging seems to set their minds running along these lines. English fairies live underground, and the ground is also where you find treasure. A lot of diligent but unsuccessful digging follows. And yet digging seems risky; a previous inhabitant of the house has also become obsessed with treasure, with grim results; the digger who helps them, Pywall, gets sicker and sicker as he goes on digging, eventually dying. Yet when the spirits return, they suggest more digging, this time telling Susan to dig in a field where a pot of gold is said to be buried. Susan cannot find it. Instead, she meets the queen of the fairies, and refuses to kneel to her, returning to Rye very sick and frightened. Anne Taylor is by now eager to use the fairy money to buy back her property, and Susan and Anne give gifts to the fairies to secure their goodwill. Gift exchange was a common mode of interaction with the fairies, as all readers of fairytales know. Fairies often ask for food or gifts, and in exchange offer excitingly transformed circumstances. But now we seem to be in a very factual, pragmatic world, a world of business ventures, investment and clientage:

And she further sayeth that Mistress Tayler the next time that she this examinate came to her house, did make four Nosegays and delivered them unto this examinate to give unto the Four Fairies as she termed them, the which Nosegays she did lay in the window for that the familiars were not there at her coming/ And afterwards they were taken way as she thinketh by the spirits for that no body else could come there, the doors being shut.

Such gift-giving was central to the *modus operandi* of London's most inventive criminals. Anyone who urges you to buy an expensive present 'for the Fairy Queen' is using gift-giving to trap the unwary. The whole innocent story of leaving nosegays for the fairies implicates Susan and Anne as already enmeshed in a net of greed and trickery, or the wrong kind of fiction, if you like. And yet we never find out for sure who is tricking whom. In her analysis of this case, Annabel Gregory has shown that Anne Taylor, at any rate, was set up by her political opponents in Rye, so they at least are tricksters. But in besmirching Anne with witchcraft accusations, her enemies are drawing on stories she may actually have told and believed, stories that have their own murky logic, fairy logic, fictive logic.

Whereas many of the Scottish depositions have strong and obvious links to folklore, in the Rye depositions these links are much more attenuated. The townspeople of Rye may have needed different things from fairy lore than did the Scottish rural dwellers and other rural communities on which folklorists concentrated. Yet the fairy stories told by the people in the Rye case do resemble the Scottish stories and folklore narratives in two respects; they are about the desires of the people who tell them, and they convey and record knowledges about land – who owns what, why and when – especially knowledges that might otherwise be consigned to the past. So memory and desire are still central to fairy narratives; it is just that in England, memories and desires are different. They are desires arising from the struggling economies of a failing town, rather than those arising from the per-petual miseries of a rural economy; they are the memories of people who now have ways of recording land ownership, and are looking not simply for memory but for authentication. These English fairy stories are no more nor less 'authentic' than the more familiar and more obviously mythic stories of Scottish witches like Bessie Dunlop and Janet Trall.

With all these caveats, however, certain issues are central to all the stories told in this case: health, marriage, money, land ownership, motherhood. Bodily health was something commonly negotiated through stories about fairies in almost every culture which had such stories. Susan's encounters with the fairies begin simply, as part of a search for health, but almost at once that search for health is diverted into a search for buried treasure. Susan is supposed to plant a sagebush, and instead becomes engrossed in a series of digging projects which terrify her, and which lead nowhere, but from which health apparently comes. Digging for health; what is the relation between bodily healing and digging for treasure? Twofold. As we have seen, fairies live in a world underground, an underearth; this means that they know things – they know where buried treasure lies, where it can be found, where the dead are – for the dead too are in the ground. When other people are taken by the fairies, they are taken underground, or, like Janet Trall, they eat dirt in their despair. So earth and the ground are fairy domains. And yet the wholeness of the ground, its inviolate nature, is also a fairy preserve – digging or building on fairy sites arouses their wrath, and stories warn against such digging. So Susan's digging is both an attempt to confront the fairies, to get closer to them, and also a transgression of their laws, however licensed by them. The mixture of transgression and close approach characterizes some healing magic, which involves abstracting something from the being who caused the illness, stealing it, taking possession of it, in order to control and take possession of the owner. Is this what Susan is doing in going after fairy treasure?

Partly. For Susan is also, straightforwardly, and practically, equating money with health. She is a townswoman, and a poor one; she knows that bodily wholeness can be bought. But money also has symbolic significance. It allows the owner to escape from the poor self, to don a new self, to (so to speak) turn the coat to turn away whatever bad luck had dogged the person when poor. In more ways than one, Susan is hoping that money will save her from her illness.

And yet Susan does not want to change *too* much; she also wants to keep hold on herself. The place where Susan's story comes closest to fairy folklore is the point at which Susan fears that she will be 'taken' and asks her husband to save her. From the ballad Tam Lin to the numerous Irish stories superbly documented and analysed by Angela Bourke, the story of the lover who must dare and sacrifice everything to keep the beloved from the fairies or to rescue him or her is central to folklore. In this story, though, it is Susan's story, a story she lays over events, a grid she uses to interpret them. Susan needs her husband to protect her from being 'taken'.

But what did it mean to be 'taken', and what does it say about her that she was so afraid of it? Angela Bourke suggests that for women, being 'away' was often a metaphor for difficulty in adjusting to married life or to a new household. Susan is pregnant when the fairies threaten to take her with them. Like childbirth, pregnancy might make fairy abduction seem more likely, since fairies were believed to long for human babies and also to need human nurses to give them milk. Susan's pregnancy somehow divides her uncomfortably from the everyday world, making her different, special, but also vulnerable. Many women when pregnant feel alienated from bodies that are no longer their own; in a nightmare version of pregnancy, the pregnant woman has already been possessed by another, already taken from herself. Like the other states to which fairies are attracted – birth, adolescence, childbed – pregnancy is a liminal state. To be pregnant, especially in early modern England, and especially for a poor woman, is to be committed to a desperately life-threatening process; eventually there will be birth, with all its agonies and risks. The fear of losing both baby and life must have been very real – very factual – for such women. Since fairies take babies, and since they represent the dead come back to haunt the living, Susan's terror of fairy abduction may be a way of talking about fears she cannot utter, fears of losing her baby and her self, her very life.

Given Susan's preoccupations, it is significant that the figure of a pregnant woman recurs in her visions, a pregnant woman who is also from folklore, though a different layer of folklore:

one spirit in the likeness of A woman great with child did appear unto her in her house in the daytime and did wish that she had some Apples, whereupon this examinate went to Mistress Tayler and told her of it and she Answered that if she had any she should have some, And so she went and fetched three Apples and deliv[r]ed them to this examinate and willed her to give it unto the woman, w[hi]ch accordingly she did, and two of them she did eat and the third she cut in four quarters and flung away.

The story about the apples is confirmed by another witness, albeit a very hostile one. Margery Conyers deposed that Anne Taylor had been coming to her for food for the spirits:

she hath come to me for Beef out of my pot, and diverse other things, and she came the other day for Apples for one of them [spirits] that was with child. And I asked her whether she gave her any, and she said; 'I faith, that I did, and a piece of sugar too.' And then this deponent asked Mistress Tayler what they were that she sent the apples to, and she said she knew not what they were.[2]

Stories about pregnant women with unnatural cravings for food, especially fruit and vegetables, are very common in early modern culture, and such stories often attribute to the fruit some prognosticatory power. The best-known survivor is the 'Cherry Tree Carol', in which the Virgin Mary announces her pregnancy by telling Joseph to pick her some cherries. He responds angrily that the one who got her with child should pluck them, whereupon the cherry tree obligingly bends down and offers itself to her. There are also the apricots in Webster's *Duchess of Malfi*, and the radishes in Rapunzel, so longed for by the expectant mother that she says she will die without them. But her desire for them seals her baby's fate. It was thought dangerous to resist such cravings, and dangerous to give in to them as well; they could leave marks on the child, and worse, they could put the child in the power of supernatural forces if the mother broke significant taboos to satisfy the craving. Witches are often bearers of suspicious gifts of apples in early modern stories of witchcraft, with which they seduce both children and women in order to gain power over them. Yet here, the story is reversed; it is the supernatural being who wants earthly apples; it is the fairy woman whose gravid state demands food from outside her realm. Susan Swapper may see this pregnant fairy woman as a version of herself, herself breaking the boundary between the human world and the fairy world because of her own desires, herself risking harm to her baby by acting on those desires, and above all, herself out of control. Stories of pregnancy cravings are always stories about being out of control, about losing the will to regulate desires for food and drink, as women ordinarily must. This is not just scary. It is also exhilarating, carnivalesque; pregnancy is a time when women have a kind of licence to stop controlling themselves and act on impulse.

The queen also cuts the apple in four quarters and throws the quarters away. A stone or core fruit bearing seeds of new life within a swollen exterior is an obvious metaphor for a pregnant woman's belly. In these palmy days of ultrasound, we can hardly understand the passion of earlier cultures to see, know and control the growing baby within, to know its sex, for example, and such longings find expression in numberless divinatory rituals. This may be one of them; the disposition of apple seeds is often of divinatory significance in pre-industrial culture. The fairy woman is once again acting out Susan's longings, Susan's desires.

But . . . but . . . like other rituals of its kind, this one is actually quite transgressive, even violent. The cutting, and even more, the throwing away – it may sound trivial, but is there an additional fear of loss of self here? I have suggested that the digging, too, is a kind of tearing open of what might have been closed, and it is also about looking for something hidden, hidden inside. Feminists see such fantasies as purely male, but they may be shared by women too, to whom the whole process of generation is as much of a mystery as it is to men, but to whom it happens. It is as if Susan's pregnancy has begun for her a process of uncomfortable fantasizing about the interior of her own body, a process she projects on to the outside world. Early modern culture encouraged such anxious probings because it was the responsibility of the mother (then as now) not to ingest anything which might conceivably damage the growing foetus.

Susan's stories of digging and cutting ask: Is the body working properly? Is it a proper body – a womb? Or a tomb? Does it contain treasure, or nothing? Or a monster? Pregnancy links the expectant mother with the dead, too; she is passing on their names, their identities, and she is herself brushing up against death, a death that waits for her, for her baby, visible, not far off, but not yet a fact. Like the Fairy Queen, this is a death that may mirror her – that may be hidden in her body – but also a death that may come and take her away. Is Susan in the end digging for safety?

We cannot know, though we do know what happened to Susan Swapper. Convicted of witchcraft, she was sentenced to be hanged, but was a beneficiary of her richer neighbour's efforts to extricate herself from the same charges; the sentence was never carried out, and she was released from gaol under a general pardon in 1611. We do not know what happened to the child. We do not know many facts that we might like to know – might need to know if we are to interpret the fictions rightly. But this is a familiar bind; we're in it with Shakespeare and just about everyone else whose fantasies sing to us of desires and fears – our own and theirs.

English fairies and treasure

Desire for gold is the prime motive in many a fairytale. Accustomed by romantics to think of any supernatural encounter as uplifting, we may be dismayed to find that for the English, in particular, fairies were part of the growing enterprise culture of Elizabethan England. Like modern punters buying tickets in the National Lottery as a way of magically transforming their lives, early modern people sought out fairies and begged them to work their magic, not in the interests of morality or soul uplift, but as a way of getting rich – and the quicker the better. While Scottish witches sought money indirectly, through marketable occult powers, the English sought it directly. The result is that most, though not all, English encounters with fairies are tonally different from Scottish accounts. To meet a fairy in Scotland is at best an equivocal experience, and can be downright disastrous. In England, fairies are still risky, but the sense of risk is defrayed by an even clearer and more optimistic sense of the possible benefits.

John Webster, for example, tells the story of a man in dire trouble who is helped by the fairies. In all essentials it is the same as Bessie Dunlop's story, but whereas Bessie's story is haunted by her fear of and guilt about her dead baby, Webster's story has an entirely untroubled conscience. I shall leave the story in Webster's own words so that readers can assess the calm tone for themselves:

Then one night before the day was gone, as he was going home from his labour, being very sad and full of heavy thought, not knowing how to get meat or drink for his Wife and Children, he met a fair Woman in fine clothes, who asked him why he was so sad, and he told her it was by reason of his poverty, to which she said, that if he would follow her counsel she would help him to that which would serve him to get a good living; to which he said he would consent with all his heart, so that it were not by unlawful ways; she told him that it should not be by any such ways but by doing of good and curing sick people; and so warning him strictly to meet her there the next night at the same time, she departed from him, and he went home. And the next night at the time appointed he duly waited, and she (according to promise) came and told him that it was well he came so duly, otherwise he had missed of the benefit, that she intended to do unto him, and so bade him follow her and not be afraid. Thereupon she led him to a little Hill, and she knocked three times, and the Hill opened, and they went in, and came to a fair hall, wherein was a Queen, sitting in great state, and many people about her, and the Gentlewoman thus brought him, presented him to the Queen, and she said he was welcome, and bid the gentlewoman give him some of the white powder, and teach him how to use it; which she did, and gave him a little wood box full of white powder, and bid him give two or three grains of it to any that were sick, and it would heal them, and so she brought him forth of the Hill, and so they parted. And being asked by the judge whether the place within the hill, which he called a Hall, were light or dark, he said indifferent, as it is with us in twilight; and being asked how he got more powder, he said, when he wanted he went to the hill, and knocked three times, and said every time, 'I am coming, I am coming', whereupon it opened, and he was conducted by the aforesaid woman to the queen, and so have more powder given him. This was the plain and simple story (however it may be judged of) that he told before the judge, the whole court, and jury, and there being no proof, but what cures he had done to very many, the Jury did acquit him, and I remember the judge said when all the evidence was heard that if he were to assign his punishment, he should be whipped thence to Fairy-hall, and did seem to judge it to be a delusion or imposture.

Webster says the man was 'a very simple and illiterate person to any man's judgement, and had been formerly very poor, but had gotten some pretty little means to maintain himself, his Wife, and diverse small children, by his cures done with this white powder'.[3]

The man tells the story when the judge asks him how he came by the powder. Neither he nor Webster find the story important or exciting; it is just interesting, in a calm, easy way. Welsh fairies too were guardians of treasure. In the 1540s, one of these soothsayers, Harry Lloyd, confessed to a Welsh court that he had conference with the fairies every Tuesday and Thursday and that they gave him plenty of gold.[4] Why do fairies offer special knowledge of treasure? Three reasons: their association with ancient monuments, and hence with the kind of places where people might expect to find it; their link with the dead, and hence with knowledge of the dead, and their association with wild places, places where finders are keepers, and especially with underground caves; this means they know about *buried* treasure in particular. More importantly, folklore borrows here from literature and vice versa. Literary fairies get richer and richer as the seventeenth-century aristocrats got further and further into debt, until Margaret Cavendish – who had even more debts than most – writes of fairies who live among mountains of pure gold studded with diamond rocks and entire quarries of rubies and sapphires.[5]

Cunning folk and fairies

Both the stories of fairies as familiars and the story of the changeling and the cunning man raise the issue of the connection between fairies and the practice of magic, an issue implicit in some other stories, including those of many of the Scottish witches.

To be a cunning man or woman was to take up a trade, to adopt a profession, one that might have been frowned upon by the élite, but was welcome within village society. A cunning person could do some or all of the following: heal animals or people by magic, unwitch those who had been bewitched, find buried treasure, identify burglars, murderers and other malefactors, and find missing objects.[6] Contrary to wishful New Age thinking, most cunning folk did not use medicinal herbs, though many did use herbs magically, and (again contrary to our own fantasies) descriptions of exactly what they did tend to be alienating accounts of their power to take an illness off their client and divert it into a dog or similar beast rather than pioneering medical experiments.

But these are our prejudices; early modern villagers seem to have found cunning folk helpful. At least they listened. At least they tried. At least they offered hope. There was no one else when your own knowledge and hope had failed. And they probably had stupendous stories to tell, because all persons who claimed supernatural powers naturally had to be willing to explain how it came about that they were so much more gifted than their neighbours. One explanation, to which numerous cunning folk resorted, was contact with the fairies. Fairies were less intimidating and less culpable than the devil; yet they were not beings with whom most early moderns felt at ease. Stories about fairies created awe without terrifying the client away. Perhaps for this reason, cunning folk often began their stories by telling of how one day they had met a man or woman who had shown them how to scry (to look for missing objects, buried treasure or future events), heal or see. Others claimed constant access to the fairy folk, or to one particular fairy, who could be consulted about whatever was perplexing the client, with the cunning person acting as go-between and interpreter. Another way of saying all this is that stories of fairy encounters were part of what the cunning person had to offer, such stories were told to entertain as well as advertise, to pass long winter nights, to take people's minds off their troubles.

This sound commercial imperative to talk about fairies may explain why fairies crop up so often in the confessions of accused witches. For on the face of it, the accused, especially in Scotland, would have done far better not to bring up the subject of fairies at all. For the godly élite, fairies were simply, conclusively, devils: to admit to dealings with them was – in Scotland, and in England too after Elizabeth I's reform of the witchcraft statute – to admit to witchcraft, to plead guilty. Scottish examiners often asked about demons – or fairies, using the terms interchangeably, so that anyone could see what they thought. And yet women and men persisted in telling long and involved stories about fairies. One explanation is that if you have been entertaining the entire village with stories of your encounters with the good neighbours for thirty years, it may be both impractical and imprudent abruptly to deny all knowledge of them in court.

Magicians and fairies

More sophisticated magicians – magicians with a university education – also conjured fairies, or spirits with fairy names at least. The Witch of Ey, who in *A Mirror for Magistrates* indiscriminately calls up fiends, fairies and the dead, may have been an inspiration for some.[7] One set of papers reveals how the knowledge of conjurations was passed around in magical circles in early modern England, like court gossip or village news. Magicians networked; they heard of the doings of other magicians, and sought to emulate them. A conjuror named

Robert Allen, arraigned for matters of astronomy and suspicion of calculation, left papers which include spells to cover the full range of cunning practices: spells to find thieves, to find out liars, and so on. He also possessed the papers of another magician of similar kidney, William Wycherly, who claimed to be able to 'invocate' the spirit into the crystal glass 'as soon as any man, but he cannot bind the spirit so sure as other[s] from their lying lies'. Like half the country, William was hoping that the spirits he conjured were going to make him rich:

Item, as concerning the sword and the use thereof he saith that he hath not used the same, save only about two months past he used holy water, a sword unconsecrated, and therefore was uneffectuous, at Hale Oak beside Fulham, where they digged for treasure and found none. But, as they were working in the feat, there came by them alonst the highway a black blind horse, and made this deponent and other with him to run their ways, for it was in the night.[8]

This is the sort of thing the English do when they find a magical thingummy; they at once begin grubbing about for buried treasure. The remarkable claims made for the enlightening effects of the mildly Paracelsian magic being used here are far less important than the profoundly practical goal: hard cash, on the nail. Fantasies of birth, sex and death are replaced by fantasies about money. At the same moment, stories about people finding pots of gold at the bottom of the garden with supernatural assistance begin to multiply; perhaps the most charming is the story of the pedlar of Swaffham, who dreams that if he stands on London Bridge he will become very rich. Haunted by the dream, he duly goes to London, and stands on the bridge for three days without result, until he impatiently tells the man standing next to him about his foolishness in coming. 'Ha! Dreams!' says the man. 'Now, I dreamed last night that there was a pot of gold buried under a tree in the garden of a pedlar's house in Swaffham. Can you beat it!' The pedlar waits for no more, but rushes home, where he duly finds the riches the dream foretold in his own garden.[9]

The same set of papers contain a list which shows how astoundingly widespread was the practice of this kind of practical magic. Among his list of scryers he cites a Fleet Street broderer, two priests, a man named Thomas Owldring, 'a conjuror, and hath very good books of conjuring, and that a great number', and an Aldersgate labourer who uses 'the sieve and shears'. So do a plasterer and his wife, while a Norwich painter uses 'invocation of spirits'. Among this motley crew of inexpert but startlingly bookish magicians is 'one Croxtons wife, in Golding lane in St Giles parishe [in London]', who 'occupieth the sieve and shears, and she only speaketh with the fairies'. Shuttling up and down the vertical hierarchy of Tudor society, fairies were themselves socially mobile as well as being agents of social mobility.[10]

There are very many written records of spells to catch fairies, and such knowledge circulated orally too, making it impossible to separate 'authentic' popular culture from high culture. An example from Elias Ashmole's manuscript collection, very prodigal of such charms, makes it clear that the kind of entity being summoned is a kind we have met before, perhaps a deceased person or relative, one with an ordinary proper name. It is headed, 'An excellent way to get a Fairy, but for my selfe I call Margarett Barrance but this will obtaine any one that is not already bound.'

First get a broad square crystal or Venus glass in length and breadth 5 inches, then lay that glass or crystal in the blood of a white hen 3 Wednesdays or 3 Fridays: then take it out and wash it with holy aqua and fumigate it: then take 3 hazel stickes or wands of a year groth, pill them fair and white, and make so longe as you write the spirits name, or fairies name, which you call 8 times, on every stick being made flat one side, then bury them under some hill whereas you suppose fairies haunt, the Wednesday before you call her, and the Friday following take them up and call her at 8 or 3 or 10 of the clocke which be good planets and hours for that turn: but when you call, be in cleane Life and turn thy face towards the east, and when you have her bind her to that stone or Glass.[11]

The same manuscript also offers a spell for an ointment which allows one to see the fairies, giving physical form to a magical product which is elsewhere just a figure in folktales:

An Ungt. to anoint under the Eyelids and upon the Eylids evening and morning, but especially when you call, or find your sight not perfect. That is, an ointment to give sight of The Fairies.

Not all such strenuous efforts at conjuration were effective. A letter from William Stapleton to Thomas Cromwell is about a notable failure of fairy magic. William, like the women of Rye, was a diligent treasure-hunter, and after an abortive search for treasure and an even more abortive attempt to summon the spirit of the treasure for helpful advice, eventually resorted to a magician, who told him that the parson of Lesingham had recently called up Andrew Malchus, Oberion and Inchubus. 'And when they were all raised, Oberion would in no wise speak.' So the parson asked the other spirits why Oberion did not speak, to which Andrew Malchus smoothly explained that Oberion was already bound to the lord Cardinal, meaning Wolsey.[12] This charming little calumny may have been the point of the story; Wolsey was known for his personal ambition, and this reputation accords only too well with the attempted conjuration of a fairy. Other conjurations abound, and Oberon was an especially popular choice, especially after the publication of Lord Berners' translation of the French romance *Huon of Bordeaux* in 1534 made Auberon a familiar name. A six-teenth-century manuscript in the Bodleian Library, for example, gives lavish directions for the conjuration of Oberon into a crystal stone, using Catholic prayers in Latin, which after the Reformation became imbued with magical power as a kind of unintended riposte to those Protestants who kept insisting that the Mass was nothing but hocus-pocus:

First say in the name of the father & of the son and of the holy ghost and Amen. Then say a paternoster, Ave and Creede and the childe also and bless you and the child.[13]

This recipe is followed by another with advice on how to conjure other fairies, using a fairy ointment made from the rime left on clear water by the fairies who wash in it. Thereafter, the procedure to be followed owes far more to romance and ballad than to Paracelsian magic:

then set yourself down by the fire in a chair with your face towards the table, and anoint your eyes with the same cream or oil aforesaid. Then you shall see come by you three fair maids, and as they pass by they will obey you with becking their heads to you, and like as they do to you, so do to them, but say nothing. Suffer the first whatsoever she be, to passe, for she is malignant, but to the second or third as you like best reach forth your hand and pluck her to you, and the next morning for to assoil such questions as you will demand of her; and then if she will grant you suffer her to depart and go to her company till the hour appointed.

Refuse the first thing you are offered – this is fairytale logic. So is the courtesy of imitating the fairies' actions. This text, in which folklore and folktale overlay the higher magic of conjuration, both shot through with the hopeful greed of the questioner who seeks not occult knowledge but treasure – all the layers of English fairy belief are compressed into this one short passage.

The origins of such miscegenation are complex. The English sceptic Thomas Jackson once confronted an English cunning man, and asked him about one of his rituals, which the man said was directed at the king of fairies. 'Yet,' says Jackson, with an audible grin, 'he had entirely forgotten this King's name, until I remembered it unto him out of my reading in *Huon of Bordeaux*.'[14] You can be sure that the poor man never failed to call the king of the fairies 'Oberon' after that, even if he had never heard the name in his life before. So, expertise is acquired; so, what counts as knowledge is altered.

The story of Joan Tyrrie: folktales

Other, mere splinters of story point to other concerns. One story might be taken straight from the annals of folklore. A Somerset cunning woman, Joan Tyrrie, claimed that

at one time she met with one of the 'fair fairies', being a man, in the market of Taunton, having a white rod in his hand, and she came to him, thinking to make an acquaintance of him, and then her sight was clean taken away for a time, and yet hath lost the sight of one of her eyes.[15]

This motif of stolen fairy 'sight' is common in folktales; mortals who have used the fairy ointment can see fairies who are invisible to others, and as a result have their sight taken so that they cannot reveal the fairies' secrets. Usually such women have been nurses to the fairies, women who have been taken so that they might nurse a fairy baby or stolen human, women whose presence at the fairy court is guaranteed by maternity. The fairies give them fairy sight, but later take away from them all sight. This tiny piece of story may point to a fantasy that illuminated a whole life: Joan Tyrrie, midwife to the fairies. On the other hand, it may be another case of a woman who, on being asked a series of questions she could not answer, groped desperately for something to say, and hit upon a story she knew, one she told to the children on winter's nights when they asked her how she lost her eye. Joan was a cunning woman, like Bessie Dunlop and Elspeth Reoch, and like them she derived her power from the fairies, who would, she said, tell her who was bewitched and who was not. Here there may be a trace of an even bigger story, the story of the opposition between the fairies and the witches, a story told all over Europe at this time, and a story which will be told here in due course.

Similarly, Agnes Hancock, in 1438, was a healer who professed to cure children afflicted by the spirits which the common people call 'fairy'. In order to heal those afflicted, she had communication with the fairy herself.[16] In other stories, the fairies are both cause and cure of mysterious ills. In *Britannia's Pastorals*, a similar story of a cunning woman is given:

When any man hath caught a fall upon the ground, forthwith he starteth up again on his feet, and turneth himself round three times toward his right hand, with his sword, skein, or knife he diggeth, into the earth, and fetcheth up a turf, for that, they say, the earth doth yield a spirit; and if within some two or three days he fell sick, there is sent a woman skilful in that kind unto the said place, and there she saith on this wise: I call thee from the East and West, South and North, from the forests, woods, rivers, meres, thou idle wood-fairies, white redde, blacke, &c.[17]

A similar story with strong links to folklore materials is told by Richard Bovet; it describes fairies at a fair.

Those that have had occasion to travel that way, have frequently seen them there, appearing like men and women of a stature generally near the smaller size of men; their habits used to be of red, blue, or green, according to the old way of country garb, with high-crown'd hats. One time about fifty years since, a person . . . was riding toward his home that way, and saw just before him, on the side of the hill, a great company of people, that seemed to him like country folks, assembled, as at a fair; there was all sorts of Commodities to his appearance as at our ordinary fairs . . . At length it came into his mind what he heard concerning the Fairies on the side of that hill: and it being near the road he was to take, he resolved to ride in amongst them, and see what they were; accordingly, he put on his horse that way . . . He found himself in pain, and so hasted home; where being arrived, a lameness seized him all on one side, which continued on him as long as he lived, which was many years.[18]

Like Joan Tyrrie, the countryman who sees the fairies is punished for the sight with a deficit, in this case lameness, which could in other pre-industrial cultures itself be a sign of fairy identity in the form of abnormal feet. What is striking here is that the fairies are just like country folks; their only distinguishing characteristic is their old-fashioned clothing. Like ghosts – which they partially are – fairies belong to the past, as their clothes suggest. What Bovet's traveller sees is the past, alive again. No wonder the sight is blasting. Yet it is not without its uses. For the more practical cunning folk, to see the past is to see lost objects, to see missing persons, to see people hiding wills and burying treasure. What cunning folk like Joan Tyrrie 'see' is the past, the past translated into an estate, a vault of money.

Fairies and men: Andro Man's story

To this day, fairies are considered a girl's thing. My son's ballet teacher refused, at his first lesson, to let him dance with a tinselly, spangly wand like the rest of his class, issuing him with a sword and the stern injunction, 'Little boys can be princes, not fairies.' (My son cried heartbrokenly. He felt left out, like the poet at the women's festival of the *Thesmophoria* in Aristophanes' play.) And it is true that the fairy stories I have been retelling so far are stiff with women's concerns: childbirth, babies, children, caring for the sick, caring for the dead. Yet there was one point of entry for men into the fairy realm: men could, like women, take up the unofficial profession of cunning or knowing, acting as counsellor, healer and diviner for a village community, building up a practice as one who could remove bad magic and find that which was lost. When men did this, their profession often obliged them to enter a woman's world. Like my son at ballet, part of what they may have hoped for, apart from the obvious rewards of esteem and hard cash, was a glimpse of those parts of life normally sealed off from men: birth, death, the ongoing relationship with the dead signalled by care of the body. This longing to belong to a world often seen as inferior, and even polluted, is generated by the separation of gender roles; as long as femininity has its sphere, some men will feel a passionate curiosity to see what lies inside it. And many standard folktales about men's encounters with fairies, and particularly encounters with the Fairy Queen, reflect this sense that the man is boldly going where it might be better not to go, entering a realm that is profoundly not his, a realm dominated by a woman. This is especially true of the Thomas the Rhymer type of story, where encounters with the queen both define and reduce masculinity. So it is interesting that the Scottish cunning wizard Andro Man identifies himself so eagerly with Thomas the Rhymer. Andro's story is no less interesting than those of the women accused of witchcraft, but it is more conscious of its sources and more careful in referencing them, as if an educational protocol had brushed off on Andro. Like Carlo Ginzburg's miller, Menocchio, who invents his own heresy, Andro is using a wide range of cultural materials to make his story, materials to which many of the women accused of witchcraft may not have had access.[19] His repertoire of sources are not all nameless to everyone but folklorists, as theirs are, though his source for Thomas's story may well have been oral – a circulating ballad or a story based on one.

The same themes recur in Andro's story – birth, copulation and death – but seen from his perspective as a male outsider:

[the Queen of Elfame] . . . came to thy mother's house, in the likeness and shape of a woman . . . and was delivered of a bairn, as appeared to thee there, at which time thou being but a young boy, bringing in water, the Queen of Elphen promised to thee, that thou should know all things, and should help and cure all sorts of sickness, except stone [?] dead, and that thou should be well entertained, but would seek thy meat or thow deit, as Thomas Rymour did.[20]

There are echoes here of Bessie's story, and of Susan Swapper's: the queen comes to the house of Andro's *mother*, and comes there for the purpose of delivering her baby. Themes of birth and babies are still uppermost. Like the queen who came to Bessie, and like male fairies, too, she offers her votary knowledge and healing power. Here, however, the recipient of knowledge is male, and the teacher is female, and as a result Andro is able to cite a role model from story, one we have met already: the prophet Thomas Rhymer, whose uncanny abilities were believed to come from his liaison with the queen of the fairies. What the reference points to is the nature of the contract between Andro and the queen. At first it might seem as if the queen takes Andro on because of his mother, rather as Titania takes on the changeling boy for the sake of her mortal votaress in *A Midsummer Night's Dream*. But just as that relationship is sexualized by its very hierarchy, its overtones of service and dependency, so too is this one. Like True Thomas's queen, like Morgan le Fay, and like the male fairies who greeted Elspeth and others, the queen of the fairies seeks sex:

be the space of thirty-two years since or th[ereabouts], thou [began] to have carnal deal[ings] with . . . the Queen of Elphen, on whom thou begat diverse bairns, whom thou has seen since; and that at her first coming, she caused one of thy cattle die upon an hillock called the Elphillok, but promised to do him good thereafter.

Andro's usefulness to the queen is like Bessie's: he is a giver of babies. And just as Bessie's relationship with the fairies begins with death, the death of her child and the death of her cow, so Andro's relationship with the queen is sealed over the death of a cow on a fairy hill. However, there is a difference; the agony implicit in Bessie's story, the agony of two women struggling over a child both want is completely absent here. As a man, Andro can give the queen as many babies as she wants without having to give them up. It is all cleaner, easier. And yet the knowledge Andro acquires is feminine knowledge; it is as if his sexual relationship with the queen of the fairies allows him access to a world of female sexuality and gestation normally closed to men. Thus equipped, he is able to cure a wide range of diseases, and also to act as an unwitcher, a person who can cure bewitchment. He is particularly linked with women's mental maladies, curing one woman of the falling sickness, and another of 'being heavily diseased with a furiosity and madness'. So he assumes some real importance in his community. But his most remarkable act has no parallel in any of the very numerous women's testimonies; he claims land rights:

Thow has meted and measured diverse pieces of land, called wards [the oldest form of feudal land tenure, by military service] to the hind [last, or ladies'] knight whom thou confessis to be a spreit, and put four stones in the four nooks [corners] of the ward, and charmes for the same, and thereby heals the [people], and preserves them from the lunsaucht [lung disease] and all other diseases, and thow forbids to cast [soil] or divet theron, or put ploughs therein; and this thou did in the Manids of Innes, in the Manis of Caddell, and in diverse other places, which thou confesses thyself, and cannot deny the same.

Here, Andro seems to be acting as a kind of land-agent for a mysterious entity called 'the hind knicht', said by Andro to be 'a spreit'. This probably means a fairy. 'Hind' could mean 'last', the knight who rides last, or even the dead knight. But it seems much more likely that it means 'maiden', so that the knight is the lady-knight. If so, it may refer to Andro himself. Andro's land claim is part of a curative ritual which will prevent lungsickness, but it is also a kind of land reform; he forbids the earth on the hind-knight's land to be turned or ploughed. It is all too easy to interpret this in crudely Freudian terms; the hind-knight's land must be kept virginal – or perhaps merely exclusively female – unsullied and unbroken by the violently phallic plough. And this strand of thought may be present. However, before we are carried gustily into unfounded syntheses about ancient pagans disliking the plough, we might consider something more practical. The point may be more prosaic, and about land use. Andro is an animal healer, and he is also someone who himself keeps cattle. Common land is often grazing land, in both Scotland and England, land on which poor men and women can pasture their beasts. Enclosed land, on the other hand, is often arable land, on which crops are grown for the owner. If so,

Andro may be thinking of the hind-knight as someone who protects the maidenhood of the land and through doing so protects the grazing rights of the people, and perhaps also a traditional Highland way of life, under some threat from landlords here as elsewhere in the British Isles.

What makes Andro Man's case even more fascinating is that the queen of the fairies is not Andro's only contact with the supernatural. He is also in touch with a mysterious being called Christsonday. The name of this mysterious spirit illustrates the rashness of distinguishing too sharply between pagan and Christian in this context; Christsonday may be a fairy, and he may hang out with the queen of the fairies, but his origins are biblical and Christian: he is given to apocalyptic prophecies, such as:

at the day of judgement, the fire will burn the water and the earth, and make all plain, and that Christsonday will be cast in the fire because he deceives worldly men: And this yeir to come shall be a dear year, and that there shall be twice seven good years thereafter.

In setting himself up as a prophet, Andro nonchalantly blends together his very different role models: Thomas the Rhymer, Joseph, and St John, the author of *Revelations*. He does not distinguish very sharply between these entities, just as Jeanne D'Arc and perhaps also Bernadette Soubirous do not distinguish very sharply between the queen of the fairies and the queen of heaven:

the Quene of Elphen has a grip of all the craft, but Christsonday is the goodman, and has all power under God, and that thou knows sundry dead men in their company, and that the king that died in Floddon [James IV of Scotland; this battle has a special place in Scottish folk-memory] and Thomas Rymour is there.

It is as if Andro has suddenly become nervous with the idea that he is being taught by a woman. The queen may technically be in charge, but plays second fiddle to Christsonday, who is, it seems, the one who has all the power, who is the goodman or husband, who is in authority. As dramatic as the taming of Titania, this reduces the stature of the queen of the fairies with stunning speed, and from this point we hear more and more about Christsonday and less and less about her in Man's confession. It is as if a little boy is growing up, moving – as little boys in the early modern period did – from the world of the household, dominated by mothers and nurses, to the public world of education, church and state, overwhelmingly dominated by men.

This entry into the adult world of masculinity does not remove the threat of femininity, however. The queen's power surges up again, as – in a breathtaking retelling of the myth of Diana and Actaeon – Andro describes a ritual in which Christsonday in the form of a stag is hunted by his wife:

Upon the Rood-day in harvest, in this present year, which fell on a Wednesday, thou confesses and affirms, thou saw Christsonday come out of the snow in likeness of a stag, and that the Quene of Elphen was there, and others with her, riding upon white hackneys, and that they came to the Binhill, and Binlocht, where they use[d] commonly to convene.

Despite the gratuitous addition of an obscene kiss, which does not seem to fit with the story Andro is telling and was probably dictated by his questioners, this story does show the relation between the meat culture of the Scottish wilderness, and the Scottish nobility as a metaphor for relations between the dead and the living, and hence as a powerful Christian symbol. It is entirely orthodox and quite commonplace for Christ himself to appear as a hunted unicorn or stag – as in the legend of St Eustace, for example – but here that symbol is given meaning by its context in a culture where hunting was a class privilege, and meat derived from it an impossible upper-class luxury. The Christian idea that the humble are slain by the great and that from the death of the humble comes life, together with the more basic Christian notion that the deeds of those now dead affect the living, are all implicit here. In other words, this story makes sense in the culture of which Andro is actually part. We do not need to think in terms of ancient paganism to interpret it.

The queen's intimidatingly comprehensive sexuality is a theme to which Andro returns: 'the queen is very pleasant, and will be old and young when she pleases; she makes any king whom she pleases, and lies with any she likes'. Again, one must note the literariness of Andro's fantasy and its evident affinities with the medieval romances discussed earlier, romances which he may not have known directly, but may have known in ballad form. The queen is like the loathly lady, and she is a kind of sovereignty hag, determining the legitimacy of kings. She is also out from under paternal control. Like Hermia, one of the heroines of A *Midsummer Night's Dream*, this queen's desires do not need to be approved by an authoritative man. This puts the queen at variance with the society of which Andro was a part. And yet she is also a fantasy produced by that society, and in this case, by a man within it. She is not a woman's fantasy of power, but a man's fantasy of the terrible, inscrutable power of realms of femininity from which he is forever barred.

John Walsh's story

By contrast, the Devon cunning man John Walsh is entirely practical in his response to the fairies and his fantasies about them are far less arcane and complex than Man's.

Unlike Man, Walsh is straightforwardly part of the class of semi-learned conjurors, or cunning men; to him, the fairies are not even interesting, but a way of getting important information. They do not interact with him socially, but can be compelled by a simple ritual; like other conjurors, Walsh uses books. Walsh has moved even farther towards a modern, urban interpretation of fairy lore than Susan Swapper. Literacy and money elbow fairy nature from his mind:

being demanded how he know[e]th when any man is witched he saith that he knew it partly by the fairies and that there be iii kinds of fairies white green and black.

wh[i]ch when he is disposed to use he speaketh with upon hills whereas is great heaps of earth namely in Dorsetshire and between the hours of xii & one at noon or at midnight he usethe them.[21]

These are standard times for fairy encounters, from the ancient world and its dread of noontide nympholepsy. But there is nothing rich or deep about Walsh's evocation of this history. It is simply useful practical information, nothing more.

Whereof the glacke [*sic* for black] fairies is the worst / also he saith that he had a book of his said m[aste]r which had great circles in it where he would set two wax candles – a cross of virgin wax – to raise the familiar spirit of who[m] he would then ask for a thing stolen who did it and where the thing stolen was lost and thereby did knowe

Again, this is all knowhow, DIY fairy magic. Like later figures of a similar sort, Walsh claims not a supernatural but an earthly source for his magic; he learnt it from his master, Sir Robert of Drayton. The evocation of the normal craft relationship between master and apprentice is of course exceedingly common in magical writings, and it again throws the emphasis on the practical. Fairies are simply beings you learn to summon. There is a right way and a wrong way. End of story. Unlike the Scottish deponents and accused, Walsh is if anything less interested in the fairies than his accusers are:

he being demandyd whether that any of the iii kyndes of fairies whe[n] they did hurt whether they do it of their own malignity or of the p[ro]vocat[ion] by any wicked man: he answereth that they do hurt of their owne malignity not p[ro]voked by any ma[n] & that they have power upon no man but on suche as only do want the faith, w(hi)ch is the cause why they have pow[er] more of some persons then of any others.

Just what Walsh means by 'the faith' is important. It may, of course, be Protestantism, but it is much more likely to be Catholicism, or at any rate a form of Protestantism less strict than that advocated by the Church of Walsh's day. The pamphlet based on the case certainly thinks Walsh is Catholic, and spends a good deal of energy fulminating against papists. This may seem paradoxical, because in many ways Walsh represents the new world in which occult knowledge is transmitted just like any other skill: through books, through a master who teaches an apprentice. But he also represents adherence to the old ways, to a Catholicism increasingly proscribed, increasingly the object of suspicion. As a businessman – a cunning man – Walsh was at the cutting edge of change; as a man of religion, he adhered to a past that was vanishing because of persecutions. In 1549, not quite twenty years before Walsh's arrest and investigation, the villagers of Sampford Courtenay in Devon refused to allow their priest to use the new Protestant prayer book, forcing him to say Mass in the old style. This sparked off a dramatic demonstration against the new religion; people from Devon and Cornwall banded togther and laid siege to Exeter. It was late summer before the government was strong enough to defeat them. To be sure, the rebels were not campaigning for the return of Roman Catholicism, but for the less vehemently and bleakly Protestant services of the last years of Henry VIII's reign, though the rebels did campaign explicitly against the Bible in translation, arguing that with it in circulation the clergy would be unable to control the rise of heresy. However, their beliefs were widely seen as 'popery' by their opponents. The pamphlet which describes Walsh's trial reports his statements very accurately, but interprets them in the light of the menace posed by the succession of wicked conjuring Popes whose dubious activities it recounts.

All uses of the fairies are therefore uses of the past. Whenever the fairies ride, the past rides with them. The link between fairies and Catholicism, fairies and other ancient customs, is explained by their links with the dead. For Protestant reformers, Catholicism, like the fairies, was constantly threatening to rise from a shallow and uneasy grave and ride again through the land. Like all revolutionaries, the Protestants were terrified of the primitive undertow of custom and tradition. It may be that Herne the Hunter, who might have been imagined by Shakespeare for that bogus fairy play *The Merry Wives of Windsor*, is the leader of a fairy ride. Like Buccleigh, whom we shall meet later in a ballad, he represents the past, but in early modern England, it was the past which revolutionaries sought to restore. The poacher-protestors of fifteenth-century Kent, too, may have been thinking of themselves as an avenging fairy ride, scouring the land from newfangled injustice.

Fairies and night battles: good companies
of Europe

Others saw their relationship with the fairies differently, and far more
exotically. For some men and women, involvement with the fairies
meant being part of a great battle between good and evil, light and
dark. For some, to ride with the fairy host did not merely mean an
opportunity for learning magic or getting money, but a chance to take
part in raging conflicts for the soul of a community. For others, to join
the fairy host was not so much a question of embattlement as an
allegiance, not unlike a later secret allegiance to a Masonic order. Like
the Masons, the fairy society could protect its members, both from
supernatural forces of evil and from more obvious earthly perils.
Also like the Masons, the fairy society could prove the gateway to a
profession – the art and craft of cunning folk. Such societies strongly
resembled the guilds which were part of the basic social glue of medieval and early modern European society, only instead of becoming a
blacksmith or a weaver, one became a shaman or a magician. Like
guilds, the good society was responsible for training its members, and
also for protecting them; also like guilds, it functioned as a team, as
an aspect of identity, something like football team support in 1990s
Glasgow. It may never have existed, or it may have had a basis in
reality. But for those who felt they 'belonged' to it, belonging was
what it gave.

For example, the Romanian cathartic dancers and healers, the *calusari*'s speciality is to cure diseases caused by the fairies, while their
secret society is itself under the rule of the queen of the fairies. The
calusari also do their cures by trance dancing.[22] The Romanian fairies
are the *iele*: they dress in white, dance and use herbs to cure; they
also possess people, including the *calusari*. In some places, there was
certainly a trace of the paganism of the Roman world in such beliefs
and activities, since the good people were led by a goddess often
called Diana. Diana survived, however, because her cult made sense
to people: she was the special protector of women, children, animals
and the poor. Her Celtic equivalent, the goddess Epona, whom Carlo
Ginzburg sees as central to all these stories, was also responsible for

ferrying the souls of the dead over to the land of death, a role that links her naturally with fairies in their roles as links between the living and the dead, or as the dead or almost-dead themselves.[23]

The *Canon Episcopi* of *c.* 900 by Regino of Prum, abbot of Treves, later to become part of canon law, describes a practice which some have seen as relevant to popular beliefs:

Some wicked women, perverted by the devil, seduced by illusions and phantasms of demons, believe and profess themselves, in the hours of night, to ride upon certain beasts with Diana, the goddess of pagans, and an innumerable multitude of women, and in the silence of the dead of night to traverse great spaces of earth, and to obey her commands as of their mistress, and to be summoned to her service on certain nights.[24]

Others would see Regino as simply copying out late-antique materials unquestioningly. Diana/Artemis, from St Paul's Epistles through to the Middle Ages, is often seen as a kind of concentrated essence of paganism, the opposite of Christianity, a personification of the paganism the Church must oppose. It is always tricky to use a learned and hostile source to interpret popular culture, and matters are not really made easier when the remarks of various inquisitors are taken into account, since they too may well have been very familiar with accounts of heroic Christians dispersing pagan cults and destroying pagan temples; they may have identified, too, with such heroic Christians. This in itself should make us mildly suspicious of any text in which the name Diana occurs in connection with night riders or good folk; the goddess may be tacked on by the learned Christian in an interpretation of popular culture which harmonizes well with church history. Regino may be reflecting a popular belief, but assigning his own, church-sanctioned meaning to it. Later, matters are complicated still further by the eagerness of some nineteenth- and twentieth-century scholars, influenced by Romanticism, to see paganism everywhere in folklore. For Jacob Grimm, for example, in Germany, Diana was a mother deity who awoke just after the darkest night of the year; she led her 'furious army' through the skies, but also helped with crops and spinning; she rewarded industry and punished laziness. In her night journeys she was followed by the souls of the dead, especially the souls of unbaptized children.[25] She sounds very like the Scottish queen of the fairies, especially in her enthusiasm for spinning and her special link with dead babies, but we should be cautious of allowing ourselves to leap to the conclusion that the Scottish queen of the fairies is therefore the goddess Diana – at any rate, without knowing far more about Grimm's sources. *Dives and Pauper*, for example, repeats Regino almost word for word: 'women who ride by night on diverse beasts and pass sundry lands and countries, and follow a glorious queen called Diana or Herodia'.[26] Similarly, James I refers to Diana in his *Daemonologie*, equating her with the fairies: 'The fourth kind of spirits, which by the Gentiles was called Diana, and her wandering court, and amongst us was called the Phairie (as I told you) or our good neighbours.'[27] This is plainly an attempt to interpret popular culture through the lenses of learning.

However, there are several references in both inquisitorial materials and in witchcraft and sorcery depositions to a series of beliefs which appear to have less to do with organized paganism than with a more loosely knit world of shadowy and fairy spirit entities. Bernardo Gui, made rather unfairly notorious by Umberto Eco's *Name of the Rose*, wrote that one must ask those suspected of sorcery about 'the fairy women (*fatis mulieribus*) called the good things (*bonas res*) and who go out at night'.[28] The suggestion occurs in a passage about the conjuration of the souls of the dead, which would seem to tie it in more strongly with fairies. Inquisitors listened, and the stories duly poured out.

Most like Andro Man and his Christsonday was a Milanese witch of 1384, Petrina from Bripio, who followed Madonna Oriente, the lady of the east. The lady's followers included both the living and the dead, but those who were beheaded or hanged do not dare to lift up their heads in that company. The company learnt herb and healing lore from Madonna Oriente, and at night went on visits round the houses, and when they found a home clean and orderly, they gave it their blessing.[29] Madonna Oriente rewards her followers with delicious meats taken from slaughtered animals, but after the feast the animals' bones are placed back in their skins, and the lady strikes them with her staff, whereupon the animals revive, but are never much use for work thereafter. The myth embodies the idea that dead bodies may contain a dormant vital force which can be reawoken. This motif of the resurrection of the dead links the food of the company with their own state as recently dead, and unites feaster and feast in a cycle of death and rebirth. It also recalls a well-known Norse myth in which the gods dine on goats whose flesh can be renewed in a similar fashion, but it is very common in European witch-trials as a motif.[30] The society that formed around Madonna Oriente was called the 'good people', the 'good society', a phrase that recalls the Scottish witches who called the fairies 'our good neighbours'.

Similar stories abound. In 1457, two women of the Alpine Tyrol confessed that they went travelling with 'Mistress Richella' to a place where there was feasting and dancing.[31] The magician and prophet Chonrad Stoeckhlin, like many Scottish witches, spoke of travels to the beyond, of being snatched away to the Mountain of Venus. There, just as Andro Man had met the famous dead of Scotland, Chonrad met the famous dead of his region, Meister Eckhardt and Tannhäuser. There was feasting, drinking, eating; as usual, no sex, because for the poor desire for food outweighs and drives out other desires. In the Dolomites, women spoke of the 'mistress of the good game', and 'the game' was the feast and the dancing. In France, Lady Abundia led the 'good ladies' in nocturnal house visits. Some villagers went with them in spirit, travelling into homes where, if they found food and drink ready for them, they partook without diminishing the food.[32] The motif of leaving food and drink out for night visitors, and particularly for the dead, is common to many pre-industrial cultures, including Scotland. In Corsica and Friuli, men and women saw themselves as part of a good company whose role was to keep the forces of evil at bay; though neither group linked themselves with the fairies, the story is similar.

In northern Morocco, too, a similar cult surrounded the jinn, whose special votaries were healers who perform a trance dance with a beautiful female jinnee called A'isha (like Haggard's Ayesha) Quandisha. She can appear beautiful or hideous, but again, her feet always give her away: she has the feet of a camel or some other heavy animal. Like the queen of the fairies, A'isha likes to seduce men before they discover her true identity: many cunning men claim to be among her husbands. Moha, for example, was a healer said to be married to her.

Sick people could bring a thread from their clothing to him, and he would place it under his pillow and dream of A'isha, who would tell him what to do to heal the person.[33] In Tunisia, too, jinn are believed to possess people, causing illnesses; the disease is cured by a holy woman who dances in the mausoleum of an Islamic saint.

Similarly, Croatian, Hungarian and Slovenian witches have truck with the fairies. Hungarian witches, politely called 'beautiful women', interact with fairies who appear among humans very much like classical nymphs; they are beautiful, they dance in groups, or occasionally they ride on thunderstorms. These dancers appear both inside and outside houses, and witnesses describe their whistles and drums. Those who go with them are transformed; one witness recounts how 'in the group they all seemed of beautiful and gentle colours, and even if they dress in rags at home, in the group they wear clothes of great beauty'. The fairy celebrations centred on a feast both sumptous and magical, for the fairies often created it from scarcity, feeding all their votaries to bursting point on ten millet seeds.[34] This is a transparent metaphor for the fairies' function in imagination; they turn peasant scarcity into abundance, a process that requires powerful magic. And yet such magic could prove nothing but a trick, as bitter commonsense overcomes fantasy, illusion fades and the victim may realize that the food was in fact unsatisfying, the sumptous settings illusory. Or so the church authorities always wanted to say; as supernatural beliefs became more violently polarized between good and evil, so fairy feasts were more subject to this kind of stark exposure. This is not just a matter of the Church trying to prevent people from having any fun; it is not about insisting that they know their place, even in fantasy. It is about insisting that only God can make things better.

The fairies of Eastern Europe are also associated with forest animals (remember Andro Man's story of the deer). And like Scottish fairies, they are connected with the dead. During the period between Easter and Pentecost, the dead, who are also the fairies, seek out humans, and this is when connections can be made with them. However, it is also the time when they bring illness.

What did people gain from these stories? What purpose did they serve for the individuals who told them and the communities who listened? To answer these questions, we can look more closely at two particular stories. In Palermo, Sicily, a group of witches investigated by the sceptical and lenient Spanish Inquisition described themselves as *donas de fuera*, a term which means both a fairy night-rider and a witch who travels with her. Like Romania and most of Eastern Europe, Sicily had healers who specialized in curing diseases caused by the fairies; these healers (men and women) had *sangre dulce*, sweet blood, and could as a result go out on Tuesday, Thursday and Saturday night in spirit to take part in the journeys of 'the company'. A company was a group of such persons, organized by region and social class. The fairies themselves are markedly Greek and ancient in character, and are indeed called 'the Greek ladies'; they share with the ancient fairy demons the identifying characteristic of abnormal feet. Some have cat's paws, others donkey feet. The company members evidently described their deeds with great garrulity, perhaps telling the same stories over and over, perhaps making up and inventing new ones, for there are often over twenty witnesses for each story. Like most of the Scottish witches, the Sicilian fairy followers had each a particular tutelary spirit who introduced them to the fairy gatherings and conducted them there. And again like the Scottish witches, all these women were poor, and the fairy religion was a compensatory fantasy that allowed them to experience in imagination the splendour and specialness denied them in life. Their meetings involved dancing, beautiful clothing, sweet music and above all, splendid food, the kind of food normally eaten only by the rich.

Like fairy followers everywhere, the Sicilian women were offered wealth, through fantasy, through helping women with their spinning (again like Scottish fairies) and other housework (like English fairies), and through the marketing of their occult status by setting themselves up as healers and unwitchers. As a healer, the wise woman would suggest that human or animal illness was caused by giving offence to the 'ladies', the fairies; she would then suggest that the sick person make an offering to them, and significantly the offering was usually a meal rife with luxury, honey-cakes for example, which the fairies have favoured since ancient times. Sicilians, unlike Friulians, did not think of 'good' and 'bad' witches, but of fairies and their votaries who could do both good and harm. Association with both aspects of fairydom gave the votaries of the 'ladies' great power: the power to heal, and the (implied) power to harm. If the former could be a source of payments, the latter could be used to blackmail a community into indulgence. Finally, one must not overlook the tremendous self-aggrandizement implicit in such stories. The men and women of the good companies, all over Europe, were able to see themselves as the linchpins of their communities, elevated not only to the lifestyle of the nobility, but also to their ability to make history, to make or prevent things from happening. There is a famous Philip K. Dick short story about a man who is a menace to the state. It is decided to control him by giving him a false sense of self-esteem by implanting in him the memory of saving the world from alien invaders.[35] But more efficient than any implant is the power of story. The Sicilian women were garrulous even to inquisitors, because to them these were stories that reflected well on them, could hardly reflect better, in fact.

Such elaborate fairy mythologies may have reached the British Isles. In Britain, too, fairies can be followed by something like companies, though these are not an inevitable or even a common feature of fairy interaction. In Wales, a pastor complains about the 'swarms of soothsayers and enchanters', who

claim that they walk on Tuesdays and Thursdays at night with the fairies of whom they brag themselves to have their knowledge. These sons of Belial, who should die the death (Levit. 20. 6) have incited such an astonishing reverence of the fairies into the hearts of our silly people, that they dare not name them without honor.[36]

As always, though, with learned sources, there is a risk that quite disparate popular beliefs are being falsely interpreted through the lenses of alien theory. This may also be the case with a pamphlet from Ireland, one of the earliest popular accounts of Irish fairy beliefs. In it a man called Dr Moore, plainly an English settler, is 'swept away' from his friends by strange powers, despite their convulsive grasp on his legs. His experience is the standard British Isles experience of 'revelling and dancing, together with variety of meat and liquors'; a simple hoedown, as ever. This seems to be an individual experience, but it resembles the experiences of others, and the pamphlet may merely be ignorant of the folklore context.[37] By 1632, such experiences had become profoundly enmeshed in literary culture: in *The Pinder of Wakefield*, for example, Merlin appears to summon a troop of 'pretty night-walkers', including Oberon, for revelling and feasting.[38]

When we turn to witchcraft trial depositions, there is much less support for the idea of a British Isles fairy society. In Scotland, Andro Man envisages fairy meetings as collective encounters, though far more confessions understand such meetings as individual experiences. The case of Bessie Dunlop discussed earlier is striking in this context. The third time her fairy guide Thom Reid appears to her, at midday of course, he takes her to the hill-end, where he forbids her to speak, no matter what she hears or sees. And when they have gone a little way forward, she sees twelve people, eight women and four men, the men clad in the clothing of gentlemen, and the women with plaids around them, 'very seemly to see'. So far, so like the continental tales: the fairy society is a place where common people can be gentled, can be and seem like the rich of the earth. But now the first subtle difference emerges. Asked if she knows anyone present, Bessie says she does not, except for Thom. The question clearly points to the continental-inquisitorial agenda, but Bessie has not learned the 'right' answer. To her this is not a 'good society', but something else. Now the fairy folk ask her to sit down, and they welcome her, and ask her to go with them. Bessie, primed by Thom, says nothing. And a short time after, they all vanish, with what she calls 'a hideous ugly [gust] of wind'. And yet when asked who the people were, Bessie's answer seems in keeping with the stories of the continent: they were, she says, the good folk from the Court of Elfame, who came there to desire her to go with them. But Bessie is not going to join unless she can see some benefit in it for her. 'She saw no profit to walk in that kind of way, unless she knew what for!' Thom urges her on: 'Don't you see me?', he asks, 'well-fed, well-clad, and good enough in person, better than ever I was?' Bessie's answer opens up a large conceptual gap between her story and those of the continental members of 'good society'. She answered, 'That she dwelt with her own husband and bairns, and could not leave them'.

Two things are at once plain: first, for Bessie, joining the fairies would be not a night-time activity, but a permanent removal to a different community. This reflects the bulk of Celtic folklore from the British Isles, in which those who go with the fairies and ride with them are generally lost to earthly society for a long time, and often for ever. Secondly, for Bessie to join the fairies would be an act not of loyalty to her community, but of faithless desertion of her husband and children. She might climb socially herself, but doing so would leave them behind. Of course, in saying this Bessie may be being strategic, trying to show off her womanly virtues to the court, but it nevertheless reflects her belief about what she was being invited to do, a belief profoundly unlike continental 'good society' stories. Like other Scottish witches, Bessie is describing not a fairy ride or gathering, but the risk of being swept away – a belief also shared in Ireland and England.

The testimony of Alesoun Peirsoun is analogous to Bessie Dunlop's. Alesoun describes being 'away':

she would be in her bed hale and feir, and would not wit where she would be or the morn: And that she saw not the Queen [for] seven years. And that she had many good friends in that court, but were all away now. And that she was seven years well handled [treated] in the Court of Elfane and had kind friends there, but had no will to visit them after the end. And that it was they, good neighbours, that hailed [greeted; also named] her under God.

Yet the ballad about Alesoun is far closer to the continental idea of the 'good society' than Alesoun's own words:

> A carling [servant] of the Queen of Fairies,
> . . .
> Through all Breadalbane she has been
> On horseback, on Hallow even;
> And ay in seeking, certain nights,
> As she says, with our silly wights;
> And names our neighbours six or seven,
> That we believed had been in heaven.
> She said she saw them well enough,
> And specially good old Buccleigh,
> The secretary, and sundry other.[39]

The ballad-writer knew more about 'good societies' than Alesoun herself did.

In England, a traveller claimed, the fairy society met in a big house full of the light of candles, full of men and women feasting on fine things, dancing, singing, far from the nearest village.[40] Similarly, Reginald Scot – steeped in European demonological writings, and no folklorist – writes that

you must also understand that after they have delicatlie banketted with the divell and the ladie of the fairies; and have eaten up a fat oxe, and emptied a butt of malmesie, and a binne of bread at some noble mans house, in the dead of the night, nothing is missed of all this in the morning. For the Lady Sibylla, Minerva or Diana with a golden rod striketh the vessel and the binne, and they are fully replenished againe.[41]

When the continental and learned idea of a witch's sabbath filtered through to English interrogators, the suspects they questioned often responded with long tales about being taken to a place – a house, a ruin – in the remote countryside, where they were plied with luxurious food and drink.[42] Paradoxically, the fact that in England those looking for fairies must go to the remote countryside may just possibly support the idea that the story of societies of 'good neighbours' had reached the British Isles.

Where to find fairies

On the other hand, finding fairies in the wild may simply reflect the much better-established notion that fairies live in the past. Early fairies are not found at the bottom of any garden, and they do not on the whole hang about in places of natural beauty. Rather, fairies tend to like areas that are distinguished by being nameless, unmapped, uncharted, and above all unowned. This is why they prefer woods to fields and pastures, and ruins and caverns to houses. Fairies also associate themselves with places linked with a past that is visibly disappearing, and hence they are attracted to ruins, especially the ruins of monasteries destroyed at the dissolution of the monasteries, and to raths or Daneforts, as the Scots and the Irish call them, that is, to neolithic sites. For the same reason – their links with the dead – fairies are attracted to graveyards. Richard Gough sums up most of this knowledge when he describes where his parishioners in Myddle believed fairies lived:

And if you take notice of the situation of the place, you will find it more unlevell with banks and deep glades, than any other low grounds in the lordship. This may confute that idle conceit that the superstitious monks and friars did formerly persuade ignorant people that there were fairies, or furies, and hobgoblins. And this wood, being a thick, dark and dismal place, was haunted by some aerial spirits, and therefore called Devlin Wood.[43]

Same story again? Perhaps. Yet there is no record of a developed tradition of fairy riding and night battles in the isles. No English witches report being summoned to such houses for the purpose of meeting as a society. Given this, it seems at least possible that the impetus for such stories comes not from the accused, but from the well-read accusers, so that English fairies, like others from the British Isles, retain their essential distinctness from the 'good society'.

The misuses of fairies: familiars and brownies

If fairy stories had their uses for those who told them, there were also times when telling a fairy story was a mistake, out of place or out of time. One example of this misuse of fairies is the predominance of fairies and fairy lore in one of our principal sources for it: witch-trials. As we have seen, it was probably unwise for Scottish witches to be so forthcoming about their connections with the fairies. They thought the fairies useful, but inquisitors simply saw them as diabolical. English witches, as we shall see, were also prone to this misuse of fairies.

Fairy stories surface surprisingly often even in the hostile, sensible climate of the English witch-trials. A distinctive feature of English witch beliefs is the familiar, the small household-demon who hovers around the witch, doing her will, but also seducing her farther and farther from her true self, from salvation. Familiars are often tiny, often taking the form of the kind of small animal that might be found around a house or farm; they can be as big as a weasel, and as small as a housefly or a wasp. (English magicians, as we have seen, had fairy familiars too, though these were rather grander demons, with grammar school or university educations, who came to circles cast by the magician to give knowledge.) Witchcraft historians have long puzzled over why England has this strand of story, unique to it. In the context of the Scottish materials, however, in which each witch has a personal fairy who is the source of her occult power and knowledge, the role of the familiar and its origins may become a trifle clearer. There is a functional link between familiars and Scottish fairies: both are met by chance, and both are inclined to offer occult services which turn out to come at a price. In Scotland, the price is use of the woman's body or the child born from it; in England, the familiar demands the use of the body for other purposes, suckling the woman's blood. Both are blood-prices. There are many tangled associations here; Scottish fairies behave like lovers, and often want children, while English familiars behave like children and often want love. Both entities are enmeshed in the stuff of women's bodies and their lives: birth, copulation.

Comparing the stories women told about familiars in court with English folklore stories about fairies points to some other resemblances. An English familiar called Malekin (note that this name remains common: Greymalkin) had the voice and shape of a little child. Sometimes he spoke English in the Suffolk dialect, but now and then he conversed in Latin. Fairies too were apt to speak in the tongues of the past, so that Gerald of Wales's fairies spoke Greek. Malekin asked for food and drink and these were left for him on a chest, and always disappeared. He lived in the house of Sir Osborn de Bradewell.[44] One of the standard fairies of English folklore is the brownie, or hob, a household spirit that helps housewives, or more often servants, with their work in exchange for food, usually a bowl of milk or cream. A striking number of witches' helpers also demanded milk as payment for their services; occasionally they also provided it, as did the familiar of the Windsor witch Elizabeth Stile.[45] Ursula Kempe, an Essex witch of the sixteenth century, confessed that her familiars had been sent to her to drink her milk, and when they deserted Ursula, the same spirits took to demanding milk from another woman, Elizabeth Bennet. There is also a fragment of another brownie story embedded in these accounts. Brownies were notoriously hard to please and capricious. If the woman they were helping was rash enough to substitute skimmed milk for cream, or to make a naked and furry hob a set of clothes, or even just to thank the hob, he would usually take his services elsewhere, crying, as Reginald Scot notes, 'Hemton hamten, here will I never more tread nor stampen.' (To us, the most familiar version of this story is the Grimms' tale of 'The Elves and the Shoemaker'; often sweetened as a tale of pious gratitude, the story is actually a warning not to make clothes for fairy helpers.) Similarly, accused witch Ursula Kempe's familiar abandons her, as do the familiar toads of Joan Upney, who repeatedly desert her for other people.[46]

Occasionally, instead of leaving, hobs turn malevolent, ruining the housework with which they once helped; this may lie behind women's ambivalent relations with their familiars, who can heal but can also harm. In witchcraft trials, the malevolent kind of fairy, who seeks to play tricks on a household, surfaces as a kind of poltergeist. In folklore, some of those are hobs who have not been treated properly by their own perverse standards; others, like the Norse trowies and the Greek *kallikantzaroi*, are mischievous by nature. The Italian Monaciello, a demon analogous to the ancient demons discussed in the first chapter, serves no mortal, delighting instead in tricks like pulling off the bed-clothes. English writers often compared poltergeists to fairies, suggesting how closely the two categories could overlap: a 1650 pamphlet, which sees the malevolent creature as the familiar of a local witch, describes its activities in terms of fairy lore:

Peerking the ladle out of the wives boyling pot below, as high as into the Husbands bed above, putting the husbands breeches upon the Wives head (as though the Grey mare were the better horse) not enduring that a boy should be too captious or capritious throwing the boyes cap into the chimneys smoke, yee as a Lord of Misrule, breaking earthen pots (as fast as some merchanes and bankrouts in these broken and breaking times) with other such reakes and mad merry pranks, as strange as ever Hobgoblins, pinching fairies, and Robin Goodfellow acted in houses in old times among Dairy Wenches and kitchen Maids.[47]

Some of the names given to familiars are also fairy names: Robin,

Dick, Piggin, Hob, Puckle.[48] As well, some familiars appear to be the dead, like Scottish fairy guides; Margaret Moor's familiar calls to her in the voice of her dead children, 'Mother, Mother'.[49] Similarly, Scottish fairy guides are usually kin to the person they guide, though they are more usually ancestors than descendants. Or it may be that Moor's familiar is a child she gave to the fairies, as Bessie Dunlop gave her child. Moor is oddly guilty about her dead child, and it then seems to want her to kill her other children; is this a macabre and faint echo of the idea of giving a child to the fairies? In Moor's case, as in many others, fairies have anyway been blurred with demons. For godly Protestants, fairies were demons, and the idea may have begun to reach some of those who had dealings with them. This is what Reginald Scot inveighs against when he writes that

what sorts of witches so ever M[alleus], Mal[ificarum] or Bodin saie there are: Moses spake onlie of foure kinds of impious coseners or witches (whereof our witchmongers old women which danse with the fairies, &c., are none).[50]

What helped the blurring process was the incorporation of fairies into learned Paracelsian magic and conjuration, a process we have already seen at work.

German familiars also sound like fairies; Claudia Bruyne had a spirit called Cajy, who was carried around in a phial; he advised her on how to cure, how to find missing objects, and how to detect witches. Learned demonologists wrote of spirits who did the housework, called the 'white ladies' or 'good ladies', who could be helpful to the householder in drawing water, lighting fires and preparing food. The 'devils' of Neuchâtel are green, blue and yellow, and while historian of witchcraft W. Monter suggests that there may be a link to the pagan gods of the Jura forests, it seems more likely that these are fairies, or elves, beings who inhabit the remote regions of the wilderness and embody its characteristics.[51] In the same way, the animal form of the English familiars recalls the English hob's fondness for animal-skin clothing, and for suits of leather, also an animal hide. In some parts of Europe, such figures were understood to be the good opponents of evil witches, which may be why they feature so often in witchcraft confessions; the accused may have believed that they were excusing rather than condemning themselves by confessing to dealings with hobs or with the 'white ladies'.

None of this is to suggest that all familiars are fairies. Instead, familiars seem to be a name under which various creatures and apparitions of folklore can be named and their stories told: ghosts of dead children, demons, monsters of the imagination. But it is none the less possible that some of what the interrogators heard as familiars were stories about fairies.

Changelings

The other local fairy belief which persisted in early modern England was the belief in the changeling, a belief we have already seen working in the legend of St Guinefort. But even here, certainty was often tinged with pragmatic scepticism. A woman named Mary Pennyfather had a little girl who could not walk, or talk. She consulted a cunning man called Thomas Harden, 'because it is noysed in the country that he is a wise man and can skyll of many thinges'. Harden made a standard diagnosis; he told Mary that her child was a changeling, and promised to help her. She made a return visit, and he proposed a cure which in some ways recalls the fairy woman's spell with the apple in Susan Swapper's story. Mary was to take a nut, pick out the kernel and fill it with mercury, stopping the hole with wax and then binding the nut with a thread. Then she was to lay the nut under the pillow where the child slept. Mercury is a poison and a medicine; its equivocal nature, cocooned within the nut, symbolizes the equivocal nature of the fairies. Perhaps, too, there is some idea that the child might be symbolically reborn from the nut; just as the kernel of the nut has gone, so will the fairy intruder.[52]

However, Mary was not a satisfied customer. Her child, she said, had had no help by this method, so she went back to Thomas, who agreed to offer her another remedy. This time what he suggested was more brutal, more reminiscent of the tradition of harming the changeling to charm the baby: 'He bade her to set the childe in a chare uppon her dungell [dunghill] by the space of an hour uppon a sonny day.' Mary did it. But still it didn't work. The child remained incapacitated. Mary had not lost faith in Thomas, however, and gave him sixpence, promising more. But her faith did not lead her to imagine her child was cured, and the two remained unreconciled. Neither fairies nor fairy stories were of any use to poor Mary, with her wailing baby; they did not canalize or justify cruelty or infanticide because what Thomas Harden suggested was also useless – or was it useless because Mary did not believe?

Was empiricism creeping into the world of folklore, chasing away the stories that had comforted and healed the pain of subsistence culture? It was certainly the task of empiricism to make fairies seem useless to their former devotees, a process that begins with Reginald Scot, as we shall soon see. But the fairy's uses were still more gravely threatened by Scot's most carelessly intelligent readers. Science had powerful allies in its task, allies whose power over the English language allowed them to turn fairies from useful beings to useless adornments almost overnight.

5

The Fairy Goes Literary:
Puck and Others

So far, the fairies we have met have been about birth, copulation and death, and also about money as a lubricant of all three. Yet at the same time as these stories were being told and recorded, another kind of fairy was emerging, costumed, from the wings, a fairy whose characteristics are not darkness and death, but tininess, endearing sweetness – and freakishness. This fairy reaches its apogee at the hands of the Victorians, as we shall see, but it is largely introduced to the world – fabricated – by one man: William Shakespeare. And we shall see that Shakespeare's invention is so powerfully seductive that no one afterwards can quite escape its influence.

Puck: the biography of a famous fairy

Like a jobbing tailor using up the ends of fabric rolls, Shakespeare pieced together his sweetly tiny fairies from a number of sources, but none was directly folkloric; indeed, it is questionable whether Shakespeare knew *anything* about fairies from oral sources at all, as opposed to from the writings of the burgeoning folklore industry, especially those of Reginald Scot. After all, Shakespeare was a townie; in the streets of sixteenth-century Stratford people were less interested in fairy lore than in how to turn an honest penny, or even a dishonest shilling.

Take Puck, for example. Most people tend to assume that Puck is famous before Shakespeare writes about him. So he may be, but he is not – or not quite – Shakespeare's Puck. Reginald Scot, Shakespeare's chief and often his only source for English folklore, certainly mentions 'Robin Goodfellow' on a number of occasions, though the earliest reference to him describes a being not very like the one Scot and Shakespeare describe. William Tyndale in 1531 describes those for whom 'The Scripture ... is become a maze to them, in which they wander as in a mist, (as we say) led by Robin Goodfellow ... they cannot come in the right way.'[1] This is a trickster, but not a household one like Scot's Robin; rather, this is a will of the wisp, a marsh-spirit or moor-spirit. Another early reference is different again; for Thomas Harman, Puck is a thief who steals the clothes of men lying asleep: 'I verily suppose that when they wer wel waked with cold, they suerly thought that Robin Goodfellow (accordinge to the old saying) had bene with them that night.'[2] Here Robin is likened to a plain robber, a criminal, and his subversive, even demonic, energy becomes a representation of the criminal classes.

What these disparate beings have in common is that all are tricksters, and it is tempting to begin adding one story to another to make a corpus of folklore. However, what if we don't? What if we entertain instead the suspicion that these learned, disinterested men were simply assigning the name Robin Goodfellow to whatever apparition or fairy story came their way? The entity Scot describes, however, is not quite the entity Shakespeare gives the world, and not quite the being Shakespeare's imitators seek to evoke.

Scot has had an undue influence on English writers on fairies; most take it for granted that he is describing authentic folk beliefs of his own day when he writes about Puck. This is certainly the simplest explanation of his many references to fairies, but there are two obstacles. First, Scot himself says that fairies are *not* the folklore of his own day, but the folklore of an earlier day. Just how he can *know*, of his own knowledge, what stories 'our grandam's maids' used to tell is never clear, but it sounds as if the knowledge that fairies are an older knowledge is itself not learned from any maids, but from other books. Other writers, including Chaucer, say exactly the same. Take, for example, Scot's most celebrated passage, a delicious piece of Elizabethan prose, well worth reading for its pleasure value, but one whose status as serious folklore is deeply compromised:

But in our childhood our mothers maids have so terrified us with an ugly devil having horns on his head, fire in his mouth, and a tail in his breech, eyes like a bason, fangs like a dog, claws like a bear, a skin like a niger [black person], and a voice roaring like a lion, whereby we start and are afraid when we hear one cry Bough; and they have so fraid us with bull beggars, spirits, witches, urchins, elves, hags, fairies, satyrs, pans, fauns, syl[v]ans, kit with the cansticke [candlestick], tritons, centaurs, dwarfes, giants, imps, calcars, conjurors, nymphs, changelings, Incubus, Robin Good-fellowe, the spoorne, the mare, the man in the oak, the hellwain, the firedrake, the puckle, Tom Thumb, Hobgoblin, Tom Tumbler, Boneless, and such other bugs, that we are afraid of our own shadows; in so much as some never fear the devil, but in a dark night; and then a polled sheep is a perilous beaste, and many times is taken for our fathers soul, specially in a churchyard, where a right hardy man heretofore scarce durst pass by night, but his hair would stand upright. For right grave writers report, that spirits most often and specially take the shape of women appearing to monks &c; and of beasts, dogs, swine, horses, goats, cats, hairs; of fowls, as crowes, night owls, and shriek owls; but they delight most in the likeness of snakes and dragons. Well, thanks be to God, this wretched and cowardly infidelity, since preaching of the Gospel, is in part forgotten.[3]

That entire gorgeous list of names is not fathered on 'our mothers maids', as too many assume, perhaps because it is hard to resist the lovely picture of the authentically peasant maids passing on their rich oral culture to the upper classes in kitchen and nursery. However, the maids' culture – in Scot's narrative, at any rate – may not be quite what we would like it to be. The maids, we learn on close examination, terrify by their evocation of a very authentic and indeed Protestant-sounding devil, one who could be seen above any church door before iconoclasm, shovelling the damned into hell. Such deep, 'personal' devils did indeed become very common among the less literate, and were certainly used by childcarers to try to frighten their charges into obedience, or simply transmitted out of pure fascination; Robert Louis Stevenson's nanny, for example, terrified him with her tough and monstrous Calvinist devil. But this devil is not the kind of 'authentic' old wife's tale people fasten on; rather, we would like to think that the list of bogeys is a window on to the mental world of 'our mothers maids'. Yet this is not what Scot says. The list of 'bugs', on the other hand, is much more vaguely attributed to a mysterious 'they'. The passage invites us to equate 'they' with 'our mothers maids', but stops just short of doing so. And this is just as well. For of the list of thirty-three named 'bugs', no fewer than seven are classical (satyrs, pans, fauns, sylans or silvans, tritons, centaurs, nymphs) and unless Scot's mother had very overqualified maids, it is doubtful that they would have heard of such creatures, nor of elves, dwarfs, conjurors or Incubus either, all of which derive from strictly continental materials, and the last from continental demonology. For the rest, only a few names are specific enough to suggest a real story, and we have seen, too, that even when under interrogation, women and men alike tended to be reticent about the names of the entities with whom they had dealings.

What Scot seems to be saying – alongside the idea that all this is outdated claptrap – is that the role of the maids was to fill him and others with fear of a literal and monstrous *devil*, which fear then led them to become afraid of anything not-quite-human of which they subsequently heard, from any source. Like the polled sheep, the cows and the crows, the apparitions in the list are simply encountered – for the most part in books – and become objects of terror because of the framework in which the encounter is set. And that is why preaching the gospel can help drive them out.

Secondly, Scot is writing not in response to popular superstitions, and not in an effort to record them. For Scot, such stories are not rich, exciting folklore, but a label for popular incapacity and muddleheadedness. Inveighing against those who see witches as seducers of the people, Scot says that 'God knoweth they have small store of rhetoric or art to seduce; except to tell a tale of Robin Good-fellow be to deceive and seduce.'[4] While it is interesting to notice Scot equating witches' rhetorical skill with tale-telling, and in particular with telling tales of fairies, perceptions amply supported by trial evidence, the name of Robin here seems to act less as a reference to a character in whom people believed, than to one in whom they didn't. Because you don't believe in Robin Goodfellow, says Scot, incessantly, to the reader, disbelieve in this.

And know you this by the way, that heretofore Robin Goodfellow, and Hobgoblin were as terible, and also as credible to the people, as hags and witches be now: and in time to come, a witch will be as much derided and contemned, and as plainly perceived, as the illusion and knaverie of Robin goodfellow. And in truth they that maintaine walking spirits, with their transformation, &c, have no reason to deny Robin Goodfellow, upon whom there hath gone as many, and as credible tales, as upon witches; saving that it hath not pleased the translators of the Bible, to call spirits by the name of Robin Goodfellow, as they have termed diviners, soothsayers, poisoners.[5]

So Scot is not writing to record such despised popular beliefs, but as a response to the writings of mostly continental demonologists. Now demonologists and inquisitors, as we have seen, are prone to interpret local fairy beliefs through a haze of stories about the Christian defeat of paganism. This has the side-effect of working up anxiety about the 'pagan' threat to Christianity from such beliefs, and it is this idea that Scot is out to undo. Like his foes, he yokes fairies and spirits together with pagan deities of the countryside in his list, but he also wants to strip fairies of their grand pagan associations, and with this in mind he mentions stories of hobs, equated by him (how reliably cannot be determined) with Robin Goodfellow, or Puck:

In deede your grandams maids were wont to set a bowl of milk before him and his cousine Robin Good-fellow, for grinding of malt or mustard, and sweeping the house at midnight: and you have also heard that he would chafe exceedingly, if the maid or goodwife of the house, having compassion of his nakedness, laid any clothes for him, besides his messe of white bread and milk, which was his standing fee. For in that case he saith; What have we here? Hemton hamten here will I never more tread nor stampen.[6]

We cannot know from Scot whether these ideas are a reliable tracing of English folklore, or an interpretation of it by him, and one of the reasons we cannot know is because Scot is so very influential. Thomas Nashe reproduces a kind of edited version of Scot's voluptuously long list, writing of 'Robbin-good-fellowes' (plural) which 'idolatrous former days' called 'Fawns, Satyrs, Dryads and Hamadryads', as does William Baldwin, who writes of 'the ayry spirits which we call Demons, of which kind are incubus and succubus, Robingoodfellow the Fairy, and goblines'.[7] For Robert Burton, too, Robin is as Scot describes him:

'a bigger kinde there is of them, called with us Hobgoblins, and robin goodfellows, that would in those superstitious times grind corne for a mess of milk, cut wood, or does any manner of drudgery work', though Burton suggests that such beings are really Scandinavian trowies, a fascinating possibility which might help explain the distinctiveness of the British Isles hob.[8] After Scot, many other literary sources seize on the figure of the hob, with his penchant for a bowl of milk or cream and his attention to housework. Robin is given milk and bread in *Albions England* and in Rowland's *More Knaves Yet?*, and in Samuel Harsnet's *Declaration of Egregious Popish Impostures*, where 'the bowle of curds and creame' set out for Robin Goodfellow is mentioned.[9] Harsnet, like Scot, is an arch-sceptic, eager to argue for belief in Puck in order to claim that its unreliability is proof that other beliefs – in exorcisms, for instance – are even more unreliable. By 1632, Robin is featuring in ever less distinguished and more infantile company. In *The Pinder of Wakefield*, he is tumbled together with Oberon, but also with King Twuddle, King of the Pygmies, and with Tom Thumb. As before, but more crudely, a dash of folkloric 'authenticity' is added to give colour and to pretty it up: Robin dances with a broom, the same motif used by Shakespeare at the end of the *Dream*. Even as Robin's career begins to wind down among the second-rate fairies of popular print culture, the wine still smells of the grape.

There is something faintly artificial, even Frankly Fake, about Robin as folklore. This is revealed in a series of texts which link Robin – master of tricks and disguise – with another London subculture, the clowns of the London stage. *Tarlton's Newes out of Purgatory* is a fairy text, all right, in that it is a text about the dead; it is spoken by the ghost of Tarlton, the brilliant clown actor of the 1580s. And Tarlton makes a link between himself as apparition and Robin:

sith my appearance to thee is in a resemblance of a spirit, think that I am as pleasant a goblin as the rest, and will make thee as merry before I part, as ever Robin goodfellow made the country wenches at their creambowls.[10]

Though this does betray a real streak of folklore, it is also part of an intrusive élite fantasy, that Robin represents an idyllic world of jolly, rural pleasures – Merrie Englande, in fact. Yet Robin is put to a tendentious service, in this case to lament the decline of traditional hospitality. This was almost as constant a jeremiad in Shakespeare's time as laments about late trains are today:

This makes Robin good fellow that was so merry a spirite of the butterie, to leave all, and keep himselfe in Purgatorie, for Hospitalitie is so cleane runne out of the countrie, that he needes not now helpe the maides to grinde their mault, for the drinke is so small, that it needs little corne; and if he should helpe them, where he was wont to finde a mess of cream for his labour, scarce get a dish of floate milke.[11]

To make its derivation from Scot even clearer, the dissatisfied hob who does not get his cream will 'say as I was wont: What hemp and Hamp, here will I no more grind nor stamp'.

The 1628 jestbook of the *Mad Pranks and Merry Jests of Robin Goodfellow* repeats all these familiar motifs:

Once upon a time, a great while ago . . . about that time (when so ere it was) there was wont to walk many harmless Spirits called Fairies, dancing in brave order in Fairy rings upon green hills . . . (sometime invisible) in divers shapes; many mad pranks would they play, as pinching of sluts black and blue, and misplacing things in ill-ordered houses, but lovingly would they use wenches that cleanly were, giving them silver and other pretty toys.[12]

This is the beginning of a motif in texts aimed at the educated that repeats and repeats: fairies as a sign of the Good Old Days, the Good Old World before whatever change the writer deplores. The good old world before the Protestant Reformation, before the decline of Christmas, before prices rose so high. It is a role fairies have played ever since, and it was this role that appealed to politically and ecclesiastically conservative poets like Ben Jonson and Robert Herrick, both of whom eagerly imitated Shakespeare's tiny fairies and put them to work as propagandists for the Old Ways.

For the concomitant of fairies as people who symbolize the Old Rules is fairies as a means not of breaking rules, but of making rules, particularly for women, and this too is seized on eagerly by an élite eager to get their money's worth out of their servants. *Tell-Truth's*

New-Year's Gift (1593) depicts Robin as 'one who never did worse harm than correct manners, and make diligent maids'.[13] Here, Robin is simply an incentive to cleanliness, a motif later repeated almost endlessly by Jonson and his imitators. Shakespeare's mischief-making Mab, who plaits the elf-locks in foul sluttish hairs, quickly becomes the kind of woman who draws her hand along the shelves to see if you have dusted them: 'She that pinches country wenches/ If they rub not clean their benches'.[14] Robert Herrick, for instance, turns fairies into a dogmatic litany of dos and don'ts for servants:

> If ye will with Mab find grace,
> Set each platter in his place:
> Rake the Fire up, and get
> Water in, ere Sun be set.
> Wash your pails, and cleanse your dairies;
> Sluts are loathsome to the Fairies.[15]

One wonders whether the servants fell for it.

There is something about the whole idea that is faintly reminiscent of the tooth fairy, and perhaps from this association comes its unpleasant tang: maids are like children, to be bribed and cajoled. Maids are tricked into cleanliness by Lord Smartyboots, who leaves a silver tester in the maid's shoe as a sly form of tip, to make her be good. The servants – they are not like us anyway. Why not make use of their superstitions, their difference from us, to get more work out of them? Or at least, why not mark their difference from us by showing how funny and odd, even how *cute* such beliefs can be. By William Lilly's heyday in the Civil War, the fairies had become guardians of an entire moral code, loving 'neatness and cleanness in apparel, a strict diet, an upright life, fervent prayers unto God'.[16] Such morality might seem a far cry from Shakespeare's playful sprites, but he was nevertheless the originator of the beings who gave it authority.

Shakespeare on fairies

In order to understand the pivotal role of Shakespeare in setting forever the limits of what Robin and other English fairies could be and do, we can look in particular at two speeches about fairies from his *oeuvre*: Puck's speech about himself in *A Midsummer Night's Dream*, and Mercutio's Queen Mab speech in *Romeo and Juliet*. Both are digressions that halt the action of their individual plays.

The Queen Mab speech first: a group of young men are about to crash a very posh party. The audience knows that Romeo is going to meet Juliet at the party. What cinema critics call 'helping work' – the process of identification where the audience tries to get the characters to their destinations – urges them on to the Capulet mansion. And yet their progress stops for a discussion of dreams and omens, culminating in a long speech about a fairy that no one believes in. In *A Midsummer Night's Dream*, too, we have an exciting situation – desperate, divided lovers lost in a wood, hilariously inadequate actors, quarrelling fairy rulers. But again the play stops for a speech about a fairy. Yet it is just at these moments where things look most wayward that Shakespeare's tyrannical brilliance asserts itself. Both plays explore the delicate ground between comedy and tragedy, and both speeches are revealed as turning-points in their individual plays by comparison between them. They mark the moment when the plays divide, one turning towards the tragic, one towards the festive comic.

There are obvious parallels between Mab and Puck. Both are mischief-makers, tanglers-up of what ought to run smooth and straight, reflecting the desires of others in a distorting fairground mirror. Both are related to Cupid, but in opposite ways. Mab is Cupid's way *out* of *Romeo and Juliet*; Puck is his way *into* *A Midsummer Night's Dream*. In *Romeo and Juliet*, playing Cupid is explicitly dismissed before Mab's entry: 'We'll have no Cupid hoodwinked with a scarf'.[17] By contrast, Oberon asks Puck to play Cupid; the god of love is ushered into *A Midsummer Night's Dream* through the story of the begetting of Love-in-Idleness, and although no one acknowledges it, it is Puck who plays his role, wielding his powers of desire. In his speech, Puck talks about what fun it is to pull chairs out from under ladies, but he does nothing like this in the play; all this Merry Prankster material is there as a symbol for the comic arbitrariness of desire, which interrupts 'the saddest tale'. Why should Demetrius like Hermia? The same reason Puck likes to spill people's drinks: no reason at all. Mercutio would approve, because he expresses the same idea of arbitrariness in the Queen Mab speech: why should each estate harbour its futile dreams of advancement? Why should Romeo long for Rosaline? Why for Juliet? Yet the play will not allow us to go on thinking this way for long, which is why it becomes a tragedy.

In *Midsummer Night's Dream*, Puck's debt to Cupid has been noted before, but its relevance to the genre of the play has not been noticed. Seneca's *Hippolytus* is one obvious source for Puck's Cupid-like activities and demeanour, and we know Shakespeare had been reading Seneca's play, taking Helena's pursuit of the unwilling Demetrius from Phaedra's pursuit of Hippolytus. Puck's headlong plunges around the earth explicitly allude to the moment where Phaedra's Nurse describes Cupid: '*natum per omnes scilicet terras vagum Erycina mittit, ille per caelum volans proterva tenera tela molitur manu*' (the goddess of Eryx sends her son to wander through all lands, and while flying through the heavens he has wanton weapons in his boyish hands).[18] Yet Seneca's play is a *tragedy*; why should such a festive comedy as *Midsummer Night's Dream* borrow from it, borrow a Cupid, and what has to happen to allow this modulation from minor keys to major? One factor is the introduction of a festive aesthetic from another source.

To us, the lyrics known as the *Anacreontea* are late and obscure, but to the Renaissance they were important, thanks to Henri Etienne's edition of 1554. In the *Anacreontea*, the god of love is the Puckish agent of mischief and mistakes. Intriguingly, the second anacreontic lyric addresses precisely the subject of genre: '*Dote moi luren Homerou/ Phouies aneuthe khordes*' (Friends, give me the lyre of Homer, but without the murderous string). Murder (the leitmotif of tragedy more than epic, or so it might have seemed to Shakespeare) is replaced by the anacreontic festive aesthetic of drink and desire. Cupid is part of that festive aesthetic, which influenced the general and the specific poetics of the *Dream*. The *Anacreontea* are full of rich evocations of the seasonal festivities associated with the vintage, and with weddings and wedding-songs; likewise the *Dream*. As well, some of the anacreontic Cupid poems are a direct influence on *Midsummer Night's Dream*, especially no. 15, in which a dove from Peleia flies about the earth as Anacreon's courier in a manner that recalls Puck putting a girdle round the earth, and no. 31, in which the god Eros/ Cupid leads Anacreon through woods and rivers to love.[19]

Other Renaissance writers placed the anacreontic Cupid in a wood; in Lady Mary Wroth's sonnet number 93, for instance, indebted to *Anacreontea* 33, Cupid is lost in a wood, and is rescued by a nymph.[20] In texts of this Anacreontic kind, Cupid becomes a way of understanding the events of the heart, interpreting the apparently heartless randomness of love. As such, he imparts comic distance to love, for as long as love can be seen as outside the self, something that is done to you by someone else, there is some faint hope of getting away from it.

Shakespeare also borrows lavishly from *Hippolytus'* chorus, who like Puck fills the woods with stories of the ragings of arbitrary desires. The chorus is also the digressor in ancient tragedy, usually so purposeful: it is the chorus who explains events (often wrongly) via parallels and mythic stories, just as both Puck and Mercutio do. But only Puck *is* the chorus of his play, speaking its epilogue, surviving its action unchanged. Mercutio is not a survivor, and yet he performs a choric role in the action. Shakespeare modifies his classical generic paradigm by replacing the role of the chorus as a commentator on events as they unfold with a *character* who is vulnerable to the outcome of such events. This goes far further than the kind of intervention in the action associated with transgressive choruses like that of Sophocles in *Antigone*, a play Shakespeare may have known later in his career through Latin translation.

Choruses in both Greek and Senecan tragedy characteristically explain the actions of Eros; even the gods are victims of Cupid. Mercutio attempts such a choric analysis of events at several points in *Romeo and Juliet*, but (like many choruses) he is utterly ineffectual in getting others to agree with his interpretations. So it is with Mab; Mercutio uses Mab as Cupid, as a way of interpreting desire as merely random. For Mercutio, love is a blind bow-boy, the child of an idle brain. Sweeping away the glamorous mask of Cupid to reveal a ridiculous female face, Mercutio is clumsily trying to demystify love, to sweep away what Romeo has romanticized. Mab is not some import from Irish or Warwickshire folklore; she is a joke, like the fairies of *The Merry Wives of Windsor*, a quean and whore, as her name suggests: she is *nothing*, in both senses, the simple and the bawdy. Beneath the lyrical rhetoric of love that Romeo espouses, Mercutio argues, is a whore who distributes her favours with a random hand. Mercutio is a supreme rhetorician: he can invent and invent; his invention overtops anything provided by God or nature. And he is in superb control of his invention. Every bit of Mab's equipage gets one line; every segment of society gets two or three lines, at most; only the soldier, when Mercutio is running out of characters, gets more. It is as regular as a metronome. (Compare Romeo's early speeches, where his images and metaphors run away with him.) He is like a child playing with a dolls' house, making the inhabitants do this and that. Or rather, he is like Oberon and Puck, like Cupid himself, playing with mortals and gods like puppets.

Perhaps Mercutio could go on talking for ever, and then none of the rest of it need happen; he might live in the comic neverland with the lost boys of Verona for ever. (This is, after all, pretty much what his lineal descendant Hamlet is sometimes attempting.) Like the clock in Colette's libretto for Ravel's *L'enfant et les sortilèges*, Mercutio might lament that if Romeo had not wantonly stopped him talking on and on, no one need ever have died. There is room for melancholics like him in Shakespearean comedy – Benedick, Jaques. Yet no prank, no clever Touchstone-fool, draws Mercutio into the action of desire. He remains alone, and alone he is powerless, and must fall, dragging the play into tragedy with him. Mab is as much Mercutio's servant as Puck is Oberon's, but Puck is the instrument Oberon uses to control the plot. Mercutio's Cupid-substitute is a thing of words only. Mercutio's control over Mab and her activities, his rhetorical prowess, mocks his inability to manage the play's events, to manage the feud, manage Romeo. Mab is a consolatory fantasy, dreamt up by a man who cannot control anything larger or more important.

Keeping Mab out of the action is what turns *Romeo and Juliet* from a comedy to a tragedy. The Queen Mab speech turns on the contrast between Mab's activity and the passivity of the sleepers. Their desires do not activate them, and hence they remain stories; estate satires like this are always static. Such stasis is comedic; comedy is about a reordering of desire that will eventually affirm sameness. Tragedy, on the other hand, is about permanent changes; desires that are not reordered become the agents of actions which cannot be reversed, symbolized by death. In *A Midsummer Night's Dream*, the helpless randomness of human affairs is pushed into the foreground by Puck and all the misuses of Love-in-Idleness. In Shakespearean tragedy, whatever Mercutio may like to think, acts originate from within. The Queen Mab speech is an effort to push *Romeo and Juliet* on to the same comic ground as *A Midsummer Night's Dream*. But it is Mercutio himself who will turn it for once and forever into a tragedy by being killed by mistake in another's quarrel, itself an arbitrary *substitution* which owes much to his own comic understanding of the universe, but which in this play cannot be rectified because it solidifies into the cold fact of his death. And from that death, the rest of the tragic action must follow.

In *A Midsummer Night's Dream*, everyone is inside the dream, which allows the audience to be outside it. We are shown its workings in Puck–Cupid. In *Romeo and Juliet*, only Mercutio is outside the dream; only he knows how it works. And paradoxically, that is fatal knowledge, because it is knowledge of the wrong kind. Like Lady Macbeth, like Richard III, he is caught in the wrong play, and he dies for it, giving birth through comedy to tragedy.

Producing dreams

How little this can be liked or understood by most modern audiences is amply displayed by the Hollywood Dream Factory's latest assault on *Romeo and Juliet*. Baz Luhrmann's much-hyped film of *Romeo and Juliet* is a dazzling piece of cinema that deliberately shuts its eyes to the play. The ho-hum gangland scenario – *de rigueur* for the feud since Bernstein's *West Side Story* – is the beef here. The point is that it renders life and death not tragic, but arbitrary. No one here knows how the dream works, because it has no works, only random lurches. This cannot help but make the audience indifferent to every death except those of the lovers, and in this case even those of the lovers are so rubbed smooth by repetition, so worn by meeja overhype, that the tears they wring are themselves second-hand. (And Leonardo Di Caprio can't act, and he's far too young for the part – but let that pass.) Amidst the stylish muddle, though, there is one moment of real inspiration, though it is hard to read. Before making the Queen Mab speech, Luhrmann's Mercutio, himself a drag queen, holds in his hand a blandly smiling tab of E. Now, in one sense this is drably literal; gee, I bet those people in the past who saw fairies were all on something, yeah? But the drug is an apt metaphor for the power of speech in Renaissance times; like E, rhetoric was seen as subversive, too much fun, and likely to persuade people to do Bad Things. In another sense it marks the *difference* between Shakespeare's Mercutio and Luhrmann's; Shakespeare's could be drunk on words, but Luhrmann's needs a chemical to be high enough to see a fairy who isn't there.

Puck's posterity

Once *A Midsummer Night's Dream* is produced, Pucks grow and prosper, and in ballad and chapbook the story of Puck becomes a story of Pluck, a story of how tough prole energy and high spirits can overcome the dreary prudence and economy of the middle classes. Typical is 'The Merry Pranks of Robin-Goodfellow: very pleasant and witty', a ballad in which Robin is Oberon's son by a mortal woman. While retaining some faint traces of folklore, this is heavily derived from *A Midsummer Night's Dream*; Oberon's nocturnal wanderings through houses at midnight, and his promiscuity, are straight lifts from the play.

> In time of old, when fayries us'd
> To wander in the night,
> And through key-holes swiftly glide,
> Now marke my story right,
> Among these pretty fairy elves
> Was Oberon, their king,
> Who us'd to keep their company
> Still at their revelling.

And sundry houses they did use,
But one, above the rest,
Wherein a comely lasse did dwell,
That pleas'd King Oberon best.
This lovely damsell, neat and faire,
So courteous, meek, and mild,
As sayes my booke, by Oberon
She was begot with-child.[21]

The midwife soon spots that Robin's father must be a fairy, and Oberon comes through with some Child Support in the form of delicacies for the mother and linen for the baby. But before long, Robin's mother is receiving complaints from the neighbours about her son's naughty tricks, and this leads him to leave home. No one says he is going to seek his fortune, but that is what it amounts to. Robin is living a fairytale version of the experience of middling and lower-class boys in Stuart England; they become unruly, and are then sent out to be apprenticed to a master.

Nothing could be further from the dreaminess of the *Dream*: here the gap between Robin and the mechanicals collapses when Robin becomes apprenticed to a tailor, like Shakespeare's Robin Starveling, perhaps his namesake. And Robin is almost as intelligent as his mechanicals; when asked by his master to whip the sleeves of a gown, he proceeds to flog them unmercifully. Robin is like the rebellious apprentices who dogged the streets of London in Shakespeare's day, stirring up strife. Here Robin is also like those dimwitted sons who go out to seek their fortunes and inexplicably succeed: Dummling, who acquires the Golden Goose, and the various characters named Jack, who are all stupid enough to swap a cow for a handful of beans, but manage in a topsy-turvy world to profit by it. Again like such heroes off to seek their fortunes, Robin finds his identity: he meets his father and discovers his power to transform himself into an animal. Here again, Robin overlaps with Bottom; the ass's head put on the weaver becomes Robin's proper garb. This link with animals confirms Robin's association with carnival and with what Russian literary critic Mikhail Bakhtin calls the carnivalesque: all those parts of the body and of life which well-mannered, middle-class people try to exclude. The lower

Ancient mother demons

1. Athene holds the gorgon-headed aegis, whose terrifying grin drives away foes in battle. Greek vase painting, *c.* 525 BC.

2. This nymph exemplifies sensuousness, but not the fear nymphs could also arouse. Relief from the lid of a Roman pyxis, *c.* 130 BC.

3. Lilith, seductively nude, but betrayed by deformed, birdlike feet. Terracotta relief from Mesopotamia, *c.* 2000 BC.

4. Half-monstrous sirens swirl around Odysseus and his crew. Greek vase painting, *c.* 490 BC.

Comment melusine sen volla en forme de serpent par la fenestre

Coment melusine venoit tous les soirsvisiter ses deux enfans.

Medieval dreaming

5. and 6. In these depictions, the medieval fairy Melusine shares the features of ancient mother-demons: a monstrous lower body and a yearning for babies. Woodcuts from *Melusine* by Jean d'Arras, *c.* 1500.

7. Mortal and immortal: the Lady of the Lake presents her pupil Lancelot to Queen Guinevere. Illumination from *The Story of Sir Lancelot*, a fourteenth-century French manuscript.

Mortals in the fairy realm

8. A ring of fairy-witches assemble outside a fairy mound. Undated English woodcut.

9. A man is caught in the act of becoming a fairy. His feet are already furred, though he has yet to grow horns. Flemish woodcut, 1558.

10. The Royalist prophet, Ann Jeffries, in 1645; the nineteenth century seized on her contacts with the fairies, but had less to say about her politics.

Troublesome Things through time

11. A sun- and moon-spangled Robin Goodfellow may link this fairy with astrology. Sixteenth-century English woodcut.

12. Fuseli's Puck, *c.* 1790s, is a night-flying demon, driven by madness across a dark sky.

13. Goya's hobgoblins, 1799, are a malign view of fairies as servants or workers; they are not obedient, but monstrous and rebellious.

14. Very domestic brownies, but servants or plagues? Causes of or cures for piles? This Victorian advertisement isn't sure.

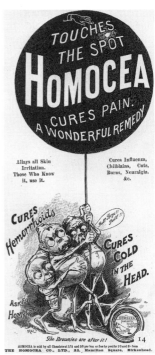

Royal fairies

15. Paton's *Oberon and Titania*, 1849, bring the solemnity of the formal classical nude to the fairy realm.

16. Fitzgerald's tiny fairy queen, *c.* 1860, is oblivious as her goblins taunt a helpless captive robin redbreast.

The Folk of the Air

17. Fairies playing in a snuffbox: the archetypal tiny wisp
of Victorian dreams.

18. And the reality: fairies made of girls, gaslight and glitter at
Drury Lane, 1853.

19. How the folk take to the air in the Victorian theatre; note the
display of leg. Magazine illustration, 1871.

Outside Over There

20. A forlorn Peter Pan sits on a branch, both baby and bird. Illustration by Arthur Rackham for J. M. Barrie's *Peter Pan in Kensington Gardens*, 1912.
21. The Rackham Goblin with his big nose and cap has faintly anti-semitic overtones. From *Peter Pan in Kensington Gardens*.
22. The Celtic Twilight and its seductions: *The Riders of the Sidhe* by John Duncan, 1911.

And the dreams go on ...

23. One of the notorious Cottingley fairy photographs, 1920. Note the Edwardian fairy hairstyles.

24. The fairies' maker Elsie Wright in the 1980s.

25. The contemporary fairy as frothy child-femininity.

26. There are alien shops as well as fairy shops through which people can express their fascination with other beings with a credit card. A souvenir shop in Roswell, New Mexico, 1997.

body, but especially the bowel and its sounds, and the lower orders of being, but especially pigs and their sounds, are disproportionately worrying for clean, tidy, middling people. Robin, who learns how to transform himself into a 'gruntling pig', is similarly disruptive; his animal nature is a sign of his intractability, his endless capacity to disobey.

Yet Robin is a force for social order against those who would disrupt it by too much authority, just as he is in the play. He retains his Shakespearean role as Eros/Cupid when, in a plot that echoes those of Jacobean city comedies, he punishes the lecherous old uncle who pursues his beautiful niece, and arranges the niece's marriage to a more acceptable suitor. This aspect of Robin is also found in *Tell-Truth's New Year's Gift*, which stresses his insistence on tidiness, but also portrays him as a Cupid who helps true lovers escape from parental tyranny. Robin is a kind of spirit of stage comedy, standing both for good and tidy order and for the pleasures of emotional liberty.

What makes reading these texts so difficult is that many of them were either originally composed or copied by an élite. It is a good rule that the English élite so long for authentic folklore that they resort periodically to its manufacture, and one result of this practice is that what purports to be authentic folklore gives cachet to modest literary works. The song 'The Pranks of Puck', sometimes attributed to Ben Jonson, and certainly Jonsonian in style and manner, is a fine example. It celebrates Shakespeare's Puck, knowing nothing and caring less about folklore. It rehearses all the tricks Shakespeare's Puck says he performs, and expands gracefully upon Puck's alleged household role, knitting in other bits of genuine fairylore on the way and tacking them too on to the supreme figure of Puck. Thus it is that Puck comes to swallow up all other English fairies, like some multinational fast-food outlet driving the idiosyncratic greasy spoons out of business. The trouble is that in the hands of an élite, and misattributed to a fairy in which no one believes, fairy activities lose their meaning and potency; when Jonson writes of Puck moving through the house at night, the fairy seems no more disturbing than a cleaner. All associations with death and the dead have been dropped, as has any sense of a difficult relationship of gifts and placations. This fairy is a good chap, and a good man in the pub:

Yet, now and then, the maids to please,
I card, at midnight, up their wool;
And, while they sleep, and take their ease,
With wheel to thread their flax I pull.
I grind at mill
Their malt up still,
I dress their hemp, I spin their tow.
If any wake,
And would me take,
I wend me laughing's ho, ho, ho!

Such stories are no longer told as a warning, and they do not shiver on the edge of fear; they are entertainment, of a streamlined and predictable sort.

Thus having told my dreame at full I'le bid you all farewell.
If you applaud mad Robin's prankes, may be ere long I'll tell
Some other stories to your cares, which shall contentment give.
To gain your favours I will seeke the longest day I live.[22]

The fairy has been tamed just as surely by Shakespeare and Jonson as by Walt Disney.

The romance of fairies

Is Oberon, then, equally tame? Not in his origins, at least; we have already seen that Oberon retained a position within magic as a powerful spirit to be conjured for luck, or power. However, this seems to derive less from popular culture than from high romance. Oberon comes not from fairy lore as Susan Swapper or Bessie Dunlop knew it, but from high romance, and in particular, from John Bourchier, Lord Berners' translation of the French romance *Huon of Bordeaux* into English. Huon is one of those influential romances that few people now read; it is extremely long, and the plot is elaborate and convoluted. Reading it, though, one can still see why it took writers like Spenser by storm. In it, Oberon is a fairy king, one who lives in a wood 'full of the fairy and strange things.'[23] He is deformed, only three feet high, and 'crook-shouldered', but he has 'an angelic visage', so that no mortal man who sees him fails to take pleasure in his face. He speaks to anyone who enters his wood, and anyone to whom he speaks is lost for ever, yet anyone who fails to speak to him is plagued with storms so terrible that the silent traveller cannot help but believe that all the world will perish. Oberon can also make a flooding river appear across your path, but you can cross it easily. The Oberon Huon meets is wearing not plaid, but a gown so rich and so garnished with precious stones that it shines like the sun. He also carries a magic bow, one that can bring down any animal, a horn made by the fairies of Avalon, that can cure any sickness and any hunger when blown, and can make anyone who hears it happy. Somehow, though, Huon does not suffer in the prescribed way. When he refuses to speak, Oberon does indeed raise up storms, phantom rivers and castle mirages to torment him, eventually ordering his warriors to slay the churlish knight, but he accepts the advice of one of his retinue to try negotiations one last time. This he does, and Huon is amazed by his beauty, and by his resemblance to a child of five years. At last he greets Oberon, who is so delighted that he agrees to reward him lavishly for his courtesy.

And yet despite the evident gulf between elegant, prestigious Oberon and the fairies of the witch-trials, Berners is closer to those popular stories than the elaborators of the cult of Puck. Oberon, it transpires, is the son of Julius Caesar and a lady of the Secret Isle, a lady who was the grandmother of Alexander the Great. Thus like the fairies of folklore, Oberon is linked to the powerful dead, and in particular to the dead patriarchs, the conquerers and founders of nations. All the fairies were invited to attend the birth of Oberon except for one, and she was so angry that she put a curse on the baby which made him stop growing when he was three years old. Later repenting of her curse, she also made him 'the fairest creature whom ever nature formed'. This Sleeping Beauty fairytale of gifts and curses continues as Oberon recounts the way other guests enhanced his magical powers; he gains clairvoyance, the ability to travel wherever he likes by wishing, the power to tame any bird or beast, the power to make a castle grow at his command. Oberon will never look any older, and when he leaves the world he will find a place ready for him in Paradise. Feasting Huon and his company with a magical banquet, an upper-class fantasy of pleasure and excess with much emphasis on the setting and the gold plates, Oberon resembles the humbler fairies of Scotland in his ability to elevate those he wishes to the absolute sky-limit of their own social ambitions. He also gives power to Huon, just as humbler fairies do to humble people; he gives Huon a magic horn which when he blows it will bring Oberon and a hundred thousand knights to his side. Such links may be less an outcome of popular stories finding their way into Berners than of romances gradually making their way via ballads and storytelling into oral culture.

Whatever their origins, these are Oberon's characteristics. They are endlessly elaborated through his tempestuous relationship with Huon, who always behaves like Oberon, and eventually becomes his heir and replacement. Huon joins the fairy host himself, just as many cunning men and women did, and it is an irrevocable change, just as it usually is in Celtic cultures. Huon and his queen Esclaramonde will remain in fairyland until the day of judgement, says the author confidently. Perhaps Shakespeare did not get quite this far with Huon's story. He and other dramatists of the 1590s continued to write of Oberon as the king of fairies. In Robert Greene's *James IV*, for example, Oberon is king, and not only Oberon but all the fairies are small. Oberon is so tiny that he 'lookest not so big as the King of Clubs'.[24] He also retains some of the links with the dead suggested by his status: he cannot endure the coming of morning light. We will return to the question of size, but Greene's reuse of the tiny Oberon of Berners' romance is proof of its influence, and may directly have inspired Shakespeare.

Shakespeare's Oberon, however, like his Puck, is translated, translated from a folk figure through the crib of the classics. Although he resembles the Oberon of *Huon* in his possessiveness, his jealousy, his exotic location in India (II.ii), and his proneness to moodiness, he is in essence a classical deity of the seasons, a vertumnus. Vertumnus was the Roman god of the changing year, a trickster who wins Pomona, Roman goddess of ripening fruit, by deceit and disguise. In Ovid's *Fasti*, Vertumnus impersonates a series of rustics to get to the goddess – the same symbolic pattern as Oberon's efforts to win Titania's allegiance by using the disguised, rustic Bottom.

Later, Ben Jonson, whose head was even more thoroughly stuffed with classics, created an Oberon who is an English prince, and no more exotic than that implies. His masque for the successful but all-too-mortal Prince Henry, James I's heir, likens the young prince to Oberon just as other masques had likened Henry's papa to Hercules, and with no more frisson. Powerful males are powerful males. The masque is also thronged by Silenus, Sylvans and other classical beings, hugger-mugger with fays; following Shakespeare's lead, Jonson is not interested in making a difference of kind between Oberon and the ruck of classical walk-ons, but only a difference of degree. Even the romantic Oberon of *Huon* is more or less subsumed.

If Oberon is a classical deity, then his queen, Titania, is an Ovidian goddess-nymph. Huon does of course feature a fairy queen, and a very unruly one, Morgan le Fay. Yet apart from the standard unruly-woman-desires-mastery plot, little is left of her in Titania. When Arthur Golding translated Ovid's *Metamorphoses* into English, Ovid's nymphs became fairies; this follows a tradition first established in Gawin Douglas's translation of Virgil's *Aeneid*.[25] At first glance, it might seem similar for Shakespeare to give to his fairy queen an Ovidian name for Diana, but in fact it is the opposite; turning fairies into nymphs and goddesses, not vice versa.

If there is a surviving strand of folklore in Titania, she herself remains ignorant of it. That surviving strand is the changeling boy, the little boy over whom king and queen quarrel. Titania's account of how she acquired this child is serene, courtly, and completely unruffled:

> His mother was a votress of my order,
> And in the spiced Indian air, by night,
> Full often has she gossip'd by my side;
> And sat with me on Neptune's yellow sands,
> Marking th'embarked traders on the flood:
> Which we have laughed to see the sails conceive
> And grow big-bellied with the wanton wind;
> Which she, with pretty and with swimming gait
> Following (her womb then rich with my young squire),
> Would imitate, and sail upon the land
> To fetch me trifles, and return again
> As from a voyage rich with merchandise.

but she, being mortal, of that boy did die;
And for her sake do I rear up her boy;
And for her sake I will not part with him.[26]

How *sisterly* it all sounds – the two women sitting together, enjoying each other's friendship. Louis Montrose found it glowingly matriarchal, Amazonian, a kind of perfect pre-patriarchal continuum of female solidarity. And yet, and yet . . . what if Bessie Dunlop were to tell this story? What if this *is* Bessie's story, as seen by the queen of the fairies? What if all the pain Bessie suffers, the mortal woman's agony, her hard and deadly childing, her loss of her baby through death, are simply things Titania does not or cannot see? Perhaps jolly and supportive sisterhood exists only for immortals; for mortals, being the fairies' votaress meant loss and death, a loss and death the fairies themselves cannot even understand. The fact that Titania is Diana, goddess of childbirth, and the one who determines whether women in childbirth live or die, might have strengthened this interpretation. Here, however, Titania is very serenely simply one of the immortals; for her, death does not unite her with the birthing mother, but divides them, and allows her to take the child with a clear untroubled conscience, less fairy queen than fairy godmother.

And there is a trace of something else: Titania is Diana, and when Diana's votaries got themselves pregnant, the goddess was not exactly a fountain of sympathy; she exiled or killed them for their transgression. The way in which neither mother nor baby get to enjoy each other is reminiscent of those grim Ovidian stories. While Titania plainly accepts the pregnancy of *her* votary, the images of the woman's pregnant belly as a kind of trading voyage signals the possessiveness with which she does so. Even when still inside its mother, the baby is '*my* young squire', it is goods for the queen, not its mother.

As Diana, Titania is not amenable to the desires or rules of men. In evoking Diana, Shakespeare repeats a classic plot of Renaissance bodice-ripping romance, in which a virtuous virgin who rejects men is pursued – and sometimes caught – by a particularly determined lover. Just so does Oberon pursue Titania, eventually forcing her into a particularly rough piece of trade through the old rapist's trick of drugging her. The drug he uses is itself the result of an older duel between Cupid and Diana, one in which Cupid's arrow missed its mark; that duel is now restaged in Puck's encounter with Titania, and this time it is Cupid who is victorious. What made all this fairy play seem both relevant and deeply risky politically was the virgin at whom Cupid aimed his arrow: not Diana, not Titania, but a 'fair vestal throned in the West'. The arrow does miss Elizabeth I, but the rest of the play seems designed to insist that this was really rather a pity, that Cupid ought to win.

On the other hand, the very comparison between Elizabeth and the Fairy Queen thus implied does Elizabeth no favours, and here Shakespeare is drawing on Edmund Spenser's *Faerie Queene*, another fairy text that both flatters the queen and agonizes about her continuing single status, and one far less comfortable with its queen than is Shakespeare. Shakespeare can knock the queen about, make her marry a worker with an ass's head. Spenser hardly dares to write about or invoke her – Gloriana is by no means a major character in the poem that ostensibly bears her name. And yet Spenser can by devious ways, ways he himself might not fully realize, ways which the poem cannot speak about, use the stories of the Fairy Queen to get a kind of fantasy revenge on the queen who so unnerves him.

For example, the vision of Gloriana experienced by Arthur looks far from straightforwardly complimentary to Elizabeth in the light of the Fairy Queen's associations with sex and death in the medieval romances which Spenser emulates. However highminded it seems, the vision remains sexualized: when

> Her daintie limbes full softly down did lay:
> . . .
> Most goodly glee and lovely blandishment
> She to me made, and bad me love her deare,
> For dearely sure her love was to me bent.[27]

Even the impress of the queen's body on the grass as the trace of her presence has a faint whiff of sexuality; this queen is fully incarnate (as opposed to a mere vision). Arthur's misery at Gloriana's departure, a misery which leads him to embark on a quest to rediscover her, casts him as another of the Fairy Queen's votaries, gifted perhaps, but gifted by virtue of having encountered femininity at its most other, most alien. That encounter shapes his giftedness. Arthur also represents Elizabeth's courtiers, men who were forced to pursue her favour endlessly, often at the expense of forming more reliable ties, without ever securely grasping it. Walter Ralegh was, after all, closely concerned with the poem's development and one of its dedicatees.

Here, then, is an aspect of *A Midsummer Night's Dream* overlooked by recent combatants disputing whether the poem rebukes Elizabeth's power or her sex.[28] It matters that Titania is not just any old queen, but the fairy queen. As he was to do in *The Merry Wives of Windsor*, Shakespeare was indulging Elizabeth's enthusiasm for the role of the queen of the fairies or her votary, while slyly undermining her through the same figure.[29] All the stories we have been discussing are caught up and reworked in this play. The similarity of Titania's love for Bottom to the narratives in which the Fairy Queen elevates a mortal are evident. Here, the queen's choice is desperately inappropriate, of course: Bottom is not capable of elevation. That inappropriateness casts doubt on both female rule and male attempts at social advancement. There is also a sense in which both Bottom and Titania are victims of deception, trickery and masquerade, but with a difference. Whereas both the authentic and the trickster fairy queens were firmly in control over their own impersonations, this fairy queen is the butt of the joke. Removing from femininity its power to deceive, and rendering it as deceived, is a very effective disarming of an otherwise terrifyingly unstable power. Oberon is able to subdue Titania through masquerade. This is not, then, just about the taming of a queen. It is about the taming of a fairy queen, and hence about subduing the very dark anxieties generated for masculinity by a female ruler.

And perhaps it is this process of taming Elizabeth which leads Shakespeare to tame the fairies altogether. The fairies of *A Midsummer Night's Dream* are far more kindly and benevolent, far less dangerous, than the fairies of medieval romance, and they are also much more manageable than the fairies of witch-trials, English or Scottish. Unlike Janet Trall and Susan Swapper, Theseus and Hippolyta can sleep safely in their beds while the fairies trot through the house; Puck may be sweeping the floor, but there is no fear here of being 'swept away'. The sweet fairies of the *Dream* are indeed the remote ancestors of every wholly benign fairy, right down to pink-clad Sugar Plum fairies in tights. In taking the sting of death out of fairies, Shakespeare robs them of their complexity.

The sorrows of the small

Size does matter.

The job of sweetening and simplifying fairies was continued by and through a trend in literary depictions of fairies. The Elizabethans and even more the Jacobeans loved the miniature. In their hands, fairies shrank to tininess. Though there are scattered references to tiny fairies in literature before Shakespeare, they are small rather than insect-like, like the three-foot childlike Oberon of *Huon*. In the Queen Mab speech, Shakespeare gives the world fairies who come in shape no bigger than an agate-stone, and they proceed to multiply like malaria mosquitoes. Just as editors' desks a few years ago were suddenly and mysteriously clogged with books about tulips, so the early Jacobean printers were kept sweating over one teeny-weeny fairy after another. The grandfather of such exotic description is Michael Drayton, whose *Nimphidia* describes a tiny fairy court at absurd, laughable length. Here is his fairy palace:

> The Walls of Spiders Legs are made,
> Wel mortized and finely layd,
> He was the master of his trade,
> It curiosly that builded:
> The Windows of the eyes of Cats,
> As for the Roofe, instead of Slats,
> Is cover'd with the skinns of Batts,
> With Moonshine that are guilded.[30]

Drayton's fairies are at once primitive and sophisticated; they use the natural materials associated with savages, but the miniaturization has an effect of sophistication and civility. Yet Drayton does not try to prevent miniaturization from collapsing into the grotesque, or at least into burlesque. *Reducing* the other to miniature scale reduces it to manageability too, making it laughable. Drayton's tiny fairies are part of a trend for miniaturization as a luxury which began in the late sixteenth century but continued well into the eighteenth.[31] Tiny printed books were produced: the *Diurnale Moguntinum*, printed in 1468, represents a microcosm. Tiny almanacs were especially popular. Such productions offered to encapsulate the whole world in a small portable artefact through the principle that the microcosm reflected the macrocosm. They were images of conquest, as were Nicholas Hilliard's miniatures of languorous, eroticized courtier-lovers. Tiny fairies came to be described in micro-forms; the octosyllabic couplet, for instance, extending the effect of miniaturization to the verse-form itself. The transformative effect of miniaturization is to make the everyday remarkable. Drayton's fairy city is not adorned with gold and silver, but with bats' wings and spiders' legs, transformed in theory by the labour of the fairies, but in reality by what it signifies, the labour of the poet, into a luxury item. Such luxuries are described so thickly that there can be little narrative development; the poems of this kind keep getting 'stuck' at the level of *enargeia* and never progressing to romance. Yet this inertia is also a sign of luxury. Reading in so much detail is a sign of the reader's leisure. Civilization is about not being in a hurry. Hence these representations of luxury are also representations of the reader, as well as the other. Distinctions between the homely and the exotic founder in consumerism.

What the fairies do is exotic because they are so tiny. In William Browne's *Britannia's Pastorals*, for instance, the fairy palace might be under a hill, as in folklore, but Browne is less interested in its location than in a minute description of the exceptionally exotic viands: sitting down to dine at a table covered in a rose-petal cloth, the fairies eat stuffed grasshopper and roast ant, while the Fairy King discourses pleasantly of hawking and coursing, though their hawks are only wagtails. The resemblance to children's literature of the nineteenth century is not, as we shall see, coincidental. This is a toy fairy set of the mind; it lacks corporeal form, but it is none the less a kind of dolls' house. Examples of such tininess could be multiplied endlessly, since the tiny fairies troop on into the Restoration and eighteenth century, finding miniature homes everywhere from Margaret Cavendish's

poetic attempts to explain the discoveries of science to Purcell's nostal-
gic operas of Englishness.

Such attractive tininess is also central to Robert Herrick's fairy
poems, and Herrick is in any case a poet who uses the miniature to
represent control and power. To keep things small is for Herrick to
keep them elegant and orderly. In this way, style reflects content, for
as we have seen, some of his fairy poems exhort others too to work to
maintain order and cleanness.

Elsewhere, the octosyllabic couplet represents the elegance and aristocracy of fairy life; in Herrick's hands, fairies are already taking up
their long historical role as the only true aristocracy, all *noblesse* and
very little *oblige*. Like Drayton and Browne, he is keen to describe a
miniature banquet, a poetic equivalent of the marchpane miniatures
that adorned real banquet tables at the courts of James I and Charles
I. Like such sweetmeats, Herrick's fairy food is about the luxury of
not needing sustenance, of being able to think about food without
hunger, even without interest. This fairy banquet springs from the
absence of those savage gnawings that led the Scottish witches to
imagine fairy food. It is a dream of satiety. It also reflects an era of
culinary innovation. Of course, no one was really going to try out the
'unctuous dewdrops' of the snail, but this was an era in which food –
from an emerging trading empire – was becoming prized for its rarity
value. Again, Herrick provides a literary equivalent of the inventiveness
of real chefs.

Herrick does understand that fairies are sexual, but his are so
formidably civilized about it that all edginess is lost. Escorting Oberon
to bed with Mab, always the queen of little fairies, Herrick is full of
sly winks and grins; isn't it amazing, he seems to say, that such small
creatures can – well – do it? Herrick's fairies are precursors of the
copulating animals at whom we goggle on wildlife television pro-
grammes. The joke outstays its welcome, of course, as such whimsy
must. Yet tiny fairies proved to have a long shelf-life, and to this day
the conceit that fairies are the same size as flowers is endlessly recycled
in the cuter fairy books for children, as we shall see in due course.

As symbols of an ideal, simple aristocracy, Herrick makes the fairies
Catholic. In a poem describing the chapel of Oberon – a nice variation
on the more usual tours of fairy palaces – Herrick throws up his hands

at the sight of saints so numerous that he cannot possibly describe them all. This is of course a slyly Protestant take on Catholicism; in likening saints to pagan idols, Herrick is toeing a standard Church of England line.

> Now this the Fairies we'd have known,
> Theirs is a mixt religion,
> And some have heard the elves it call,
> Part pagan, part papistical.
> If unto me all tongues were granted,
> I could not speak the saints here painted.[32]

A move followed by others, most famously Bishop Corbet, whose poem 'Farewell rewards and fairies' has been kept in the repertoire by Kipling's use of it:

> Lament, lament old abbeys,
> The fairies lost command;
> They did but change priest's babies,
> But some have chang'd your land:
> And all your children stol'n from thence
> Are now grown Puritans,
> Who live as changelings ever since,
> For love of your demaines.

Fairies also evoke other past fractures and ruptures. John Selden famously recorded the common saying that 'there never was a merry world since the fairies left dancing and the parson left conjuring'. John Aubrey, the antiquarian and scholar, tells the story of a boy he takes to be a changeling, who enacts the Battle of Bosworth with two wheat-sheaves, correctly predicting the outcome: the fall of the last Plantagenet. A Civil War pamphlet allows Robin Goodfellow to narrate the first battles of the war, which he does from an early pacifist perspective, but he is himself assumed to be delighted at news of Queen Henrietta Maria's arrival because he is like her a Catholic. For Aubrey and for Corbet, the Civil War was itself a rupture that removed for ever the smooth continuity of rural life: as Aubrey wrote, 'the Civil Wars coming on have put out all these rites, or customs quite out of fashion'.[33] Rather than assuming that this is a merely factual comment, we could see it as a comment on the way the Civil War imposed on people a felt need to stress the seamless continuity it had disrupted. Fairies, invented to display the glories of the aristocracy on the one hand and the cloddish charm of the servants on the other, were the ideal mortar for an edifice of fantasy about the antebellum past, a past in which servants knew their place and aristos knew theirs.

The fairy-taken believer

Ironically, we began this chapter with a sceptic and finish it with a true believer, in defiance of expectation. Belief in fairies actually warmed and grew as people began to be afraid that scepticism was a bottomless black vortex into which Christianity itself might be drawn. Such a true believer was Robert Kirk, a Scottish clergyman whose remarkable book *The Secret Commonwealth of Elves and Fairies* was first brought to public attention just in time to fascinate the early Romantic folklorists such as Walter Scott. Surviving in a number of eighteenth-century manuscripts, Kirk's book purports to describe the world of fairies, though actually for at least half its length it is more concerned with trying to verify the doctrinal value of second sight, with reference to Plato and Cornelius Agrippa as well as the Bible. There have been lengthy discussions of how far Kirk's material on fairies might legitimately be treated as a source for folklore; recently, leading folklorist Stuart Sanderson has made a vigorous case for its validity. Certainly some of Kirk's material will be familiar already: he writes, for instance, of

women . . . yet alive who tell they were taken away when in child-bed to nurse Faire Children, a lingering voracious image of their being left in their place, like their Reflexion in a Mirror, which (as if it were some insatiable spirit in an assumed bodie) made first semblance to devoure the meats that it cunningly carried by, and then left the carcase as if it expired and departed thence by a naturall and common death. The Child, and Fire, with Food and other

Necessaries, are set before the Nurse how soon she enters; but she nather perceaves any passage out, nor sees what those people does in other rooms of the lodging. When the child is wained, the Nurse dies, or is conveyed back, or gets it to her choice to stay there. But if any Superterrneans be so subtle, as to practice their slights for procuring a Privacy to any of their Misteries, they smite them without paine, as with a Puff of Wind, and bereave them of both the naturall and acquired sights in the twinkling of an eye . . . The tramontains to this day put Bread, the Bible or a piece of iron in Womens Beds when travelling, to save them from being thus stollen.[34]

So far, so popular. Kirk also reports on women taken from childbed, and women who can no longer eat; he knows about brownies, and like Scot he is a kind of grab-bag of half-heard and half-understood spells, only some of which have anything whatsoever to do with fairies. Nevertheless, and despite Sanderson's disclaimers, Kirk's argument, like Scot's, is distinctly 'interested'. It is highly likely that *The Secret Commonwealth* was written not in a Scottish village manse, but in London, amid the hurly-burly of the Sadducee controversy. As documented by Ian Bostridge, this was an intellectual ferment among the London clergy, who had become afraid – reasonably enough – that growing scepticism about the workings of the supernatural in witchcraft and other superstitions portended a crisis of belief in God himself. Kirk's efforts to make fairies part of an educated world may be an attempt to defend God.[35]

Yet it was not Kirk's earnestly Neoplatonic spirits who dominated the imaginations of men and women, but Susan Swapper's spirits of the national lottery, laden with gold. If most early modern people feared fairies, they also longed for them, for exactly the same reason children hoped to meet a fairy in a later era: they were hoping for personal wealth. And where the greedy are gathered together, there surely will be the Brooklyn Bridge sellers in the midst of them. If Robin Goodfellow is transmogrified from household brownie-demon to stage clown, his altered state aptly symbolizes what happens to the fairies themselves. They too become tricksters. They too are inhabited, a disguise, by one con-artist after another. A late seventeenth-century ballad links the two themes:

> Of Robin Goodfellow also,
> Who was a servant long ago,
> The queen of Fairies doth it know,
> And hindered him in fashion:
> She knew not what she did herself,
> She chang'd him like a Fairy elf,
> For all his money, goods and pelf,
> She gulled him.[36]

Here the biter is bitten, the trickster is tricked.

Sexual licence allowed some women to tell a very simple version of this story to men and women with great effect. The story goes like this: in exchange for sex, the king/queen of the fairies will transform your goods into gold. Two such tellers of tales were Judith Phillips and Alice West, both of whom impersonated and spoke for the queen of the fairies.[37] Alice West's story was told in a 1613 pamphlet. She did not pretend to be the queen of the fairies, but to be one of her votaresses, like Titania's dead friend. In this role, she persuaded a goldsmith's apprentice who 'had charge of more wealth than wit' that 'the queen of the fairies did most ardently dote upon him'. If Bottom could be loved by Titania, and served by her fairies, why not any other rude mechanical? Shakespeare had written the script; all Alice West had to do was to fill in the blanks. She persuaded him to bring his master's silver plate to be turned into gold while he should 'confer with the amorous queen of fairies'. However, what awaits him is not sexual exhaustion, but a beating:

The young man next morning got up early according to his hour, went to the close, and placed the plate in the four corners, still expecting the queen of fairies, and then this Alice West had placed in a ditch four of her consorts, who came forth, and with stones and brickbats, so beat the poor prentice, that he ran home, and forgot to take his plate with him.[38]

In the fantasy Alice West offers, the alchemy of sex, translating blood into seed, is mimicked in the Fairy Queen's alchemical translation of silver or base metal into gold, also a process of making the sterile into the fertile. This way of making money – literally *making* money, making it breed and grow from nothing – is the antithesis of the virtuous, godly notion of prudent profitability, whereby money and goods could not be 'made', but only gathered and stored. Whereas the mainstream notion of enterprise involved a virtuous storing up of the fruits of labour, the Fairy Queen offered a way to short-circuit all that, a chance for a miraculous rise that was intrinsically undeserved, as was Bottom's. That was, of course, its main attraction. As well, the entire fantasy is so evidently based on a system of government where bribes and gifts function as ways to ingratiate oneself with the powerful that its constant denunciation as trickery and theft might itself make uneasy reading for the ruling classes. The practice of gift-giving became less a taken-for-granted way of doing business and more a sign of corruption as the seventeenth century wore on; here, the notion of buying favour is shown to be a cruel delusion.[39] What, after all, is the difference between the queen of England and the queen of the fairies? Ordinary people never meet either, but have unsustainable hopes of both.

The exchange of sex for cash in Alice's story of the queen establishes an analogy between the two, an analogy developed when the pamphlet says that Alice 'drained' one of her victims 'completely dry'. This refers to his loss of money to her, but might equally mean his loss of bodily fluids; the witch in *Macbeth* threatens to drain her victim 'dry as hay' in like fashion.[40] No wonder the man's courage was 'cold' for meeting the queen of the fairies. Similarly, the celebrated astrologer and cunning man William Lilly had a client who was eager to meet with the queen. However, when it came to the point:

As it happened not many years since with us, a very sober discreet person, of virtuous life and conversation, was beyond measure desirous to see something of this nature; he went with a Friend into my *Hurst wood*, the Queen of Fairies was invocated, a gentle murmuring Wind came first; after that, amongst the hedges, a smart Whirlwind; by and by a strong Blast of wind blew upon the Face of the Friend, – and the Queen appearing in a most illustrious Glory. No more, I beseech you, (quoth the Friend) my Heart fails; I am not able to endure longer, nor was he; his black curling hair rose up, and I believe a bullrush would have beat him to the ground.[41]

Desiring the queen of the fairies is accompanied by terror of her. Here, she presents herself almost as God did to Moses, preceded by a roaring wind. But the queen's glory, too, seems terrifying, Medusan, reflected in the upstanding hair of Lilly's client.[42] What kind of incapacity is he confessing? An inability to look, to see, undoubtedly, but perhaps another incapacity also, an incapacity in meeting the demands of the queen. What if I'm not (so to speak) up to this?

Another of the queen of the fairies' eager votaries was Goodwin Wharton, the younger son of a prominent gentry family. Like Lilly's friend, Wharton was both dazzled and terrified when the cunning woman he had encountered, Mary Parish, introduced him to the amorous queen of the fairies. Wharton was acutely anxious about his own ability to meet the sexual demands of the queen and Mary. He began to suffer from a backache. At first he thought this was due to a riding accident, but it turned out to have another cause, a cause for which he gained a cure when he realized that his back seemed worse after sex with Mary. He felt half-dead afterwards. Thinking it over, he remembered Mary's story that the king of the fairies had once told her that he could make himself invisible and enjoy her whenever he liked. Wharton began to think that a female fairy was using him similarly. It turned out to be the queen herself, whose passion for him was so great that she had taken to consorting with him several times a night. Once, she had had intercourse with him three times in a row, and had then 'sucked up her breath' at the moment of climax, so that she had drawn 'the very substance of the marrow' out of his bones.[43] She had almost killed him. We might read this as a naturalization of the fears evoked by the rivers of blood and the teind to hell in the ballads, fears of engulfment, exhaustion, female sexual excess. Yet Goodwin Wharton is also frustrated, for he never sees the queen who desires him so much.

If ever there were stories of deferral, dilation and delay, these are such stories.[44] The whole point of every romance narrative is to stave off for as long as possible the inevitable moment when the lovers confess their love, for once that has happened there is no more to say. Similarly, Scheherazade-like, Mary had to keep Goodwin at her side by never finishing her story, for once it finished, he would be bound to see that it ended in nothing. Far from being constrained by the

non-existence of those on whom her story depends, and by the impossibility of consummation, Mary is inspired by them to create a rich and
elaborate web of story, one with more plot twists than romance writer
Aphra Behn or French fairy-tale teller Madame D'Aulnoy could hope
to boast. This is the need to avoid the ending that is constantly
foreshadowed which makes Mary's story a romance. A glittering future
of money and prestige can be *told* and retold, but cannot ever quite be
reached. That future is symbolized by the queen of the fairies. In
all these tales of cozenage, the Fairy Queen can appear only as a
non-appearance. Her presence generates a desire without an object, or
with an object that can exist only as further story. What if the Fairy
Queen's excessive and unruly desires are simply reflections, mirror-
images of the insatiable desires she generates by her perpetual absence?
What if her lust for man's seed, for men's bodies and blood, is a
reflection of their desire for gold? For in these stories it is only the
queen who is driven by lust. The men are driven by a longing to make
money from their royal paramour, and from another motive too: a
wish to be somebody, to be elevated into the world of nobility and
royal supremacy. Getting on paradoxically involves overcoming or
coming close to a horrendous threat to masculinity, a devouring femininity which might well 'drain' the victim.

Yet this fantasy is not just a selling strategy aimed at a consumer.
Mary was a good saleswoman, and all good salespeople believe their
own stories. At times, Goodwin Wharton seems more interested in
recording Mary's stories for their own sake than in making them his
own. Her story is also just that – *her* story – and the fact that it is
told in Wharton's diary and not in her own personal statement at a
witch-trial should not lead us to ignore her role as its begetter. In fact,
Mary seems to have set out systematically to learn the arts of a cunning
woman – learn to tell stories – after her sojourn in prison for debt. She
studied alchemy and astrology from books, though she herself claimed
to have learned about the possibilities of buried treasure from her
grandfather, who had, she said, found a pot full of fairy gold and
silver, with the standard folkloric direction, 'Where this pot doth lie,
there stands a better by'.[45] Such family anecdotes are plainly crafted
from folklore, but they lend authenticity to Mary's credentials as a
woman acquainted with the fairies. Mary also claimed to possess a

book 'worth more than the world itself', a book written partly in Greek, the language of magic to Stuart England, a book that came from Germany, home of high magic. Mary draws on both book-learning and folklore to make her fairies – she also receives visits from the dead, setting herself up as a kind of shaman. A dead woman who visits Mary may even be a kind of fairy to her – though Goodwin may be too well-educated to notice – since like the Fairy Queen she is knowledge-able about buried treasure. Mary's fantasies sound a good deal like Susan Swapper's, in fact:

After this day as she was sitting alone in her chamber, appears a man to her, and tells her thus: Mary, if thou wilt come down to Glastonbury Tor, we have a great treasure, thou shalt have some of it, but there will appear a great fierce bull, who will come furiously at thee as if he would have thee to pieces but be not thou afraid of him, for he cannot hurt thee nor hinder thee. And then disappeared.[46]

Here, legends of King Arthur and of 'ancient' monuments, the Scottish motif of the elfbull and the folktale motif of earning treasure by confronting some fearful apparition are mixed together to make a powerful story of fairy guidance to wealth. Yet all these elements are also subordinated to the simple desire for money which animates both Mary and her client. There is no pleasure in seeing an elfbull unless it leads to something practical. Devoid of romantic interest in the supernatural for its own sake, Mary's concerns are severely practical. Like Susan Swapper, Mary is poor; when Goodwin Wharton first meets her, he is horrified by the squalor in which she lives. Like Susan, and like Bessie Dunlop, Mary is simply hoping that fairies might be a way out of the despair of her situation. Like Susan, too, she was at odds with her society in matters of religion: Mary's family were Cath-olic, and Mary's fairies, like Herrick's, were Catholic too; the king's principal adviser is a Father friar; and there is a church headed by a fairy pope.[47] And like Susan, she has lost children – fourteen of Mary's enormous brood of seventeen died in the Great Plague of 1665 – so Mary's links to the realm of the dead were exceptionally strong. According to Mary, the fairies lived under Hounslow Heath and in Cornwall and at Shirburn Castle in Oxfordshire. The realm could be entered through a door in the earth: down in a spiral path, the visitor progressed to a level plain, and there stood a royal palace with many marble-paved courts.

Also like the Scottish witches, Mary had a personal guide to the world of the dead, someone who was himself dead. While in Ludgate prison for debt, Mary had met a gentleman named George Whitmore, also a debtor, to whom she became romantically attached. Suddenly, however, George was thrown into Newgate prison on charges of highway robbery, and hanged for his crimes. That is how he became Mary's spirit guide.

Yet other, new elements of fairy lore also creep into Mary's stories. Goodwin Wharton's fairies are small; though able to assume normal size if they chose, they were naturally 'not above a Yard in height' and they rode horses the size of 'masty dogs'.[48] Their size is also rationally explicable; they are human beings who simply happen to possess some magical skills which humans have unaccountably lost. Yet their smallness shows how Shakespeare, Herrick and other creators of literary fairies are coming to shape what people who were not themselves especially literary thought about them.

These are also the first English 'fairy tales' known to me that are genuinely influenced by courtly fairy representation and by French *précosité* and its aristocratic *contes des fées*.[49] The queen of the fairies who so tired Goodwin Wharton was named Penelope La Gard, a name both exotic and aristocratic, and like the wife of Charles II she was Portuguese, the sister of the reigning Fairy King of Portugal. After her husband's death she becomes the ruler of the kingdom, and it is not long before she declares her intention of marrying Goodwin and making him the new king of the fairies. Meanwhile, the queen's sister, Princess Ursula La Perle, the most beautiful woman in the world, came to be attracted to him too and made even more lavish promises than had the queen: she offered to make him rich beyond his wildest dreams, agreed to live above ground with him, or in Italy if he preferred. Snobbish though all this sounds, it stands in direct contradiction to Wharton's own desperate efforts to transcend his own position as impoverished younger son through spectacular deployment of occult resources. He was not content to accept his place, but sought to improve it, and politically he was an ardent Whig, keen to restrain the power of the monarch, and in trouble himself for having so many family members connected with the Meal Tub Plot. In inventing fairies to suit Goodwin Wharton's needs and desires, Mary seems to have consciously evoked them as the moneyed, privileged goal that he was pursuing, while using their by-now-built-in conservatism to reassure him about his own daring in challenging the social order.

It is impossible to retell Mary's stories without making her – however admiringly – the villain of the piece. Yet Goodwin's intentions were never altogether honourable; the relationship between them is not straightforwardly one between victim and con-artist. Mary convinces him of her supernatural prowess, true, but his reaction is to see her as a commodity which he can exploit as her manager. As we shall soon see, the habit of seeing fairies and those linked with them as sideshows was growing on the English.

6

Into the Enlightenment

As fairies moved forward into a new era of trade, empire and industry, that era's preoccupations acted upon them. Shakespeare and Herrick's tiny fairies and Goodwin Wharton's money-making miniatures gradually became marked by the exciting new world of colonialism, slaves and shopping that opened up for Europeans. And the reverse was also true. Gazing, bewildered, at pygmies or Amazon Indians, white colonists were apt to see the more familiar figures of fairies. The habits of thought used to understand native peoples and those used to describe the realms of fairy began to coalesce.

A fascinating anthology called *A description of the King and Queen of Fairies, their Habit, Fare, their Abode, Pomp and State* was printed in 1635. It is prefaced with a poem which makes explicit the connection between describing fairies and describing other strange peoples:

> Deep skilled geographers, whose art and skill
> Do traverse all the world, and with their quill
> Declare the strangeness of each several clime,
> The nature, situation, and the time
> Of being inhabited; yet all their art
> And deep informed skill could not impart
> In what set climate of this orb or isle,
> The king of Fairies kept, whose honor'd stile
> Is here inclod'd, with the sincere description
> Of his abode, his nature, and the region
> In which he rules: read, and thou shalt find
> Delightful mirth, fit to content thy mind.

As well as making descriptions of the fairies analogous to exploration and travel-writing, the poem also suggests that such descriptions are a burlesque of geographers' ambitions. Fairies are that which elude geographic observations, that which cannot be so known and described. The detailed descriptions of fairies undermine the effort of early anthropology, even as they echo its rhetoric, because the fairies' habitation, fare and clothing are fictional, drawn from the imagination and not from empiricism. Fairies problematically exceed description, restoring play and fancy and theatricality to a central position, and also restoring control to the artist. Fairies offer writers the opportunity to Make Your Own Colonial People. Such manufactured entities are bound to be more reassuring than the real thing.

Fairy freaks

But of course such reassurance applies only to the European viewer, for some attempts to manufacture an ideal colonial people use real colonial people as raw materials. However far we seem to have strayed from it, even the very literary sources I have been discussing retain a faint but traceable continuity with more popular oral culture. Now, however, we meet a fairy who is in every way the opposite of what we expect and hope fairies will be. Its only link with Mary Parish's fairies is through the marketplace, for this is a fairy who can be seen and sold for hard cash:

To be seen the next door to the Black room in West Smithfield, during the time of the Fair, being a living Skeleton, taken by a Venetian Galley, from a Turkish Vessel in the Archipelago. This is a fairy Child, suppos'd to be born of Hungarian Parents, but chang'd in the Nursing [it's a changeling], Aged Nine Years or more, not exceeding a foot and a half high. The Legs, Thighs, and Arms so very small, that they scarce exceed the bigness of a man's thumb, and the Face no bigger than the Palm of one's hand . . . It has no teeth, but is the most voracious and hungry creature in the world, devouring more victuals than the stoutest man in England.[1]

The sheer unaffected cruelty of this advertisement text, its Gothic quality, has little to do with the Merrie Englande the fairies are normally thought to inhabit. The idea of the changeling, as we have seen, was used to legitimate cruelty to children and even infanticide. This changeling, too, is a child, a real child, whose appetite lets us know it is alive, but who is presented as nothing but an 'object' on a fairground stall. It is a person who has become a symbol.

One word for such a person is a freak. The freak show is one instance of what has been called domestic orientalism – tourism without the tour, looking at scenes at home for their strangeness, seeking out the strange within a familiar setting in order to marvel at it, goggle at it, for 'it' becomes an it through the process of being looked at as one. The advertisement for the fairy freak marks its strangeness, its difference from us. Our cosy identities are stroked, caressed by its barbed and terrible difference. As Europeans encountered more and more difference, as 'new' worlds they did not understand were heaped up and threatened to overwhelm them, such meditations became imperative and were staked out on the seemingly unpromising site of the body of the fairy. When Europeans met Indians, they were confronted with something they didn't have a word for, a holding place for; the very name 'Indian' betokens European willingness to confuse something new with something old. So the familiar old supernatural strangers of Europe offered ways to interpet such new worlds, and vice versa; ways of writing about new worlds could be road-tested on the European supernatural. The freak fairy is like the eskimos brought to London by explorers searching for the Northwest Passage; she is strange, and her strangeness, her exoticism, is marvellous; it enlarges the world, and with that enlargement, the European ego also swells.

The apparent interchangeability of racial and natural oddity is shown by the peculiar status of dwarfs and midgets in the fairground freak show. Cultural critic Leslie Fiedler points out that alone of fairground freaks, dwarfs – or fairies – exist not just as sports in a normal population, but in imagination as a whole tribe, a people, a nation.[2] This is one simple reason for thinking of fairies as a 'race', or one way in which they came to be so understood.

Nor were such spectacles solely the province of the vulgar. Early modern dwarfs were displayed at court as well as in sideshows, and their popularity in Jacobean and Caroline England coincided with an enthusiasm for fairy poetry and fairy theatricals. As showman P. T.

Barnum was to do in nineteenth-century New York, the Caroline court celebrated the wedding of two dwarfs, Richard Gibson and Anne Shepherd. Charles I gave the bride away himself, and the event was celebrated with praise-poems which emphasized the spectacle of the miniature.[3] Henrietta Maria had her own dwarf, Jeffery Hudson, who was presented to her baked in the crust of a cold pie, like a girl in a cake at a businessman's party. Only eighteen inches tall, very handsome, and said to excel at cuckolding the men of the court, Jeffery's entire life was a kind of exotic, erotic romance; captured three times by pirates, he later hinted that the indignities to which they had exposed him had made him grow.[4]

It might be fair to call both Jeffery and the dwarf wedding by the highly modern word 'cute'. What happens in cuteness? What happens when we coo over something 'Oh, how cute!'? What kind of desire is this? It is the desire to rescue the cute object, cuddle it, take it home, nurture it, give it love – in other words, to buy it. The beginnings of female consumption – I shop, therefore I am – lie not in the Victorian era, but in the mid to late seventeenth century, precisely the moment when the court dwarf and the fairy baby freak surface. Why? Because there was so much more to shop for, so many exotic, delicious luxuries, trade goods, the spoils of a growing empire, spoils which included cute fairy freaks. Consumer, consumption – not, perhaps, such fun for the thing consumed. Maternal erotics can also be a love of conquest.[5] In the hazy alliance between the longing to cherish and the longing to possess, applied to dwarfs and fairy freaks, is the first, faint outline of the double-faced figure of the child-fairy who was to dominate the Victorian and Edwardian nursery.

How cosy – how centrally homelike. Yet fairy narratives always gather in whatever place is not home: the Middle East, the New World, the forests, moors and marshes of England, the Celtic terrains of Ireland and the Scottish Highlands. Literary and folkloric fairies begin to proliferate at precisely the moment when a culture begins to encounter other cultures. The first big literary starburst of fairies occurs during and after the Crusades, and centres on the Middle Eastern kingdoms; the second, in the Renaissance, after the conquest of the New World and the beginning of the slave trade, and has numerous epicentres, from the wild countryside to the Americas. I shall be exploring these strange persons and lands in due course. But first I want to visit the map-makers who charted them. For the idea that fairies were somehow like a native people meant that they were among the first subjects of anthropology.

The fairy seekers

The sixteenth and seventeenth centuries were beginning to treat 'popular' beliefs as amusing curiosities; to be recorded and described in minute detail for their quaintness. Love of such 'cute' and funny old stories became a way of marking the civility of the observer; only the really urban sophisticate could take an obsessive interest in the hilarious fancies of his forebears. Civility consisted not just in rejecting popular beliefs, but in knowing them, recording them, inscribing them – all without for one moment believing in them. The scepticism about the supernatural which resulted was the foundation of Enlightenment sciences. Edward Fairfax, who investigated and wrote about a case of demonic possession in his own family, observed that

so many are the strange follies, rooted in the opinion of the vulgar, concerning the walking of souls in this or that house, the dancing of fairies on this rock or that mountain, the changing of infants in their cradles, and the like.[6]

Seventeenth-century clergyman Richard Gough, as well as distancing himself from the beliefs he carefully records, writes that

This may confute that idle conceit that the superstitious monks and fryers did formerly persuade ignorant people that these were fays, or furies, and hobgoblins . . . Butt, truth and knowledge have, in these days, dispersed such clouds of ignorance and error.[7]

Here, the disappearance of the fairies is a symbol of the coming of 'truth and knowledge', while in Fairfax their perseverance is a sign of the persistence of folly and superstition. Either way, fairy beliefs are distinguished from the positions taken by the authors, even as those beliefs are recorded. The study of fairies and the study of beliefs in fairies are apt to blend together when early writers offer descriptions of fairy customs and appearances, for these treat both fairies and believers as objects of attentive scrutiny. In the Restoration demonologist Richard Bovet's description of country fairies near Taunton, describing fairies becomes a way of describing and understanding the people of the countryside: 'their habits used to be of red, blew, or green, according to the old way of country garb, with high-crowned hats'. The man who sees the fairy fair sees

a great company of people, that seemed to him like country folks, assembled, as at a fair; there was all sorts of commodities, to his appearance, as at our ordinary fairs, pewterers, shoe-makers, pedlars, with all kind of trinkets, fruits, and drinking booths.[8]

This conflates people of the countryside with the fairies in whom they believe. The reader is distant from both.

Yet it is the detail of the description that is striking, the apparent need to catalogue, to make a kind of reference-work of fairy behaviour and hence of rural folk behaviour. What motivated this obsessive scrutiny? This was an historical moment crowded with anxiety about the lower orders. The Elizabethan Poor Laws and their enumeration of vagrants, the enumeration of underclass criminals in conycatching pamphlets are other manifestations of the same anxiety. The thrilling list of fairies in Reginald Scot's treatise comes to stand in for the lists of troublemaking proles found in pamphlets warning against criminals. Fairies are emanations of a populace increasingly seen not as subdued, but as dangerously insubordinate. At the same time, because of fairies' associations with dutiful servants, the anxieties aroused by the lower orders can also be soothed by conflating them with fairies or symbolizing them through fairies. Better wholesome rural fairies than the restless poor of London – an idea that the Victorians took up and amplified.

In the proliferating fairy poetry of the Elizabethan, Jacobean and especially Caroline lyric, the folk fairy is both delightfully incredible and a symbol of all that is pure, pre-print, pre-civil strife. Nothing could possibly be more cosy canny than the fairies of Milton's 'L'Allegro':

Then to the spicy nut-brown ale,
With stories told of many a feat,
How faery Mab the junkets eat,
She was pinched and pulled she said,
And by the friar's lantern led
Tells how the drudging goblin sweat,
To earn his cream-bowl duly set.[9]

Milton's pastoral jollities in 'L'Allegro' include 'stories told' of Mab and Puck. Milton knows them mainly from Ben Jonson's *Entertainment at Althorp*, but describes them as if they were oral stories told by simple shepherds.[10] Just as in Shakespeare, the literary pretends to be above and beyond literacy, pretends to be anthropology, in fact. The poem could fairly be described as proto-Romantic, offering to lay bare to the reader's eye the doings of simple people excluded from the circulation of print and hence inaccessible to urban sophisticates – except, of course, through the offices of the poet himself. So what we are shown by Milton the sideshow showman is not too different from what crowds at Bartholomew Fair could see: a fairy that we cannot believe in, and so a fairy that confirms us in our urban worldliness and cleverness. Whether condemned as primitive or Popish superstition or lauded as the simple life, the fairy opposes and hence confirms urbanity, print, sophistication, scepticism.

The best-known and most influential of those who turned their obsessive, disbelieving gaze on to fairies is John Aubrey, and like the others he establishes a critical distance from what he studies:

Old customs and old wives fables are gross things, but yet ought not to be buried in Oblivion; there may be some truth and usefulness be picked out of them, besides 'tis a pleasure to consider the errors that enveloped former ages, as also the present.[11]

Old wives' tales are gross things, not refined, the opposite of civility. Yet it takes civility to appreciate them. Aubrey's pleasure depends on distance for its value. Yet he was a tireless recorder of folktales, especially tales of the occult, including several concerning fairies.

What motivated Aubrey to record, and hence to possess, a body of story that by his own account was already consigned to the past? And how did he manage to evade the tendency, which dogged other early folklorists, to convert the popular into the high by substituting Greek and Roman antiquities for the popular stories that act as clues to them? Though he was also riding the Zeitgeist, in Aubrey's case there were perhaps additional personal reasons for his interest in fairies and in the folk. Aubrey's mother stopped him from going to view more refined things by preventing him from taking the Grand Tour: 'my mother to my inexpressible grief and ruin hindered my design'. Perhaps the origin of the feminization of popular culture lies in the son's failed separation of himself from a maternal world of space and discursive authority. Having failed to enact this separation through education (the Grand Tour), Aubrey performs his own tour of the unlettered world, returning to it as an adult distant from it. The stones of Avebury and the sayings of wives must stand in for Greek and Roman antiquities, they must be objects of study in their own right, because Aubrey has been confined to their study, confined to the maternal world of old wives by the maternal refusal of the wider world of the Grand Tour.[12] So a separation that cannot be physical has to be mental. Aubrey must control the old wives' tales with his mind. It is a conquest, and a colonizing one, but also an incomplete one. Personal as Aubrey's anxieties are, they point to the way colonization is precisely that – personal, carried out by individuals as well as by cultures, and hence perhaps always anxious, uneasy under its glossy and self-assured façade.

Fairies of the empire

If we turn now to another advertisement for fairy freaks, we will be able to see the connections between Aubrey's fake fairy anthropology and questions of race:

The Lest Man and Horse in the World
The First being a little Black-Man, being but 3 foot high, who is distinguished by the name of the Black Prince, and has been shown to most Kings and Princes in Christendom. The next being his wife, the little woman, not 3 foot high ... straight and proportionable as any Woman in the Land, which is

commonly called the Fairy Queen, she gives a general satisfaction to all that sees her, by diverting them with dancing.[13]

We are so used to thinking of fairies as Caucasian, even as English, that this text is bound to come as a surprise. Robert Bogdan, an expert on freaks and fairs, writes that there are two ways to present freaks: the elevated and the exotic. The former means emphasizing the freak's civilized qualities, calling him or her by royal or noble titles, representing him or her in luxurious surroundings. The latter involves exoticizing the freak with colonial origins (like the nineteenth-century 'wild man' of Borneo).[14] Bogdan attributes both these to the nineteenth century, but actually both are evident in the wonder cabinets of the Renaissance, and in the freak show fairies in this advertisement, who are high and royal, and also exotic, tribal. In nineteenth-century freak shows, midgets and dwarfs are often given grand titles, like Count, Prince or Princess, titles reminiscent of the those given to black comic figures in minstrel shows, such as Apollo and Senator. This might appear to blur categories of high and low, but it also ridicules the pretensions of the low to the status of the high: a *black* Senator can only be funny, or at any rate odd. And a black Queen? How – cute!

Yet surprising as this text may be, it is actually part of an old fairy story. Mixing the exotic and the fairy supernatural has medieval origins. The first fairy romances are products of the Crusades era, an era when Western Europe's cultural certainties were subjected to progressive shocks through encounters with other cultures. In particular, the encounter with Byzantium was disconcerting, in part because Byzantium was so much bigger and more spectacular than anything the Crusaders had seen in Western Europe. The authentic note of hick wonder at the bright lights of the big city resounds in what Geoffroi de Villehardouin wrote in 1203:

those who had never seen Constantinople before gazed very intently at the city, having never imagined that there could be so fine a place in all the world. They noted the high walls and lofty towers encircling it, and its rich palaces and tall churches, of which there were so many that none would have believed it to be true if he had not seen it with his own eyes, and viewed the length and breadth of that city which rules supreme above all others.[15]

The first crusaders saw a city ten times the size of Paris or London, one with markets full of rare silks, spices, jewels, streets full of extravagantly dressed nobles, palaces, churches. The ante on luxury was decisively and permanently upped. Thereafter all fictional cities were attempts to go on gazing at Byzantium with the intensity it demanded. Arguably, even the later romance of Venice, the Queen of the Adriatic, is merely the continuation of this romance with Byzantium by other means, since to Venice went the silks, the artworks, the mosaics looted by the Crusaders in their fury that anything could so thoroughly outshine Western Christendom. And Byron called Venice 'a fairy city of the heart'. A mixture of acquisitive rage and admiration was provoked, a mixture that inaugurated what Edward Said identifies as orientalism: a stress on luxury, wealth, pleasure.[16] Medieval romances, however, often refuse to understand or look at Byzantium directly, but instead rationalise its splendour by making it supernatural; it is much easier to bear being outshone by fairies than by a heretical human civilization. Chrétien de Troyes uses the exoticism of the Byzantine empire in his romance *Cligés*, where the hero is the son of the Byzantine emperor. The thirteenth-century Charlemagne romance *Huon of Bordeaux* features the fairy capital Monmur, which also owes something to Byzantium. Later, drawing on these medieval traditions, the city of Ariosto's fay Alcina, in the East Indies, with a seaport and a golden wall around it, and Spenser's Cleopolis both owe something to the romance of Constantinople.[17]

Capturing Byzantium meant bringing back luxury to Europe in the form of desirable new consumer goods – come buy, come buy. Romances, too, often feature people who escape from fairyland bearing just one treasure. Perhaps the clearest and finest instance of this is the story of the Luck of Edenhall, an exotic glass cup decorated with enamel which the butler is said to have brought back from an encounter with fairies on a picnic. Unable to regain it, the fairies shouted after him, 'If the cup should break or fall/ Farewell the luck of Edenhall.' The cup is now in the Victoria and Albert Museum, where they say it is actually Syrian, probably mid-thirteenth century, and probably brought home either by a Crusader, or via a trade route opened up by the Crusades. At some point, one kind of exoticism was substituted for another; the luxury of the East was metamorphosed into the luxury of the fairy realm.[18] Exotic trade goods were fathered on the fairies, and fairies given concrete visibility by their presence in goods.

Medieval romances, dream-visions and travel literature went on to shape early modern encounters with the New World. Notions of the marvellous, and ideas of how to manage culture shock, were filtered through the stories of how heroes had encountered obstacles and strange beings and overcome them. Sometimes fairies were the obstacle, sometimes, as in *Huon of Bordeaux*, the helpers. The terms 'pigmies' and 'tribes' were used interchangeably for both fairies and peoples. In particular, the notion of a 'secret commonwealth', as Robert Kirk called the fairy kingdom, a space alongside but outside the homely, the idea of two societies living side by side, was a paradigm for the colonial situation.[19] The descriptions of fairyland that proliferate in Elizabethan, Jacobean and Caroline literature can thus be understood as a conspectus of possible descriptions of the colonial marvellous.

In England, fairies are particularly associated with uncultivated ground, wilderness. Jonson's *Oberon* begins with 'a dark rock, with trees beyond it, and all wildness that could be presented'.[20] In *Britannia's Pastorals*, the fairy court was found by descending through

> An arched cave cut in a rock entire,
> Deep, hollow, hideous, overgrown with grass,
> With thorns and briers, and sad mandragora.[21]

The country of the fairies is underground, under mountains and lakes or under hills, or, in Scotland and especially Ireland, under 'raths', or neolithic graves. The association of fairies with wild nature places them beyond the borders of what could be known, and also links English fairylands with their alternative, oriental and colonial sites.

What all these locales have in common is their opposition to the known and the homely. Fairyland is always just beyond the boundaries of the known. It began in the Holy Land. When Huon of Bordeaux encounters Oberon, it is in a wood near Jerusalem. Then fairyland gradually moved to the Middle East more generally, locating itself in northern Persia, or in central Asia. As the pace of exploration accelerated, so fairyland moved onward. Ariosto takes Boiardo's Alcina, who lives by the Black Sea, and places her in the East Indies, responding directly to the explorations of the Portuguese and Spanish. Spenser's fairies go beyond exploration as the age did. His fairyland is no longer a trading port from which exotic luxuries might be obtained, but a tract of colonial territory, sited in England's principal colonial targets, India and America, and controlled from the fairy capital, Cleopolis, or London. Spenser's fairies do not merely live in these exotic spaces; they rule them:

> The first and eldest, which that scepter swayd,
> Was *Elfin*; him all *India* obayd,
> And all that now *America* men call.[22]

Portrayals of fairyland in high romance often drew on colonial description. The East is associated with jewels – Marco Polo described the rubies, sapphires and pearls he found there; geographers associated the East with gold and silver, as well as with spices. With each new traveller's tale of untold wealth beyond the seas, the fairy marvellous had to be refurbished to provide the same frisson of wonder.[23] Guy of Warwick's fairyland is fairly simple: jewelled, moneyed, but still a plain spectacle of marvellous wealth:

> The walls were of Crystal,
> The ceiling was of fine ruwal [ruby]
> That shone swithe bright.
> The resins were of fine coral,
> To-gether joined with metal
> Within and eke without.[24]

Rather later, Boiardo's Morgan le Fay is a treasure fairy, an aristocratic version of the local fairies who left a silver coin in the shoes of tidy maids. She presides over wealth and metals found in mines. In India, the ants dig gold out of inexhaustible mines for her.[25] This fantasy of inexhaustible imperial treasure is clearly related not just to the age of exploration, but to the era of Aztec and Inca gold flooding the European money market. Perhaps a modern fairyland might be located in a Manhattan skyscraper, or an Upper East Side triplex.

Spenser retains and modifies all these ideas in his fairyland. Cleopolis is of course London, but it is not described as if it were. Instead, so strong is the association between fairyland and the Holy Land, fairyland and the Crusades, that when we finally 'see' Cleopolis, we see it in the context of and in comparison with Jerusalem, which of course surpasses it. Looking at Jerusalem, we are given a vision of Cleopolis:

> That great *Cleopolis*, where I have beene,
> In which that fairest *Faerie Queene* doth dwell
> The fairest Citie was, that might be seene;
> And that bright towre all built of christall cleene,
> *Panthea*, seemd the brightest thing, that was.[26]

The exotic seduction of fairyland is used to represent Spenser's imperial capital as a wonder, to put it on the map of the marvellous. This is getting your own back on Byzantium, for now urbanity, wealth and sophistication can be associated with *us* instead of with them. And yet the association between fairyland and the Middle East persists. It always arose partly from a longing for an ally in wars of religion; one version of Huon's story imagines a fairy army helping the Christian Franks to capture 'Babylon'. Spenser also imagines the fairy kingdom of Gloriana as an instrument in helping the British confront the Saracens.[27] Although these fantasies seem on the face of it to be harking back to the Crusades, they re-enact them because the Crusades exemplify the colonialist terror of isolation in a space not yet willing to conform itself to the maps held in the mind.

Mapping fairyland, like mapping the New World, became a way to chart the unknown. Romance narratives and the 'wonder-tale' had been used to understand and make the New World. Renaissance Spanish explorer and travel writer Bernal Díaz wrote of Tenochtitlan that

When we saw all these cities and villages built in the water, and other great towers on dry land, and that straight and level causeway leading to Mexico, we were astounded. These great towns and *cues* [pyramids] and buildings rising from the water, all made of stone, seemed like an enchanted vision from the tale of Amadis. Indeed, some of our soldiers asked if it was not a dream.[28]

Precisely the same breathless tone is found in Ben Jonson's masque *Oberon the Fairy Prince*, written for Prince Henry and performed in 1611:

There the whole scene opened, and within was discover'd the Frontispiece of a bright and glorious Palace, whose gates and walls were transparent.

'Look! Do not his Palace show/ Like another Sky of lights?', gasps the rustic Silenus.[29] This is civilization glimpsed by the low, the folk, like Geoffroi's vision of Byzantium. Here, however, we in Europe are revenged on Constantine and Montezuma. It is *our* cities and palaces that astound the locals.

Robert Kirk's *Secret Commonwealth of Elves and Fairies* describes cultural differences existing alongside ourselves in the manner of one venturing into new lands. Kirk comes complete with his own captivity narrative; his knowledge of the fairies was said to be the result of his imprisonment by them to serve them at Mass. Like Mary Rowlandson and other Indian captives, Kirk exploits his status as both inside and outside the tribe he describes. Kirk himself makes the analogy nearly explicit by calling the fairies 'the wandering tribes', and by comparing them to the native populations of the Americas. Some of what he writes figures fairies as like us, as knowable in anthropological, even in human terms:

They are distributed in tribes and orders, and have children, nurses, Marriages, Deaths, and burials, in appearance, even as we, (unless they so do for a mock-show, or to prognosticate such things among us).

He also tries for exact descriptions of fairy activity, travellers' tales:

Their women are said to Spine very fine, to Dye, to tossure, and embroider: but whither it is as manual Operation of substantial refined stuffs, with apt and solid Instruments, or only curious Cob-Webs, impalpable rainbows, and a fantastic imitation of the Actions of more terrestrial Mortals, since it transcended all the senses of the Seer to discern whither, I leave to conjecture as I found it.[30]

But such descriptions can only draw attention to fairy difference. They act like us, but the likeness dissolves under pressure from the acting. So they are *like* us, but not *the same* as us. Described as if they were a tribe, the fairies come to behave like one; they are our imitators, and hence they disturb our certainties about our own identities. This is so evidently analogous to the colonial regimes being established in America, Ireland and India, that it probably expresses colonial anxieties. In particular, both Ireland and India were already sites of experimentation in persuading the natives to take up working with cloth. Elizabeth Cary's project as wife of the Lord Deputy to Ireland, to civilize Irish women by setting up a workshop where they could learn to spin and weave cloth, is reminiscent of Kirk's fairies; *they* learn to spin in imitation of *us*, but their imitation keeps drawing attention to itself, opening up awkward splits in their – and our – identities.[31]

Such carefully colonized fairies prompted a kind of cultural exchange with the teeny-weeny fairies, so neat and dainty, as neat and dainty as servants and natives were supposed to be. We have already seen the spread of tiny fairies like Drayton's. Later, a little-known poet called Sir Simeon Steward described the fairies as a foreign court, a society coming under the anthropological or traveller's eye:

> Then did the Dwarfish Fairy Elves
> (Having First attired them selves)
> Prepare to dress their Oberon king
> In his light Robes for Revelling
> In a cobweb shirt more thin
> Than our Spider fine could spine.
> Bleached by the whiteness of the snow
> As the stormy wind doe[s] blow
>
> . . .
>
> A riche waistcoat they did bring
> Made of the Trout-flies gilded wings.
>
> . . .
>
> On every seam there was a lace
> Drawn by the unctuous snails slow trace
> To it the purest silver thread
> Compared did look like dull pale lead.
> Each button was a sparkling Eye
> Tane from the speckled Adders fry.[32]

Note the contrast between 'our' spiders and their cobwebs, which figures us as in a foreign country. The entire description relies on contrasts, of course; contrasts between the Brobdingnagian vastness of us and the tininess of them. But those contrasts can symbolize and imply others: cultural and geographical contrasts. Fairies become an empty space as oral traditions fade, and hence become a space for thinking about difference. The description parallels and recalls such descriptions as that of Sir Thomas Roe's of the Mogul king:

the King came; who at last appeared clothed or laden with Diamonds, Rubies, Pearls, and other precious vanities, so great so glorious! . . . his fingers every one with at least two or three Rings Diamonds, Rubies as great as walnuts (some greater) and Pearls such as mine eyes were amazed at.[33]

The hefty signs of wealth of the Mogul king are sometimes registered in fairy poems, as we have seen. In Steward's apparelling, however, the king's wealth is signified more obliquely than in Roe's portrait, but just as unmistakably. The king's clothes are symbols of civility. Detail in clothing was already associated with labour-intensive production, and hence with wealth. Their tininess represents labour and also leisure, as does their fragility. Garments sewn with snail slime wouldn't be very hardwearing in the woollen mills, or for that matter in the jungle. They also represent exotic cloth, exotic trade goods, for they are exotic in the sense of being unobtainable except through the medium of textual description, as well as being exotic because they are signs of riches. The 'splendour of the Orient', so central to the Western imagination, is mediated and transformed through these fairy poems. As well, these garments are insanely refined, the antithesis of both godly dress-codes and working clothes. Their preservation depends on a life of absolute – perhaps even decadent – leisure.

Yet at the same time, the Fairy King's pretensions to splendour are undercut by his smallness. His idea of himself is always burlesqued, because he does not know how small he is; he is unaware of the gigantic eyes trained upon him, of his place in the scheme of things. This lack of awareness can signify an unknowing barbarism – albeit civilized barbarism – and justify the superiority of the viewing eye. Ultimately the king, however splendidly dressed, is just a freak.

Fairies and the slave trade

A different set of pressures on the sense of self came from the beginning of the slave trade. The first significant English penetration of Guinea and Morocco began in the 1550s, and this is also when first West Africans were brought to England – to act as interpreters, but also as objects of interest in their own right, as freaks, in other words. The first African slaves are sold by John Lok in 1552, though they are eventually sent home; two English captains journey to Guinea in 1553 to break into the gold trade. The English slave trade is created by John Hawkins in 1562, beginning with a group of slaves lifted bodily from the hold of a Portuguese slaving ship.[34]

Now it is in the 1550s and 1560s that literary fairies begin to proliferate. The ostensible cause is the publication of Gawin Douglas's translation of the *Aeneid* in 1553. However, why should writers have picked up Douglas's use of the word 'fairies' and ramified it so extensively? It was natural to Douglas to translate 'nymph' as 'fairy' because he was drawing on a tradition of Scottish romance and trying to graft on to it the cultural prestige of the *Aeneid*, but his English successors did not share this motivation in quite the same way. True, Spenser and Shakespeare eagerly Anglicized fairies. But fairies also remained suspiciously 'foreign', as we have seen.

It may be worth beginning to demonstrate the connection between fairies and slaves by reminding ourselves that fairies were understood among other things as spirits that could be summoned by magicians. Numerous spells to conjure a fairy exist in manuscript, and there are also many references to fairies as familiars in witchcraft trial depositions and pamphlets.[35] The whole point about a conjured spirit is that it is your slave; it must do what you say. At the same time, conjured spirits were like slaves in other ways, could be subversive, disturbingly acting on their own desires rather than those of their master. Supposedly nothing more than the willed embodiment of those desires, they could create a worrying split in the integrity of the self by proving themselves different rather than reassuringly the same. In particular, they constantly tried to reverse the relation of ownership, seeking to enslave the master who had enslaved them. (This might seem more familiar if you think of the Faustus legend; summoned fairies are often little different from Mephistopheles.) The spectre of the slave's disobedience and even revolt lurks within fairy spells of conjuration. Most significantly, the fairy summoned, according to one spell, could not be dismissed, but had to remain with the summoner for ever. The idea of the slave trading society as bound to its slaves, unable to escape from their uncanny and imperfect replication of its desires, is represented in the permanence of the fairy–master relationship.

One might even argue that such fictive slaves were woven into stories which allowed people to imagine – perhaps even to long for – real slaves. Like slaves, too, and especially like slaves in the New World, fairies summoned by magicians could transform rags into riches instantly, overturning the old social order in which people knew their place. Like the slave and the slave trade as a whole, the fairy advances his master's social position by apparent sleight of hand; the wealth he produces is unearned. We have already seen the number of people hanging about the English countryside desperate to meet a well-heeled and benevolent fairy who could decisively advance their class position. This get-rich-quick logic is rather like early notions of what colonialism and empire meant; getting away with the wealth of native peoples and using it to advance the position of oneself or one's country. The first sea captains to penetrate Africa were simply after gold; then John Hawkins realized that the slave trade was so profitable that he was able to persuade various Tudor grandees to invest in his trading voyages, making profits of as much as 60 per cent on his investment. Hawkins himself was eventually knighted, taking as his crest a black female African, thus signifying the origins of his spectacular social advance.

Fairies give form and narrative shape to anxieties which are retold later about slaves and Africans, as well as about all other peoples not 'white'. Miscegenation fears can be expressed through the story of the changeling, the fairy baby substituted by the fairies for a human child kidnapped by them. The kind of worry about sameness and otherness represented in these stories can be glimpsed in the figurative use of the term 'changeling' in Thomas Nashe's polemic against inkhorn terms. Nashe calls his opponent 'the factor for the fairies and night urchins, in supplanting and setting aside the true children of the English, and suborning inkhorn changelings in their stead'.[36] The fairy changeling is a foreign upstart. The changeling is invariably ugly, and by contrast the human baby is beautiful and charming, like the significantly Indian page-boy that Oberon and Titania both covet in *A Midsummer Night's Dream*. The changeling is a mark of the terror of a society that could no longer feel confident of its own perfect self-replication.

Finally, we always think of fairies as Caucasian. Not so the early modern period. Rather, fairies are often described via what has been called 'the trope of blackness', the figuration of a proto-racial polarity via the language of dark and light.[37] John Walsh, tried for witchcraft in 1566, contended that 'there be iii kindes of Feries, white, greene and black', while Scot wrote of 'white spirits and blacke spirits, gray spirits and red spirits'. Black fairies were also, said John Walsh, 'the woorst'.[38] Milton's 'swart faery' in *Comus* is 'dark' (435). He is a dwarf, but he recalls the Indian and African slaves in the treasure mines of the Spanish empire. Milton's 'fairy of the mine' also gestures at the wealth of fairies like Alcina, guardian of the precious metals of the New World. Mine-spirits generally are apt to be black, providing an explanation for their colour which harmonized only too well with the notion that blacks were the natural people to work in such places. In *The Masque of Cole-Orton*, mine-spirits are connected with gypsies: 'Ye dancing spirits of the Pits, such as look to Toms Egyptians here, & help them hole & drive sharp their Picks & moindrils.'[39] Ben Jonson refers to 'olive-coloured spirits' in *The Gypsies Metamorphosed*. Most crucially, an incident at the Woodstock masque brings together this rhetoric of blackness and enslavement with the logic of identifying fairies with the homely and hence with Englishness in a moment when a fairy is 'whitened' by contact with Elizabeth. Presenting herself to the queen, the fairy explains her transition from blackness to whiteness as follows:

> This love hath caused me transform my face,
> And in your hue to come before your eyes,
> Now white, then black, your friend the fairy Queene.[40]

The benign beams of Elizabeth's love translate the fairy from blackness to whiteness, wash the Ethiop white. Alternative images – where an encounter between the white and the black result in blackening, miscegenation, were prolific enough for the effect to be understood. Fairies too are blackeners; in Thomas Randolph's *Amyntas*, for instance, the fairies 'tattoo o'er thy vulgar skin/Until thou art an Indian king', or as they have it (for these fairies, like others, are fond of Latin verse): 'Statim Dices tibi datam/ Cutem valde variatam' ('immediately you have been given a highly speckled skin').[41] What if the natives turn us black? It may not be irrelevant either to note that the fairy who most resembled a household slave was called the 'brownie', a name which suggests darkness. Brownies, like slaves, did household and farm chores in exchange for enough food to stay alive; a bowl of milk or cream was the usual payment. Brownies were capricious, however; they could and did rebel, absconding if skimmed milk were substituted for cream. Both the pleasures and anxieties of slave-owning were displaced on to fairies, and later fairies and fairy stories were used to further interpret relations between master and slave.

In Shakespeare's *The Tempest*, magic and fairies come together – not without jarring and quarrelling – with questions of rule, authority, knowledge and control over unknown terrains. As many post-colonial critics have noted, Ariel no less than Caliban is a native of the island, and like Caliban becomes a servant to a colonial master. Ariel is not only fairylike in being a summoned spirit, but also fairylike in being a slave, and a slave who advances his master's social position. Of course, Prospero's advancement is *really* a restoration, since he *is* the Duke of Milan and no upstart. Prospero may not be an upstart, but his dark counterparts Stephano and Trinculo are as upstart as they come. Their efforts to obtain Caliban for a freakshow not only parallel Prospero's enslavement of the monster, but also connect Caliban to the freaks shown at Bartholomew Fair. By displaying him, they hope to make their fortunes, and we have already seen that displays of this kind were prototypes for the slave trade: 'If I can recover him, and keep him tame, and get to Naples with him, he's a present for any emperor that ever trod on neat's leather.'[42] Like Prospero, and like John Hawkins the first slave trader, Stephano and Trinculo kidnap their slave from another, earlier slaver; Caliban changes masters, consents to his captivity. It is just this consent that Prospero keeps trying to wring from Ariel, who has likewise been released from another enslavement.

Prospero appears to be Ariel's rescuer, but in fact enslaves him; perhaps it allowed Hawkins to excuse his actions in a similar fashion, for Elizabeth I urged him strongly not to carry off slaves without their consent, a thing 'which would be detestable and call down the vengeance of heaven upon the undertakers'.[43]

Ariel is not *really* consenting, however. He is a spirit – no one in the play ever calls him a fairy, and he lacks the social context normally shared by fairies. But he resembles fairies in his abilities, his tendency to enforce behaviour by pinching, and above all his miniaturization: 'Where the bee sucks, there suck I' is stylistically a reversion to the cute teeny-weeny fairies of the *Dream*. But unlike unruly Puck, who in the play and its imitators frustrates his masters, Ariel *must* obey Prospero, even when he wants only his freedom. In his first debate with Prospero, Ariel enunciates the slave's touching faith that meritorious behaviour might lead to freedom:

> Remember I have done thee worthy service,
> Told thee no lies, made no mistakings, served
> Without or grudge or grumblings. Thou didst promise
> To bate me a full year.[44]

Of course Prospero at once explains that Ariel must remain a slave because he, Prospero, rescued him from slavery. And for the rest of the play Ariel's pattern of behaviour is repeated again and again; he performs, he wants his freedom, he is rebuffed. This relationship between spirit and magician is a representation of that between master and slave. It is upon Ariel that Prospero's mastery of the island depends, his symbolic wealth. And yet eventually Prospero does give Ariel his freedom, though that 'freedom' seems contingent on the end of the play in a manner that reminds us yet again that the prototype of the slave trade was the side-show, the court attraction. When the show is over, the showman is freed from his role, as are his attractions. 'Let your indulgence set me free', begs Prospero himself in the final line of the often-discarded epilogue. Prospero ceases to be a magician – or an actor – and dismisses the slave who gave him power. And an audience. In doing so, he liberates himself from the terrible burden of colonialism, and returns to the comfort of the pre-colonial world.

Tiresome tinies

After such spectacular and majestic outbursts, it is depressing to revert to the mundane repetitiveness of eighteenth-century fairy poetry, in which many a hack author recycles the teeny-weeny fairy motif without charm, and without either the twin pressures of folklore or empire. Only Pope makes much of tininess, but the sylphs of *The Rape of the Lock*, though owing a little to fairy poetry, are also comprehensively devoid of its vitality, and that is the point of them. Like the teeny-weeny fairies we have already met, the sylphs preside over the commodities brought by empire, from tea and silks to all Arabia in a box. But unlike Drayton's king and queen, the sylphs flutter hopelessly in a world of giants, giants whom they are supposed to serve, as Ariel serves Prospero. But while Prospero's Ariel is triumphantly obedient, not all Ariels were so successful. The heroine of *The Rape of the Lock* is also attended by an obedient Ariel, but he fails utterly to protect and serve his mistress, Belinda. Perhaps the colonist had by now lost faith in his 'inferiors'? How stupid the servants are, Belinda might have murmured. Pope was the first to see that the tiny fairy was becoming debased currency, comic rather than touching. Just as the sylphs are really too flimsy to withstand the pressures to which the mock-epic subjects them, so fairy poetry was likewise exhausted, left limp and gasping by the onslaught of imitativeness.

But rescue was at hand in the shape of a Romantic revival, which in fairy lore began with the publication of Thomas Percy's *Reliques of Ancient English Poetry* in 1765. Soon eager imitations of folklore, particularly what was taken to be Scottish folklore, were on hand to breathe new life into the dead of fairyland; Herrick's milk-drinking fairies pack their bags for the Celtic fringes in William Collins's *Ode on the Popular Superstitions of the Highlands* (1788). As always, fairyland is pushed out beyond the boundaries of the known; in British Isles terms, this means that as the English countryside filled up with towns and canals and industry, fairyland is consigned to the edges of the land, as well as the edges of memory.

William Blake did not offer renewal, but a kind of uncanny anticipation of Victorian sanitization. Or did he, like other Romantics, need inauthentic fairies to believe in real ones? Blake believed he had seen a fairy funeral in his own garden, and he was capable of writing poems which were simply a more rustic version of the standard, tired old take on the wee, wee folk, not even worth quoting. At other times, though, Blake went out of his way to link fairies with the coquettishness which repels the proper desires of the body. In 'Long John Brown and Little Mary Bell', Blake uses the cute, pseudo-rustic form of teeny fairy poems to mock the prudishness which certainly went with them by the Edwardian era. Little Mary Bell had a fairy in her nut, which leaves her to inhabit the guts of her would-be seducer. Blake, then, follows Pope in linking fairies with a kind of feminine disembodiment. But he had few followers, and all he really added to the fairies was an anxious though prescient diagnosis of what they would come to mean by 1900.

The Magic Flute

When rescue came, it was from the German-speaking world, in the form of the Queen of the Night. Mozart's *The Magic Flute* is often seen as misogynist, because the women-only world of the Queen of the Night is eventually defeated. However, most audiences are more likely to remember the searing violence of the queen's coloratura than Sarastro's sensible, moralizing baritone. An elegant parody of a shrill woman's voice it may be, but it is also steely, powerful beyond imagination and as sharp as shards of glass. Vocal display and virtuosity make the Queen of the Night's aural power the equivalent of seeing a vivid kingfisher in a flock of rooks. It is not virtuous, like Pamina's creamy soprano, but it is chillingly, spine-tinglingly powerful – and about as inhuman a sound as the human throat can make. It is in fact the perfect musical correlative for both the old fairy queen of folklore and the new emerging fairy queens of glittering stage. Only Mozart could have created a death-fairy that is also a panto and even a drag queen, and in doing so anticipated, and heretically combined, what Victorian England would work out carefully and laboriously.

The Romantic fairy: Goethe and Keats

In 1782, a German poet wrote a terrifying, sharp-edged story of the death of a child at the hands of a monster whose existence cannot even be acknowledged by his father.[45]

The boy and his father are riding together on a windy night. The boy is wrapped warmly in his father's arms. Suddenly he covers his face; he sees the *Erlkönig*, the Erl-King, with his cloak and crown. It is only the mist, says his father. And now the Erl-King begins to sing to the little boy, whispering in his ear. 'Come with me dear child./ I'll play such lovely games with you,/ And we'll find bright flowers on the shore./ My mother has such lovely golden robes.' But the father cannot hear the Erl-King's song; it was just dry leaves, he says, dry leaves that rattle in the wind. The Erl-King promises the child that his daughters will dance for him all night in a ring, that they will hold him and rock him and love him. The daughters beckon to the child. The father insists they are only willows.

Does he know? What is it with adults who cannot see things? Is the father merely clinging to the everyday, the incontestably real, when confronted by the terror of what can never be known? His refusal to know, the poem implies, dooms his son. Now the Erl-King's seduction has failed, and he proceeds to force. 'I love you, I am drawn by your beauty/ If you are not willing, I'll force you to come!' And now the child gives a great heartbreaking cry: 'My father, my father, his fingers grip me,/ The Erl-King has hurt me so!' And at last his father believes him, realizes the danger, riding fast, holding his child in his arms. But when he reaches home, the boy is dead.

Thirty-seven years later, a young man in England who knew he was dying of consumption also told the story of a youth taken to death by the fairies. A young knight is lingering by a lake, under the frost of winter. He looks ill, pale. He begins to tell a story of meeting a lady, a lady who sang to him, picked flowers for him, became his lover. And she lulled him to sleep, and he began to dream. This was his dream: pale kings and princes, death-pale, call to him, and they warn him that he is under a spell, held captive, by the beautiful lady without mercy.

And he wakes, alone, on the cold hillside. And now he sings his own, winter song. He will sing it till he dies.[46]

What does the Erl-King want with the boy? Sex? Service? What does La Belle Dame want with the knight-at-arms? Sex? Death? Service? Neither poem explains. The desire of both the Erl-King and La Belle Dame is a cypher, a riddle that neither the reader nor the poet can answer; it baffles and frustrates their victims, the boy, the knight. To be a Romantic poet is not about being the one who desires, the one who pursues. On the contrary, Romantic poets are haunted by poetry which threatens to possess them in its longing for them. Think of Coleridge's three great poems: 'The Rime of the Ancient Mariner', 'Kubla Khan', 'Christabel'. Each concerns a person taken from themselves by strong, violent, supernatural forces. Think of Keats's odes, where the speaker is reft away from himself by contemplation. The myth of Romantic poetry is that the poet is like a prophet possessed by the choking, rapturous presence of the god; what emerges from such possession is not the poet's desire, but the god's. And how can mortals know the desires of gods? Both the Erl-King and La Belle Dame are muses; they speak through poets. But the unknowability of their own wants and needs stands for their terrible difference from us and from the other mortals in the poem. It is a privilege to be loved by them, to be chosen by them, but a deadly one. Both the boy and the knight literally die of incomprehensible difference.

Coleridge's pixies and the cave

In Coleridge's poem on a pixy's cave, the prologue is more striking in some ways than the poem itself.[47] Coleridge describes a pixies' cave, one that contains a trace, a text, from his own childhood, the autographs of his brother and himself. The pixies are literally guardians of the poet's past, and the interior of the cave is inscribed with his childhood. These inscriptions, key to a lost past, are *also* a way of describing the poem, which evokes a past of rural folklore which for Coleridge is assumed to be fading, dying. The poem *also* commemorates another piece of the past, because the young Coleridge conducted a party to the Pixies' Cave, a party of young ladies. One of the young ladies is 'of stature elegantly small, and of complexion colourless yet clear', and she 'was proclaimed the Faery Queen'. From childhood to adolescent sexual awakening in one breathless Romantic leap; both childhood and adolescence and their sudden changes are conflated with the supernatural pixies, made magical by a link with magic, so that magic can come to represent both the time before sex and sex itself. The cave is now a place of encounter with a magical woman, a cavern haunted by the spectres of the past. The commonplace pixies' cave is the forerunner of that much grander cavern, 'measureless to man', with its mighty fountain and mourning woman wailing for her demon lover, the cavern beneath the palace of Kubla Khan.

For this woman, wailing is not part of the oriental mythology of the poem, nor part of its classical antecedents. She comes from Scottish folklore, from a ballad that tells a story, a familiar story, the story of a woman who meets a man in the woods, a man in black and green, and lies with him, and is betrayed by him. She intrudes into the poem; she is not in the cavern beneath Kubla's palace at all. Rather, she is in some different, undescribed cavern, one to which Kubla's cavern is merely compared. Her story is the usual one, the story of the Erl-King, the story of La Belle Dame sans Merci. 'Mister, I met a fairy once', it goes. When Coleridge wants to create a romantic cavern – a Romantic cavern, if you will – it requires a fairy.

And not just any fairy. A fairy who imparts a hurt, a grief, that can only find utterance in poetry, in song. Like the knight, the woman with the demon lover is telling her story: she is wailing. The role of the fairy muse is to break silence, to force speech and sound from those visited by that deadly inspiration. She is the last incarnation of the sovereignty hag, and the power she brings is the power of poetry. The fairy muse was later to receive a new lease of life from a new generation of poets on the other side of the Irish Sea, but in the meantime some strange adventures were to befall her.

7

Victorian Fairies

It is in Victorian England that fairyland, like everywhere else, undergoes a population explosion. Fairies, elves, gnomes and small winged things of every kind multiply into swarms and infest writing and art and the minds of men and women. Perhaps it is only natural that people should explain this expansion in the same way that they explain the terrestrial population explosion: as the result of urbanization and industrialization. Romantic fairies, as we have seen, are part of the Romantic opposition to the world of work, professions, cities, factories and confused identities. But just as the Victorians by no means accepted the entire programme of the Romantics, choosing which parts to keep and which to throw away, so they did not accept Romantic fairies completely, untransformed; fairies changed with changing fashions. As Regency gowns ballooned into hoops, so fairies altered too. The main reason for the alteration was not only pragmatic. Many Victorians – rather like us – wanted somehow to have the countryside and also the benefits of the Industrial Revolution – to have fairies, but not Queen Mab. In an age of progress, one way to square this circle was to see ideal, unspoilt innocence as a phase. The Victorians took up the Romantic notion of the child as perfect innocent, and linked that innocent child with fairies. A lot was lost along the way. A fairy linked with a childhood innocent of, among other things, sexuality, could never be a beautiful lady without mercy. But other things were retained, including – particularly at the end of the nineteenth century – rather rebellious portraits of fairies who were indeed children, but children as savages, animals or amoralists.

Cinderella

Cinderella's fairy godmother is not a fairy in every version of the story. In George Cruikshank's moralized version, the godmother is a dwarf, though Cinderella realizes she must really be a fairy. A nineteenth-century attempt to turn Cinders into a kind of frothy drawing-room comedy leaves the fairy godmother on the cutting-room floor, replacing her with a kind, earthly godmother with a helpful servant who is always dashing out to the shops for a fresh gown.[1] At this point, the jig is up, for such transformation scenes reveal what the fairy god-mother has stood for all along: class advancement. The magnificent dress she gives to Cinderella signifies perfect *civilité*; the glass slippers are signs of ladyhood, because no one could hike down a country road nor clean out the grate wearing them without breaking them. Glass slippers are a sign of a life of leisure, like long fingernails. In the countless pasteboard souvenirs produced for children, to be sold after pantomimes – penny plain and twopence coloured, as they were called – Cinderella's inability to be a servant while *en grande tenue* is further shown by her tall coiffure, which would fall down at once if she tried to scrub the floor. Now that Cinderella is dressed for the part, she can be the part. The recent film version of Cinderella, *Ever After*, made this even clearer by showing that court dress was actually a kind of disguise. And this modern Cinders isn't really an upstart; she deserves to get on because she is kind and good. The fairy godmother is a means of obtaining all this largesse without evil consumption; indeed, from Perrault onwards, Cinderella's prudent housewifery is routinely con-trasted with the doomed and fashion-conscious consumption of her stepmother and stepsisters. If the fairy godmother is simply replaced with an American Express Platinum Card, the fear that anyone might simply buy status is aroused. The story gets around this by delegating the bills to someone for whom they have no meaning. In *Ever After*, there is no fairy godmother, but there is (believe it or not) Leonardo da Vinci, who comes up with a pair of wings to signify and legitimate Nicole/Cinderella's ascent. Genius in the modern sense does duty for genius in the ancient sense; not a spirit but a Great Mind can elevate Nicole. Elsewhere, though, the credit card has come quite calmly to take the place of the fairy, as in *Pretty Woman*, the saccharine film about a hooker who is transformed into a businessman's consort. It is his credit card that transforms her, and this is not a matter of discomfort to the film. Rather, it gleefully celebrates her elevation, literally figured by her daily ride to the penthouse in a lift. The moral drawn by Perrault – that it pays to have a fairy godmother – draws attention to the National Lottery win aspect of fairy tales, which of course was the reason the powerless enjoyed them. And as if to confirm the tradition, the National Lottery itself took to using the image of a fairy's wand to symbolize its power to change lives.

It is Dickens, with characteristic flair, who makes the fairy of Cinderella a respectable helpmeet of the bourgeois rather than an unfair liberator of the underclass. In his fairy tale 'The Magic Fishbone', Princess Alicia, unlucky member of a royal family which has fallen on hard times and is living the life of the struggling middle classes, has a fairy godmother, the fairy Grandmarina. But Grandmarina has no intention of giving Alicia an effortless passport to the aristocracy. She gives the princess a magic fishbone, but firmly and testily urges her not to use it until her own resources are exhausted. Alicia, Cinderella-like, is obliged to look after her seventeen younger siblings, tend the baby and nurse the queen, 'for there were not many servants in that Palace'. In every domestic crisis Alicia copes gamely, ignoring her father's hints that she should use the magic fishbone, until finally her father confesses that he is very poor, though he has tried his best. Alicia at last invokes the fishbone, but only to wish it was quarter-day, when her father's salary arrives.[2] The gross incompetence of Alicia's father, and his slothful longing to rely on magical aid, is the kind of cold-eyed critique of grown-ups which becomes ever more frequent in fairy literature, reaching an apogee in Barrie's grossly unjust Mr Darling. By the standards of fairytale morality – the very morality enjoined by adults upon children – adults themselves can be found wanting. And if fairies were later to become an adult fantasy of childhood, perhaps the fairy godmother is a child's fantasy adult: appearing only when required, and then at once willing to hand out the readies without argument or exhortation. A kind of disembodied credit card indeed. But not here; here the credit card has a very definite upper limit. Alicia is eventually provided with a prince and a splendid wedding feast as a reward, but since she is destined to have thirty-five children, it is evident that her patience, tact and domestic capacities will still be required. This is a Cinderella for whom the grate is not a punishment, but an opportunity to use talents and capacities that would be wasted in a life of greater luxury.

The early Victorians were afraid of fairies and tales. As late as the 1860s, they were associated for some with the revolution in France, and perhaps that makes sense when we consider their dizzying power to alter the social place of individuals, and their place at the forefront of radical and Romantic poetry. They were also, of course, insufficiently moral – Sarah Trimmer, writer and moralist, complained that Cinderella 'did not supply any moral instruction level to the infantine capacity'.[3] The early Victorians tried to correct the problem; the first really moral fairies are perhaps those in Catherine Sinclair's *Holiday House* (1839), a curious irony in a book famed for its breaks with the literature of improvement. Harry and Laura's uncle David tells them a 'nonsensical story about Giants and fairies', in which the protagonist, a wicked and idle glutton called Master No-Book, is visited by 'two magnificent fairies, just arrived from their castles in the air'. One strongly resembles the pantomime fairy:

the fairy Do-Nothing was gorgeously dressed with a wreath of flaming gas around her head . . . Her cheeks were rouged to the very eyes – her teeth were set in gold, and her hair was of a most brilliant purple.

The fairy Teach-All, on the other hand, is simply dressed in white muslin. The former offers a life of ease, while the latter offers purpose. Naturally, No-Book chooses the former – as who would not? – but is soon surfeited by luxury, particularly when it transpires that the fairy has a deal with a local giant, who periodically eats her idle followers. (It is all rather reminiscent of *Watership Down*, in which the luckless rodents who lead leisured lives are really the victims of a farmer who regularly snares them.) Of course a happy ending looms – Fairy Teach-All kills the giant, liberates No-Book and reforms him. Here the fairies have no reality of their own, and their reality is not central to the story. Simply alligators, who should stay on the banks of the Nile, they do not make any appeal whatsoever to imagination or even fancy. They derive from the stage, and what works on stage backed by spectacle does not entrance in book form. More eccentrically, and far more worryingly, the best-selling *Better Than Fairies* imports into moral tales the anxieties provoked by theatrical fairies. Set in Germany, home of the Brothers Grimm and their *märchen*, it tells of poor children who live in a great forest with their widowed mother. Soon one of the children falls ill, while another asks, 'If a fairy came – what would you choose?' At last, they agree to write a letter to Jesus Christ asking for food and shoes. Jesus smiles at such simple faith, and through the goodness of the postal clerk and others, who of course see the letter, the children get their shoes and food. Plainly worried that wishing on fairies would undermine faith in Jesus, the book is nevertheless obliged to resort to selling Jesus to the young as a kind of superior fairy. Eventually, one of the children dies, in an ecstasy, knowing that Heaven yawns before him.[4] To die is not an awfully big adventure.

Natural fairies

The fairy and the fairytale were eventually rescued. Not long after, however, the idea of the countryside fairytale, rustic and peaceable, became thinkable after publication of the first translations of the stories of the Brothers Grimm. Urban stories about social-climbing hussies might be revolutionary, but the 'simple' stories of the Common People could be as conservative as you please. The Merrie Englande of the Young England movement, in which happy peasants danced round maypoles, was also the place where fairies could roam without alarming conservatives. In this non-existent rural idyll, rich and poor are benevolently linked, with no awkward and bumptious middle classes. The demonization of industrialization and urbanization was short lived in political reality; Young England folded in 1846.[5] But aesthetically it effectively drew the teeth of the Romantic fantasies of natural and supernatural aesthetics. For Victorian thinker John Ruskin, fairytales were all well and good in their local setting:

they belong properly to districts in unblemished country, and in which a healthy and bustling town life, not highly refined, is relieved by, and contrasted with, the calm enchantment of pastoral and wood-land scenery ... under conditions of this kind the imagination is ... never so much impressed with its supernatural phantasies as to be in danger of retaining them as part of its religious influence upon the character of the mind.[6]

So the proles can be entrusted with fairy stories provided they are living in controlled conditions. From then on, nothing could check the spread of Victorian fairies across the countryside. However, as we shall see, some fairies stubbornly refused to conform to the ideology they were supposed to exemplify, and fairies could serve several purposes.

The dazzling fairies of the footlights

When we think of Victorian fairies, what comes first to mind is probably a poem, or a painting, or a children's book. But for many Victorians, particularly early Victorians, fairies would have conjured up a vision of theatrical splendour. At the climax of an entertainment full of songs, jokes and a fairytale plot, the lights go down. New lights dawn. There is music – yearning, lyrical. First the gauzes lift slowly one after the other, giving glimpses of the realm beyond. Clouds and banks of flowers are revealed. Diverse lights in brilliant colours illuminate girls – dozens of girls – slowly ascending, apparently by magic, dressed in filmy fronds of tulle and tarlatan, glittering with tinsel. Girls perch on pedestals draped in material to look like clouds, jewels, banners. As the clouds and banks slowly part, new ascending groups of fairy girls are revealed, with a pyramid of fairies mounting slowly in the centre. Some of the fairies seem to float in the air, or rest on the fragile branches of trees. Finally at last, at the back, the brightest light comes to rest on the most beautiful, the most elaborately robed, the Fairy Queen. The music rises in a crescendo of triumph. The transformation scene is still. It is complete. A stout man in black comes out and makes an awkward bow.

This is based very closely on a Victorian description of a Transformation Scene – scenes which could take place in pantomimes, or in what were called 'spectaculars' and 'fairy extravaganzas', highbrow pantomimes with less comedy and more visual display.[7] Such scenes could last upwards of twenty minutes. There is a Busby Berkeley feeling about some of these scenes; perhaps the only way we can really grasp their impact and their attraction is by a re-viewing of prewar musicals. Alternatively, we might think of special-effects movies, where the goal is simply to show the audience something it has not seen before. In *Harlequin and Sindbad the Sailor* (1881), the fairies of the Valley of Jewels carried white wands surmounted by capital letters in copper, spelling out the names of jewels in words of blazing light. Others reached for High Art, for the target audience was not the working classes, but the middle classes, the better-off. Collins's *Sleeping Beauty* sought to evoke Venice, with a crystal fountain made of Venetian glass. In the 1830s, such scenes were innovations, the acme of modernity.[8]

These pantomime fairies are the antithesis of the Romantic fairies who were a version of pastoral; they may represent a pure visual realm apart from everyday life, but the means by which they are produced are constantly subject to scrutiny, and those means are industrial, not rural. The paradox of presenting an ideal at odds with the means by which it is presented is especially clear in a drawing published by the *Strand Magazine* (1893), entitled 'Lifting a Fairy'. Four burly stage-hands raise a fairy on a small trapdoor – a kind of elevator, employed for appearances and disappearances, to make the supernatural appear at will. The fairy's femininity, ethereal costume and rapt, elevated expression contrast sharply with the burly stage-hands and practical, rough wooden trap and surround. This contrast, as we shall see, was something of a source of anxiety to the spectators.

Such illustrations, and the articles about How It Was All Done which accompanied them, were the Victorian equivalent of today's pieces on cinematic special effects and CG animation. Everyone understood that they were watching not a triumph of the supernatural, but a triumph of technology. Books like *The World Behind the Scenes* explained how every trick was done; how the Fairy Godmother transformed Cinderella's dress from rags to riches with a wave of her wand, for instance. They mean that everyone knew that watching the supernatural really meant watching machinery. Similarly, when electricity was introduced to the London theatres in the 1880s and 1890s, it was at once used to ornament fairyland: from *Iolanthe* (1881) onwards, tiny electric lights powered by batteries sparkled in the hair, among the floral ornaments and on the costumes of female dancers. Fairyland was a chance to display the latest technological wizardry – it is not insignificant that we still refer to techno-*Wizards*. The more romantic such fairies appear, that is, the more 'authentic' they look, the more they can hardly help celebrating and advertising the advanced technology that creates them. Whereas Romantics and, later, the creators of cute nursery fairies wanted to see fairies as the antithesis of machinery, the stage told a different tale. Machinery had brought fairies to heel, tamed their capriciousness, reduced their wills. Now it was the trap-plan and the trapdoor hand who decided when a fairy should appear. Such modern invocations could make fairies appear at the same point every night, could show the audience things that had never been seen before, could garner treasure – box-office takings.

Of course, it took more than clumsy men in black coats to make such transformations. It also took hundreds of girls. The pantomime fairy, aged between seven and twelve years, emerged every winter to enhance the Christmas spectacles. There were about 1,000 such children in London every Christmas, and 5,000 or so nationwide. The majority of these children were extras, adornments, part of a large-scale spectacle. Such spectacles, crowded but ordered, were often visions of the urban crowd redeemed, and the habit of 'framing' fairy transformations with everyday urban life emphasized the idea that what was being transformed was the unruly mob of the modern street. By making an alliance with urban life and with industry, the fairy could transform them into something that accorded with Victorian ideas of what was beautiful and elevating. So had the fairy lost altogether her uncanny quality?

No. For the stage fairy, more than any other, trod some very dangerous borderlands, and she was not empowered to tread them. For the whole point of a special effect is that we know it isn't real even while we treat it as if it were real. The pantomime and spectacular fairies were not really fairies, but fairy impersonators. They straddled a number of divisions central to Victorian society, divisions between adulthood and childhood, artifice and sincerity, industry and country, machines and imagination. To understand why the pantomime fairy seemed a dreadful hybrid, a fearful spectacle of things combined that ought to have been forever separate, we have to understand the context in which the Victorian raptures about children were produced. The Romantic invention of the child as the holy innocent coincided with the increasing employment of children in factories, with urbanization, with growing child poverty, with child prostitution. At the very moment when Wordsworth, and later Dickens, extolled the purity of the child, children were rising at dawn and returning home from work at midnight. The Victorians were deeply and anxiously alive to the contradiction.[9] Some responded to the anomaly by equating the Romantic child with a kind of Hobbesian vision of savagery. In the 1840s, particularly, there was anxiety about the idleness of children, especially the sinister street children. This mentality sought to rectify the anomaly in the direction of seeing the child as a citizen, deleting the Romantic aspect of the child. Just as African savages needed to be saved and civilized, so the street child also needed attention. Constantly compared to an Arab, and like an animal too: 'all within the desolate creature is barren wilderness', worried Dickens.[10] Work, regular work, and the obligations it brought with it could be the saviour of such savages. The future, however, lay with those who responded to the pressure by pleading that the contradiction be resolved in favour of the Romantic child. Childhood was to become a refuge from the increasing demands of the world of work and capital. For these social reformers, childhood was the antithesis of work, and childhood a time of play, innocent pleasure or enjoyment. Children were not supposed to contribute to the family purse, and any sign that the family actually needed their contributions reflected very badly on the parents. The happiest situation for young children was a free life in the country. Working came to seem inimical to the very idea of childhood – just as it does to us. Henry Mayhew, author of the classic social survey *London Labour and the London Poor*, interviewed a little girl who sold watercress in Covent Garden, and was horrified to find her

in thoughts and manner a woman. There was something cruelly pathetic in hearing this infant, so young that her features had scarce formed themselves, talking of the bitterest struggles of life ... I asked her about her toys and games with her companions, but the look of amazement that answered me soon put an end to any attempt at fun on my part.[11]

The idleness of fairies, who had at most a few light household duties, was the perfect symbol of the new childhood.

All the more reason, then, to worry over stage fairies. Children of the stage were workers. Yet they worked at representing the ideal child. The child-actor impersonating a fairy in a spectacular transformation scene encapsulated in her small body both the glittering ideal of the innocent child and the reality of the working child. Deconstructing the gap between the child and work, and unpicking the duality of child-hood innocence and elaborate artifice, the stage child threatened to show the ideal child as nothing but a manufactured image, an image manufactured at the expense of the real child. As such, she was a threat to the image, a threat that had to be neutralized. This contradiction was lovingly reiterated and worried at by those moralists who found it offensive:

Most children to whom a visit to a pantomime is one of the greatest treats of Christmas have, at one time or another, imagined that nothing could be more delightful than to be one of the fairies posing in glittering garb around their queen, in halls of splendour and brilliancy. The young fairies themselves, however, take a very different view of the case. To them the pantomime means business ... [they] belong for the most part to the poorest classes, and fortunate they deem themselves if they are ranked among the numbers of the elect of fairyland ... They get into bad company ... amid the tinsel splendours of the stage, they acquire a taste for finery which later on leads them to all kinds of mischief, and unfits them for work in any other station of life. The acting and posing deprive them in many cases of the naturalness of children, and convert them into coquettes before they have even reached their teens.[12]

Note the objections: the fairies appear a cut above the middle-class audience, but are really a cut or two below. Impersonation becomes social confusion when the poor acquire a taste for finery, for tinsel splendour. (Without the stimulus of the stage, the poor would of course happily wear worsted.) This is about class, but it is also about sex. The fairies are female, and here a taste for finery and glitter probably means a consciousness of oneself as an object, someone to be looked at, and this is only a ha'penny away from recognizing that the way one looks has redeemable cash value. For if money and concern with money is the antithesis of childhood, what may lie behind this is fear of prostitution, fear that children will begin to sell themselves. What especially worried the moralists was the possibility that young girls would be led into sexual unruliness by the stage. Arguing against a defender of child-actors, the women's rights campaigner Millicent Fawcett refutes her argument that child-actors do not become whores, because in a home for fallen women only two are former actors:

It would certainly be a rather startling development or religious revival that would bring a Miss Jocelyn Montague and a Miss Nina Montmorency, who make five toilettes a day, whose persons are adorned with diamonds, laces, and furs, who drive a smart victoria by day and a neat brougham at night, on the modest salary of £2 per week, if they trooped to a home.[13]

The whole worry was not that children would fail to become successful whore-actresses, but that they would succeed.

The same anxiety lay behind worries about scanty costumes. The children's lack of clothing was also a concern – a health concern, and also a concern with defined childhood: 'Dressed in the airiest and alas! the scantiest of costumes . . . the clothing of the children was of the scantiest kind, and many were in flesh-coloured tights.'[14] Finally, the acting and posing are themselves sinister. The Romantic child is valuable because unversed in the ways of civilization. To act is to be part of civilization, to be capable of lying and deceit. The loss of childhood itself by the working child was one of the main fears, a fear especially associated with the stage. Of a troupe of acrobats, 'nothing of the child [was] remaining with them but their stature', complained one moralist.[15]

Theatre moralists described the day of the pantomime child as an overlong, unimproving nightmare:

[She] has been up at six, has attended school before rehearsal, has had hardly anything to eat, and has fallen asleep in some cobwebby corner, protecting as well as she can with a frowsy, beaded mantle her two little sisters of five and six who are being trained with her. The long hours go on, midnight passes, the small hours begin to grow into tolerably big hours . . . the pantomime child is still to be seen in the cold, wet, slippery streets, dragging two smaller and still more weary children homewards over Waterloo Bridge or towards the Vauxhall Road.[16]

This is a lonely child, and there is an unspoken contrast between its solitude, its unsupervised solitude, and the grand masses of fairies, apparently a community. Another contrast emerges, too. The contrast between the privileged children who watched the pantomimes and the luxury they saw, set against the means of its production, were also acutely felt:

When the curtain, however, falls, and the excited little ones return to their happy homes, and still under loving care sink to sleep in their downy beds, how few parents, we fear, give a thought to that curtain's reverse shadows, or inquire into the well-being of the human machinery which provided their evening's amusement. Turn off, however, the gas, slip off the tinselled raiment, and follow those other little ones, too often through pitiless rain and biting cold, to their so-called 'Homes' in some fireless London garret, and compassion will surely arise to learn what Transformation Scenes await them there.[17]

Again the fairy appearance is contrasted with the stark reality.

Whoa, the fairies!

After this kind of talking-to, one could be forgiven for simply equating fairies with the false and the bogus. And, of course, the sexual. 'Oh, the fairies! Whoa, the fairies! Nothing but splendour/ And feminine gender!', as the old music-hall song has it.[18] Worries about the sexualization of pantomime were not wholly irrational; just as musical chorines were associated with sex by a later generation, so the younger chorus of fairies was sexualized. This sexualization was in part imported from the visual arts, where for some the licence previously applied to the pagan gods and goddesses was now extended to the fairy; these subjects were an excuse to paint a nude or enticingly draped body. Sir Joseph Noel Paton's portrayal of Oberon and Titania's quarrel (1849) is a case in point; both are inexplicably nearly naked, and posed in recognizably classical ways. She in particular resembles the Venus of Milo. Later affairs were more thoroughly abandoned to sexuality, like Richard Dadd's bare-to-the-waist fairies in *Come Unto These Yellow Sands.*

This is most evident in a flagrantly immoral text, a pornographic fairy pantomime called *A New and Gorgeous Pantomime entitled Harlequin Prince Cherrytop and the Good Fairy Fairfuck, or the Frig, the Fuck and the Fairy* (1905). The tedious plot is a kind of catalogue of Victorian sexual anxieties. The bad demon Spermatorrhea puts a spell on the kingdom which compels everyone to masturbate instead of having sex. When this curse is lifted by Good Fairy Fairfuck, another bad fairy gives the entire kingdom syphilis. The fairy kingdom is a kind of spoiled pornutopia, a place where lots of sex can go on amid whole troops of beautiful and willing women. Fairies are directly and simply objects of desire, and slavering with desire themselves. They also play their folkloric and pantomimic role of facilitating other people's sexual development. This was probably not what went through the heads of the men in the audience of some modest spectacular, but it does point to the perceived sexiness of the scantily clad fairy in her flesh-coloured tights.

A fruity melodrama of a novel entitled *Fairy Phoebe; or Facing the Footlights* sums up the moralists' cares and fears. It begins with a woman throwing herself and her bastard child into the Thames. They are saved by a waterman, who remarks, 'My! What a pretty fairy the little 'un is.[19] The guilty mother dies, leaving her innocent child to be brought up by a poor-but-honest policeman, his Quaker wife and their blind son, a family so moral and sensitive that they make the Cratchits seem positively depraved. Throughout, they call the foundling Fairy, as a tribute to her smallness, 'for Phoebe seemed to him stately and grave for such a wee mite'. This is an ironic reversal of the changeling story; here, the fairy baby is loved, and no attempt is made to return her to the fairies. But they take back their own. The child of unspoken immorality is naturally drawn to the stage. Inevitably, the little girl grows up to be unusually beautiful, and this is of course her downfall: soon she is 'exposed to influences as perilous . . . as can fall to the lot of any English child'. In other words, Phoebe falls into the hands of the theatre. A little old woman, 'extremely dirty', whose job it is to train children, spots Phoebe and thinks she would be perfect for a job. This woman is at the centre of a traffic in children, disgraceful because it treats children as commodities: 'some were sold to her outright', and because she corrupts them by introducing them to adult pleasures: 'Gin, too, was freely administered to such diminutive performers who, from their small size, were particularly valuable, and whose healthy growth was very undesirable.' Treating children like adults paradoxically keeps them children. The life of child-actors is drawn directly from the pamphlets campaigning against them:

the public must be entertained at any cost – what matters the sacrifice of young lives, the suffering inflicted on tender limbs, the exposure to almost unparalleled temptations, the slighting of all childish innocence, the imperilling of all womanly virtue, so *this* end be attained!

Rechristened 'Fay', which of course means 'fairy', her name lost in her new role, poor Phoebe is soon Exposed to Moral Danger. One of her fellow baby chorines has a sister called Jessie, suspiciously well-dressed and adored by the other children. The young sister is called Spangles, a name which – like Fay – conflates the actress with what she represents. Spangles confirms this: she likes 'my pretty dresses' and the 'trans. scene', in which the fairies wear 'short gossamer skirts glittering with tinsel ornaments . . . a scene of fairy-like splendour'. But the distinction between the illusion produced and the reality underlying it is made clear:

How brilliant was the scene! How complete the illusion! How lightly step those dainty little fairies, appearing and disappearing as if by magic, though well enough Fay knows the trap-door arrangement, and the unpleasant sensation of being swallowed up thereby, the horror, indeed, which had possessed her when undergoing her first lesson in this mysterious mode of exit. And the transformation scene – how it holds her spell-bound – Enchanted! Those sparkling, radiant fairies rising – like Venus from the ocean-foam – each from the centre of some gorgeous blossom; that shining winged angel poised aloft; that mimic cascade dancing over its flowery bed; that shower of golden rain in a haze of prismatic colours; and the flood of changeful light over all, now white as moonlight, now glowing as with sunset rays . . . Yet none knew better than Fay what a miserable sham was the whole concern . . . she knew that every lightly-poised fairy was strapped securely in her place to an iron support.

To illustrate the dichotomy between the brilliant scene and the suffering it causes, a child who plays an angel goes into a decline, attributed to hanging about in draughty corridors wearing nothing but a flimsy costume. Eventually she has a haemorrhage and dies, alone. To further illustrate the dangers, the gauzy costumes of a troupe of fairy dancers actually catch fire, 'changing in a moment the songs of the fairy-ring into shrieks of terror'. However, at this point Fay is rescued by her policeman, marries his blind son and retires to a lovely house, safe from the deadly dangers of the stage. Of course, the lovely house is in the country, unlike the depraved theatre from which she has escaped. The effect of innocence is gained at the cost of terrible experience.

Or so the novel would have us believe. An alternative telling of a similar story might end entirely differently. In fairytales, brave and resourceful heroines are allowed to rescue their families rather than symbolically rescuing a society. Instead of symbolizing innocence, their youth simply stands for the ability to work and to stand long hours of labour. The pink and tinselly fairy is a working-class dream of the child who rescues the family from poverty and herself from the dreariness of school, the misery of the factory. From a middle-class point of view, these fairies are bringers of undeserved wealth, wealth obtained through the rejection of female and childhood innocence. From a working-class point of view, Spangles and Miss Nina Montmorency are salvation, and aspiration. If the rules say that there is no other way to get a victoria and a nice toilette, the stage will be a popular career.

Actually, the theatre's critics tended to overstate the theatre's enthusiasm for the romantic childhood they were trying to promote. Spectaculars were not against industrialization or urbanization. There were often jokes in which fairies were aligned with precisely the kind of intellectual and scientific discourses to which they were supposed to be the antithesis. *The Bee and the Orange Tree*, for instance, features the Fairy Trufio, Honorary Member of the Horticultural, Botanical, Zoological, Entomological, Astronomical and all other learned societies, a Director of the Grand Atmospheric, Fairy-land (Theatre Royal, Haymarket Junction, 1845), while the fairy in *The Wolf and Little*

Red Riding Hood is called Industria (Theatre Royal, Birmingham, 1869–70), meaning hard work, but also gesturing at hard work as a virtue. In *Beauty and the Beast*, Rose D'Amour, the Fairy of the Enchanted Gardens, is a benign and beauteous being, seraphic and sylph-like, in silver spangles and pink tulle. She looks traditional enough. But the fairy regrets that her godson, the Beast, has become a fast young man who smokes.[20] Still other fairies of spectaculars owed a lot to Shakespeare: in *Cherry and Fairstar*, the Fairy Queen is Mab, and she is attended by such literary fairies as Hobgoblin and Puck, who even promises to put a girdle round the earth in forty minutes. But alas for Puck, Mab rejects his offer:

> What would that be worth?
> Mortals would beat you hollow, sweet simplicity, –
> It's done in half the time by electricity.[21]

This jokey tradition, mingling contemporary reference and traditional fairytale, is deployed in W. S. Gilbert's lyrics for the comic operetta *Iolanthe*, which was a pretty spectacle as well as a series of elaborate digs at the House of Lords. The fairies, who marry the 'very wicked peers' of the Upper House, end up in control of parliamentary business, using their spells to advance the cause of the son of one of their number. They contrive this by threatening to make peerages available by competitive examination if the Lords refuse to comply, a threat which has the Lords quaking in their boots, but which the Blair government might wish to consider. What they are not is an investment in a pre-political world of merry peasants. By contrast, the most seductively lyrical moment in the intrigues and comic plottings of the cast of *The Merry Widow* occurs when the heroine sings 'Vilya', a song of her childhood about a fairy of folk tradition. The fairy offers an escape from the brilliance and decadence of the court. It also offers a route back to childhood and to childhood love. This was Adolf Hitler's favourite opera, despite his better-known liking for Wagner, and it shows at precisely this point.

Glittering Dreams

Despite constant worries about the lowbrow character of spectacles, they reflected Victorian ideas of beauty and visual splendour so precisely that they had great influence on stagings of Shakespeare. The production of *A Midsummer Night's Dream* at Covent Garden by Madame Vestris revived the play's fortunes. Hazlitt had said that it was impossible to render the world of the *Dream* on stage, but new technology made it seem possible. Vestris had herself staged fairy extravaganzas in her management of the Olympic with J. R. Planché, who advised her on the *Dream* production: Planché was the Steven Spielberg of extravaganzas. Vestris also had contacts in the world of Romantic ballet, and her dance scenes were influenced by Marie Taglioni's *Sylphides*. In the final scene, the fairies could be seen darting 'from side to side, flying round and round . . . waving their tiny lamps until the whole palace seemed sparkling with the countless hues of light'.[22] This is a transformation scene, self-consciously so. Like the fairies of transformation scenes, these fairies are pure spectacle, spectacle consciously put in place with the help of technology. Ventris also used Mendelssohn's overture, in which the musical treatment of the fairies allies them with the supernatural beings of Romantic ballet. This production established the framework that was to dominate stagings of the play for more than half a century. Samuel Phelps's Sadler's Wells production in 1853, for instance, followed similar lines:

it is dreamland with its curious population of fairies and elvish sprites, whose fantastic outlines the eye can scarcely make out, presented most dreamily before the spectator. There is a misty transparency about the figures that gives them the appearance of flitting shadows more than of human beings.[23]

Mistiness signifies fairies' difference from people, but also makes them hard to see, symbolizing the inadequacy of the empirical eye to the supernatural world. Technically, the effect was achieved with a huge gauze that filled the proscenium opening. The fairies in this production were seen as a break with stage fairy norms:

the fairies, as they glide in and out of the trees and foliage, give you a notion that they have actually stepped out of them, as though the trunks and the flowers were their natural abiding-places . . . There were none of your winged white muslin fairies with spangles and butterfly wands.

These fairies were, in other words, even more Romantic and Rousseauan than previous fairies; they were part of nature, despite the enormous artifice which went into producing them. Kean's fairies in 1856 had clockwork wings – five pairs – to enhance the belief that they could fly. Another fairy machine imitating nature? Act 3 of the play concluded with fairies dancing around a maypole, which rose out of the stage, dropping garlands of coloured flowers when it reached its full height. A maypole: the very symbol of those safe rural villages in which fairies entertained the peasants? Yes, but everyone knew that this was really the London theatre, that the maypole was mechanical.[24]

This did worry some people. A critic called Dutton Cook complained that 'the scenic embellishments . . . and the musical accompaniments, without which the work could hardly be presented to the playgoers of today', reduced the play 'to the level of a fairy spectacle of commonplace quality'.[25] Others mourned the decline of imagination, the audience's need to be spoon-fed with fairies. Spectacle and spectacular tried to represent a perfect rural past, but the more perfect the replication, the more obvious it became that it was a replica. We can see at this precise historical moment the beginning of the link between fairies and the synthetic rather than the natural products of the imagination. Meretricious, fake fairies: they are commercial, they are shiny, they are the antithesis of real, authentic childhood. From the moment when fake fairies were identified, the race was on to distinguish real fairies from them. The familiar dichotomy between the fake, inauthentic Disneyfied fairy and the authentic, real fairy of folklore, reiterated by every folklorist and children's literature guru, is a product of Victorian anxiety about the fairies of the stage. Once the panto fairy's tinsel was tarnished, true fairy quality became what she excluded – the real Romantic child, who had not risen at dawn to take part in a panto, who remained innocent of sexuality, who imagined fairies rather than wanting to see them acted out mechanically. To this day, most people interested in fairies are at pains to distinguish real from fake, to mark the difference between real proper authentic fairies and tinsel ones. They probably do not know that they are reiterating Victorian morality, disdain for sex and class values as they do so.

There were still attempts to bring real fairies to the stage. Edward Saker's 1880 production of *A Midsummer Night's Dream* was characterized by the use of children to play the fairies.[26] The difference between adults and children became a metaphor for the difference between mortals and fairies. No moralist came forward to opine that such acting would corrupt the children in question. Such children, unlike the stage children in pantomimes, could be perfect images of the glorious pre-industrial past; they represented the childhood of the nation as well as the past of each individual adult. They were educative for adults; adults needed them. In Shakespeare extravaganzas, as in fairytale spectaculars, the fairies were pushed around, handled, shot up into the air from star traps and suspended by vast hoists. If Puck could put a girdle round the earth, it was only through the help of revolving dioramas. Fairies were no longer outside human control. Victorian toy theatres made this even clearer: the occult in an age of mechanical reproduction. Still remembered as penny plain and twopence coloured, they were originally sheets of card from which children could cut out favourite characters. These fairy paper dolls, fragile yet infinitely manipulable, allowed children to act the part of the man in the black coat, staging their own fairy extravaganzas, albeit with a more limited cast. This way, they could have their own fairies, like a pet, or a toy. One of the earliest toy theatres was a depiction of *The Fairy of the Oak, or Harlequin's Regatta*, a pantomime so early that it still featured Harlequin. *A Midsummer Night's Dream* was also produced as a penny plain, twopence coloured toy theatre, as was the *Lady of the Lake*, showing how 'serious' adult fairies could be absorbed into children's play and spectacle. More traditional pantomimes, with titles like *The Good Fairy*, were also on offer (1922); the Good Fairy is a buxom, motherly-looking woman, a fat fairy, old-fashioned, cosy and distinctly lacking in 'whoa! the fairies' appeal.[27] But possessed of the same capacity to be an object, to be pushed around, looked at, played with. To be desired.

Sex and shopping?

Other fairies also had to do with desire, but they were far, far more difficult to manage. No one really knows what Christina Rossetti's 'Goblin Market' means, but it is probably the finest Victorian fairy poem. It is the story of two sisters, Lizzie and Laura, who every evening hear the enticing cry of the goblins, 'Come buy! Come buy!' Eventually Laura succumbs, pays the goblins with a golden lock of her hair, and eats the goblins' fruit; 'she sucked and sucked and sucked the more . . . She sucked until her lips were sore.' Thereafter, Laura longs for more fruit, but can no longer hear the goblins' cries. She withers, like a changeling, and Lizzie cures her by resisting the goblins' lures herself to bring back a fruit for her sister, which now tastes as bitter as wormwood: 'She loathed the feast'. Thus Laura is saved from death, and the poem concludes with an encomium to the power of a sister's love. For generations, readers have felt the poem's sexual meanings; the fruit is so excessively pleasurable, so tempting, and yet its consumption is death, not only the death of the soul but the death of reputation. Laura and Lizzie together enjoy an innocent sensuality – they share a bed – which is the antithesis of the violently erotic goblin-fruits. Ancillary evidence supports this reading; the same year, Rossetti composed another poem about two sisters, in which one yields to the seductions of a rich man while the other, obdurately virtuous, becomes his wife. As well, Rossetti worked in a Christian home for fallen women, and herself did lifelong battle with her own passions, though rage rather than lust seems to have been her chief temptation. 'Goblin Market' is dedicated to her own sister Maria, who later became a nun.[28]

However, the poem is not just a lightly disguised story about sex. The process of buying and selling goblin fruits marks the entry into adulthood. Once Laura has bought the fruits, she is unable to hear the goblin voices, and we have already seen that an inability to hear or see fairies is the mark of the adult. Laura might be deflowered when she eats the fruit, but if so defloration is simply a metaphor for growing up. A specific Victorian anxiety often voiced in fairy stories was how it would be possible to grow up while retaining some elements of childhood; this was usually seen as especially important for women. Lewis Carroll's Alice is congratulated on her power to retain the heart of childhood when an adult. It is Lizzie who works out a way to meet the goblins, to grow up, without losing childhood; by taking but not eating the fruit, she becomes its master. It is difficult – and pointless – to translate this into a parable about sex. The point is that it is an answer to the desire to be an adult, a desire equated with illness and death here. Only by remaining in perpetual, arrested development can Laura and Lizzie stay alive. To grow up fully is to die. And here the jig is up for the whole Victorian fantasy world of childhood. It is a kind of Great Pyramid, an attempt to stop the clock, to beat death. Victorian children are little mummies, bathed in the nitre of their parents' longings for immortality.

Fairies are complicit both in the desire to stay alive at all costs – they are, after all, immortal – and in the desire not to. For the goblins of 'Goblin Market' are unlike other, sweeter fairies; they are on the side of the grown-ups, and we are not allowed to like them for even a moment. Whereas other deformed fairies are objects of pity, even love, the goblins of Rossetti's poem are simply held at arms' length; they are a menace, and that is all. This is perhaps why some of the poem's recent readers have insisted – perversely, and in tune with the 1980s rather than the 1860s – that the poem is about shopping rather than sex. Now we know the answer to the poem's riddle: poor Laura has evidently spent up to the limit on her storecard, which is why she cannot buy next day, and the goblins, who seemed such good pals, are not interested in her any more. Only Lizzie, with her intact storecard, is able to brave the store without purchasing anything, and cancel both accounts . . . Of course it doesn't work. Shopping – having your own credit card, your own power to create your own image – is the principal, sometimes the only, mark of citizenship and adulthood in the *fin de siècle* West of today. An earlier generation of hippies were equally eager to see the goblins' fruit as drugs, for similar reasons. As ideas about what constitutes the lapse into adulthood shift, so too do ideas about what the goblins' fruit really is. Whether the fruit is sex or designer clothes or a tab of E, however, it is something that you can't have as long as you are a child, and therefore something that having makes you into an adult. We might explicate this symbolism differently every ten years or so, but its inner meaning is constant. Fairies play exactly the same kind of role in the paintings of John Anster Fitzgerald, and of course in Richard Dadd's overhyped fairy deliriums. Precisely because they are both part of childhood and outside it, they can represent a threat to it, like drugs in the playground. The enemy within.

The heroic Lizzie, inexplicably popular with feminist critics, is of course against such walks on the wild side from the beginning, playing the thankless fairytale role of the Sensible Sister who resists desire. Rossetti was writing under the influence of the Victorian mania for fairytales, and she knew well the stories of two sisters, one greedy and the other restrained. It was as a folktale that Rossetti's first reviewers read 'Goblin Market', and what is interesting is their comprehensive lack of interest in what to us are its glaring sexual undertones. It is true that Rossetti in this poem restores fully a sense of the otherness and menace of the fairy world, a sense missing from literary evocations of it since the death of Keats.

Her hairy goblins come not only from the tales of the Brothers Grimm, however, but also from her major literary model, Milton's *Comus*. *Comus*, like 'L'Allegro', is full of references to the more rustic kind of fairy, but it is also the story of a girl who is tempted to drink a drink which will put her irretrievably into the power of the strange half-animal, half-god being who offers it. She is rescued at the last minute by her brothers. Now, if we assume that the Victorians were apt to read the human characters in *Comus* as children, an idea strongly supported by Victorian illustrated editions, we can see that Rossetti has elaborated its plot and simply changed the sex of the rescuing sibling, thus allowing rescuer and rescuee to be subject to the same temptations. In *Comus* the temptation is to sex, yes, but to generalized sensual indulgence, to an opening of the body to pleasure. There is an evident overlap between the evocation of the Lady's body as closed by chastity and Lizzie's tightly closed body:

> Lizzie uttered not a word,
> Would not open lip from lip,
> Lest they should cram a mouthful in:
> But laughed in heart to feel the drip

Of juice that syrupped all her face,
And lodged in dimples of her chin,
And streaked her neck which quaked like curd. (428–36)

The sensuous abandonment of juices dripping on Lizzie's body is however itself eroticized, especially when Lizzie herself becomes food, a quaking curd. Rossetti's chief modification of Milton's much more self-confident moral programme is the eroticization of deprivation and restraint. Most readers of *Comus* are disturbed to find the temptations more enticing than the refusals; Rossetti is taking no chances of that, and though the fruit is dripping with allure, the goblins are decidedly not. But she takes a different risk in making restraint as erotic as submission. Ultimately, Laura's desire is redirected towards Lizzie, who urges her, 'Hug me, kiss me, suck my juices' (468). But it would be a mistake to read this as lesbian, though it might be fun for lesbians to read. Rather, and as often, fairies are the gatekeepers of a realm where sensuous play without sexual guilt is always available. Here the fairies represent guilt and the girls innocence, an innocence that can find, at least in fantasy, an adulthood of which death is not the end.

Originally such seductive visions of a non-adult adulthood might have been offered to adults only, but 'Goblin Market' found its way into the Edwardian children's book market. A book of stories from the poets, by the girls' school stories author Christine Chaundler, retold Keats's 'La Belle Dame Sans Merci', Arnold's 'Forsaken Merman' and Rossetti's 'Goblin Market' for children. The illustrations remove the goblins' ugliness; instead, there is a troop of sanitized dwarfs. When Arthur Rackham illustrated Rossetti's poem in 1933, however, he began the process of transforming it into a secretive sexual allegory for adults. His illustration 'White and Golden Lizzie stood' shows Lizzie held roughly by many goblins, coded as male by their hairiness and priapic noses. Once fairies became firmly tied in with sexuality again, readers could hardly help reading 'Goblin Market' as their own fantasy of taboo lusts. Eventually, even *Playboy* came to take a misguided interest in Rossetti's masterpiece, with an introduction calling it 'the all-time hard-core pornographic classic for tiny tots', and a series of sad, lurid illustrations by Kinuko Craft, one showing Lizzie's white body almost lost amid a mass of caressing goblin hands.[29]

The trouble is that in the poem the goblins do not caress Lizzie; they merely try to force her to eat.

The Dark Tower

Robert Browning's 'Childe Roland to the Dark Tower Came' is perhaps the greatest and most unflinching Victorian fairy poem. It tells the story – if that is the right word – of a squire who has to cross a bitter landscape of hardship and fear to reach a dark tower. When he arrives at the tower, he finds unimaginable forces arrayed along the hills against him, but he is last seen defying them, blowing his horn and preparing to die without surrender. The poem is also about the split between a fairyland seen as ideal and a terrible reality that underlies it, but this is not clear, because Browning starts his story of Roland's quest to free his brothers in the middle. One of Browning's sources may be a ballad recalled by a Victorian folklorist as told to him in childhood. This ballad – or folktale, for the memory of teller and recounter is inexact – may well be as much a Victorian work as Browning's; many experts think it a fake. But it is a fake by someone who has read a lot of fairy folklore. In this story, Roland is the son of King Arthur. His sister is carried away by the fairies to the castle of the king of Elfland. Roland's brothers first set out for the Dark Tower, where they are beguiled by fairylike visions of beauty into trusting its inhabitants. Only Roland, with some magical help from Merlin, succeeeds in rescuing his sister.[30] In Browning, Roland alone sees fairyland without illusion. In many folktales, visitors to fairyland see magnificent palaces and comely people until they accidentally rub the fairy ointment on their eyes. Then fairyland is revealed as a charnel-house, grey and grim, with the fairies as the grinning dead. It is as if Roland has always had this fairysight, for to him the kingdoms of Elfland are simply places of nearly unendurable trial, haunted by dead people, by nameless fears:

> Good saints, how I feared
> To set my foot upon a dead man's cheek,
> Each step, or feel the spear I thrust to seek
> For hollows, tangled in his hair or beard![31]

When he spears a water-rat, its cry sounds like a baby's shriek. The terrible land Roland has to cross is also the waste land, of course, the kingdom of Arthur made infertile, reeking of death. Fundamentally, the land is simply the wild, the place to which knights must go to prove themselves, but having made themselves regard woods and mountains as simply sublime or pleasant, Victorian writers are obliged to produce something much more obviously unnatural to challenge their heroes. Roland's dream-landscape also owes a little to the despoliation of the countryside by industry; its barrenness is made, not born.

Roland's land is also inside him, subjective. Perhaps it is his interpretations of the land as hostile which make it hostile. For the first time, an author may be saying with full consciousness of the implications that fairyland is inside us; inside our longings, our guilts, our unfulfilled desires, a dream or nightmare that we have made. Fairies become objects for the scrutiny of the new army of psychologists and mental health practitioners. This process, already implicit in Romantic poetry, is closer to explicitness here. What makes fairyland terrible to Roland? Memories of treachery, his own and other people's? Or something that the poem cannot talk about, cannot even allude to, a terrible white silence at its heart? The ballad of Roland and his sister Eline ends in their passionate incestuous coupling, and we have seen before that incest is special to fairyland, a transgression fairies allow and even demand. This is not addressed in Browning's poem, but Roland could be read as about crossing the bleak and broken landscape of his own perverse longings and their guilts. The brothers have each their crime, but Roland does not tell what his is.

Nevertheless, something has blasted this land, and blasted Roland too; he sounds exhausted, old-young, and he has forgotten why he has come. The land speaks to him and the land is him and he cannot read it, but it maddens him. Like the poem, it is a story without a beginning, without an end, a story that cannot be told. And what else is incest? Browning always refused to explain the poem himself, saying it came to him in a dream. Perhaps it contains a story that he could not tell directly, did not want to read there. However, taken together with the eroticization of the fairy, the internalization of fairyland meant that fairies increasingly came to be seen *consciously* as symbols for what could not be said. The trouble was that once they became *readable* as little images of sex and murderous desire and incest – once everyone could nudge each other as they did last time I saw Victorian fairy paintings on display, and say, 'Oo, look – phallic symbol – Freud', they could no longer be used as such. Once 'the love that dares not speak its name' is a known euphemism, it ceases to be euphemistic. Such symbols can work only if people are unconscious of what they mean. Once everyone became knowing about fairies and sex, fairies could no longer be an unknowing symbol for sex, a way to slip something past the ever-vigilant super-ego, the bit of us that absorbs and reiterates all the rules about desire that we have learnt since infancy. From about the mid-Victorian era to the present, certain super-egos got into a way of saying, 'Fairies, eh! Who do you think you're fooling?'

The *roman d'aventure* and the strangeness of the fairy country fascinated the Victorians just as they had their pre-industrial ancestors. The changeling stories, too, found an echo in Victorian anxieties about children, already seen in action in their battles about pantomime fairies. Whereas pre-industrial peoples had used the changeling story to talk about their terror of losing their children to death or even to the influence of strangers, the Victorians saw changeling stories through the metaphor of the romantic fairy. They recast the story, and it was told not by the parents of the kidnapped child, but by the child itself or its fairy substitute. As such, the changeling story could become another chance for the Victorians to think about the perpetual pleasure and oddity of childhood. Children were always changelings, always different from their parents because they were still young. At the same time, the Victorians were so set on a single immutable model of child upbringing that the fairies often acted to rectify any deviation from it. One obvious and chilling example is the moralizations of the changeling story to become a story of child death. In one tale, an unhappy orphan is given the opportunity to die and rejoin her longed-for mother by the fairies' magic.[32] In Kipling's story 'Cold Iron', the fairies look after a child unloved by the human world. The idea of the changeling as the unloved child, or the idea that an unloved child might become a changeling, meant that the fairies pointed obliquely to the inadequacies of human parenting.[33] In Charlotte Mew's poem 'The Changeling', the changeling struggles desperately to stay human, even though he has been rejected by the human world. He concludes

> I shall grow up, but never grow old,
> I shall always, always be very cold,
> I shall never come back again![34]

This changeling can only be reclaimed by the fairies because his parents have failed to love him enough. If his mother had only left a night-light burning, they could never have taken him, an idea expressed also by J. M. Barrie in *Peter Pan*. Far from fearing the changeling, the poem asks the reader to make up for the shortfall in parental love by her investment in the pitiable figure and its desolation. The object of pity and love is the dreamy child, the one who is unproductive in adult terms. Mew's changeling can't do its sums or lessons because it is always listening to the fairy noises of the world outside the window. The fewer sums you get right, the more special you are. Though this is a child's revenge on its pushy parents, the poem is also comforting for adults, reassuring them that they are empathetic and warm-hearted, not themselves pushy, by the feelings it evokes. Also, the moral is hearteningly clear: accept your child's imagination. Closer to folklore is Walter de la Mare's poem on the changeling, 'Peak and Puke', which impartially portrays parental and sibling cruelty to the changeling child:

> It we'll neither rock nor tend
> Till the Silent Silent send,
> Lapping in their waesome arms
> Him they stole with spells and charms.[35]

Yet such cruelty is also a form of steadfast loyalty to the child who has been taken. The mother and brother must resist the wailing of the changeling, must constantly reassure themselves as well as the changeling that they intend to resist. Here, refusal of love is a form of love; cruelty is kindness. Yet Victorians mostly expressed extreme dismay when it became apparent that belief in changelings was licensing child cruelty. Such events as the murder of Bridget Cleary, which I discuss later in this book, were threatening because they implied that belief in fairies was not always linked to innocence and tenderness.

Far from it; the Victorians also produced fairies who seemed the epitome of frightening female sexuality, mostly in the context of Arthurian legend. Here, fairy difference from mortals became an emblem of female difference from the male. Take Waterhouse's *La Belle Dame Sans Merci*.[36] A Knight is drawn towards a young girl because her hair is entangled in his armour. A sexual enchantment, a spell of hair. She is very young, slender, intent on his face. They are in a wood, the wood of adventure. His lance points directly at her belly, in a piece of phallic symbolism so obvious that it cannot have escaped the artist. What does she want with him? What he and what the viewer wants with her is projected on to her, as her wants. The wickedest fairy in Victorian art was, however, Morgan Le Fay. Frederick Sandys' picture of Morgan (1864) is described by a critic in the *Art Journal* as 'a petrified spasm, sensational as a ghost from the grave': sexual language.[37] Edward Burne-Jones's *Morgan Le Fay* is a beautiful seductress holding a poisonous plant between her lips; her body is clearly robed, with no flesh showing, but the picture somehow suggests that her robe is a deception, a cover-up of her sexual nature, of the horrible truths of her body.[38] The Victorians only sporadically thought of Morgan as a fairy, even though her name says she is one. Perhaps by now it was awkward to acknowledge the unruliness of fairy sexuality, having assigned it to so many young girls in flesh-coloured tights and scanty tutus. Pantomime fairies are not *tempting*; you can look at them all you like, because they are not actionable. You look and that is the end of it. Morgan is different; look at her, and you may end up who knows where. Your own desire will be turned against you.

The fairy that dares not speak its name

For children, Hans Christian Andersen was eager to expound the same displaced sexual terrors. For someone who made the fairytale famous and respectable, Andersen's stories contain curiously few memorable fairies, or few being named as such. There is the Fairy of the Garden of Paradise, attached to the story of an Eden arisen only to be lost again apparently solely to provide sexual temptation. Generally, however,

Andersen dealt with female beings more overtly sexual and far less childlike than the nursery fairy: post-pubescent women, driven by desire to act out appalling rites of bloodshed, self-sacrifice and self-loss. His Little Mermaid is not a mermaid because she is a temptress. While the Fairy of the Garden of Paradise is an unwilling seductress, the mermaid completely lacks seductive powers. Or rather, she gives them up in an effort to seduce. Once voiceless, she is the hapless victim of the seductive powers of humans. Reversing the power relations of the usual mermaid story, Andersen gives the human prince all the destructive delight of the mermaid, and gives the mermaid the burning desire of the sailor-victim. What did such a reversal mean? Andersen seemed to want to explore realms of forbidden desire. The mermaid cannot possess the prince because of their difference. But here, difference might represent sameness. As Andersen's recent biographer Alison Prince suggests, Andersen himself was from late adolescence passionately and hopelessly devoted to a boy who was debarred to him not only by gender, but also by social class. The mermaid simply cannot become human enough, or become human fast enough, for her Prince, and so she is lost, losing both the sea and her natural, pagan span in it, and the human world. Only the *dea ex machina* of the Daughter of the Air role saves her from annihilation. And oddly, it is the Daughters of the Air who seem most like nursery fairies, or at any rate like sprites, fairies purged of all desire except the desire to lose themselves in helping others. Like fairies, they are particularly concerned to serve children, fanning hot faces, and like nursery fairies, they are particularly subject to children's opinions. In a kind of precursor of Tinker Bell's resurrection, the Daughters of the Air depend on children's good behaviour to progress; bad children set them back a whole year.[39]

By contrast to the Daughters, there is Andersen's most brilliant, menacing and evocative fairy presence, the glittering, fatal Snow Queen, who more than any other fairytale entity haunted my own childhood with wild dreams of terror and desire. Though not exactly a fairy, the Snow Queen owes a lot to Titania, sharing with her fellow queen a penchant for abducting the beautiful mortal boy. She also shares with fairy queens a tendency to kill the thing she desires, or perhaps it is actually death and the dead that she wants? Like the Erl-King – to which her airborne, rapturous abduction owes a little –

her desires are never explained, which is what makes them so haunting. Her palace, a mass of ice fragments that can be arranged in endless, meaningless patterns, is quite without heart. This is not merely femininity at its most menacing. It is fairyland as its most untransformed and raw, a place of pure power and seduction with no moral input whatsoever. Under the power of the queen, Kay becomes not merely passive, like the earlier victims of Titania and other early fairy queens, but insensible, unable to complete the task of spelling out Eternity, unable to desire, even, the skates held out by the queen as inducement. Such comprehensive emasculation is beyond even the most diabolical fairy confronted by Arthurian knights. Kay is autistic, trapped in a world of numbers from which he cannot escape, like some savant who can recite every date until the end of the world, and at this point one cannot help recalling that some people think autism is the real explanation for the myth of the changeling. He is, or he is meant to be, the antithesis of the Romantic poets abducted by vision and fairy. And yet, as always, good seems so much more feeble than evil. Kay's rescuer Gerda is persistent, diligent, virtuous; she has some interesting adventures, but somehow it is all pallid compared with the memory of being swept up by the Snow Queen into the great vast vault of the sky, amid the stormy wind singing its old ballads, over the shrill howling of the wolves of winter. The moral song about the roses really stands no chance against such powerful magic, every snowflake instinct with the terrible darkness of the Northern winter, its power to kill and maim.[40]

All Oscar Wilde's characters in every single one of his fairy stories die of hopeless, unrequited, sometimes unrequitable love, in a world too careless to see its beauty. That this was how he understood himself, and his own homo-erotic passions is self-evident; what is more interesting is that it was the fairytale which gave such ideas expression. The otherness of fairies licensed the fairytale as an expression of the otherness of homosexual desire. As the literary critic Alan Sinfield has remarked, one of the puzzles for us is why Wilde was not arrested for sodomy sooner; never was there such a perfect instance of a man who looked, sounded and wrote like a raging queen. And yet no one cottoned on, which must mean, as Sinfield rightly remarks, that the image of the raging queen was formed after Oscar Wilde's trial and because of it.[41] It is because Oscar Wilde wore purple dressing-gowns and wrote pretty poems and fairy stories and walked mincingly that we are apt to think that gay people might do these things. The fairy, image of a heightened sensibility, was drawn by Oscar Wilde into this image. The link between the fairy and the perverse, the unsayable, was present in folklore, but Wilde gave it a local habitation and a name that was eventually to prove more fatal to the fairy than Captain Hook's poison. We shall explore this later. For the moment, the fairy is still walking about, unaware of the deadly draught she has imbibed. Even as Edwardian fairies multiply, their fate has been sealed.

Mad fairies

And they were walking about in some forms so perverse, so irredeemably and absolutely personal, that we cannot understand them. Take the lurid visions of Richard Dadd. Dadd is likeable because of his extreme lunacy; what everyone enjoys is the stark contrast between the putative innocence of fairies and Dadd's very striking crime sheet. Dadd murdered his father in 1843, and at once fled to France, where he stabbed a fellow stagecoach passenger while on a self-appointed errand to kill the emperor of Austria. In Bedlam, he was allowed to paint, and he chose to paint fairies, fairies tangled in the grey-green mist of undergrowth, fairies engaged in cracking nuts. *The Fairy Feller's Master-Stroke*; Dadd worked on it for nine years. His enthusiasm for parricidal acts squares all too neatly with the nutcracking fays, but it is difficult, however we try, to see his paintings as self-expression; they are too obscure. We are always eager to see the supernatural as merely an outcome of a psychic state of error, but Dadd does not quite let us do that; his fairies are not as readable as we would like them to be. Rather, their inscrutability seems to point to the secret languages and meanings of madness, indecipherable to the sane. His paintings are congested; the eye is led purposelessly from one tense fairy figure to another. We simply cannot read them, though they tease us with their knowledge – their fairylike knowledge – of a suffering so particular that we cannot share it.[42]

Dadd's fairies are remarkably ugly, like Rossetti's goblins. Such ugly fairies hark back to Fuseli, who used ugliness to signify malice and desire. Even the habitually smooth Millais could not quite keep the grotesque at bay when he portrayed the boggling faces of the fairies who convey Ariel to Ferdinand. Bald, with narrow black eyes and mouths exuding air, their bony hands held to their faces, their smiles twisted, cunning, these fairies are the antithesis of the beautiful child-fairy they carry, or perhaps its unacknowledged underside.[43] In the 1855 revival of *A Midsummer Night's Dream*, Puck wore a grotesque outsize pantomime head, and some fairies were given odd appearances, large hands, for instance. This reminded the *Times* reviewer of the illustrations to Croker's *Fairy Legends*.[44] The equally frightful fairies of John Anster Fitzgerald, vividly and even violently coloured, are smooth like children's book illustrations, but with hideously dark subtexts. Tormented birds and mice look up helplessly at the viewer as cruel fairies pinch or imprison them. His portrayal of a man dreaming of painting fairies, a man whose dreams are brought to him by fairies, is a perfect depiction of the cherished fantasy that fairies are themselves a psychic fantasy. Here their origin in the mind of the dreamer is revealed. Similarly, his *The Stuff That Dreams Are Made Of*, misquoting *The Tempest*, shows a woman lying on a bed, dreaming of wicked imps and tender lovers. All the tiny elf and fairy figures are reduced to images of the woman who dreams them; they are like midnight secrets revealed at noon. They are her true self. But in becoming so, they have lost for ever any real otherness. Fitzgerald is trying to say that fairies are the part of ourselves that we cannot accept or like or agree about, the part of ourselves that we cannot own.[45]

Perhaps the part of children we cannot own, either; Doyle's illustrations to the stories of the Brothers Grimm are among many that show fairies as uncomfortably neither children nor adults, a mixture of adult features, big hands and heads, and child torsos and limbs. Another element is added: the animal. This depicts beasts and children, the purely animal that cannot or has not been civilized, but also the adult, the sly, sophisticated, knowing adult, dreaded by parents. Elsewhere, fairies are more pleasant bits of the self, bits of the self that their originator would like to own. R. Huskisson's panel *The Mother's Blessing* depicts a madonna-like woman with a plump baby in her arms; engrossed in his gaze, she does not appear to see the tiny, benign fairies who circle about the pair, apparently attracted by their mutual bliss. These are fairies of maternal love, fairies anyone might be proud to own. And once art has decided that fairies are us, we are bound to make ourselves more agreeable fairies, fairies we can live with. The cute fairies, in other words.[46]

The fairies rebel

The Grand Riposte to all the moral fairies that beset Victorian nurseries was eventually administered gloriously by Lewis Carroll. Just as *Alice in Wonderland* is full of savage debunkings of moral verses, so Carroll's lesser-known *Sylvie and Bruno* sets out to teach all those oh-so-virtuous fairies a good lesson:

I want to know why fairies should always be teaching *us* to do our duty, and lecturing *us* when we go wrong, and we should never teach *them* anything? . . . I'm almost sure (only *please* don't repeat this loud in the woods) that if you could only catch a fairy, and put it in the corner, and give it nothing but bread and water for a day or two, you'd find it quite an improved character – it would take down its conceit a little, at all events.[47]

Yet despite its elegant debunking of the moral fairies, Carroll's work is also the precursor of a new and in their way equally moral wave of fairies destined to infest Edwardian nurseries. These are child-fairies, fairies who represent what the late Victorian and Edwardian adult wanted – had a right to expect – of children. Here is Carroll's description of Sylvie:

she seemed so good and gentle that I'm sure she would never expect that anyone could wish to hurt her. She was only a few inches high, and was dressed in green . . . she was so delicate and graceful that she quite seemed to belong to the place, almost as if she were one of the flowers.

Sylvie is so delicate, so evanescent, so close to disembodiment and yet so fragilely feminine that she can only represent a femininity cleansed of disturbing adult solidity and sexuality. Carroll was in any case prone to conflate children, especially girl-children, with spirits and angels: 'Now here, now there, a childish sprite,/ Earthborn and yet as angel bright,/ Seems near me . . .'[48]

Bruno: Think of any pretty little boy you know, rather fat, with rosy cheeks, large dark eyes, and tangled brown hair, and then fancy him made small enough to go into a coffeecup.

Like Barrie was to do later, Carroll also uses Bruno for a careful, awkward portrayal of what a child is actually like. Bruno is engaged in wrecking Sylvie's garden because she will not play with him until he has done his lessons. Lewis Carroll, a character in his own story, talks Bruno into rebuilding the garden instead of wrecking it. This is the storyteller's ironic awareness of his own role in fairyland, or of the adult's role in childhood, which in Carroll comes to the same thing: to sweeten, to civilize, to moralize.

Fairies are to Carroll a kind of concentrate or distillation of what makes children desirable: not sexuality, but their lack of connection with it. Children's bodies are not suggestive of sexual acts; bodies the size of coffeecups are even less so. The tiny body effectively blocks eroticization. So there can be sensuous pleasure in looking at the body, sensuous pleasure devoid of erotic intent, devoid even of an obvious and therefore suggestive bar to erotic intent. Similarly, the naked fairies that sport in Victorian fairy paintings are the antithesis of Fuseli's sexual visions. Yes, they are nude, and yes, there is plenty of body contact. What is crucial is that these little visions do not exchange desiring glances with each other; the viewer's eye is not directed with desire. Rather, fairies like these direct the eye out of the prison of desire and its pains, and into another realm, a realm free of sex.

Fairies making children

Meanwhile, as the nineteenth century went on, industrialization and urbanization simply went on too. The poor did not move *en masse* back to the countryside to absorb the woodland scenery and dream of fairies; they misguidedly scrabbled to better themselves with jobs and consumer goods. So the rural idyll symbolized by fairies could not, it seemed, be actual. It had to become a country of the mind, a mental, artistic escape from the cities and from the industries they contained. Luckily, there was one group of people who could, at least in imagination, inhabit this idyll all the time, and so keep it open for those who had to hold literary soirées and give lecture tours. This group of people were children, the children of the better-off initially, but gradually, people came to feel, all children:

God has given us each our own Paradise, our own childhood, over which the old glories linger – to which our hearts cling, as all we have ever known of heaven on earth.[49]

The link between children and fairies came naturally. Children were associated with fairies anyway; childhood is a boundary of life, and many folktales, as the Victorians well knew, told of children stolen by fairies. Increasingly, the Victorians came to see such stories not as horrific abductions, but as signs that children and fairies were somehow akin, even as merciful releases for the child from the world of cities and machines. The Victorians also believed that each individual had to go through the same stages as civilization as a whole. After the barbarian baby stage, children must reach the calm, attractive rural idyll of Ruskin's dream. Each child was not its parents' future, but their past.

It goes without saying that the results were designed to gratify adults and to mould children. To this day, we tend to see children's imaginations as sacred and liberating, but of course they are invariably well stocked with materials placed there by adults. In the mid to late Victorian era, imagination became a necessary feature of childhood, and the child had to demonstrate it by believing in fairies. Any child heartless enough to insist that fairy rings were caused by mushrooms was dismissed as an emotional cripple. If such children were unluckily discovered, their parents or schools were usually to blame; for Edith Nesbit, books merely dimmed the bright fairy-seeing eyes of childhood, while for Compton Mackenzie, the progressive Newalls who surround their children with mechanical toys and aeroplanes neglect to tell them 'stupid stories about fairies or ghosts of the heroes of the past'.[50] The most famous of such children is perhaps C. S. Lewis's Eustace Clarence Scrubb (not Edwardian, but consciously retro), who almost deserves his fearful name, and whose academic parents make him preternaturally sceptical. Of course he soon unlearns all that. Such unlearnings are invariably portrayed as liberations for the child in question, but really in the Edwardian era it was almost compulsory to be so liberated. Children *had* to be dreamy and sensitive, gazing into corners and peopling them with supernatural beings, in order to qualify as appropriately childlike. Any resistance to this behaviour was regarded as precocity and ruthlessly shunned. It is just as burdensome to be obliged to see fairies lurking around every corner as it is to be obliged not to see them.

What is more, the fairies such children were required to see suffered from a very bad case of the cutes, a phrase coined by American critics in the 1920s in a desperate effort to banish the serried infestations of sweetly tinkling fays, gnomes and elves. There are thousands of such cute fairies, dizzying amounts of them, and even the most ardent cultural critic might balk at a survey of all of them. Perhaps the best-known cute fairies in literature are those of Rose Fyleman, the author of the breathless 'There are Fairies at the Bottom of our Garden!':

> There are fairies at the bottom of our garden!
> They often dance on summer nights;
> The butterflies and bees make a lovely little breeze,
> And the rabbits stand about and hold the lights.[51]

For children, cuteness is a guide to conduct. A feature of cuteness is gaiety, cheerfulness, at worst – optimism. Think of Shirley Temple: the cute childlike figure is only allowed to be sad briefly, and must accept consolation and encouragement. Cuteness must never brood or mourn. So there is an insistence here that children be happy, be made happy by the poem – which was really directed at adults, though spoken by a child – and by fairies. That happiness must find visible expression, which is why there is always emphasis in images of cuteness on spontaneity and playfulness. The late Victorian child and the Edwardian child simply must be happy, simply must gratify their parents by being in paroxysms of soppy joy every time they venture into the nursery. In literature, child gaiety serves another purpose; it allows adult narcissism to flower. Adults can enjoy imagining that they too were once just as attractive as the fictional children prancing before them, while luxuriating self-pityingly in regret for the loss of the innocence fictionally grafted on to the young.

Cute fairies are adults' attempts not to recover but to repair their childhoods, to make them over as simpler and nicer than any real childhood can be. We do not long for what we had, but for what we never had, which is why fairies always seem so hideously disjunct from real childhood, real children. Adults who indulge in cases of the cutes often believe they are entering into a child's world, but the opposite is the case; the Cute World exists just for the adult, and the child must play along. As a result, some Cuties were invented by children themselves, perhaps in obedience to adult demands and desires. The eleven-year-old Helen Douglas Adam, for instance, wrote a poem called 'The Elfin Pedlar':

> Hush! The fairies are dancing
> Dancing in the dell
> The dickie birds are watching
> The fairies weave their spell.[52]

'Where a child got such insight and art is a question that baffles us,' gasped a Dundee clergyman in the foreword, and he urges readers 'to simply believe that there are elect minds that can mediate between us and the father of light', making it painfully clear that this effusion is meant for adults. Fairy cuteness arouses a profound maternal desire to nurture, a maternal longing, a desire to rescue the cute object and put it within a family context. People – not me, I hope, but other people – long to own what is cute, to take it home, to cherish it as it deserves. The cute is often seen as forlorn, lacking something, somehow sad, needy. As the RSPCA can tell you, such longings are short-lived; once the cute object has been taken home, adopted, it is forgotten; the drama is about acquisition, not about care. In fact, it is about shopping. Shopping is about the longing to possess something cute – 'oh isn't it *cute*' – and to take it home, add it to the home. In this way, the fairies become virtually a brand-name, a way of saying that here is a desirably cute child-object, a way of arousing and satisfying the maternal desires of the shopper, the bookshopper, the shopper for prints and products, for nurseryware. To have such desires aroused becomes proof that the woman about to make the purchase is herself properly maternal, properly desiring. In *Peter Pan*, it is Mrs Darling's devotion to buying things for the nursery which proves her a good mother, a sentiment still peddled by the companies eager to persuade us that no baby can be happy (and that is the goal, remember) without nursery wallpaper and matching duvet covers and mobiles.

As in *Cinderella*, motherhood remains central to cute fairies and fairy stories. Cute moralizations of traditional folktales are often about the sweetening of the role of the mother; the familiar tale of the fairies' wetnurse becomes a tale of a widow's determination to help the fairy whose love for her child mirrors her own love for her baby.[53] Such moments of maternal solidarity are at least still achieved through biological processes; generally cuteness excludes precisely the processes of maternity that are awkwardly biological or sexual. The idea that babies are brought by the fairies runs rampant through this strand of Victorian fairy writing. Fairies bringing babies has a faint, a very faint, echo of the role of fairies as borderers, agents of change, but all the risk has gone out of it. Cute fairies find babies under cabbage patches, on rainbows and in flowers. Even relatively frank fairies manage to romanticize the whole process; the fairies in Edith Howes's *The Cradle Ship* tell Win and Twin that 'baby grew in a silky baby-bag under your heart, mother'.[54] In another story, the fairies lack 'human babies', and that is their favourite thing of all. Why? Because 'the only people who provide babies are the storks, and they live miles from here'. Eventually, the fairies manufacture a baby out of ingredients like rose-petals and bluebells and the pure gold of sunset clouds. The baby is eventually delivered to a cottage – a cottage, and not an urban tenement – by a way of a rosebush.[55] The story successfully covers every possible way of explaining the arrival of babies except the right one.

Win and Twin: another inexorable part of fairy cuteness is cute baby-names. Invented fairies of the late Victorian and Edwardian eras often had names suggestive of children's lisps or coinages: Widdy

Winkums, Wuffly Worples. (These examples could be multiplied, but I don't have the heart.) Often in cute literature the children themselves use baby talk; 'Poor Goldylocks, it was all "very drefful", as he said.' Cute fairies have cute names, like Pinkle, Widdy Wunkum and Worry.[56] If readers can control their rising gorges – for a different aesthetic has made this kind of talk look worse than last year's fashions – they might want to ask themselves what such words mean. They mean a failure to control talk, which itself sets a conduct norm for children. Children should be seen, and not heard very clearly. One of the things that keeps them children, keeps them safely in fairyland, is the inability to make themselves understood, to understand others. If Latin is a Victorian puberty rite, then English acquisition marks the end of the nursery days. *En passant*, Tinky Winky, Dipsy and Laa Laa would not look out of place in these lists, and their endearing – well, intended-to-be-endearing – talk of Tubby Tustard would fit into Goldylocks's mouth. Is this why Jerry Falwell worries so about Tinky Winky's handbag? The Teletubbies do not waft children to fairyland, though – they waft them to TV land. A point to ponder.

Fairy learning

Fairy coercion is not confined to the insistence that children be imaginative and ceaselessly overjoyed and not very articulate. Sometimes coercion is more obvious. Some fairies work, and the kind of work they do is suggestive: 'Every flower has a fairy living in it, and it is the fairy's business to wash and dust the flower and keep it nice and fresh.'[57] Cute fairies might appear to be all about leisure, but they also make the child work. Take, for instance, *The Grammar Fairies* (1891). Or *The Fairyland A B C for little folk* (1885). Here are the fairies, unluckily embarked on the fearful business of Making Learning Fun. *The Fairies' Annual* is a Case of the Cutes wrought, as many such are, by the importation of the fairies into another children's genre. The framing story explains that the fairies have reproduced the annual themselves for the instruction of mortals. What makes the whole production unbearably cute is the application of educational discourses to fairyland. 'Fairy life had just emerged from nebulosity, soon after the Tertiary

Period'; 'the Cloud System Light railway', and so forth.[58] Other, moral lessons might also be learned. In *Fairy Fingers; or, 'A little child shall lead them'* (1889), a temperance league uses a magic lantern show of pictures of fairies to entice poor trusting children into taking the pledge themselves, then putting pressure on their unlucky families. The title refers to one child's campaign to get ten pledge signatories in a year, as many as the fingers on a fairy's hand. Amid the soft soap, it is notable that the fairies here are a special effect, as in the theatre.

Most remarkable of all is an attempt to use fairies to teach history, a rewriting of Queen Victoria's biography as if it were a fairytale with herself the heroine. 'Once upon a time', it begins archly, 'there was born a pretty little baby girl as pink and white as a blush rose. She was so pretty and so pink that the fairies came to see her.' Victoria is selected to be Queen by the fairies, who have to overcome the enmity of the envious Duke of Grumble-land (Cumberland), and then find her 'another heart as good as her own, which should throb by her side'. The story is not without sly criticism, however; the fairies decide to test Prince Goldenheart by dressing Victoria from the ragbag, to see if he is able to recognize quality in disguise. The Prince soon recognizes Victoria, and the result is 'a dream of love, softer than the soft vapours of evening' loved by the fairies because 'the fairies could not help loving them when they loved each other so much'. The fairies are on hand to stop Victoria being shot by an evil toad, and to guard her babies, said to be exactly like dolls.[59] This tiny volume elegantly combines the highly conservative political ideology of Young England with its principal metaphor. It is not just a history lesson; it is a lesson about how history ought to go. No revolutions, please. It is notable that Swinburne, in the flush of youth, wrote a hymn to Queen Victoria on her visit to Eton which likens the Queen to Gloriana:

> Lo! From the time-worn turret's deep recess,
> A virgin train pass forth in youthful loveliness;
> 'We tend by night the Fairy Queen's loved walks, . . .
> With footsteps light as dew upon a flower,
> When all is hush'd at midnight's solemn hour.'
> They cried 'till from her fairy kingdom bright
> She deigns to bless us with her favouring sight.[60]

This is a history lesson too, a lesson in literary history. Self-consciously basing his work on Spenser and Shakespeare, Swinburne thus educates his fellow pupils in the legitimacy of the Queen. How can she be anything other than legitimate when she comes backed by such powerful literary voices? How can mortals question her, when she exists on another plane from them? These are of course old tricks, but still good ones.

Children were supposed to learn grammar and history, but to shun naughty materialism and consumerism: in *The Fairies' Annual* there are three children who do not believe in fairies. The fairies themselves write that 'they are the children of a wealthy mortal, who spends all his time accumulating metal discs which, as you know, correspond to our Honey-Nuts'. The mother of these children spends most of her time playing cards, the consequence being that the little ones are left to the guidance of 'a stolid silly servant with no imagination'.[61] The lower orders cannot provide the higher fancy and imagination necessary for true childhood, at least not without the benefit of living in the country. Increasingly, it is the mother's role to nurture imagination, an idea that reaches its apotheosis with *Peter Pan*. A series of tales 'commanded by Gloriana' features a fairy called Affection, who comes to the narrator's bedchamber and offers to cure his insomnia (quite the scandal!). She says that by telling his children the stories he will help the Fairies in their battle against

the hideous Gnome-King, Red Gold; that powerful king before whom I see so many millions kneeling – nay, grovelling in the dust. Justly is he styled red gold, for all his glitter cannot hide the blood-stains that have always been his – blood-stains wrung, alas, from poor, unhappy, starving, dying people![62]

Of course, it is only ever the upper classes that can afford to be so dismissive of money, and as had become usual, the fairies side with the nobs. On the other hand, fairy unworldliness could have other meanings: fairy primitivism is often linked to the sentimentalization of other races for nursery delectation, for if children are really themselves man's primitive past, and fairies are also the past, then fairies might be pygmies, or American Indians. In Edmund Dulac's *Fairies I have Met* (1907), 'the sea-fairy's name was Laughing Sapphire, and he lived in a Nautilus-shell; the land-fairy was called Sweet-of-the-Mountain, and his home was a tuft of heather'. One might note the resemblance of these names to the (romanticized) version of Plains Indians names (Great Big Little Panther, and so forth).

Innocent?

We cannot proceed much farther with the Cute Fairies without noting something else about them, something disturbing. They seem so innocent. And yet . . .

They [mischievous elves] had crept up to a daisy and were blowing and puffing out their cheeks and scattering all her pretty white petals. They called it snipping off her kirtle. The poor daisy could do nothing, they held her fast, and were so much stronger than she was. Soon she was left alone crying over her lost kirtle, while the naughty elves ran away laughing. Goldy was so distressed he came down and kissed her, and tried to comfort her. He told her not to cry, but the poor little thing could not help crying, for she knew her pretty mantle couldn't be made again quickly, and this made her sad.[63]

Here we have a little girl held fast by little boys, and stripped, and left distressed. Is this some kind of sexual assault? Is the description worryingly eroticized? A daisy-ripper? We have to bracket these tricky questions in thick masses of Awful Warnings. We in the post-modern world are apt to be convinced that sex is at the bottom of everything, that we know far more about sex than the Victorians did, and that we can read their unconsciousness like a book. These are all dangerous thoughts. Just because sex seems to us at the bottom of everything, does not mean this is equally true for all others; just because we know a lot about our own sexualities (and do we really?) does not mean we know a lot about Victorian sexualities; just because we read something in a text doesn't mean it is there for everyone. Paedophilia might be in this text for us, and not for the Victorians; for us it is sort of remotely Catherine Cooksonish, the rape of the innocent. The Victorians, however, had not had the benefit of reading Catherine Cookson. They had, however, had the benefit of reading Shakespeare and increasingly, as the century wore on, folklore, and both understood fairies in relation to human sexuality. So in Mark Lemon's *Tinykin's Transformation*, Tinykin is a beautiful child with whom Titania is passionately in love; repeatedly touching and kissing him, she tries – but fails – to keep away from him. Tinykin is a Sunday child, which is why he can see fairies, and his fascination with an Undine is almost his undoing because it arouses Titania's passionate jealousy.[64] Such stories owed rather more to folkloric researches than an earlier, tamer generation of tales. Folklore suddenly seemed an attractive way of writing about fairies. It legitimated feelings and desires for which the fairytale was a natural outlet by associating them not with deviance but with the new if non-existent rural ideal.

Kipling's differences

'Dymchurch Flit' is often read as a conventional Victorian redoing of a quaint folktale, but it is much more than this in the expert hands of Rudyard Kipling. The story of a child led back through history by a fairy was by no means unique to Kipling. In *Jim Crow*, for instance, the hero – who bears no relation to the American slaves for which the name Jim Crow became a soubriquet – is a boy who becomes too ill to take his part in the local pantomime. Instead, he meets various storybook characters, not only the fairies, but Guy Fawkes and Alice in Wonderland and Jack Frost. All of them are huddled together in a feverish muddle.[65] Kipling, by contrast, makes something of the notion that the fairies are a memory-trace, a living voice of the past – a way, in fact, to speak with the dead. The plot is as follows: the fairies of England (or Pharisees, as the story calls them) all crowd into Romney Marsh, horrified by the Reformation, less because they are Catholics than because they realize that they are reckoned among the images, and because they dislike strife. They disorder nature because of their vast numbers and distress; there are fires, plagues. They decide to take ship to France, helped by a poor widow with two sons, one of whom is blind and the other dumb. The fairies leave the family a special gift; there will always be a child in the family who has deep intuition, but no real wits.[66]

There is such a child listening to the story as it is told: the Bee-Boy, who understands and loves bees, but is a kind of 'natural', not unlike a changeling child. However, his family accept and love him – because of the legend, Kipling implies - so that the story becomes another story about children, a story about how children who are 'different' or difficult might be loved if they were sponsored by the fairies. Of course, this is also the story of Cinderella, and in Kipling's case it is related to the stories he wrote about his own childhood, notably 'Baa Baa Black Sheep', in which a sensitive, difficult little boy called Punch – Kipling – is understood as different and half-witted, prevented from reading or playing by a cruel relative who is looking after him while his parents are out in India.[67] In another sense, all Kipling's best-known fiction – from the Elephant's Child, through Mowgli and Kim to Stalky and Co – is about the acceptance of difficult children through the discovery of their special talents, but usually this discovery happens when the child makes contact with a realm apart from the home, a special, supernatural realm with different laws, not a cosy place, but one where challenges will bring out the child's gifts: a jungle, or the Indian frontier. For Kipling, the Sussex fairies offered yet another way to dramatize this profound and painful story. While undoubtedly over-optimistic about the reaction of traditional communities to those who had been in touch with the fairies, Kipling does resemble their story-tellers, Isobel Gowdie and Elspeth Reoch, in turning folk-stories into personal stories.

Of course there is much more going on in *Puck of Pook's Hill* than this; it is one of those outpourings of Kipling's absolute fresh genius where you keep stubbing your toe on the Empire. Puck is not so much a fairy as a kind of memory-trace; he contains all the stories of England which have to be understood, even internalized, in order for the Empire to flourish. Puck is also an English working-class countryman, maverick, tough, liking spontaneity and fond of puns, tricks and jokes. Using the extensive folklore collections published on Sussex at the end of the nineteenth century, Kipling was able to undo the more usual connection between the fairies and the upper classes, presenting a fairyland not as a land of leisured consumption, but as a place of hard work, craftsmanship and fun. (Puck's lineal descendants – though in far duller and tamer form – are J. R. R. Tolkien's beer-drinking, gardening hobbits, which is doubtless why the phrase 'Oak, ash and thorn', the phrase that summons Puck, is quoted in a song near the end of *The Hobbit*.) Puck's realm is contrasted with the refined idea of both children and country: Puck is also and self-consciously not tame, and through him Kipling asserts his anxiety about the over-refinement of *fin de siècle* England. It is also interesting that Kipling's fairy is solitary and quite self-sufficient; he is in fact the model for the empire builder, able to go on alone indefinitely because he has so securely internalized English culture that nothing can ever make him doubt himself. Dymchurch Flit is a necessary good. But more than any other fairy, Puck is also the precursor for that most famous of all near-fairies, Peter Pan; however, the world of enchantment into which he leads the children is far more serious than the Neverland, and his own place in it far less complex. Una and Dan are not there to complete him; he is complete already. They need him far more than he needs them. What made Kipling gloriously unlike his contemporaries is that in his world, the world of the Black Sheep, growing up is not a curse, but a blessed relief. We have only to turn briefly back to the stage, the stage written for rather than by children, to see why Kipling's stance might look desirable.

8

Tinker Bell's Magic and the Fairies' Call to War

Bluebell and Tinker Bell

Bluebell in Fairyland was *Peter Pan*'s precursor, *the* major influence on Barrie, and yet it is very different from *Peter Pan*.[1] The play is fascinating for revealing what Barrie left out, Bluebell's interest in and anxiety about working-class children. The arrantly middle-class Darlings are not in any real difficulty, despite having only one servant and a dog for a nurse. By contrast, Bluebell is a kind of apotheosis of Victorian fairy anxieties, in which the fairies themselves are brought on board, fairly enough, to resolve the problems created by their cult. Bluebell is a London flower-girl, one of the child-adults about whom the Victorians worried so. Dickensianly virtuous, unselfish and family-oriented, Bluebell's one aim is to give her little sisters a happy Christmas, 'and now – I've hardly enough to buy them dinner'. Bluebell's beau, a crossing-sweeper called Dicky, would like to help, but can't. He is a former pantomime actor, and irresistibly reminiscent of Bert from *Mary Poppins*. Yet though he is part of the meretricious world of the stage, Dicky knows that there is a beautiful, ideal, and of course rural, world beyond Covent Garden. The poor children of London are innocent of the pleasures of the country, and in a heart-rending scene, Dicky tries to explain them:

1ST BOOTBLACK Country? What's that?
DICKY Why, out of London –
1ST BOOTBLACK I didn't know there was any place out of London.
DICKY Oh! Hark at Livingstone! Corse there is; Where they've got the sky all painted blue!

ALL Gon!

DICKY Yus, – straight – and flowers everywhere.

Dicky then sings a tragic song, 'Just imagine 'Ackney with the 'Ouses took away'. Designed to inspire settlement work and other attempts to bring the workers into line with middle-class ideals, *Bluebell* wants to equate the green country with the fairyland Bluebell visits. Yet it also wants to see fairies as working Covent Garden children, which in theatre terms they often were. The flower-girls double with fairies, Dicky with the Sleepy King. But the play by no means sides with the moralists against the theatre. The fairy Water Lily sings a song:

> Fairyland is waiting when the dustman calls
> With the dustman for your friend
> There's a land of golden weather
> At the dreamy journey's end.

Eventually the rich Joplin, having tested Bluebell's honesty by giving her half a sovereign instead of sixpence, gives her a whole sovereign. Bluebell and Dicky want to spend it on a theatre or a music hall, the closest thing to the country available to them, a touch of beauty in their grey lives. Self-congratulating as this is, it is perhaps more realistic than the children's yearnings for the fields. But goody Bluebell goes home to her sisters and reads them the story of the Sleepy King. It was this story which fascinated the Llewelyn Davies boys and hence inspired Barrie. The King is doomed to sleep by a fairy because he is greedy and refuses to share his wealth with the poor (Hint!). He must sleep until a child comes to wake him. Thinking of the story, Bluebell falls asleep and is wafted to fairyland by the violet fairies of her unsold flowers. The king and queen of fairyland have put on a big party to try to distract all the children from searching for the Sleepy King. The party is all about greed. The queen announces that 'No children's party is a success unless they all feel thoroughly ill twice during the evening'. So wicked consumption is the key to deprivation, a neat way of preaching middle-class values of restraint while appearing to support the poor. The king and queen refuse Bluebell admittance because she is shabbily dressed, and so she goes off to search for the

Sleepy King on her own. She wakes the Sleepy King, who promises to be good to those in need. Recognizing him as Dicky, she rejects the chance to marry him and be king and queen of fairyland, choosing instead to return to her sisters. Joplin arrives to adopt her and her entire family, but the hard-to-please and Dorothy-like Bluebell rejects fairy and material splendours alike, choosing instead to marry Dicky in his role as street sweeper. Fairyland is only available to those who are willing to be dustmen – or perhaps to Those Who Know Their Place.

This was the play that inspired the work which more than any other manages to combine all the Victorian manifestations of fairies that I have been discussing, and some more ancient beings besides. Magnificent, magical; yet it also froze all those fairies, made them unchangeable. People's great love for this incarnation of the fairies was the second great blow to fairies after the trial of Oscar Wilde, and their enthusiasm was matched only by their queasiness at its whimsy, its advanced, full-blown and protracted whimsy. We all know *Peter Pan* so well. Or should we call it *Peter and Wendy*? Or *Peter Pan in Kensington Gardens* – which was originally called *The Little White Bird*? What should we call the innumerable alternative manuscript versions?[2] They do matter, because more clearly than any extant version of the story of Peter Pan, they reveal the origins of the play in Victorian fairy spectaculars and the traditions associated with them. Tinker Bell was once called Tippy Toe, and the original name marks her link with ballet girls in flesh-coloured tights. Originally, too, Barrie envisaged a Victorian-style fairy finale in Peter and Wendy's treetop house: 'flocks of fairy lights arrive like flocks of birds'.[3] Barrie told the press one scene of the new play was called 'The Birth of a Fairy'. There was a final scene closer to *Bluebell in Fairyland* than was the finished play. There was a scene in Kensington Gardens, at the Round Pond, where the newly posh Twins disdain Slightly, who has become a street-seller, selling balloons. Their mother calls him 'a vulgar boy'. Tootles, on the other hand, gives Slightly a cigarette end. The infamous scene known to Barrie and his entourage as the Beautiful Mothers scene matters too, for it illustrates the link between Peter Pan and other theatrical attempts to reform adult behaviour, other moral fairies whose goal it was to make adults behave and stop seeking naughty goblin Redgold. In the scene in question, candidates as mothers for the Lost Boys are put through a series of tests so coy and noisome that one balks at writing them down. Those who are not affected by the sight of baby clothes are not true mothers. The true mother can kiss her child without waking him, and at a fire alarm turns first to save her child. When hit by her son, her first thought is to see whether he has hurt his hand. She is patient when shoes are kicked off, and knows a child is hurt without his having to mention it.[4] (NB: I would fail this test.) It seems to be about the same anxieties about parenthood expressed in the moral fairy literature. Were parents properly fostering imagination? Were they spending enough time with their children? Were their children absolutely central to their lives? Buried in *Peter Pan* is a strikingly contemporary anxiety about who is minding the children – also expressed in the *agon* of having a dog for a nanny; no doubt this was all the agency could send. But Nana is the last faint trace of such moorings to social reality. It is as if Barrie used social issues as scaffolding, and then kicked the supports away to reveal a structure apparently timeless. This is, however, theatrical illusion.

We might as well begin with Tinker Bell, the play's only fairy and the book's only fairy with, as it were, a speaking part. Barrie explained Tink's origins with reference to the twin sacred cows of the nursery fairy, the child's imagination and the rural idyll:

It was one evening when we climbed the wood carrying [Michael] to show him what the trail was like by twilight. As our lanterns winked among the leaves, [Michael] saw a twinkle stand still for a moment, and he waved his foot gaily to it, thus creating Tink.[5]

Barrie just has to father Tink on a child, and if we listen to this sort of explanation we may forget to read the play and notice what she is really like. First, Tink is not a girl, but a special effect, and a rather headache-laden one at that. At first, on stage, they tried little cut-out figures, then a silhouette fastened on a spotlight and flashed about. Finally, a small mirror was held in the hand offstage, reflecting a little circle of light from a powerful lamp. Tink was a reflection, then, of nothing. More than any pantomime fairy hoisted to glory on a trapdoor, she existed solely as technology dictated, while pretending to represent its opposite. She did enjoy one season in 1911–12 of being played by a real girl, who could be seen dancing and tucking herself up in bed. She was only visible to that section of the audience who could see the end of the miniaturizing glass through which this effect was achieved. No one knows who this girl was, and the idea was short-lived.[6] Nowadays, at the National Theatre, Tink is a projected hologram. Reflected light and hologram are alike bodiless, more bodiless than miniaturization alone can achieve. And perhaps it is this radical disembodiment that allows Tink to be the most embodied, most sexual character in all versions of *Peter Pan* in which she appears. Tink is the only character in the play with adult sexuality, and that is because she derives from the erotic, near-naked fairies of the spectacles and extravaganzas, and not from the cuties of the nursery. Her morals are elaborately of the gutter; she is a would-be murderess, constantly trying to seduce the uncomprehending Peter. In fact, she exists in part to show that Peter is perfectly, seamlessly uncomprehending of sexuality; she guarantees his innocence, patrolling his sexuality, fiercely seeing off any other women who might make him more experienced. Yet Tink is also firmly under Peter's thumb, sometimes literally under it. Tink is also a pet, like a dog. Tink shouts that she is Peter's fairy, angrily insisting on her own complete submission. One can imagine Mick Jagger rejoicing in the correctness of the sentiment of the line in the Sixties.

Book-Tink is not a special effect, and the obtrusive narrator insists on her embodiment. Tink is 'slightly inclined to *embonpoint*'. Normally translated as obesity, *embonpoint* was actually the word that the women of the French aristocracy used to describe graceful curves short of obesity. Tink's antique furniture plainly proves her a member of the same class, though an upstart, for she mends the pots and pans. She has aristocratic leanings, however, to go with her aristocratic body. Barrie is having fun with the eighteenth-century idea of the fairies as ideally upper-crust.[7] In later visual versions of Tink, *embonpoint* becomes an excuse for a jokey sexualization. Disney's Tinker Bell was based on Marilyn Monroe, a kind of joke, of a sort Disney animators have always liked, an extrusion of adult sexuality into the sanitized world of Disney. As a sexual being, of course, poor Tink-Monroe was not immune to the seductive and gentlemanly wiles of Hook, and thus she betrays Peter, like some *noir*ish gangster girl in a Cagney movie. The fate of Tink-Monroe was interesting. Despite her leanings towards a life of whoredom and crime, she eventually became a pantomime fairy, changing scenes, introducing new places or stories by acting as curtain-raiser for the Disneyland television series, aired in the 1960s and 1970s. Like them, she carried on the still-older tradition of fairy-as-guide, fairy as guardian of the portals, fairy as transformer. Tink also became a logo, one of many fairies who ended their days as twentieth-century trademarks; she and her wand signified Disney's 'magic', the most artificial, meretricious magic ever made. More recently, Tink was doomed to be impersonated by the toothy, leggy, but breast-free Julia Roberts in Steven Spielberg's *Hook*. Unlike the intelligent Disney animators, Spielberg brought to Tink sexuality without sexiness. Roberts had played a whore in *Pretty Woman*, but a very, very clean one. Now, her Tink was more eager boy than woman, despite her love for Robin Williams's Peter. (In this film, it is Peter who inclines to *embonpoint*.) Roberts does not look like Tink, but like a Rackham fairy; thin, genderless, slightly deformed, ultimately sexless despite her status as a paid and praised object of desire. Thus, ironically, Roberts brought Tink back to being something like a dancing light reflected from a mirror, something mildly pleasing but completely unthreatening. The script also deleted Tink's Queen Mab furniture, her bad temper and her seductive wiles. Tink was purged of the pantomime fairy at last.

Tink is simple enough, once we have acknowledged that she is a pantomime fairy, a Miss Nina Montmorency. What about Peter? What is he? Children, at any rate, understand him as closer to Tink in the order of things than to the Darling children because both can fly without assistance. After each showing of the play, the cast were inundated with letters, very practical letters, from children. 'Dear Peter. Come to my house for tea and show me how to fly?'; 'Dear Tinker Bell, will you blow some Fairy dust over me, to make me fly. Love from Katherine.' The brighter children urge Peter to lend them one of those wires which allows him to fly himself.[8] For child-correspondents, Peter Pan is the power of flight. (My own son cried for three days after seeing the play because he couldn't learn to fly like

Peter Pan. He has been in a Jumbo Jet, but it's not the same.) Children also know that fairies have wings – if you ask a child to draw a fairy, you will get wings – and the play makes the connection explicit by showing that the Darlings can fly when sprinkled with the fairy dust. So Peter might be a sort of fairy? Maybe. Apart from his power to fly, Peter Pan is difficult to grasp. We can't get away from the diversity of him, not only what one might call the merchandizing, but the innumerable versions into which children's classics descend, in his case inaugurated by Barrie himself. There are the numerous actresses and latterly actors who have incarnated him. There are the innumerable stagings – every year Peter Pan came on in London a few days before Christmas and played until well into the New Year; every production went on tour for 10–12 weeks until the war put an end to revivals. There is the statue in Kensington Gardens, 'rather niminy-piminy for a boy who struck Hook from the lists of men', grumbled Patrick Chalmers.[9]

So let's begin with the obvious. Peter Pan is a hero of the empire. Adventurousness in remote and strange places is a language of empire. Peter subdues the Redskins and makes them his allies; if you think about it, it's a John Wayne part. Barrie was also influenced by Ballantyne's *Coral Island*, one of his favourite books. Peter clears the pirates out of the Caribbean: the Nelson touch. The boys refuse to become pirates on the grounds that they will not say 'Down With the King!' and doggedly sing the National Anthem against the pirates' choruses. In what she says is a message from their real mothers, Wendy urges her boys to die 'like English gentlemen'. Of course, this is all ironized a little, bracketed off. When Wendy says she hopes the boys will die like English gentlemen, it is impossible not to snicker, even though the sentiment is sincere enough. The snicker comes from the perception that Wendy is acting a part – she is only playing at being mother, just as the boys are only playing at death. This exposes such sentiments in general to the charge of play-acting. Patriotism and self-sacrifice are not the innate feelings of innocence, but carefully crafted and constructed sentiments. But not everyone saw it that way. After all, it would not be long before some real mothers were pushing their sons into the trenches on the Western Front with similar hopes. The founder of the Boy Scouts, Baden-Powell, used to visit the theatre night after night to see Peter Pan because he found it so moving. In 1915, the famous line 'to die will be an awfully big adventure' was omitted on account of the war, but this only points to the uncanny way in which the play defined Edwardian masculinity.[10] Peter was, first and foremost, the perfect Edwardian boy.

But he was also more, and in some ways less. The name, for instance? Pan is a goat-footed Greek god, already celebrated by Kenneth Grahame in his hymn to children-as-animals, *The Wind in the Willows*. Though not a fairy, one might call him a modified fairy, or rather an attempt to restore to the fairy image the vitality which was leaking away from it under the over-tender ministrations of the cuties and their makers. Descended from the Romantics, the cult of Pan embraced a kind of putatively amoral but innocent paganism. Maurice Hewlett's play *Pan and the Young Shepherds* similarly evoked Pan as a figure for perpetual boyhood. These connotations of rural beauty, childhood paradise and animality helped Peter Pan and abstracted him a little from normal boyhood. It allowed Peter to be presented as indescribably old and well-known, known even to your mother and grandmother. It also buries Peter in a past of memory, a lost realm of play, lost to adults.

So that is Pan; why Peter? Barrie used to walk his enormous St Bernard dog Porthos in Kensington Gardens, and there he met a little boy, four years old, with black curly hair and a rosebud mouth, who was called George Llewelyn Davies. Some months after this first encounter, Barrie sat next to a beautiful woman at a dinner-party. She said little, but at the end of the meal quietly gathered up all the sweets. 'They are for Peter,' she said. She was Llewelyn Davies's mother Sylvia, and Peter was George's younger brother. So 'Peter' was at first to Barrie the name of a little boy with a beautiful and selfless mother, second the name of the infant brother of a beautiful and friendly little boy. Barrie became an over-frequent visitor at the Llewelyn Davies residence. He adored Sylvia Llewelyn Davies and he formed close ties with the boys, especially George, the eldest, Michael, the first he had known from birth, and Nico, the youngest. As a baby, Michael too appears in *Peter Pan*. Nowadays, every women's magazine is on hand to tell mothers not to let middle-aged men hang around their children. But Barrie did not molest the Llewelyn Davies boys – indeed, it may be that what he loved about them was not his power to force them into sexuality, but their power to rescue him from it. Like Lewis Carroll, Barrie seems not to have liked sex overmuch; his marriage was something of a washout, and the couple had no children. Adult sexuality puzzled him. The sensuousness of childhood offered bodily pleasures that evaded the Edwardian regulation of sexuality. Nowadays, when reading Barrie's stickily rapturous account of the disrobing of David in *The Little White Bird*, one can hardly escape thinking nervously of paedophilia, but no one saw it that way when first published. So Peter Pan was one of the boys whose boyhood helped Barrie escape from those parts of himself he disliked.

In another way, biographically, Peter Pan is Barrie's dead brother David. Peter first saw light in Barrie's complex, curious book *The Little White Bird*, which is narrated by a man but which is about a boy called David. David Barrie died at the age of thirteen after a skating accident. 'When I became a man, he was still a boy of thirteen,' Barrie wrote ruefully.[11] The only real way not to grow up is to die. And just as Peter finds he has been replaced by another little boy, so Barrie's mother replaced David with him; guiltily, Barrie imagines a forlorn little ghost, pressed against the window, forever young but forever excluded from the one earthly joy of a mother's arms. Like a fairy, Peter is always a lightweight; he can acquire *gravitas* if he chooses, but only at the expense of immortality. He is a little mermaid who chooses to live out his three hundred years.

The play is positively swarming with dead children, like the old Sussex house in Kipling's story 'They'. For Wendy too, in a peculiar way, is a dead child; her name, which was invented by Barrie for the play, was the name Barrie himself was called by his goddaughter Margaret, the daughter of W. E. Henley, a little girl who could not pronounce the word 'friend' and so said 'fwendy'. This became 'wendy'. The little girl died – and she is Wendy – but Wendy is also Barrie, the self Barrie was with this particular child, now lost as she. The play uncannily and in some respects unpleasantly reanimates long-dead children. There is a W. W. Jacobs story, 'The Monkey's Paw', in which a couple use a magic talisman to wish their dead son back to life. When they hear his terrible, dragging footsteps, however, they think better of it and hastily wish him dead again.[12] Like Jacobs,

Barrie seems to be saying that parental love is a terrible, unnatural force, perverse to break the bonds of death. But he is also perversely celebrating its perversity, because death is a secret in the play and novel alike. The audience is never told that the children are dead. Indeed, the whole point of their reincarnation is to argue that they should not and cannot die. Like fairies. Children, and Peter Pan in particular, turn out to be doorways to death. Again, like fairies.

Like fairies in the play, too. Tink is the one who comes nearest to making death obvious. By drinking Peter's medicine, she nearly expires. This is, of course, a piece of theatre. The children in the audience have to clap their hands to show that they believe in fairies in order to save her. For a moment, they can feel that they have in themselves the power to defeat death. It is also a brilliant reversal of pantomime conventions. Normally, fairies help stranded, beleaguered children. Now it is the fairy who is stranded, and the children who must use their magic to help her. Mortals get the chance to do that in folklore, but mostly as mothers, not as children – midwifery, breastfeeding. Tink's near-death allows the children in the audience to play the mother's role of nurturing, saving. And yet, and yet . . . once the proscenium has been ruptured, once the child has become conscious of himself as a spectator, the theatricality of the entire enterprise becomes obvious. We are not being asked to make real magic; we are being asked to make technical magic, theatre magic, the fairy magic of the spectaculars. It has the same effect as the narrator's voice in the book. It makes things less real. And death on stage is always a rehearsal, a non-death, and hence a way of managing the real thing. If Tink's death allows the children in the audience to talk to death, it is only in play, for everything here is play. If Tink's death allows them to be mothers, it is only in the sense that everyone is a mother.

Nevertheless, the play does deal, at this oblique distance, with genuine death. For, after all, Peter started life as a gravedigger, the boy – or fairy, it is appropriately not at all clear which – who buries the dead children and who break the rules by staying in the garden overnight. He is a churchyard trowie. And like them, he can fly: Barrie made up a story for George about his brother Peter flying out of his pram like a bird – the little white bird of the title. We've met the trowies, and so had Barrie, who was after all among other things a

Scot. In *Peter Pan in Kensington Gardens*, though, when Mamie is left in the gardens overnight, it is the fairies who deal with her, and they do not bury her – well, not quite. They build a house around her instead, a symbolic tomb. In the play, matters are even clearer. Wendy is shot by Tootles, and though 'really' still alive, she is believed to be dead by the boys, who at once build a house like Mamie's around her. Every Wendy House is really a grave. The children in it are dead, but also perpetually reanimate, as Peter is forever young.

A play full of dead children also had a posterity oddly streaked with death. The Llewelyn Davies boys' parents both died, leaving the guardianship of the children to Barrie, whose passionate closeness to Michael in particular was remarked by mutual friends. In 1914, when the war began, George and Peter both joined up at once. George was killed in 1915, with *The Little White Bird* in his pocket. *Peter Pan*'s producer, who more than anyone was responsible for making sure it saw the light of day, went down on the *Lusitania* in 1915 when she was torpedoed by German U-Boats. Worst of all, Michael Llewelyn Davies drowned while an undergraduate at Oxford. It may have been an accident; it may have been a homosexual suicide pact. To this list one might add even Bobby Driscoll, the American child star chosen by Walt Disney to do Peter's voice in the cartoon film; he died young-old, drug-riddled, abandoned. Finally, Peter Llewelyn Davies himself threw himself under a train, long years after the war. This catalogue of tragedy says something about the atmosphere in which the play was written and performed, an atmosphere of acute anxiety about homosexuality and at the same time a passionate wish to preserve the aesthetic movement as a definition of what was civilized. Unable to square the circle or reconcile contradictory demands, the boys were indeed badly lost. Others were lost in a war in which they felt bound to die like English gentlemen. Above all, though, the play's vague credo of 'hope I die before I get old' probably encourages middle-aged despair. One cannot be Peter Pan for ever, unless one is Peter Pan himself.

The only way to avoid death, Barrie seemed to say, is to be dead already, as Peter and Wendy are, as fairies are. This is also the only way not to grow up, a sentiment echoed very often in the run-up to the Great War. 'Smart lad, to slip betimes away', enthused the poet

A. E. Housman, on an athlete dying young. Such parallels put Peter in the mainstream of his culture, its unrealizable ideal. But Peter is also a freak, like the dwarfs and elves exhibited at seventeenth- and eighteenth-century fairs. Like the tiny queen of the fairies, he is small where he ought to be big; his perpetual youth is a swerve away from the normal and into extreme, even disconcerting, oddity. A boy who really couldn't grow up, but who simply went on living and living and living; would such a boy, in the end, retain any joy in living to impart to others? This is also a question posed by fairies. Peter, like Ariel, who as we have seen also has traces of the freak, is hopelessly forgetful, unwilling to enter into any reciprocal, loving relationships. Ariel longs to be free of all obligation, as Peter is. But what does Ariel do with his freedom? Where does he go? Does it ever pall to lie in a cowslip's bell? Is immortality always a blessing? Especially since, like the fairy throughout its history, Peter can never be free of the desires of other people.

The fairies come to town

The darker side of *Peter Pan* was not immediately apparent. It did, however, inspire a lot of imitators, most of which have now been forgotten, perhaps because they half-consciously cleaned up the deathly undertones of the Gothic masterpiece and restored cute fairies to pride of place. W. Graham Robertson's play *Pinkie and the fairies*, first printed in 1909, follows Barrie in that the children are allowed to be positively contemptuous of the adults who cannot share their world.[13] It also shared Barrie's playfulness with the conventions of pantomime: 'But we're not going to wake up in our little white beds and find it's all been a dream, are we? That's such a rotten ending.' The Fairy Queen is reassuring. 'Of course not. That's a grownup's ending.' More conservatively, the play also struggles to prise apart fairies and consumers: these fairies disapprove of shopping:

TWINKLE The shops! Why, could you buy a Seven-leagued Boot in Bond Street or a Sword of Sharpness in St James's?

> In the shops of London Town,
> Though you range it up and down,
> Fairy gifts are seldom found;
> Horns of Elfland all are drowned
> By the motors' hoots.

Not everyone felt this way. By *Pinkie*'s date, fairies had begun to move into town. Rose Fyleman sees a fairy on a London bus, and speculates that she may have come up to town for the day, an increasingly common practice for her mortal relatives. Other fairies had begun to shop, and might have proclaimed 'I shop, therefore I am' to those sceptical of their existence:

> The Fairies have their Whiteley's,
> Their Gamage's as well,
> And Selfridge's and Harrod's,
> And oh! what things they sell!

Other modern innovations reached fairyland too. The fairies no longer had to rely on pipes. 'When you're still and quite alone,/ Hear the fairy gramophone.' Even more modish fairies had radios.[14] These fairies are the lineal descendants of the fairies of the stage. They are worldly fairies. Some such fairies got very worldly indeed. In one fairy school story (yes, you heard me), called *Puck in Petticoats*, Puck has been banished from fairyland until he can perform a heroic action. The heroic action he is called upon to perform is to be the friend of a schoolgirl called Meg, who is trapped by a strict, mid-Victorian aunt who makes her do sewing. Puck is forced to dress as a school-girl and assume the name Angela (irresistibly suggestive of Angela Brazil), but he then begins to enchant the household, so that the cross old maid, Hannah, who disapproves of pantomimes, is won over and finds herself singing a Christmas song, while eventually Meg goes joyfully to the seaside.[15] Trivial as the text is, here we have, *par excellence*, the Edwardian fairy, just before the deep seas close over him. He is fancy, imagination, childhood happy, sensuous, unconfined, and entirely constructed for the benefit of adults. For he is an antidote to the little deaths of adulthood, the unremitting and boring hard work. 'The man who does not know any story to tell his children was once John.' What could be sadder? For such a man, the entire superstructure of nursery fairyland was created, Peter Pan triumphant at its apex. And now the entire edifice is about to be brought crashing down by the third terrible blow to the fairy: the outbreak of the First World War.

The fairies go to war

Before the war, fairies were what one wrote about if one was going to be a writer. A lot of people better-known for other things got their start by writing about fairies, including Arthur Ransome, who in a noisome story has an uncle who enlightens his nieces about the little folk living in the bluebells.[16] (Why were bluebells such popular fairy residences? Woodlands and rural settings again.) John Betjeman in *Summoned by Bells* hilariously recalls wandering about Hampstead Heath with a notebook at the age of seven, hoping that people might exclaim, 'Look! There's a poet!', as he gazed skyward. He also records the verses his near-rural wanderings produced:

> When the moors are pink with heather
> When the sky's as blue as the sea,
> Marching all together
> Come fairy folk so wee.

His younger self was intoxicated by the perfection he had made – 'The brilliance of the rhymes, AB, AB!' It went on:

> Some in green and some in red
> And some with a violet plume,
> And a little cap on each tiny head
> Watching the bright white moon.

But now that poem is simply 'a reproach':

> In later years I falsified the date
> To make it seem that I was only seven,
> Not eight, when those weak stanzas were composed.

At the time, however, the young Betjeman was probably hailed as the epitome of elevated childhood sensibility, a fact which is perhaps such a reproach that he does not record it.[17]

However, the reason there is such a gap between the mature Betjeman's response to his poem and the paeans of praise it is likely to have received at the time is not the gap between adulthood and childhood, but something far simpler: the war.

When the first shell was fired on the Western Front, the cute fairy was doomed. At first no one knew it. At first, the war called up the fairies. Like other idle consumers, they were forced into essential war-work. In *Britain's Defenders*, the nature fairies gather to defeat invasion; Britannia points out that wind and wave successfully beat off the Armada. Will-o'-the-Wisp helpfully offers to lead the German planes into marshes, while Thunder and Lightning fairies are at hand to frighten the enemy, and Rain to help Mist veil the sun. Once assembled, the gallant band sing a song:

> Fairy bells are ringing,
> 'Forward to the fray!',
> Fairy bands are must'ring
> Through the night and day,
> Fairy voices calling,
> 'Britain needs your aid'.[18]

The fairies are a recruiting poster, just as they had been maths and grammar lessons. The contrast between the fairies' usual lifestyle of idleness and the activity now required of them is meant to be a spur to others of the leisured class; if the fairies can join the war effort, so must everyone. Of course, there is also a crude invocation of the notion that the fairies make England a chosen nation, but this is secondary. Eleanor Gray's *The War Fairies*, dedicated to her goddaughter who had volunteered as a VAD, makes exactly the same point. The fairies' associations with youth, femininity and leisure made them ideal representatives of the middle- and upper-middle-class girls who became war nurses. Here, however, the fairies do not fight; indeed, they have a feminine fear of the violence of war:

VIOLA Makes war o'erhead the sounds that shake the air,
And terrify the lilies?
MIGNON Yes, o yes!
And fall of tears that drenches them, and sighs
That rob of joy our revels.[19]

War is a threat to fairyland; its miseries make it impossible to enjoy a life of idleness while others suffer. The feminine sphere represented by fairyland appears separate from the masculine war, but is really linked to it by feeling; even Titania's drinking cup is stained with blood. And yet the fairies (read 'women') are also miserable because they are seen as too small to be of use. However, the dying soldiers, fetishized in the usual stomach-turning ways as azure-eyed young gods, die crying 'Home! Mother!'. Having seen this, knowing they are needed, the fairies can no longer enjoy Elfland. Gamely sacrificing their gowns and coronets for Red Cross get-up, they 'grow' in the mystical, unspecific way that souls always grow through hardship – on recruiting posters.

Few people now remember that Robert Graves's first volume of poetry was called *Fairies and Fusiliers*, published in 1917.[20] Admittedly, Graves has done his best to encourage forgetfulness by excluding the fairy poems in the volume from his *Collected Poems*. This is because the volume's title straddles a kind of emerging gulf in poetry; before the war, fairies were a proper subject for poetry, but after it, fusiliers were more appropriate. In the same way, Wilfred Owen, before his fateful meeting with Sassoon at Craiglockhart, was rather surprisingly working on an epic about the Little Mermaid. And yet it is also possible that the fairies and fusiliers are not divided from each other, but equivalent; that Graves is making an analogy between the alienated, innocent soldier on the Western Front and the image of the fairy as a lost, forgotten, betrayed innocent popular in Edwardian nurseries. The troops flocked to see revivals of *Peter Pan* while on leave, booking out whole blocks of seats many months in advance, and they also liked both *Puck of Pook's Hill* and retellings of the

Arthurian legends. Later, and much more emphatically, the same connection between the blighted waste of No Man's Land and a deserted fairyland was made by T. S. Eliot in *The Waste Land*. The ur-text here is of course Browning's 'Childe Roland to the Dark Tower Came', which as we have seen reimagines fairyland as a forlorn and hostile wasteland which the hero has to traverse in order to die, apparently purposelessly, before an alien host.

Another thing connects fairies and fusiliers, however. Victorian and Edwardian writers often wrote about taboo desires through the figure of the fairy; as we saw in the previous chapter, both Hans Christian Andersen and Oscar Wilde do so. The possibility that fusiliers *are* fairies, homosexuals, hovers uneasily above Graves's chosen title; it can almost be read as an awkward in-joke, a kind of code. Owen's mermaid, too, is a natural choice for someone struggling with homosexuality, given that Andersen's story is itself a tormented account of impossible and insatiable desire for the wrong object. The *Oxford English Dictionary* records the first usage of the word 'fairy' for a homosexual in 1895, and we have seen that the slang usage arose naturally from the association of stage fairies with drag, artificial femininity. Graves certainly knew of this association, for in a letter he draws a sharp distinction between children, 'the real fairies', and inauthentic fairies marked by their make-up as part of the stage tradition:

this afternoon, after a busy morning with Fusiliers, I am going down to Rhyl for the Fairies, not the fairies with rouged lips and peroxide hair but the real fairies; the colonel's kids have invited me to a special nursery tea and tiddlywinks.[21]

Graves's fairies represent a refuge from war and sex – the twin markers of masculine adulthood in 1917 – but a hopelessly insecure refuge, one that can offer no real resistance to destructive weaponry. While in places Graves simply evokes the pleasurable pastorals of the Victorian nursery, where 'Children born of fairy stock/ Never need for shirt or frock' – the vision is apt to turn bitter almost as soon as it is limned. Fairy children 'always get their heart's desire', says the speaker glumly, implying that he will not be so lucky. In 'Babylon', Graves evokes the image of the gay, innocent, heartless child we have met so often, but with a difference: childhood does not slip away, but is battered to bits. When young, 'Spring and Fairyland are his', but later:

> Wisdom made him old and wary
> Banishing the Lords of Faery.
> Wisdom made a breach and battered
> Babylon to bits; she scattered
> To the hedges and ditches
> All our nursery gnomes and witches.[22]

There is a painful analogy with shellfire; what makes us adults may be defined as 'wisdom' here, but wisdom comes in the guise of a mysterious aerial bombardment that blows innocence away. The pastoral spring landscape of fairyland turns to a no man's land where the scattered innocent are forced to shelter in ditches. On the Western Front, at long last, Peter Pan has to grow up. And in doing so, he discovers the terrible cost of adulthood to men.

Cultural historian Paul Fussell has shown how men on the Western Front saw their experiences in terms of Victorian medievalism.[23] William Morris's *Well at the World's End* was particularly influential, a story of an epic struggle across a blasted landscape, a landscape filled with leering corpses. Morris was evoked constantly along the Ypres Salient and at the Somme. One young veteran of the Somme, retired home with trench foot, was responsible for reinventing the epic romance saga in a way that incorporated the blasted landscape and the refuges of fairylands. While the young J. R. R. Tolkien nursed his unserviceable feet, he wrote his own epic romance version of the Somme, the first of his stories about the Elves, 'The Fall of Gondolin'. Gondolin is an Elven-city, perfect in its way, and early drafts contain long, loving descriptions of its beauty. A refuge, then, from the dreadful memory of the Somme? Yes, but not for long. Like Graves's fairies and gnomes, scattered by the shellfire of adulthood, Gondolin too is a paradise lost, for it is invaded and captured by the forces of darkness. Tolkien's stories are repetitive, involving the same lapsarian narrative again and again; the Elves build a paradise, and that paradise is despoiled by war. Even as late as *The Lord of the Rings*, the Elves still inhabit and represent *refuges* from war, as if their whole business is to build enclaves, imagined enclaves, where the pressing horrors of war cannot reach. When Frodo is in Lorien, it is as if he is in another world; even time moves differently there. Thus the work imitates the mental job it is doing for its author; Gondolin, Lorien and the rest are Tolkien's imaginative refuges, longed for and enjoyed, but he knows them to be false; he knows now that the nebulous Enemy can get in and blow them to smithereens. He has grown up. And he knows it; one of the framing devices he considered for the stories that eventually became *The Silmarillion* was 'The Cottage of Lost Play', in which a nursery gnome and elf tell stories to one another while the deepening shadows close in around them.[24] For the generation that had been to the Western Front, play was always lost.

9

Photographing Fairies, and a Celtic Revival

Mortally wounded by the carnage on the Western Front, fairies limped into the twentieth century. However, at first their critical condition was not apparent. An observer might even have thought them in fine fettle, for two new and radical attempts were made to yoke them to the twentieth century and its passions. When Arthur Conan Doyle authenticated the fairy photographs taken by two adolescent girls in a Yorkshire mining town, he moved fairies from heroines of story to the objects of the voracious lenses of the twentieth century and its mania for the visual. From that moment on, the fairies were as vulnerable to the paparazzi as any other superstar. When William Butler Yeats, Augusta Gregory and Maud Gonne linked fairies with Irish nationalism, Irish volkgeist and (in Gonne's case) Irish feminism, they were also tying the fairy into the world of the twentieth century. Yet ultimately both these exciting rebirths were stillbirths, and the fairy was doomed to dwindle still further.

Seeing things?

Victorian fairy paintings had been partly motivated by a desire to prove the superiority of the painter to the mere photographer. The exactitude of the latter was seen as inimical to the festive playground of the imagination. But it was in photographs that the Victorian fairies, the cute fairies, reached their apotheosis, and in so doing the last great blow against the fairy was struck. In February 1920, a man called Edward L. Gardner received a packet containing some photographs showing two girls, a fifteen-year-old called Elsie Wright and a ten-year-old called Frances Griffiths, surrounded by fairies. The fairies had been photographed by the girls in July 1917, while the First World War still raged.

This, the greatest of all fairy stories, began simply and charmingly. Frances loved to play down by the beck, but she kept falling into the stream, and wetting her clothes. There were scoldings. There were tears. Finally, Frances thought of a magnificent justification for her recidivism; she burst out that she loved to play by the beck because that was where the fairies were. It was a little Wordsworthian, a little Barrie-esque, all those tumbles into the stream. Perhaps Frances hoped that the adults would think this cute, would think it was proof of her elevated imagination, her unconstrained Romantic childhood. If so, she was doomed to disappointment; the adults did not believe her. Like all children, Frances was indignant when disbelieved, however big the whopper told. She told Elsie, and Elsie had the brilliant idea of taking a photograph of the fairies to show the sceptical adults.[1]

So began a story of a war between belief and disbelief, proof and disproof, a war that was not finally settled even when on 9 March 1983, the *Yorkshire Evening Post* reported that Elsie admitted at last that the photos had been faked.[2] Why were the photos important? Photographs of fairies sought to reunite the parts of the fairy scattered by the stage spectacular, bringing together visual spectacle and reality. You could see it, marvel at it, and yet find it authentic. You could also have a good laugh at it, and shake your head. All those earlier articles, in the same *Strand Magazine* where the Cottingley fairies were first widely publicised, explaining how the stage fairies were whizzed about on traps, may have made an impact. People did not on the whole believe in the Cottingley fairies, even when first revealed to the world. Among their small band of devotees, however, another reason is that they offered a last hope for the theosophical project, which tried to reconcile the claims of science and religion. Founded in 1875 in New York by Helena Petrovna Blavatsky as its leading light, theosophy claimed to be 'a scientific religion and a religious science'. For theosophy, we are surrounded by invisible beings, existing as high-level vibrations not normally appreciable by human beings. As humanity evolves, we will be able to see the lower orders of the hierarchy and then successively higher ones, until identity with the deity is achieved. Humanity has not reached the stage where even the lowest order, the nature spirits, can be seen, except very rarely by specially gifted people. In 1920, Edward Gardner was president of the Blavatsky lodge of the Theosophical Society in London, and he had strong beliefs about the existence of fairies. Elsie and Frances's mothers developed an interest in theosophy, and went to a meeting entitled 'Fairy Life' at the Bradford Theosophical Society in summer 1919. Elsie's mother, Polly Wright, mentioned the fairy photos, and Edward Gardner thus got to know about them. From then on, it was only a matter of time before either Gardner or one of his other associates astounded the public with the discovery.

It was not, however, Edward Gardner who brought the fairies to public attention, but Sir Arthur Conan Doyle, the man who wrote the Sherlock Holmes stories, stories of a godlike, sceptical investigator who uses scientific rigour to discern that the Hound of the Baskervilles is a fake. Conan Doyle championed the photos, and in doing so did much to destroy his own reputation. He had to distort the facts to do so. The girls' photos were sent to three expert photography laboratories for authentication. Only one of the experts said he was sure the photos were single-shot outdoor exposures and that the fairies were not painted on the photography plate. The Kodak lab said that they could not guarantee that the photos were not a fake; another lab said they were pretty sure they were a fake, but Conan Doyle decided they were biased. In his original article in the *Strand Magazine*, Conan Doyle said that Kodak had said confidently that the photos were single exposures, which they had; he suppressed the more damning sections of their report. Why? Why did someone as intelligent as Conan Doyle believe in fairies?

Conan Doyle had many occult beliefs, and he always claimed that these were based on his own keen powers of observation. He believed in spiritualism and spirit manifestations. 'In a fair light I saw my dead mother as clearly as ever I saw her in life,' he wrote. 'I am a cool observer and I don't make mistakes.' The trouble with thinking you are Sherlock Holmes is that you are apt to think you cannot be fooled, and Holmes believes in sinister groups of killer Mormons, after all. Spiritualism was a focus for subjecting the supernatural to the thoughtful, cool observation of those who, like Conan Doyle, hoped to reconcile the unseen with science. Spirits as conjured by mediums were supposed to be visible; various attempts were made to photograph them and to 'prove' their existence. Ectoplasm, the substance which made the spirits of the dead visible, was examined through photographs and was subjected to the laws of science.[3] As the world moved from stories to scenes, from a culture of words to one of images, the supernatural too had to make that transition. Photos of ectoplasm made it seem more likely that the air and the woods were full of things visible only to a gifted few.

Fairies and seances had already been connected, too. In 1900, *Fairy Tales from Fairyland* appeared, claiming to be written by automatic writing: 'a "fairy" moved my hand, while I heard a soft, low voice whisper each word in my ear'.[4] The stories have an clear spiritualist inflection. One concerns a lazy boy, called Jack – the fairies are evidently well-acquainted with the classics of folklore – who is overjoyed when a fairy comes to tell him that this morning he can lie in for as long as he likes. Jack does not know that this is not a fairy but the Angel of Death. In the afterlife, he soon meets old friends, who ask him what he has done to account for his time. Luckily, this Awful Warning turns out to be a dream – Jack wakes up in his little white bed and beavers away diligently thereafter, eager to win the respect of those on the other side. (There is nothing more stultifyingly moral than spiritualism.) Spiritualism, of course, was a very direct way of speaking with the dead, giving them words and receiving words from them, placating them, loving them, feeding them. The huge and horrible death-toll on the Western Front, the sense among fathers especially that the war dead might not be rich, as Rupert Brooke had foretold, but angry, encouraged spiritualism.[5]

The Cottingley photos could also be forced awkwardly into the cult of the fairies and the innocent child that we have been examining. Conan Doyle's rapturous depiction of the fairies shows how deeply he felt the educated Edwardian's passion for the innocent, the child-like, and above all, the pre-war:

There is an ornamental rim to the pipe of the elves which shows that the graces of art are not unknown among them. And what joy it is in the complete abandon of their little graceful figures as they let themselves go in the dance! They may have their shadows and trials as we have, but at least there is great gladness manifest in this demonstration of their life.[6]

Rustic dances, joy, even the Arts and Crafts movement – we are back in the Merrie Englande of the Young Englanders, except now it is a country that can be reached only through death or (the same thing?) by children. The desperate, panting enthusiasm of Conan Doyle's prose speaks of the longing of a bereaved world for reassurance that spiritual realms offer happiness denied on earth. It is the old Romantic solution, garnished with fairies.

Cottingley also invokes the Romantic child. Neither Gardner nor Conan Doyle say much about the girls themselves, and what is said is often misleading. Key facts were suppressed. For instance, Elsie Wright left school at thirteen. She had a short spell at Bradford College of Art, and then got a job spotting black and white prints at Gunstone's Photographers in Bradford. She left and took another job colouring portrait photographs. This expertise in photography was not mentioned by Conan Doyle; nor was Elsie's working life generally. This was less because it pointed to photographic fakery than because it linked Elsie uneasily with an adult world of work, an industrial world of colour plates and chemicals. Conan Doyle also suppressed her stints working for a jeweller. Both girls were constantly spoken of as if much younger than they actually were, a trend followed in recent film versions of the story. This is why in every account Elsie and Frances are referred to as 'girls', even as 'little girls', when in fact both were adolescent. Fairies in adolescence would have different, less wholesome connotations. The issue is particularly plain to Gardner, who stresses the youth of the girls, their humble, simple origins, and above all their sexual innocence:

The children who were concerned are very shy and reserved indeed . . . They are of a mechanic's family of Yorkshire, and the children are said to have played with fairies and elves in the woods since babyhood . . . I am hopeful of getting more photographs, but the immediate difficulty is to arrange for the two girls to be together. They are 16 or 17 years old and beginning to work and are separated by a few miles. It may be we can manage it and thus secure photographs of the other varieties besides those obtained. These nature spirits are of the non-individualised order and I should greatly like to secure some of the higher. But two such children as these are, are rare, and I FEAR now that we are late because almost certainly the inevitable will shortly happen, one of them will fall in love, and then – hey presto!!!'[7]

Despite the fact that both girls are working, and '16 or 17 years old', Gardner insistently calls them 'children', a usage made unnatural by the very child labour laws which outlawed the pantomime fairies. He also insists that they are not yet grown-up by lamenting the fact that they may do it soon, and for Gardner to grow up is to be sexually active. Gardner is also betraying a notion of mediumship, influenced not by the history of fairies, but by Edwardian spiritualism. As we have seen, the very last thing fairies might have objected to is sexual awareness.

These are the complicated reasons, but there was also a simple one, one any writer can understand. When he first saw Gardner's lantern slides of the Cottingley fairies, Conan Doyle already had a commission to write an article for the *Strand* on fairy beliefs. He wanted to make a splash. He needed material. He was hoping that his scoop was true. Like Fox Mulder, Conan Doyle wanted to believe.

And to this day, there are those who also want to believe, who argue that even if the photos are fake, the fairies are real. For some, the fairies' reality is even guaranteed by the fake photos; the children would only go to such trouble for real fairies, argue the faithful. They proudly cite Frances's letter of 9 November 1918 to a friend in South Africa enclosing a print of the first photograph they had taken. 'I am sending two photos, both of me,' the letter reads. 'One is in a bathing costume in our back yard, uncle Arthur took it, while the other is me with some fairies up the beck, Elsie took that one.'[8] What could be more artless, say the fairy believers? Actually, children often fail to make distinctions between what they have imagined or made and what is really so. But the point is one that will be uncomfortably familiar to us; for some, a child cannot lie, and cannot be mistaken about the truth. Just as adults urged the world to believe the children in cases of alleged child abuse, so we are urged to believe Elsie and Frances. Fairies – at least, the Cottingley type of benign wingy things – are themselves a creation of the same cult of the innocent child here used to 'prove' their authenticity. Cottingley is not about a straight choice between believing the girls are lying, or believing in fairies. There are many states which are neither lying nor truth, especially for children and adolescents, for whom the boundaries between let's pretend and reality are perhaps less secure than for adults. Fairies might *feel* very real to a child who has never really seen one, just as monsters can seem uncomfortably real in the long watches of the night. Alternatively, human beings for thousands of years and in every pre-industrial society have believed in such people, largely because they fitted with their world-view. Perhaps fairies also fitted Elsie and Frances's world-view, so that it came to be a case not of why, but of why not. Fairies were in the air of childhood in 1917. Like adults, children can be induced to accept an adult view of what a child should be. When interviewed by the *Westminster Gazette* in 1921, Elsie certainly knew what a Romantic child was supposed to say. Remarking that the fairies were harder to see than in previous years, she added: 'You see, we were young then.'⁹

Perhaps there was something specific about the girls' circumstances that made fairies seem likely or natural. After all, these were girls on the border, between childhood and adolescence. Fairies and fairy photographs may have been for Elsie and Frances just what they were for Elspeth Reoch three hundred years earlier: ways to talk about changes that could not be spoken of otherwise. They may also have been a way to gain some authority, to be interesting, to be important, as they were for Andro Man; Conan Doyle and the London press did not visit every girl, after all, and we have seen that the mere writing of fairy verses made other girls into stars of the firmament of cuteness. Or perhaps the two girls had different agendas: Elsie was the one who admitted that the photos were fake; Frances, later in life, always said that the last photo was real, that the fairies were real. We cannot now know what the two girls said to each other as they set out with their camera, but perhaps what was a kind joke for Elsie, an attempt to amuse her younger cousin, was more real for Frances; Frances was younger and more apt to muddle play with reality, and Frances was the one in a strange country, without friends, with her way to make.

Perhaps, too, fairies' long associations with theatricality, trickery and daylight robbery are coming into play. 'Knowing children, and knowing that Sir Arthur Conan Doyle has legs, I decided that the Miss Carpenters [their false name] had pulled one of them,' said one press report. An American paper was blunter: 'Poor Sherlock Holmes – Hopelessly Crazy?'[10] Whatever the intentions of Elsie and Frances, tricksters did eventually gather around them. Gardner revisited Cottingley with a clairvoyant and believer in fairies, Geoffrey Hodson, author of *Fairies at Work and Play*, and someone who saw fairies everywhere.[11] Elsie and Frances both thought *he* was a fake. Still other fakers used their skill in faking to expose the photos as fake, both then and more recently: James 'the amazing' Randi used computer image enhancement to analyse the photos, and claimed to have found the strings holding the fairies up.[12]

There were no strings, however. Instead, there were hatpins. The Cottingley fairies were traced from a book, cut out of Winsor and Newton paper, stuck on hatpins, then photographed. Said the elderly Elsie in 1980,

My heart always sinks when I look at it [the photo]. When I think of how it's gone all round the world – I don't see how people could believe they're real fairies. I could see the backs of them and the hatpins when the photo was being taken.[13]

The source for some of the illustrations, too, seems properly old-fashioned: Alfred Noyes' poem, 'A Spell for a Fairy', was published in *Princess Mary's Gift Book* in 1914, just before the Western Front made the fairy aesthetic seem both desperately necessary and hopelessly anachronistic. Cottingley, in the reality of the two girls most closely involved, was not an attempt to bring fairies into the modern world, but to return to a world before the war. Despite the frisson of modernity lent to the issue by photographs, the fairies were actually refreshingly homemade. There is nothing hi-tech about cut-outs on hatpins, which instead recall pre-cinematic, pre-photographic methods of creating visual illusion; shadow shows, even puppet shows, the little cardboard theatre of the Victorian pantomime, where one cut out the characters and stuck them to sticks to make upright figures. It is such nursery games which go best with the fairy; she is and remains out of her depth in modernity.

When we look at the most famous of the Cottingley photos, what we see is so obviously fake that, like Elsie, we can't see how anyone can ever have believed in it. One of the main reasons contemporaries found the fairies less than credible was their stereotypical appearance. One photographer mentioned 'the elaborate Parisian coiffure of the little ladies'.[14] The lissom Edwardian bodies, the careful Edwardian hairstyles, the little wreaths of flowers, are all redolent of turn-of-the-century illustrations in children's books. The Cottingley fairies look as if they have stepped straight out of the pages of an Edwardian fantasy of childhood. Bluntly, they have dated. The very features which made them look like fairies at the time, make them seem hopelessly unlikely now, hopelessly of their time rather than outside it, as fairies should be. They look quaint, and by extension, they make the people who believed in them look quaint and remote too.

Some recent film-makers would disagree. The year 1994 saw two films released based on the Cottingley material. Both sought to explore the odd relations between photographs and fairies, or rather between fairies and special effects. The more successful of the two, *Fairy Tale: A True Story*, signals in its title an arch, knowing relationship with truth.[15] In the film, too, the photos are fake, but the fairies are real. But what is real? The film's swarming real fairies are special effects, another kind of cut-out, another kind of hatpin. Far more successfully than Elsie and Frances, the film seeks to make fairies come to life by visual art. And yet the film is self-conscious about a dilemma that Conan Doyle preferred to ignore: the very technology that can make fairies visible is also visible *as* technology. The film was not just about belief; it was also about the magician film-maker, with his box of special effects; they don't call it Industrial Light and *Magic* for nothing. And yet morphing and foley editing and so forth are the antithesis of the simple pastoral world of childhood that the film hopes to create with their help. Essentially, this is a dilemma – or an opportunity – held over from the special effects which made Victorian fairies appear on stage. The film badly wants to side with this simple world, but in the end it shrugs its shoulders, aware that it is now accessible to children only through its own hi-tech labours. And yet it also sells itself as a world of pastoral innocence prior to technology; the film takes place in a Hovis commercial village where everyone and everything is bathed in soft golden and blue light. We can see the longing for simple belief in the way the film's website divided its visitors into two categories by asking them if they believed in fairies; those that said yes got much richer responses.[16] Yet this too is arch, as *Peter Pan* was; it asks a question which speaks more to the longing to believe than to the reality believed in. The film's slogan, 'Believe', is an invocation, a cry into silence, one which draws attention to the difficulty of belief in a world in which the supernatural can be faked.

The Cottingley photos too had descendants: photographer Dorothy Inman made a kind of Frankly Fake Cottingley photo, though she died without revealing how she had done it.[17] Others turned up with more photos claiming to be genuine, several of which were eagerly reproduced by Conan Doyle himself. Fairy photos are still sometimes printed, and not only in the *National Inquirer*.[18] One of the most recent such photos depicts a fairy on the beach at La Jolla, California. Yet all fairy photos are subject to exactly the same problems faced by their Victorian predecessors; what can be seen can be faked. In this way, the supernaturalists failed to find a way to yoke fairies to modernity by the simple expedient of making them representable within it.

Fairies of the Celtic Twilight

While some searched for real fairies with a camera, others were searching with a notebook. In England, folklore continued to be all the rage; the establishment of the Folklore Society in 1878 saw many a nice young Englishman set out into the countryside, where there were plenty of locals who for a pint would tell him how they had once found the Holy Grail. While Gardner and Conan Doyle were trying to persuade the world to accept the Cottingley photographs, a group of Irish men and women were engaged in a far more subtle and in the long run more effective attempt to link fairies with the concerns of modern men and women. The poet William Butler Yeats, the folklorist and writer Lady Augusta Gregory, and others, seized on Irish fairy lore as a distinctive, special feature of Irish culture that could be used to give Ireland a separate and meaningful national identity, at a time when Ireland was again struggling to free itself from British rule. They succeeded to such an extent that fairies and folklore became an essential part of Irishness. Under the government of Eamon de Valera, IRA leader and later Prime Minister of the Irish Free State, folklore and folkways were promoted as essential to Irish life. To this day, every local Irish bookstore sells hefty volumes of fairy legends.

There had always been Irish fairies, or *sidhe* (pronounced 'shee'), of course, just as there are such small beings everywhere. Or had there? Those familiar with Irish legends will know that the Fenian Cycle, part of which survives in manuscripts from the eighth century, contains many fairy elements. It centres on the exploits of Fionn MacCumhaill (Finn MacCool) and his warriors, the Fianna. Fionn's first wife, Sadb, first appears as a fawn, leads Fionn to an otherworld dwelling, and gives birth to his son Oisin, who in turn takes as a lover Niamh. But Niamh is only identified firmly as a fairy in the late eighteenth-century versification by Micheál Coimin; only there does she lead Oisin to the Land of Youth, Tir na nÓg, as a fairy queen might. From Tir na nÓg, Oisin returns to Erin greatly aged. It all sounds persuasively ancient, but Coimin could have been reading Scottish ballads, Arthurian legends, or even Spenser's *Faerie Queene*, to get his ideas.[19] There is no immediate reason to imagine that they come exclusively from Irish folklore. The assumption that the spirit-women of the Otherworld of the hero sagas have anything to do with the *sidhe* who infest nineteenth-century Irish folklore is just that: an assumption. The same applies to the Tuatha dé Danann, Tir na nÓg, and all the rest of the gods who have been nominated for the role of Earliest Sighting of an Irish Fairy. Of course they have some characteristics in common, and these are important, but they are also shared with beings from all over the world. They therefore do not define the Irish national character.

And yet that was what the first wave of Irish folklorists wanted from fairylore. Thomas Crofton Croker's *Fairy Legends and Traditions of the South of Ireland* set the ball rolling, but for his successor Douglas Hyde, Croker had sinned in allowing the literary tastes of the nineteenth century to get between the reader and the folk:

when the skeletons were thus padded round and clad, they were no longer folklore themselves, for folklore can only find a fitting garment in the language that comes from the mouths of those whose minds are . . . primitive.[20]

The hunt was on for an absolutely authentic Irish culture, one not adulterated by more widespread European literary tastes. The trouble was that the very search for authenticity was itself the product of pan-European nationalism and Romanticism, but this did not deter those searching high and low for an Ireland that had somehow survived the British and that could be used to oust them.

Yeats too stressed the timeless significance of Irish folklore, and tried to connect it with the Irish epics of Cúchulain and Fionn, and with the pantheon of Celtic deities. In *The Celtic Twilight*, Yeats wrote:

One hears in the old poems of men taken away to help the gods in a battle, and Cúchulain won the goddess Fand for a while . . . I have been told, too, that the people of Faery cannot even play at hurley unless they have on either side some mortal.[21]

Bringing together every level and period of the Hibernian story around the theme of mortals and gods, Yeats neglects to mention the main classical and Norse myths that are similar. This gives his local fairy legends, and by extension his poetry, a patina of age. In his play *The Land of Heart's Desire*, for instance, Yeats begins by instructing that the characters 'are dressed in the costume of some remote time'. The daughter of the household, Bridget, has unearthed an old book from the thatch of the roof. The old book tells an even older story, the story of Princess Edain, who heard a voice singing on a May evening, and 'followed, half awake and half asleep', until she reached the Land of Faery, where no one gets old. The idea that nothing is mortal in fairyland – or faeryland, as Yeats preferred – is central; fairies stand outside the miseries of biology, and outside history too, outside its restless flux. And yet the fairies of *The Land of Heart's Desire are* history; they are a past which bypasses the years of British rule and cultural alienation. They represent an Irish culture that has been kept pure and intact from before the conquest.[22]

The IRA and Sinn Fein leadership were all involved in the Gaelic League, the Gaelic Sports League and sundry other attempts to revive true Irishness; even a pragmatist like Michael Collins changed the spelling of his name to Micheál.[23] More ardently idealistic nationalists like the poet Padraic Pearse, a leader of the 1916 Easter Rising, and Maud Gonne, the Republican beauty of whom Yeats was for many years enamoured, were apt to see their own lives and political aspirations in terms of their occult researches into the Irish supernatural. Pearse wrote:

When I was a child I believed that there was actually a woman called Erin, and had Mr Yeats's Cathleen Ni Houlihan been then written and had I seen it, I should have taken it not as an allegory, but as a representation of a thing that might happen any day in our house.[24]

Maud Gonne, in her autobiography, likens herself to Cathleen, a part she played on stage, and also reports delightedly that 'they [local people] are saying you are a woman of the Sidhe who rode into Donegal on a white horse surrounded by birds to bring victory'.[25] This delightfully self-aggrandizing vision puts Irish liberationists into a timeless tradition of Irishness. Such projections intrigued Yeats, endlessly spurned by Maud Gonne. Perhaps they could not come together in the real world because Maud was fairy-taken? While fruitlessly pursuing Maud, Yeats wrote a number of poems about encounters between mortals and fairies. 'The Stolen Child', 'A Faery Song' and 'The Host of the Air' describe mortals stolen by fairies, while 'The Man Who Dreamed of Faeryland' and 'The Song of Wandering Aengus' describe mortal men who encounter exquisite fairies only to lose them.[26] If Maud was indeed 'a woman of the Sidhe', then was she a woman taken from Yeats by them, or a fairy woman who could act as inspiration for him, as fairy women had for the Romantics? For Yeats, fairies were ambivalent; he pondered – one might almost say worried over – their mixture of benevolence and malice, eventually concluding, with great significance for his personal life and his politics, that fairies had fair faces but were chillingly malevolent underneath, like lamiae. Though slightly sanitized, the fairies in Yeats's poems bear this out. Was Maud, too, a lamia – or more importantly, were Yeats's folkloric researches skewed by his wish to find in them stories which would let him cope with her constant rejections? If so, Yeats was like the Cottingley girls, using fairies to make sense of his own life, just as the peasants he so admired did, but not with the same results.

In any case, how Irish are Yeats's fairies, really? Though he played up his own folklore researches, Yeats's fairy poems draw very heavily on Keats in particular, and 'The Song of Wandering Aengus', at least, is a kind of Celticization of 'La Belle Dame sans Merci'. Like Keats, Yeats makes the fairy both a seductive muse-figure and also an image of death, an image of death because she is so incalculably old. While practising spirit-writing with his wife George, many years later, Yeats made a point of asking the spirits about Keats and the transference of thoughts from the dead to the living, and he saw Keats's thoughts floating freely in the general mind, ready to be tapped.[27] Seductive though this sounded, it was tugging against the attempt to use folklore to map Irishness. Yeats also favours the Keatsian spelling 'faery', ever since a harbinger of the Romantic fairy. The irony is that Keats derived the spelling from Edmund Spenser's *Faerie Queene*, an Irish poem all right, but one unremittingly hostile to everything that Yeats was passionately trying to revive. Yeats's interest in the mystical and the universal was in tension with his solidarity with Irish folklorists in their attempts to salvage the Irish peasant from British rule.

By contrast, Lady Gregory was interested in the stories of the Irish peasantry, and unlike Yeats did not especially value fairies, or did not value them above her Kiltartan tenants' accounts of encounters with the Tans.[28] Her fairy stories are – not more accurate than Yeats's, for that is difficult to determine; she is however much more interested than he is in the words spoken rather than the essence of the story, because she is not trying to reconcile that essence with mythic materials from other cultures. Gregory created a new kind of Irish folklore, but it is Yeats's syncretism that has remained influential among the general public, as we shall see in due course.

Another kind of dark underside to Yeats's fairy fantasies becomes visible when we notice that the little girl in 'The Host of the Air' is called Bridget, like the girl in *The Land of Heart's Desire*. A good Irish name to be sure, but in a horrifying instance of life imitating art, it came to have other, darker connotations.[29] The name Bridget might derive from a story in William Wilde's *Irish Popular Superstitions*, in which a young woman called Biddy Mannion gives birth to a son after a year of marriage. She is abducted as a wetnurse to the fairies, and in the fairy palace meets a lady who is also mortal, and who warns her not to eat or drink within the palace. Biddy therefore refuses all food and drink, and as a result is allowed to leave, but not before the Fairy King gives her an ointment which reveals the fairy palace as a dark charnel-house: 'the place was full of dead men's bones, and had a terrible musty smell'.[30] In William Allingham's poem, too, Bridget's sojourn with the fairies is a form of death, as is her return to the mortal world:

> They stole little Bridget
> For seven years long;
> When she came down again
> Her friends were all gone.
> They took her lightly back
> Between the night and morrow
> They thought that she was fast asleep
> But she was dead with sorrow.[31]

In Yeats's poem, the eventual loss of Bridget to the fairy man is a bereavement, but also a shame; through fairy glamour the husband, O'Driscoll, is a helpless witness of his wife's adultery:

> He bore her away in his arms
> The handsomest young man there
> And his neck and his breast and his arms
> Were drowned in her long dim hair.[32]

As Bridget and her intensely erotic lover ride away, O'Driscoll is deserted by the fairy host, left to wander on a cold hillside. In place of his wife, he is offered a vision of the fairies and the sound of their pipes. The poem tries hard to make this sound more fun than marriage, but its anxiety creeps through its own defences. In any case, the poem is nervously hostile to its heroine, either because she represents the dreary workaday or because she can be welcomed by the airy and voluptuous delights of its opposite while her husband sits dull and alone on the grass. The poem was originally entitled 'The Stolen Bride', a name which points, starkly, to male possessiveness and jealousy.

Such hostility was much more apparent in the fairy abduction of another Bridget. While Yeats was dreaming of a man who accepted the sound of pipes as a substitute for the loss of his wife, a Tipperary man called Michael Cleary refused to accept the fairies' verdict. Michael believed that his wife Bridget had been abducted by the fairies too, like the Bridgets of the songs. She *seemed* to lie in bed, ill, but he *knew* that the thing in the bed was not really his wife, and he wanted his wife back. He knew just what to do. Helped by his male neighbours, he touched the thing in the bed with a red-hot poker, urinated on her, held her over the kitchen stove, all the while asking her if she were really Bridget, really his wife. When efforts to force a confession failed, Michael became desperate; he threw the woman of the *sidhe* on the floor, and held burning wood to her mouth. 'Say your name', he begged, 'three times'. She could not do it. So he doused her with lamp oil and set fire to her. Bridget Cleary died by burning in March 1895, at the age of twenty-six.[33]

Would Maud Gonne have been so eager to be taken for a woman of the *sidhe* if her class had not protected her from being taken seriously? Would Yeats have been willing to see distinctive and poetic Irishness in Michael Cleary? It is easy to use the Cleary story against the tender-hearted romantics of the Celtic Twilight – so easy that the British Empire did so at once, as Tory newspapers in London took up the story as an instance of the need of the primitive Irish for British justice and protection. While the Irish folklorists had fought to see the Irish peasant as the acme of an Irishness that had not been assimilated by British rule, the case of Bridget Cleary allowed the press to invert the argument neatly: better a degree of assimilation than being burned alive by your husband. More recently, the brilliant Irish folklorist Angela Bourke has also used the case to question the political assumptions that lie behind the studies of Irish folklore begun by Yeats and Gregory. For Bourke, the story of Bridget Cleary is not a simple story of a folktale understood too literally, but a specific story that could only have happened in that time, at that place, to those people. In doing so, Bourke is trying to undo the myth of timeless Irishness in favour of a more accurate knowledge of historical difference, and in the Republic, even now, this is radical thinking. What is even more radical is her suggestion that in the folk culture of which Yeats and co. made so much, Michael Cleary's actions may have been perfectly reasonable. She suggests an additional factor; Dr Crean, the local physician, visited Bridget during her last illness, and diagnosed 'slight bronchial catarrh', but local tradition in Tipperary asserts that she had tuberculosis. Like AIDS in the twentieth century, TB in the nineteenth century was the kind of disease that made people run away. (Ironically, Maud Gonne, that other woman of the *sidhe*, was also a TB sufferer.) If Bridget had or thought she had this dreaded disease, it might have made sense to her to see her illness as the mark of a world of death that was already drawing her away from her neighbours. At her husband's trial, it was said that she liked to walk alone on the low road near the fairy fort of Kylenagranagh; perhaps she was courting the fairies, hoping that they would cure her, or perhaps she was merely expressing her sense that her community could not accommodate someone so fundamentally diseased. She too may have seen caverns filled with human bones in the eyes of the mind. On her walks with death, however, Bridget was also saying that she was separate from her husband, and this he may not have been able to bear. Where she saw bones, he may have seen seductive fairy lords. If he felt the murderous rage and hate that lurk undisclosed in Yeats's O'Driscoll as he watches the fairy lord seduce his wife, he may have acted on them.

But like Yeats, Michael Cleary could not altogether own those murderous feelings. He spent the days after his wife's death waiting outside the fairy fort at Kylenagranagh, waiting for his real wife to ride with the fairies so that he could pull her from her white horse, bring her down, down to his level. To himself, he was not killing her, but rescuing her. He probably knew all the old stories better than any folklorist; how you had to break the iron and throw the point at the woman, what you could say. He had, after all, known all about the trial by fire. After the Second World War, a story like this was recorded in Donegal:

It was a cloudy moonless night and as they were going through a place called Alt an Tairbh, he heard a sound as if a flock of birds was coming towards them in the air. It came directly in their way and as it was passing overhead he threw the paperful of nails up in the air. He was full of anger and spoke out from his heart: 'may the devil take you with him!' No sooner were the words out of his mouth than he heard the sound of something falling at the horse's feet. He turned around and dismounted, and when he looked at the thing that had fallen what did he find but a woman! He looked sharply at her and who did he find her to be but his own wife whom he had left lying at home. He took her up and put her on the horse with the midwife who held her while he led the horse home by its head.[34]

How heroic the husband appears compared with the inertia of Yeats's O'Driscoll. And yet this resolution is bought at a price, for his wife is no more than a bundle. Both Michael Cleary and Yeats seem to have liked it that way; neither of them thought of the canny, clever young girls who study Irish folk literature, girls who avoid the entanglements of their seductive fairy suitors, girls who know their own cure and return as ghostly visitants to tell their households of it.[35] And yet most of Yeats's informants were exactly the kind of wise women to whom girls menaced might look for information. He sought and obtained fairy lore from a number of Bridgets, including Biddy Hart, who told him of peasants who met the fairy cavalcade. By contrast, Lady Gregory tells a similar story in which the husband is revealed as an incompetent:

There was a man lost his wife, and a hag was put in her place, and she came back and told him to come out at night where she'd be riding with the rest, and to throw something belonging to her after her – he'd know her by her being on a white horse. And so he did and got her back again. And when they were going home he said, 'I'll have the life of that old hag that was put in your place.' But when they got to the house, she was out of it before him, and was never heard of again.[36]

In Gregory's work it is women who are resourceful. Imprisoned by the fairies, they manage to return to suckle their babies, or to dress their babies. They are often rescued not by their husbands, but by the women of their family, sisters, mothers-in-law. Unlike Yeats's women of the *sidhe*, they remain passionately attached to their own communities; some of them even complain of loneliness among the fairies until they find a friend. They shun fairy luxuries, insisting on returning to eat leftovers in the homes of their parents: 'I have eaten no bite nor supped no drink of theirs', as the Donegal song has it, 'but cold mashed potatoes on my father's dresser.'[37] Unlike in Yeats's poems, in Irish fairy legends recorded by Gregory those taken nearly always want to escape, to get back to the mortal world of rural poverty.

As a poet Yeats often knows far more than he does as a man. He may not have been a good recorder of Irish folklore, as Lady Gregory was, but he was an exceptional listener, and as a poet he knows what all his researches cannot reveal. One of the things he heard was the contrast between ordinary rural life and fairyland. The wife who avoids the fairy food by eating cold mashed potatoes on her father's dresser rejects the realm of magic for the warm informality of the Irish kitchen. In 'The Stolen Child', Yeats uses the opposition between the humdrum and the fairy realm to magnificent, ambivalent effect. He can do this because of a shift in point of view. The Kiltartan stories – and other folk stories of fairies – are almost always told from the viewpoint of an observer. 'The Stolen Child' is told from the viewpoint of the fairies. It is a seduction song, like that which the Erl-King whispers to his boy-victim. For the first three stanzas, fairyland sounds like paradise, a wild paradise to be sure, but a paradise of wild nature. And then in the last stanza, the poem invokes the 'kettle on the hob' that will not 'sing peace into his breast' and the 'brown mice' that 'bob/ Round and round the oatmeal chest'.

> Where the wave of mooonlight glosses
> The dim grey sands with light,
> Far off by furthest Rosses
> We foot it all the night,
> Weaving olden dances,
> Mingling hands and mingling glances
> Till the moon has taken flight;
> To and fro we leap
> And chase the frothy bubbles,
> While the world is full of troubles
> And is anxious in its sleep.

Come away, O human child!
To the waters and the wild
With a faery, hand in hand,
For the world's more full of weeping than you can understand.

. . .

Away with us he's going,
The solemn-eyed:
He'll hear no more the lowing
Of the calves on the warm hillside
Or the kettle on the hob
Sing peace into his breast,
Or see the brown mice bob
Round and round the oatmeal chest.
For he comes, the human child,
To the waters and the wild
With a faery, hand in hand,
From a world more full of weeping than he can understand.[38]

The precision with which the warm kitchen is rendered contrasts sharply with the vague promises of the fairies. The reader is left asking whether this child is facing a disaster as great as the boy abducted by the Erl-King. Or rather, the reader is left to choose between the two great sacred sites of Irish poetry: the Otherworld and the mother's farm kitchen. And in the very last line, the fairies stop addressing the child; now they are talking over his head. 'For the world's more full of weeping than he can understand'. Their song has not after all been for him, but only about him. He is an object, and in the change is the faint ennui that follows a successful seduction. What can any child be to a wild nature that really has no place for him? Only cold bones on the hillside.

And yet it is this tense, ambivalent poem, rife with the knowledge that the fairy and the mortal are inimical to each other, that is sung, blithely, by the two little girls in the film about the Cottingley fairies, *Fairytale: A True Story*. For these children, fairies have no costs. And that is what makes them, in the end, empty and meaningless.

IO

Fairy Bubbles
and Alien Abductions

At last we come to the passing of the fairies. Diligent as ever in killing the things they loved, the passionate embrace of Victorian love robbed the fairy of breath. A few sad, mummified Victorian fairies survive, pressed in the pages of the *Past Times* catalogue, perhaps. Some people are devoted to these little corpses, tending them devotedly, but they obstinately refuse to flourish; they have no roots and no branches, no real resonance. This is because the fairy was not banished from all culture by the excesses of Victoriana, but only from high culture. She never found a place in modernism; indeed, she represented pretty strenuously everything modernism was against.

Remants of fairy

What is left are revenants, wraiths, sad simplified ghosts of earlier fairies, accompanied by some powerful reworkings. Cottingley, for example, has a posterity, greyer and more faded than any photograph gathering dust in a bureau. Since Cottingley, a surprising number of people have stumbled forward to say that they too have seen tiny, winged fairies cavorting in some place of outstanding natural beauty, or gnomes frolicking in a glade. Take Struan Robertson, who first saw 'them' in 1936:

Tramping near Loch Rannoch I was attracted by tuneful tones coming from clumps of rhododendrons, and advancing cautiously beheld the most beautiful dancing. I was too interested to count the number of fairies, concentrating upon how close I could get. When I was within ten paces of them one sighted me, and alarming the dancers she shepherded them in among the bushes. I shall never forget the glance she gave me as she disappeared, and the gesture, the grace of her exit, I have seen approached only by the incomparable Pavlova herself.[1]

In comparison with the fantasy fairies of the Middle Ages and the Renaissance, it lacks resonance, to say the least. And yet it was some-one's dream; it expressed someone's sad longing for something smaller and simpler than modernity. To this day, there are people who dress themselves in the fading haberdashery of Victorian nurseries, still longing for a role that was always a self-serving adult fiction. Fairies are central to such dreams.

Feeble nature

The Irish fairies had a posterity too – a dignified one of folktale and careful, sceptical folkloric research, and a more dubious one of runaway post-Romantic pseudo-Celtic New Age posturing and calendar pictures. In fantasy writer Marion Bradley's fearsomely long *Mists of Avalon*, King Arthur's old enemy Morgan Le Fay, Morgaine the fairy, is reimagined as a radical feminist of the Seventies, battered, bruised, but always Very Strong, always in touch with her menstruat-ing self. She meets from time to time with the Even Stronger Queen of the Fairies, who is even less embarrassed about her sexuality and fecundity. But somehow the whole thing never rises far above the ruck of sword and sorcery, a genre so utterly debased that little can be said for or even about it, and fairy sexuality, reduced to a formula of dull Romantic magic, loses its punch. In comparison with the medieval Ladies of the Lake, who were capable of keeping a hero from even beginning on his story, Bradley's Morgaine does not seem to have much power; her spells rarely work, and although everyone is afraid of her, the author keeps insisting depressingly that their fears are irrational. One cannot help preferring the gusto of T. H. White's Morgan Le Fay, who misguidedly builds a tempting castle to attract children out of pork and sour milk. Reeking, glistening with fat, the edifice of Castle Chariot is a terrible incarnation of raw carnality, a supreme fleshly parody of gingerbread houses. At least this retains the link between fairies, meat and death central to older fairy feasts.[2]

Bradley's weedy Morgaine is not far from the happy and skippy fairies of *Ferngully: The Last Rainforest*, an ecofable of such strenuous banality that it almost leads the viewer to pick up a sturdy chainsaw at once.[3] Here, fairies are only included at all because they represent nature, and threatened nature at that, but the symbolism is in this story so hopelessly flat and crude that it resembles a telegram. These rainforest fairies are accompanied by hordes of other animated fairies: the Blue Fairy of *Pinocchio*, a moralist in a dance frock; the goody nature fairies of *Fantasia*, Arthur Rackham fairies after a Maybelline makeover; the plump mumsy fairies of Disney's *Sleeping Beauty*, who can't make a cake or a dress worth a damn. Every one is dull and powerless and unmemorable.

Admittedly, there are more powerful fairies. Alice Thomas Ellis bravely writes of fairies old and cold – William Allingham fairies, or perhaps even Michael Cleary fairies – whose age and cruelty expose the naïvety of a young couple in thrall to exactly the myths of the countryside that produced the sweeter aspects of fairy lore. Peter Beagle's fairies, in *The Folk of the Air*, completely lack sweetness, while Alan Garner's *lios-alfar* or light elves are chillingly indifferent to everyone but themselves.[4] But it now takes an author of great talent and real courage to produce a fairy worthy of the name.

Trolls and Sith

On Internet newsgroups, a troll is a person who haunts Usenet in an attempt to stir up controversy by posting inflammatory statements. I suspect this derives distantly from the tale of the three billy goats gruff, each challenged to a fight by a troll who announces his intention of eating them. Characteristically, trolls write the most outrageous thing they can think of; to a parenting newsgroup, a troll might write, 'Breeders should be banned', and to a Catholic newsgroup, 'The Pope is a Nazi'. The aim is to draw as many responses as possible; presumably this inflates the ego of the troll, making him swell up like his antecedent under the bridge. A true troll will often keep at it for days, replying meticulously to all those who write angrily to correct him. Such tauntings are an attempt to suborn public discussion, and as such are as elegantly and disdainfully aristocratic as any fairy.

Fairies contribute, too, to other villainous personae. In the *Star Wars* series, the principal villains are the Dark Lords of the Sith. In the original trilogy, Darth Vader is the only one left, but it appears now that there were more in the past. In *Star Wars Episode I: The Phantom Menace*, there are two Sith, a master and an apprentice. They are mysterious, unknown, all-powerful. Though not exactly sexual, they are very physical. And they steal people – young girls and children – to be apprentices to them. Yet in Darth Vader's case, the Sith are also ancestors, forgotten sources of mystical power, and also the reanimate dead. Why does this matter? Because *Sith* is a Celtic word for fairy. Robert Kirk uses it throughout his book *The Secret Commonwealth of Elves and Fairies*. Far be it from me to try to see into the mind of George Lucas, but the man has read his share of comparative mythology. These updated fairy warriors, with their links with death and supernatural weapons skills, may bring back to fairies some healthy dread. Lucas's other fairies are more predictable; in *Willow*, the eponymous hero is helped by a blonde and pretty fairy surrounded by lighted 'sfx' teeny fairies. She is a spiritless force for good in a naughty world, without rhyme or reason, and without depth or meaning. The Dark Lords of the Sith, however, are glamorous and fascinating as fairies should be.

The meaning of pink fairy armadilloes

Fairy has taken on some transferred meanings, not always very explicably. In zoology, 'fairy' simply means 'small', but there is a connotative resonance of daintiness which makes the fairy penguin and the exceedingly memorable pink fairy armadillo seem quaint and endearing. If fairies were once fauna, perhaps fauna are *our* Victorian fairies – natural, unspoilt, sweet, and always in danger of disappearing or being sickened by us, our modernity, our industry. The pink fairy armadillo is endangered, in a kind of grim realization of all those myths about departing fairies.

And there's always cleaning

There was a moment in advertising when household products were all about magic. The idea was, of course, that with the help of fairies, brownies, gnomes and the leprechaun-like Mr Sheen, the housewife was spared all work. Dirt was magicked away. From a position of complete ignorance of folklore, Procter and Gamble accidentally reproduced something quite ancient in Fairy Soap and later Fairy Liquid. The early modern fantasy of the helpful hob, or brownie, a spirit eager to help those who were themselves devoted to cleanliness (or to enforce cleanliness on those who were not so devoted), bears a strong and uncanny resemblance to the fairies and other sprites who were to aid the now-servantless housewife in her drive to cleanliness. As part of that moment, Fairy household soap appeared, fairylike not only because it was clean, but because it was a small golden bar, and because it was innovative in replacing harsh carbolic with something gentle, tender and soft.

The Edwardian fairy, symbolizing innocence, children and hard work, was an apt symbol for a kinder, gentler cleanness, and the fairy logo on the box is perfectly Edwardian, betraying not a trace of the naked hairy hobs who were said to help the maids with their laundry. In the great tradition of washing-powder advertisements, she seems to represent women who are too refined to need the product, femininity whose cleanliness glows from within. And yet the echo of folklore persists. Later – and again, Procter and Gamble seem not to have known how true to tradition they were – the product took on the fairy colour, green. But the fairy did not last very long. Procter and Gamble dropped the fairy in the early 1930s, replacing Mother's Little Helper with an image of the helplessness her cleaning protects, a baby. This conveyed softness, but evaded the images of effeminacy and homosexuality which by then clustered sniggering around the word 'fairy' – though if this was a major motive, it is difficult to see why the product name was not also altered. (Procter and Gamble hotly deny that these anxieties played any part in their decision, but were unable to produce any evidence of how or why the decision was made.[5]) What does seem clear is that the overlap between fairy innocence and childhood innocence made the transition easy. The baby, whose name is Bizzie, is also alive with a demonic energy which far better recalls the hairy hob helpers of folklore than the elegant fairy he replaces. Though christened 'Billy Bettersuds' after a nationwide competition, he is always called Bizzie; his solid body and fast crawl represent the energy of the product, for it too is Bizzie, busy about keeping your house clean. In rubbing a little Fairy soap on a garment, it is as if the housewife is not performing a task, but releasing an energy source which will perform it for her. Such is the hope; some hope. By now, you know all about what fairy gold becomes – bar of soap or no . . .

Australian Fairy Margarine, too, no longer needs its stout and godmotherly fairy to connote the wonders of the dairy and the pleasures of nature, concealed, we are to hope, in a tub of hydrogenated vegetable oil. In fact, the last thing the manufacturers want to suggest is anything plump or motherly. Margarine has managed to sell itself as good because ethereally removed from the wicked world of dairy fats. Perhaps the makers should restore the fairy, but in a new, svelte form, to symbolize the restraint exercised by the buyer and the eternal life that is supposed to come with healthy eating.

Mother's helper fairies preserve some fairy lore, the dismal Victorian fairy lore of using the fairies to control the conduct of children, especially girls. Brownies, junior girl guides, were also supposed to be mother's helpers. Since I have been working on fairies, many ex-Brownies have come shyly out of the closet to tell me of their fairylike housewifely prowess, learned at the nature-loving knee of their Brown Owl. The curious alliance between breezy nature and cleanly housework is a peculiar one, since in reality housework is all about thwarting nature, with its dirt and microbes. It would look even less plausible were it not cemented by the fairy, who can dimly stand for both cleanness and nature. 'Look out! We're the jolly Pixies/ Helping others when in fixes', 'We're the fairies glad and gay/ Helping others every day', shout two ex-Brownies in Antonia Forest's delectable *Autumn Term* of 1948, one of the most intelligent school stories ever published. Their friend, Tim (short for Thalia), whose father is a real artist, looks faintly sick. 'Did you really say things like that?' she asks.[6]

Like Tim, many of us can only feel nausea when our daughters and goddaughters invest in the fairy image. At my son's Hallowe'en party, one five year old came dressed as a pretty fairy; her foamy pink skirts stood out like a wound among the ranks of matt-black ogres, vampires and Dark Lords of the Sith. The mothers hissed, 'Who's the little girl in pink?' No one actually said 'Urgh!', but everyone, like Tim, looked sick, and her own mother was apologetic. Any self-respecting North Oxford mummy would rather her daughter was a vampire than a fairy.

Why? One reason is our extreme anxiety about little girls and sexuality. Clothes that make young girls look feminine, we think, risk making them look sexual too. When six-year-old JonBenet Ramsay was sexually assaulted and murdered by an unknown assailant, press attention focused on her record as a tiny child beauty queen, the make-up she had had to wear, the 'cute' and ultrafeminine clothing.[7] Such things, it was felt, had somehow led to her death; perverse themselves, they had twisted perversity out of her killer. What were considered 'normal' clothes for little girls some thirty years ago are now considered incitements to paedophilia. And the Flower Fairies cannot be entirely acquitted of such charges. The tiny figure of the Rose Fairy, for example, with her skimpy, diaphanous skirt blowing up her leg; the Poppy Fairy, whose dress droops from one slender shoulder, the fairies whose recumbent postures recall not only erotic Victorian art, but the *Playboy* centrefold – they cause a definite frisson of disquiet. As critic James Kincaid has shown, the cute child can slide easily into the eroticized child, and certainly Cicely Mary Barker is not very adroit at keeping them apart.[8]

In such anxious times, it is important to be clear. I am not saying that paedophiles get their jollies by looking at the Flower Fairies – though Kincaid claims that most American paedophiles rely on Disney films, so anything is possible. Nor am I saying that every old lady buying a Flower Fairy book is a paedophile. What I am saying is that our consciousness of the erotization of the cute child makes it impossible for us to contemplate these fairies comfortably. An analogy: in the 1920s, Angel Brazil could write a book about a girls' school in which the main character is called Lesbia. Thirty years later, everyone would automatically snigger at this. In exactly similar fashion, our need to drive a wedge between children and sexual desire has made some of us uncomfortable with fairies.

And yet, for others, the new refusal to make little girls into little girls is also perverse, and it is to them that Flower Fairies are sold in legions. *The Flower Fairies Activity Book* features pages of the kind of pencil-and-paper games that a 'good', 'quiet' child might use to keep herself amused. The fact that these games are so exclusively for girls perhaps says something about why we as a culture so desperately prefer girls. The very association of little girls with quietness, diligence, academic prowess, stillness, bodily control – their distance from the noisy, savage, violent harum-scarum boys – is the very reason why so many middle-class parents breathe a sigh of relief when they know they are expecting one. Just as Edwardian fairies were mirrors of proper childhood – diligent, or good at grammar, or willing at tidying up – so Flower Fairies are now a logo for the 'good' middle-class girl.[9]

Such devoted diligence, and its link with femininity, is even more apparent in *The Flower Fairies Fancy Dress Book*, in which *you* can make '8 delightful Flower Fairies costumes'. Who are you? Why, mother, of course, for now it is your turn, Mother, to be diligent, to be a good girl. 'Every little girl', the blurb opines, 'loves dressing up as a fairy.' But what exactly are the little girls – or rather their mothers – buying? They are buying a glamorous femininity – one that is 'ethereal', 'dazzling'. They are also buying an imaginative landscape: 'There are hours of imaginative fun to be had skipping around a fairy circle, dancing at the fairy ball.' Like all advertisements, this one is telling us what we should be, not just how to get there. The ideal child, we learn, is quietly diligent, but also imaginative. The ideal mother has other, related virtues. 'Hand-made costumes are so much more original than store-bought costumes,' says the introduction firmly – even though the whole point of the book is that it obviates the need for invention, replacing it with diligence, working through the 'easy-to-follow' instructions. None the less, it's the right *sort* of thing to be doing, since 'children will enjoy helping you choose colours and fabrics'. This is exactly the kind of thing the guilt-ridden mothers whom cultural historian Ros Coward interviewed wished they were doing with their children – something creative, something stimulating, something that offered the child genuine expertise and opened an acceptable childhood world to it – as opposed to switching on the VCR again. Such creative play is often located in the same vanished and rural past from which

Flower Fairies come – hence the emphasis on bygone crafts in the Flower Fairy activity books. Such an idyllic motherhood brings with it other virtues, too: 'Not only is sewing satisfying, it is also economical.' The magic word indeed, 'economical' banishes the naughty gnomes of consumerism by waving the wand of creativity. Cicely Barker, too, would make her own costumes for her child-models, and when each session was finished 'she would meticulously unpick the stitches of the costume to reuse the materials'. From Barker, to mother, to girl-child, the values descend: glamour is legitimate only if it comes from, or with, diligence, care. This is indeed a doctrine for housewives, but it can be a weapon in the endless war against modernity waged by some mothers.[10]

The Paranoid Fairy of Sydney

The fairies have other warriors, too. In Australia are the fairy shops, places where the despised off-the-peg fairy costumes can be purchased, but also party venues. Fairy shops can be hired, along with their owners, for themed children's parties, in which the children are told stories about fairies, given fairy food to eat, and helped to play fairy games. The one I visited, sited at the less affluent end of the very well-heeled Sydney suburb of Mosman, was lined with black material, on which cut-out fairies, flowers, stars and fruit reposed. A cardboard model of a tree leaned against a wall, and a fairy throne covered with pink paint and glitter sat on a small dais. Everything was indescribably amateurish – the paint job was no better than I might have managed myself, and the cut-out shapes, too, had a loving-hands-at-home look – but perhaps this endearing air of craft and making-do was exactly what the punters wanted. On the other hand, perhaps not, for all was not well in fairyland. The whole shop had the indefinable air of something from which the ambience had departed; it felt like a restaurant that is empty even on a Saturday night.

Perhaps this explains the owner's extreme anxiety. She hovered behind a counter, ready for action in a pink tulle frock. When I told her I was writing a book, and asked her permission to take photos for my notes, anxiety became agitation. 'I won't let you take pictures!' she exclaimed. 'You'll just use them to open your own shop. People are always stealing my ideas.' In vain I said that I had no intention of opening a fairy shop; in vain I flourished academic credentials. 'Anyone could say that!' she spat. Without much further ado, she bundled me out on to the street. One could hardly help reflecting on the incongruous mix of strict commerce and ethereal publicity, for while fairies claim to offer an escape from mundane reality, this lady's values seemed every bit as commercial as Judith Phillips's or Mary Parish's. If so, the mix may not be a good one. In Brisbane, the Fairy Queen of Sylvanian Groves was much more forthcoming, but that shop, too, closed within a few months of my visit. (One reason was the extreme reluctance of Australian fathers to allow their sons to attend, even for an afternoon, anything with the word 'fairy' in it.) These shops were not merely commercial ventures, but standard female commerce; a hobby which had become a little business, a dream which had failed to conform to reality. Now, as ever, the fairies appear to be the friends of those who lack, but they do not always reward their votaries well. Once again, fairy gold turns to dried leaves.

Fairy glamour

Such works also induct the woman into what Susan Faludi has recently called the economy of ornament, an economy in which most jobs come not from making but from decorating. In Faludi's lament for lost manhood, *Stiffed: Scenes from the Betrayal of Modern Man*, we meet Libby, who has filled her entire house with what she calls 'antiques', tiny gnomes, elves, trolls and fairies bought at market stalls.[11] 'Every week, I'd see one, and I'd just have to have it,' Libby confesses. What was it that Libby had to have? A facile answer might be the adorable child, but Libby has three human children already. Yes, but are they adorable? She wasn't an especially happy housewife and mother; perhaps she did not feel the way she *should* about the real children who messed and spilled and whined. The adorable china fairy children, on the other hand, could be swept up, protected, taken in, sheltered; the act of buying them and bringing them home, making them part of the home, could be Libby's way of feeling like a real mother to someone. But Libby's longings are also more simply acquisitive: she nags her husband to earn more, give them more of a life. She wants nice furniture. She wants her own home. Simple wants, and perhaps the massed ranks of elves offer precisely this clean, tidy vision of suburban bliss. Perhaps they offer it most of all where it is not available; garden gnomes, after all, are a signifier of the working class. They may be just a cheap version of a fitted country kitchen by Smallbone of Devizes. So too the Flower Fairy Garden Ornaments, lovingly hand-made, or so we are told. So too the fairy china ornaments, each one 'exclusively hand-finished', words that sound the death-knell of any actual quality. You can get them on the Internet, and by teleshopping. And at *Past Times*, purveyor of a fake past to all tourists to these shores.

Yet such gewgaws constantly threaten to degenerate into exactly the kind of tat which might make us think of American junior beauty queens. *The Secret Fairy Handbook*, for example, is also aimed at little girls, but it is aimed at little girls who want to be bigger girls. It offers fairy earrings which can be pasted on to the ears, fairy nail deorations, and a fairy necklace consisting of a glittery hologram on a piece of lamé. The story, of surpassing banality and hence itself consumable, concerns the preparations for a fairy party at which conspicuous consumption seems more important than production. The parents I know justify the purchase of this lavishly doubtful product by using the phrases 'camp' and 'tongue-in-cheek' a lot, by which they mean that the violation of taste canons is so glaring as to be no threat.[12] The same might be said of the armies of winged Barbies and fairy-decorated pink toys which can be effortlessly unearthed in any toyshop. So apparent is the masquerade of femininity in such items that they appeal aesthetically more to the gay community than the straight; the sheer excess of such femininity is itself a defence against exposing the sexualization of the child associated with it.

Fairies and teeth

The last of such tidy fairies to command much assent in the way of practice is, of course, the Tooth Fairy. Though no one really believes in her, no one can quite bear to part with her either. The fairy industry churns out little faux-silver boxes with fairies on the lid, in which a milk tooth can be placed; those less committed to gewgaws make do with the traditional glass of water, or, if the parents are especially adroit, place the tooth under the child's pillow. The tooth fairy, who has a mysterious yearning to collect milk teeth, willingly swaps the lost tooth for money; the going rate at my son's school is at the time of writing £2, thanks to the genius who introduced the two-pound coin. When I was a child, the rate was twenty Australian cents, or one shilling in England. This is worth noting not just in order to launch another jeremiad about the rising costs of childhood; the rate is about the same as a week's pocket money, and is fixed at the point where it may purchase either a small toy or a really sizeable number of sweets.

Rather, the tooth fairy is an instance of the fairy-useful-in-child-upbringing, the one that keeps the little ones away from the loch or the seashore. Her use is nevertheless interesting, and quite authentic; she marks a boundary between one stage of childhood and another. The loss of milk teeth is a drama of growing up and away, a sign that a child is moving out of infancy into middle childhood. The name 'milk teeth' says it all; with the loss of those teeth, the child loses its last physical link with the infant at mother's breast. Peter Pan, Barrie tells us, still has all his milk teeth. At the time of writing, the loss of milk teeth coincides with the first or second year of school in the English-speaking world, and the loss of teeth is certainly a marker of age and status in the tribal world of playground culture. There, tooth loss is often accompanied by bravura displays of tooth-wobbling and even tooth pulling, accentuating the violence of loss. For parent and child, the establishment of routine attendance at 'big school' is the moment when the child acquires a life of her or his own, a life which can be disclosed to or withheld from the mother as the child sees fit. This is alarming and welcome to both parties, for if both feel a secret terror, both may also feel a secret relief which feeds the terror with feelings of guilt. Losing teeth may seem to both mother and child a sign of the damage done to that primal closeness, a sign that away from mother, the child will alter uncontrollably but also be damaged in the process. A kind of mini-puberty ensues. Children can be genuinely frightened by the whole business, as Freud rightly remarked. He interpreted the entire episode in terms of castration, however, though 'castration', as often in Freud, seems to mean loss of bodily sameness or wholeness, not loss of the penis in itself.[13]

This vague, inchoate sense of loss is compensated by the mediating tooth fairy, who ensures that the mother can keep the tooth – and at least a memory of all it symbolizes – without having to tell the child that she wants to, without having to make him or her aware that part of her wants the child to be her baby for ever. Meanwhile, the child is compensated for leaping ever further into the dangerous world by an offering of the one thing late childhood has to recommend it over early childhood: purchasing power.

Unlike other fairies, the tooth fairy is often stout. The tooth fairy is perhaps stout because she represents making the flesh permanent. Or perhaps her stoutness is a mixture of baby stoutness and mummy stoutness, an emblem of the soft, warm cuddly bodily relationship that is preserved, in fantasy at least, with the teeth. If other fairies are thin, almost to gauntness, this has to do with the value we give to thinness, a value that is too complex to explore in full here, but that seems to owe a lot to the whole problem, or perceived problem, of female consumption scripted into the figure of the fairy, as seen above. Fat women signify uncontrolled consumption; in order to represent the female virtues of hard work and restraint, fairies have to be lean, even skinny. Or it may be the other way around: fairies lost weight when they became associated with self-control and hard work. Their thinness now goes along, however, with sexual desirability, for in order to be an object of desire, one must be slender. The dimmed posterity of the Celtic goddess-fairy are permitted to be sexy in this predictable way, and they do make some interesting appearances in contemporary fiction, as we shall see by looking in some rather strange and underground places.

Fairy into fantasy: alien, vampire, Elvis

As well as its fierce trolls, the Internet also boasts the X-Files Fanfiction community, a group congenitally interested in the bizarre, the angst-laden, and of course the supernatural. Workaholic singles also like the *X-Files* – which is about workaholic singles. The fanfiction community, though short on Tobias Wolffs, can offer pleasant distractions no worse than those purveyed by an airport bookstall, and far cheaper. Nor is this a small group. It is impossible to estimate accurately, but at least two or three thousand people each month post to alt.tv.x-files.creative, and that doesn't include 'lurkers', people who read without posting. There are thousands of *X-Files* stories archived all over the World Wide Web.[14] Curiously, a number of such stories involve fairies, an area of the supernatural never explored by Chris Carter and the makers of the actual series. One such story is by the author of the very first *X-Files* fanfiction to be published on the Internet, a woman called Kellie Matthews-Simons. In it – hold on to something – Scully gets laid by an elf:

Dana looked him full in the face . . . Her earlier assessment of him as striking was wrong, gleaned only from brief glances. Seen this close, he was one of the most attractive men she'd ever seen. He reminded her vaguely of someone, but she couldn't put her finger on who. He had broad, prominent cheekbones, a very straight, slightly blunt-tipped nose; his mouth was full-cut and sensual. But it was his eyes that were mesmerizing . . . a luminous, leafy green, fringed with utterly spectacular lashes. The slight lines around his eyes and the gentle lift to the corners of his mouth bespoke humor, and there was something about the flare of his nostrils that hinted of passions barely held in check. Caught and held by his gaze, her lips parted on a sigh, then she remembered herself and broke eye contact . . . Fionn eased down beside her, and built a glamour, a strong one, remembering her resistance, but not strong enough to cause her distress.[15]

Fairy as Mills-and-Boon man! Despite some careful research, the author has no notion of the menace fairies generally pose to mortal women. Here, the fairy is rather less menacing than Heathcliff or Rhett

Butler. Or Mulder. He's nice. Considerate. The kind of fairy you marry. Scully ends up being called in as midwife while Fionn's fairy sister has a baby. This brings mortal and fairy together, and Scully does not seem to suffer from backache, though she is a little nonplussed when it transpires that Fionn can change sex, and even more startled to learn that he watches TV:

'Are you talking about reincarnation?' she asked, grasping at straws. He shook his head. 'No. A single lifetime ... infinitely long.' She ran a hand through her hair. 'This sounds like an episode of Star Trek!' To her surprise he grinned. 'Aye, it does. I remember that one, "Requiem for Methuselah", a good story.'

She inched away, feeling afraid for the first time. 'The stress has finally gotten to me! My god ... an elf who watches Star Trek!'

This is an affectionate in-joke for Trekfans, but it is also an attempt to make the fairy Fionn fully part of the earthly world. He may be different, but it's not a menacing difference. With just a dash of elven memory-fixing, Fionn becomes the ultimate holiday romance: exotic, very sexy and completely separated from humdrum daily life. Obeying the fanfic lore that ideally all stories have to return the main characters to their situation in the series – a law suspended by other fans – this story gives Scully and the reader a good time at no extra cost to her.

Mulder has a more difficult time, and, as fans of the series will know, that's not surprising. The fairies he meets are much more imaginatively in tune with early modern Celtic fairies than Matthews-Simons's rather airbrushed Celtic Twilight fairy. Mulder meets a fairy queen served – and serviced – by an army of midnight rambler bikers, the lords of darkness. There isn't much plot. And yet both stories show how all-pervasive Romanticism and its clichés have become in our apprehension of the supernatural. Even on Usenet, where anything might be tried, what has been discovered is those olde worlde Romantics, Shelley and Byron, the nice baddie and the nasty. These are respectively New Age and Anne Rice fairies. Anne Rice fairies represent hopeless romanticism and New Age, hopeful romanticism, but both come from the same stable. In both cases, the supernatural is simply and solely and specifically about sex – birth and death get left on the cutting-room floor.

And yet birth and death are absolutely central to the *X-Files*, in that what fans call the mytharc, the episodes which tell of a US government conspiracy to conceal the arrival of extraterrestrials from the American public, are all about the processes of birth and death. It is in the mytharc that questions of birth are debated – reproductive experimentation, cloning, bioengineering, stolen babies, strange children – and it is in the mytharc that death is debated, the deaths of characters, the death of the human race. For the X-philes who write fanfiction, fairies provide some light relief from the heavy weight of fear that accompanies the show's fantasies about aliens. And yet – and I am by no means the first to make this argument – it may be that it is aliens who work as early modern fairies did, canalizing our most potent fears and desires, beliefs and disbeliefs. When Scully is abducted by aliens, her eggs – and hence her future babies – are stolen from her, just as Bessie Dunlop's baby was 'taken'. And just as Bessie swaps her baby for occult knowledge, so both Mulder and Scully lose 'babies' – Mulder's sister, Scully's secretly spawned children – in their pursuit of forbidden knowledge. And when Scully 'finds' her baby, a little girl called Emily who has been grown from her egg, the child is doubly a changeling – she is strange to the family in which she lives, and she is, as it turns out, part alien, and could cry, like Stevie Smith's little girl returning from the fairies, 'there is nobody that I know'.[16] Like a changeling, too, Emily pines and dies; like a changeling, she is potentially fatal to those around her. She does not fit. If Bessie Dunlop's feelings of loss came from too little technical control over birth, our sense of Scully's loss comes from a fear that there may be too *much* technical control over reproduction – which for a woman may be the same as no control.

The *X-Files* scripts are based on the stories of abductees. The resemblance between modern stories of alien abduction and early modern stories of fairy abduction is certainly striking. Remember Susan Swapper, cowering next to her husband, begging him to help her? Now read on. A magisterial work called *How to Defend Yourself Against Alien Abduction* urges the victim to try her utmost to persuade a partner to join her in fighting 'them' off.[17] Remember Elspeth Reoch, who was sexually molested and may have been impregnated by a fairy? Now read on. Many abduction victims believe that aliens have experimented with them sexually, inducing orgasm to observe the results. The taxonomical urge which we have seen in fairy writings by the élite is also very much present: aliens are classified into scaly greens, small greys, Nordics, and so forth. And the channelling of anxieties about race into stories about the supernatural is also common to both fairy stories and accounts of alien activity, especially around the questions of parenting and sexual activity central to both kinds of story. Finally, the sophisticated élite awareness of the gap between credulity and scepticism is present in both fairy and alien stories. The majority of people who watch the *X-Files* do not believe in alien abductions, just as most of those who tell fairy stories do so from a position of disbelief. And yet it is still possible to be moved by Scully's lost daughter, even if you can't quite swallow her green blood. Stories of abduction fascinate, not because they are credible, but because they say something powerful about how we feel at the turn of the millennium.

I do not think I can argue that these stories come from fairy sources; I would be greatly surprised if science-fiction writer and soi-disant abductee Whitney Streiber had made much of a study of European folklore. Now that the comparison has been made, however, it is likely that some abductees will incorporate folklore motifs into their stories more or less consciously, particularly since the existence of such stories about fairies is cited as proof of the validity of abductees' experiences; to some, the fairies of the past were simply aliens. To begin with, however, the similarities are most likely to be the result of common feelings. We might say that the fears and desires evoked and managed by such stories are so powerful that they have to have an outlet, and once fairies became too tame for such wild feelings, a new bogey had to be invented. We might add that fairies always came from an unknown that was both raw nature and vanished civilization – a rath in a wood, a graveyard. Now on earth there are no unknowns, no *terrae incognitae*. But there are still the stars. And there are no civilizations about which we know nothing except the silence of what they built. But beyond the solar system, who can know? The unknown is necessary for stories; its silence is what lets them be heard. In space, everyone can hear you scream. What alien stories do show – loud and clear – is that we need something to scream about.

While Mulder and Scully fight aliens, Buffy Summers fights vampires, and her popularity is just one aspect of the extraordinary interest that vampires are currently arousing. Like aliens, vampires become important at the very moment when the darker elements of fairy myth are dying away. We have seen that a few – a very few – fairies do actually suck blood, the defining characteristic of the vampire, but this is not important. What is crucial is that both fairies and vampires are living dead, dead who do and must interact with the living. And they are in folklore the same kind of living dead, dead who live because they are killed unnaturally, taken before their time. There is even an early word for vampire that means 'wolf-fairy', and there are certainly baby revenants who are unbaptized and come to prey on other unbaptized children, mothers dead in childbirth who become angry and hungry revenants, and who must be silenced by careful reburial.

It is not, however, on such figures that modern vampire lore focuses. The most important vampires in what fans charmingly call the Buffyverse are individuals, of marriageable age. There is one child who causes nightmares, admittedly, and another whose significance is as a kind of shaman-guide to the world of darkness; mothers, however, are innocent to the point of idiocy. Generally, vampires (like their foes) are teenagers, even if they have been teenagers for hundreds of years. This does reflect a difference between fairies and vampires in folklore. While fairies need mortals in order to survive as a group – to join their group, to replenish it with sex or babies – vampires need humans individually, to replenish themselves. Fairies are communal – even solitary fairies – while vampires almost never are, and even in fictions which imagine vampire societies, the societies are distinctly Darwinian. The true apotheosis of vampires coincides with the rise of Romanticism, and the Romantic cult of the individual cut off from society, so that the vampire comes to embody this belief. As a result, the dark and brooding vampire becomes precisely the kind of object of desire which the fairy once was; he knows history – in fact he *is* history – and as such he offers himself as a shaman-guide, someone able to lead the living into the world of the dead, but also to lead them out again, though not without risk. 'My boyfriend had a bicentennial,' says Buffy of the doomiest teen-vamp, poor cursed Angel, a statement which ironically makes him a historical monument. Like fairies, vampires are always already aristocratic, from Bram Stoker's Count Dracula to Anne Rice's elegant Lestat. They are worldly and tasteful, as fairies are. Yet they are also an indictment of wealth and taste, a sign of the way in which worldly sucess leads only to the grave.

There is one final category of persons who are functioning as fairies did, and that is dead celebrities. I began with dead Diana, who was staging comebacks only days after her demise, and whose most deluded followers believe she left a child to be brought up in secret, carrying on her identity. Such notions are not confined to royalty. In a witty adaptation of the Grimm fairytale 'The Elves and the Shoemaker', the Muppets replaced the elves with Elvises, Elvises who make blue suede shoes for their grateful friends, and depart when the couple mis-guidedly make them sequined white suits. Elvises are perhaps even more like elves than some can bear to admit. Elvis is always staging little returns from the dead, offering himself as yet another shaman-guide to death and back. And like many a fairy guide, Elvis was cut off before his time.[18] But as well, the story of Elvis – like the story of most celebrities – is a story that fits with fairy stories; it is a rags-to-riches story, a story of hunger satisfied and in the end sated, a story of the world of luxury and excess and the flesh eventually overwhelming the spirit, a story of one not elevated to serene immortal status, but none the less privileged among mortals. And Elvis is, too, a possible alien abductee; the two strands of reworked fairy story come together when a woman in the film *Independence Day* says of the aliens, in a burst of post-modern irony, 'Oh, God, I hope they bring back Elvis!'

So what if no one believes her, not even she herself? No one ever really believes in fairies, either.

Notes

Medieval and early modern spellings and punctuation in the text have been modernized and some unfamiliar words translated.

1. Ancient Worlds

This chapter was inspired by Edith Hall's suggestion that I investigate certain Greek demons. I am very grateful to her.

1. Jack Winkler, 'Lollianos and the Desperadoes', *Journal of Hellenic Studies* 100 (1980), p. 163; Aristotle, *De somniis*, 2–3, 462a. 12–15; *Acts of Peter*, New Testament Apocrypha, 2nd century, cited in Winkler, p. 163.

2. Callimachus, *Hymn to Artemis*, 69. Chimney-demons: Christopher Faraone, *Talismans and Trojan Horses: Guardian Statues in Ancient Greek Myth and Ritual* (Oxford: Oxford University Press, 1992), pp. 38–40.

3. Compton Mackenzie, *Sinister Street* (Harmondsworth: Penguin, 1976; first published 1913–14), p. 231.

4. Sara Johnston, 'Defining the Dreadful: Remarks on the Greek Child-Killing Demon', in *Ancient Magic and Ritual Power*, ed. M. Meyer and P. Mirecki (Leiden: Brill, 1995), pp. 361–87, esp. 368, n. 16.

5. JoAnn Scurlock, 'Baby-Snatching Demons, Restless Souls and the Dangers of Childbirth: Medico-Magical Means of Dealing with Some of the Perils of Motherhood in Ancient Mesopotamia', *Incognita* 2 (1991), pp. 1–112.

6. Ammianus Marcellinus 29.2.17, in Jean-Jacques Aubert, 'Threatened Wombs: Aspects of Ancient Uterine Magic', *Greek, Roman and Byzantine Studies* 30 (1989), p. 437.

7. Scurlock, 'Baby-Snatching Demons', pp. 99, 101.

8. Julia Kristeva, 'Stabat Mater', in *The Kristeva Reader*, ed. Toril Moi (Oxford: Blackwell, 1988), pp. 160–86.

9. Jean-Pierre Vernant, 'Death in the eyes: Gorgo, Figure of the Other', in

Mortals and Immortals: Collected Essays, ed. Froma I. Zeitlin (Princeton: Princeton University Press, 1991), pp. 111–40.

10. Plato, *Phaedo*, 77e; Plutarch, *Quaestiones Convivales*, 5.7.1, 680d; Plato, *Laws*, 790c–791b.

11. Xenophon, *Hellenica*, 4.4.17.

12. Walter Burkert, *The Orientalising Revolution*, trans. Margaret E. Pinder and W. Burkert (Cambridge, Mass.: Harvard University Press, 1991), p. 87.

13. J. M. Barrie, *Peter Pan in Kensington Gardens*, ed. Peter Hollindale (Oxford: Oxford University Press, 1991; first published 1906).

14. J. M. Barrie, *Peter and Wendy*, ed. Peter Hollindale (Oxford: Oxford University Press, 1991; first published 1911); Andrew Birkin, *James Barrie and the Lost Boys* (London: Constable, 1979); Jacqueline Rose, *The Case of Peter Pan, or The Impossibility of Children's Fiction* (London: Macmillan, 1984).

15. Nicole Loraux, *The Experiences of Tiresias: The Feminine and the Greek Man*, trans. Paula Wissing (Princeton: Princeton University Press, 1995).

16. Calcite oil vessel in the shape of a standing pregnant woman with contorted features, her legs bent as if about to give birth (18th dynasty, Tubingen 967).

17. Scurlock, 'Baby-Snatching Demons', p. 110.

18. Gello: Sappho, fr. 178, in *Poetarum Lesbiorum Fragmenta*, ed. Edgar Lobel and Denys Page (Oxford: Clarendon, 1955); Erwin Rohde, *Psyche: The Cult of Souls and Belief in Immortality among the Ancient Greeks*, trans. W. B. Hillis (Chicago: Ares, 1980; first published 1925), appendix 6; Zenobius, *Proverbs*, 3.3; Hesychius, *Alphabetical Collection of All Words*, 'Gello'; David West, 'Gello and Lamia: Two Hellenic Demons of Semitic Origin', *Ugarit-Forschung* 23 (1991), pp. 361–8. *Aoroi*: Johnston, 'Defining the Dreadful', p. 368, n. 16.

19. Charles Stewart, *Demons and the Devil: Moral Imagination in Modern Greek Culture* (Princeton: Princeton University Press, 1991), p. 101.

20. Stewart, *Demons and the Devil*, p. 196.

21. Toni Morrison, *Beloved* (London: Chatto & Windus, 1988).

22. For instance Nigerian fiction, e.g. Buchi Emecheta's *The Slave Girl*, and Ben Okri's *The Famished Road*.

23. Leo Allatius, *De Graecorum hodie quorundam opinionibus epistola* (Cologne: 1645), section 3.

24. Adam Phillips, *The Beast in the Nursery* (London: Faber, 1998).

25. Diodorus Siculus, 20.41, 3–5.

26. *Leykinthos*, National Museum of Athens, inv. 1129, see M. Halm-Tisserant, 'Folklore et Superstition en Grèce Classique: Lamia torturée?', *Kernos* 2 (1989), pp. 67–82.

27. Mikhail Bakhtin, *Rabelais and his World*, trans. Hélène Iswolsky (Bloom-

ington: Indiana University Press, 1984); Aristophanes, *Wasps*, 1177. Lamia's testicles: Aristophanes, *Wasps*, 1035; *Peace*, 758. Lamia's 'staff': Crates, cit. scholiast on *Ecclesiazusae*, 77.

28. Melanie Klein, 'Early Stages of the Oedipus Conflict' (1928) and 'The Psychogenesis of Manic-Depressive States' (1935), in *The Selected Melanie Klein*, ed. Juliet Mitchell (Harmondsworth: Penguin, 1986), pp. 69–83, 115–45.

29. Philostratus, *Life of Apollonius*, IV, 25, trans. C. P. Jones (Harmondsworth: Penguin, 1970), pp. 94–6; retold in Robert Burton's *Anatomy of Melancholy* and John Keats's *Lamia*.

30. *Dreaming: Australian Myths*, ed. Jonas Randall (Sydney: Allen & Unwin, 1975), p. 98; Apuleius, *Metamorphoses*, I.5, trans. E. J. Kenney as *The Golden Ass* (London: Penguin, 1998).

31. Maurice Olender, 'Aspects of Baubo: Ancient Texts and Contexts', in *Before Sexuality: the Construction of Erotic Experience in the Greek World*, ed. David M. Halperin, John J. Winkler and Froma I. Zeitlin (Princeton: Princeton University Press, 1990), pp. 83–114.

32. Aristophanes, *Thesmophoriazusae*, 417; and fragments 31 and 131.

33. *Oscilla*: Christopher A. Faraone, *Talismans and Trojan Horses: Guardian Statues in Ancient Greek Myth and Ritual* (Oxford: Oxford University Press, 1992), pp. 38–40; Virgil, *Georgics*, 2.389; Macrobius, *Saturnalia*, 1, 7.11. Larva: Plautus, *Captivi*, 3, 4.66; *Mercator*, 5, 4.20.

34. Johnston, 'Defining the Dreadful', p. 375.

35. Scholiast on Aristides; cited in Sarah Iles Johnston, 'Corinthian Medea and the Cult of Hera Akraia', in *Medea*, ed. James J. Clauss and Sarah Iles Johnston (Princeton: Princeton University Press, 1997), pp. 44–70, esp. 67.

36. Maurice Sendak, *Where the Wild Things Are* (London: The Bodley Head, 1963); Humphrey Carpenter and Mari Prichard, *The Oxford Companion to Children's Literature* (Oxford: Oxford University Press, 1984), p. 567.

37. Theocritus, Idyll XV, in *The Greek Bucolic Poets*, ed. A. S. F. Gow (1953): translation very slightly modified.

38. Theocritus, *Select Poems*, ed. K. J. Dover (London: Macmillan, 1971).

39. Marina Warner, *No Go the Bogeyman* (London: Chatto & Windus, 1998).

40. Erinna: *Supplementum Hellenisticum*, ed. Hugh Lloyd-Jones and P. Parsons (Berlin: 1983), translation from *Sappho's Lyre: Archaic Lyric and Women Poets of Ancient Greece*, trans. Diane J. Raynor (Berkeley: University of California Press, 1991), pp. 121ff., extensively modified; Marilyn B. Arthur, 'The tortoise and the mirror: Erinna *PSI* 1090', *Classical World* 74 (1980), pp. 53–65.

41. Peter and Iona Opie, *Children's Games in Street and and Playground* (Oxford: Oxford University Press, 1969), esp. pp. 75ff.

42. Aristophanes, *Frogs*, 285–95; *Thesmophoriazusae*, 417. Prostitutes' names: Anaxilas, fr. 22, Koch, cited by Christopher G. Brown, 'Empousa, Dionysus and the Mysteries: Aristophanes' *Frogs* 285ff.', *Classical Quarterly* 41 (1991), pp. 41–50. Prostitutes' nicknames: James Davidson, *Courtesans and Fishcakes: The Consuming Passions of Classical Athens* (London: Harper-Collins, 1997), p. 78.

43. Burkert, *Orientalising Revolution*, p. 91; West, 'Gello and Lamia', pp. 362–3.

44. Lamashtu: Scurlock, 'Baby-Snatching Demons', p. 95. Egyptian child-killers: Geraldine Pinch, *Magic in Ancient Egypt* (London: British Museum Press, 1994), p. 45. Boney: Jonathan Gathorne Hardy, *The Rise and Fall of the British Nanny* (London: Weidenfeld & Nicolson, 1972), p. 243.

45. Gustav Henningsen, ' "The Ladies from Outside": An Archaic Pattern of the Witch's Sabbath', in *Early Modern European Witchcraft: Centres and Peripheries*, ed. Bengt Ankaroo and Gustav Henningsen (Oxford: Oxford University Press, 1993), pp. 191–215.

46. Burkert, *Orientalising Revolution*, p. 82; West, 'Gello and Lamia', p. 323.

47. Burkert, *Orientalising Revolution*, p. 82.

48. Scurlock, 'Baby-Snatching Demons', p. 97.

49. W. D. O'Flaherty, *Hindu Myths: a sourcebook translated from the Sanskrit* (Harmondsworth: Penguin, 1976), pp. 214–15.

50. M. Gaster, 'Two Thousand Years of a Charm Against the Child-Stealing Witch', *Folklore* 11 (1900), p. 133.

51. Theodore Schrire, *Hebrew Amulets: their decipherment and interpretation* (London: Routledge & Kegan Paul, 1966).

52. Joshua Trachtenberg, *Jewish Magic and Superstition: A Study in Folk Religion* (New York: Meridian, 1939).

53. Trachtenberg, *Jewish Magic*, p. 56.

54. Norman Douglas, *Siren Land* (London: Secker, 1911), pp. 126–7.

55. Keteb: Trachtenberg, *Jewish Magic*, p. 35.

56. Gaster, 'Two Thousand Years', pp. 129–62.

57. Joyce Tyldesley, *Daughters of Isis: Women of Ancient Egypt* (Harmondsworth: Penguin, 1995), p. 79.

58. Adam Phillips, *On Kissing, Tickling and Being Bored* (London: Faber, 1993), pp. 14–15.

59. Michelle Klein, *A Time to be Born: Customs and Folklore of Jewish Birth* (Philadelphia: Jewish Publication Society, 1998), p. 29; Gaster, 'Two Thousand Years'; Lucian, *A True Story*, II.46; Aristophanes, *Frogs*, 285–95.

60. R. L. Stevenson, *Treasure Island* (Harmondsworth: Penguin, 1983).

61. Carlo Ginzburg, *Ecstasies: Deciphering the Witches' Sabbath*, trans. Raymond Rosenthal (London: Hutchinson, 1990), Part 3, Chapter 2.

62. Stewart, *Demons and the Devil*, p. 158; J. C. Lawson, *Modern Greek Folklore and Ancient Greek Religion* (Cambridge: Cambridge University Press, 1910), p. 131.

63. Lawson, *Modern Greek Folklore*, p. 131.

64. Walter Burkert, *Greek Religion* (Oxford: Blackwell, 1986), pp. 150–51; *Homeric Hymn to Aphrodite*; Callimachus, *The Bath of Pallas*, 82.

65. John J. Winkler, *The Constraints of Desire: The Anthropology of Sex and Gender in Ancient Greece* (London and New York: Routledge, 1990), pp. 182ff.

66. W. R. Connor, 'Seized by the nymphs: Nympholepsy and Symbolic Expression in Classical Greece', *Classical Antiquity* 7 (1988), pp. 155–89.

67. Homer, *The Odyssey*, trans. Robert Fagles (London: Viking, 1996), 5.64–84, p. 154.

68. *Ibid.*, 5.80, p. 154; 12.53, p. 273.

69. Jean-Pierre Vernant, 'Le refus d'Ulysse', in *Le Temps de la réflexion* 3 (1982), pp. 13–19, trans. as 'The Refusal of Odysseus', in *Reading the Odyssey: Selected Interpretative Essays*, ed. Seth L. Schein (Princeton: Princeton University Press, 1995), p. 187.

70. H. Guntert, *Calypso: Bedeutungsgeschichtliche Untersuchungen auf dem Gebiet der indogermanischen Sprachen* (Halle: 1919).

71. Vernant, The Refusal of Odysseus', pp. 185–9; Seth L. Schein, 'Female Representation and interpreting the Odyssey', in *The Distaff Side; Representing the Female in Homer's Odyssey*, ed. Beth Cohen (Oxford: Oxford University Press, 1995), pp. 17–28.

72. Hesiod, *Works and Days*, 154.

73. G. Crane, *Calypso: Backgrounds and Conventions in the Odyssey*, *Beiträge zur klassischen Philologie* 191 (Frankfurt am Main: 1988), p. 27, n. 24; Artemidorus, *Oneirocritica*, 1.80 (Crane, p. 17).

74. Karl Reinhardt, '*Die Abenteuer der Odyssee*', translated as 'The Adventure in the Odyssey', in *Reading the Odyssey; Selected Interpretative Essays*, ed. Seth L. Schein (Princeton, Princeton University Press, 1995), p. 91.

75. Pindar, *Nemean Ode*, 9.6–7.

76. Plato, *Phaedrus*, 238 C f.

77. Winkler, *Constraints of Desire*, p. 120.

78. *Homeric Hymn to Aphrodite*, 256–8, 274–5.

79. Richard and Eva Blum, *The Dangerous Hour: The Lore and Culture of Mystery and Crisis in Rural Greece* (London: Chatto & Windus, 1970), p. 115.

80. Lawson, *Modern Greek Folklore*, p. 141.

81. Blum, *The Dangerous Hour*, p. 110.

82. Lawson, *Modern Greek Folklore*, p. 145.

83. *Ibid.*, p. 137.

84. Stewart, *Demons and the Devil*, p. 4.

85. Peter Walcot, 'Odysseus and the Art of Lying', *Ancient Society* 8 (1977), pp. 1–19; J. du Boulay, *Portrait of a Greek Mountain Village* (Oxford: Clarendon, 1974); M. Giselnan, 'Lying, Honor and Contradiction', in *Transaction and Meaning: Directions in the Anthropology of Exchange and Symbolic Behaviour*, ed. Bruce Kapferer (Philadelphia, 1976).

86. Peter Beresford Ellis, *Celt and Greek: Celts in the Hellenic World* (London: Constable, 1997).

87. William Butler Yeats, *Fairy and Folktales of the Irish Peasantry*, 1888; Lucy Allen Paton, *Studies in the Fairy Mythology of Arthurian Romance* (Cambridge, Mass.: Harvard University Press, 1903); Reidar Christiansen, 'Some notes on fairies and the fairy faith', *Béaloiddeas* 39–41 (1971–3), pp. 95–111; and for a far more sophisticated approach, Angela Bourke, 'The Virtual Reality of Irish Fairy Legend', *Eire-Ireland* 31 (1996), pp. 7–25.

2. Medieval Dreams

1. Ruth L. Tongue, *Somerset Folklore*, ed. K. M. Briggs (London: Folklore Society, 1965), p. 136.

2. St Guinefort: Jean-Claude Schmitt, *The Holy Greyhound: Guinefort, healer of children since the thirteenth century*, trans. Martin Thom (Cambridge: Cambridge University Press, 1983).

3. Katherine Briggs, *A Dictionary of British Folktales*, 4 vols (London: Routledge & Kegan Paul, 1970–71), vol. 2, p. 221.

4. *Ibid.*, p. 300.

5. Joyce Underwood Munro, 'The Invisible Made Visible: The Fairy Changeling as a Folk Articulation of Failure to Thrive in Infants and Children', in Peter Narvaez, *The Good People: New Fairylore Essays* (New York: Garland, 1991), pp. 251–83.

6. John Gregorson Campbell, *Clan Traditions and Popular Tales of the Western Highlands*, Waifs and Strays of Celtic Tradition, Argyllshire Series 5 (London: Nutt, 1895), p. 146.

7. Martin Luther, *Table Talk*, trans. William Hazlitt (London: 1848).

8. G. F. Black, *Examples of Printed Folk-Lore Concerning the Orkney & Shetland Islands*, ed. Northcote W. Thomas, County Folk-Lore vol. 3, Printed Extracts no. 5 (London: Nutt, 1903; reprinted Felinfach and London: Llanerch-Folklore Society, 1994), pp. 23–5; Angela Bourke, 'Fairies and

anorexia: Nuala Ni Dhomhnaill's "Amazing Grass"', *Proceedings of the Harvard Celtic Colloquium* 13 (1993), pp. 25–38, esp. 32.

9. Kevin Crossley-Holland, *The Dead Moon* (London: Faber, 1982), pp. 87–96, 101; Ralph of Coggeshall, *Chronicon Anglicanum*, Rolls Series 66 (1857).

10. Tongue, *Somerset Folklore*; Robert Jamieson, *Popular Ballads and Songs from Tradition*, 2 vols (Edinburgh: 1806), vol. 2, pp. 367–70.

11. *Sir Gawain and the Green Knight*, ed. J. R. R. Tolkien and E. V. Gordon, 2nd edition edited by Norman Davies (Oxford: Oxford University Press, 1967).

12. Wolfgang Behringer, *Shaman of Oberstdorf: Chonrad Stoecklin and the Phantoms of the Night*, trans. H. C. Erik Midelfort (Charlottesville: University Press of Virginia, 1998), p. 63.

13. Ruth Harris, *Lourdes: Body and Spirit in the Secular Age* (London: Allen Lane Penguin Press, 1999), p. 77.

14. *Documents Illustrative of Medieval Kentish Society*, ed. F. R. H. du Boulay (Kent Archaeology Society, 1964), pp. 254–5. I am grateful to Ralph Hanna for pointing out the probable mistranscription of 'sowre' as 'sose'.

15. *Six Town Chronicles*, ed. R. Flenley (Kent Archaeological Society, 1961), p. 127.

16. *Historical Manuscripts Commission*, 5, p. 455.

17. F. J. Child, *English and Scottish Popular Ballads*, 5 vols (New York: Folklore Press, 1956), vol. 1, nos. 35, 37A, 37 Appendix, 39.

18. Campbell, *Waifs and Strays*, p. 92.

19. Lady Wilde, *Ancient Legends, Mystic Charms and Superstitions of Ireland*, 2 vols (London: 1887).

20. Sigmund Freud, 'Medusa's Head' (first published 1940), in *The Standard Edition of the Complete Psychological Works of Sigmund Freud*, ed. and trans. James Strachey et al., 24 vols (London: Hogarth Press, 1953–74; vol. 18, 1955), pp. 273–4; 'The Uncanny', in *Art and Literature*, ed. Albert Dickson, Pelican Freud Library, 14 (Harmondsworth: Penguin, 1985), pp. 335–76.

21. Child, *Ballads*, vol. 1, no. 35.

22. Gearoid O'Crualaoich, 'The Primacy of Form: A "Folk Ideology" in De Valera's Politics', *De Valera and His Times*, ed. John P. O'Carroll and John A. Murphy (Cork: Cork University Press, 1983), p. 153.

23. Joan Radner, ed., *Fragmentary annals of Ireland* (Dublin: Dublin Institute for Advanced Studies, 1978), p. 78.

24. *The Romance of Thomas and The Fairy Queen*, in *Fairy Tales, Legends and Romances Illustrating Shakespeare*, ed. W. C. Hazlitt (London: 1875), p. 105.

25. Geoffrey Chaucer, *The Wife of Bath's Tale*, in *The Riverside Chaucer*, 3rd edition, ed. Larry D. Benson (Oxford: Oxford University Press, 1988), p. 116, line 859, and p. 117, line 888.

26. *Sire Degarre*, ed. Gustave Schleich (Heidelberg: Carl Winer, 1929).

27. *The Faber Book of Ballads*, ed. Matthew Hodgart (London: Faber, 1965), p. 28.

28. *Sir Orfeo*, in *Middle English Verse Romances*, ed. Donald B. Sands (Exeter: University of Exeter Press, 1986; first published 1966).

29. Geoffrey Chaucer, *The Merchant's Tale*, in *The Riverside Chaucer*, p. 163, lines 2038–40.

30. Nancy Caciola, 'Revenants and Wraiths', *Past and Present* 103 (1996), p. 29.

31. Paul Binski, *Medieval Death: Ritual and Representation* (London: British Museum Press, 1996), pp. 56–7.

32. Giraldus Cambrensis, *The Itinerary through Wales* (1191), pp. 390–91.

33. *The Works of Thomas Malory*, ed. Eugene Vinaver (Oxford: Oxford University Press, 1977), p. 149, VI. 1.8, 10–12.

34. Barbara Nolan, 'The Tale of Sir Gareth and the Tale of Sir Lancelot', in *A Companion to Malory*, ed. Elizabeth Archbald and A. S. G. Edwards (Woodbridge: Brewer, 1996), p. 172.

35. *The Works of Thomas Malory*, p. 151, VI.3.17–18.

36. Cathy La Farge, 'The hand of the huntress: repetition and Malory's *Morte Darthur*', in *New Feminist Discourses*, ed. Isobel Armstrong (London and New York: Routledge, 1992), p. 267.

37. P. J. C. Field, *The Life and Times of Sir Thomas Malory* (Woodbridge: Brewer, 1993); Felicity Riddy, *Sir Thomas Malory* (London: Brill, 1987) and 'Contextualising the *Morte Darthur*: Empire and Civil War', in *Companion to Malory*, pp. 55–74; Ad Putter, 'Arthurian Literature and the Rhetoric of "Effeminacy" ', in *Sir Gawain and the Green Knight*', in *Arthurian Romance and Gender*, ed. Friedrich Wolfzettel (Amsterdam and Atlanta: Rodopi, 1994), pp. 34–49.

38. La Farge, 'The hand of the huntress', pp. 263–79.

39. Sigmund Freud, 'Femininity', in *New Introductory Lectures on Psychoanalysis*, ed. James Strachey and Angela Richards, Pelican Freud Library, 2 (Harmondsworth: Penguin, 1973), pp. 145–69; Shoshana Felman, 'On Femininity', *Yale French Studies* 62 (1981), pp. 19–44.

40. Diane Purkiss, *The Witch in History* (London: Routledge, 1996), p. 129; Jeanne Favret-Saada, *Deadly Words: Witchcraft in the Bocage* (Cambridge: Cambridge University Press, 1980).

41. Child, *Ballads*, 37A, vol. 1, p. 323.

42. Attribution of Lanval to Marie is of course conjectural: Marie de France,

Lais, ed. A. Ewert (Oxford: Clarendon, 1960); *Sir Launfal*, ed. A. J. Bliss (London: Nelson, 1960), and in *Middle English Verse Romances*.
43. Katherine Briggs and Ruth Tongue, *Folktales of England* (London: Routledge & Kegan Paul, 1965), pp. 35–6.

3. Birth and Death: Fairies in Scottish Witch-trials

1. Black, *Examples of Printed Folk-Lore*, pp. 23–4; the original is in *Records of the Sheriff Court of Orkney*, f. 63, Orkney Record Office, Kirkwall. Barbara Rieti, *Strange terrain: the fairy world in Newfoundland* (St John's, Newfoundland: Institute of Social and Economic Research, Social and Economic Studies, no. 45, 1991), p. 21.
2. Christina Larner, *Enemies of God* (Oxford: Blackwell, 1983).
3. Robin Briggs, *Witches and neighbours: the social and cultural context of European witchcraft* (London: HarperCollins, 1996), p. 205.
4. Miranda Chaytor, 'Husband(ry): Narratives of Rape in the Seventeenth Century', *Gender and History* 7 (1995), pp. 378–407.
5. Agnes Hunter, 8 June 1649, *Register of the Privy Council of Scotland*, 2nd series, ed. David Masson, 8 vols (Edinburgh: 1899–1908), vol. 8, pp. 190–91.
6. Elspeth Reoch: *Maitland Miscellany*, vol. 2, part 1 (1840), pp. 187–91; Black, *Examples of Printed Folk-Lore*, pp. 111–15.
7. Margaret Bennet, 'Balquhidder Revisited: Fairylore in the Scottish Highlands 1690–1990', in *The Good People: New Fairylore Essays*, p. 107; Robert Kirk, *The Secret Commonwealth of Elves and Fairies*, ed. Stuart Sanderson (Cambridge: Cambridge University Press, 1976), p. 73.
8. Angela Bourke, 'Reading a Woman's Death: Colonial Texts and Oral Tradition in Nineteenth-Century Ireland', *Feminist Studies* 21 (1995), pp. 553–86, esp. 568.
9. Joan Tyrrie: Wells Diocesan Records, Somerset Record Office, D/D/CA Act Books 21–22.
10. Jonet Drever: *Spalding Club Miscellany*, vol. 1, pp. 167–8; Black, *Examples of Printed Folk-Lore*, pp. 72–4.
11. Jenny Wormald, *Court, Kirk and Community: Scotland 1470–1625* (Edinburgh: Edinburgh University Press, 1981).
12. *Sceálta Chois Cladaigh, Stories of Sea and Shore*, told by John Henry, collected by Seamas O' Cathain (Dublin: University College Dublin Press, 1983), pp. 15–17.
13. George Hickes, *Ravillac redivivus* (1678), pp. 64–5; John Lamont, *Diary*, ed. G. R. Kinloch (Edinburgh: 1830), pp. 271–2; George Sinclair, *Satans Invisible World Discovered* (Edinburgh: 1789), pp. 152–3; Robert Law,

Memorialls, ed. C. K. Sharpe (Edinburgh: 1818), p. 27; Scottish Record Office, Justiciary Court MS JC2/13, reproduced in Law, *Memorialls*; *Records of the Proceeedings of the Justiciary Court* (Edinburgh: 1661–78), vol. 2, pp. 10–15; *The Trial, Indictments, and Sentence of Major Thomas Weir . . . also his sister Joan Weir* (n.d.).

14. Judith Herman, *Father-Daughter Incest* (Cambridge, Mass.: Harvard University Press, 1981), pp. 97, 98.

15. 8 November 1576, *Ancient Criminal Trials in Scotland*, ed. Robert Pitcairn, 3 vols (Edinburgh: 1833), vol. I, part II, pp. 49–58.

16. Hickes, *Ravillac redivivus*, p. 72.

17. 'Angela', in Mark Pendergrast, *Victims of Memory: Incest, Accusations, and Shattered Lives* (London and New York: HarperCollins, 1997), p. 289.

18. 'Jasmine', Angela's 'alter', in *Ibid.*, p. 290.

19. Scottish Record Office, Justiciary Court MS JC2/13, reproduced in Robert Law, *Memorialls*, note on p. 24; *Records of the . . . Justiciary Court*, vol. 2, pp. 10–15.

20. 'Whuppity Stoorie', in *The Penguin Book of Scottish Folktales*, ed. Neil Philip (London and New York: Penguin, 1995), pp. 3–7, from a transcription made about 1784.

21. Julie Osborn, *Psychological Effects of Child Sex Abuse on Women*, Social Work Monographs (Norwich: University of East Anglia, 1990), Appendix 3, p. 38.

22. On Cinderella and the mother, see Marina Warner, *From the Beast to the Blonde: On Fairytales and their Tellers* (London: Chatto & Windus, 1994), pp. 201–17.

23. Janice Haaken, *Pillar of Salt: Gender, Memory and the Perils of Looking Back* (London: Free Association, 1998), pp. 2–5.

24. *Ibid.*, pp. 14–15, 251–5.

25. Alesoun Peirsoun: Pitcairn, *Criminal Trials in Scotland*, vol. I, part II, pp. 161–5; Melville: *The autobiography and diary of JM*, ed. R. Pitcairn (Edinburgh: Woodrow Society, 1842).

26. *Court Book of Shetland*, ed. Gordon Donaldson (Lerwick: 1991), pp. 38–9.

27. E. O. G. Turville-Petre, *Myth and Religion of the North* (London: Weidenfeld & Nicolson, 1964), p. 231.

28. Alan Bruford, 'Trolls, Hillfolk, Finns and Picts: The Identity of the Good Neighbours in Orkney', in *The Good People: New Fairylore Essays*, pp. 116–41, esp. 132.

29. *Ibid.*, p. 132.

30. Bessie Dunlop: Pitcairn, *Criminal Trials in Scotland*, vol. I, part II, pp. 49–58.

31. *Ibid.*

32. Andro Man: *Spalding Club Miscellany*, vol. 1, pp. 119–25.

33. Jonet Drever: *Spalding Club Miscellany*, vol. 1, pp. 167–8; Black, *Examples of Printed Folk-Lore*, pp. 72–4.

34. *Register of the Privy Council of Scotland*, vol. 8, p. 347.

35. Isabel Haldane: Pitcairn, *Criminal Trials in Scotland*, vol. II, p. 537; *Register of the Privy Council of Scotland*, Charles I, p. 347.

36. Black, *Examples of Printed Folk-Lore*, pp. 81–2.

37. I owe this interpretation to Carolyne Larrington.

38. *Court Book of Shetland*, pp. 38–9.

39. *Ibid.*, pp. 40–41.

40. Kirk, *Secret Commonwealth*, p. 87.

41. Janet Trall: *Presbytery Book of Strathbogie*, ed. John Stuart (Aberdeen: Spalding Club, 1843), pp. xi, xiii.

42. Isobel Gowdie: Pitcairn, *Criminal Trials in Scotland*, vol. III, part II, pp. 602–16.

43. Felicity Heal, *Hospitality in Early Modern England* (Oxford: Clarendon, 1990).

44. James VI and I, *Daemonologie* (1597), in *Minor Prose Works of King James VI and I*, ed. James Craigie (Edinburgh: Scottish Text Society, 1982), iii, 5; also iii, 4.

45. Philip Larkin, 'The Batman from Blades', in *Required Writing: Miscellaneous Pieces, 1955–1982* (London: Faber, 1983), pp. 266–71; Umberto Eco, 'Narrative Structure in Fleming', in *The Role of the Reader: Explorations in the Semiotics of Texts* (London: Hutchinson, 1981), pp. 144–72.

46. Black, *Examples of Printed Folk-Lore*, p. 47.

47. Jonet Morison, 19 January 1662, Rothesay: *Highland Papers*, ed. J. R. M. MacPhail, Scottish History Society, series 2, vol. 20, pp. 23–4, 27.

48. J. G. Dalyell, *The Darker Superstitions of Scotland* (Edinburgh: 1835), p. 531; *Presbyterie Buik of Aberdein*, 4 December 1601.

4. Desire of Gold and the Good Neighbours: The Uses of Fairies

1. Annabel Gregory, 'Witchcraft, politics and "Good Neighbourhood" in Seventeenth-Century Rye', *Past and Present* 133, pp. 31–66. I am very grateful to Annabel Gregory for lending me her meticulous transcripts of this exciting case. Any errors are mine.

2. East Sussex Record Office, Lewes, Rye Corporation MSS 13/25.

3. John Webster, *The Displaying of Supposed Witchcraft* (1677).

4. W. O. Williams, *Calendar of Caernarvonshire Quarter Sessions Records, 1541–1558* (Caernarvon: Caernarvon Historical Society, 1956).

5. Margaret Cavendish, Duchess of Newcastle, 'The Fairy Queen', *Poems and Fancies* (1653), p. 148.

6. Keith Thomas, *Religion and the Decline of Magic* (Harmondsworth: Penguin, 1971).

7. *A Mirror for Magistrates*, ed. L. B. Campbell (New York, 1960), p. 435, lines 92–8.

8. *Narratives of the days of the Reformation, chiefly from the manuscripts of John Foxe the Martyrologist*, ed. J. G. Nichols, Camden Society Publications, 77 (London: 1859), p. 333.

9. Crossley-Holland, *The Dead Moon*, pp. 27–37, 98; *The Diary of Abraham de la Pryme*, ed. Charles Jackson, Surtees Society (1870).

10. 'The Autobiography of Edward Underhill', in *Narratives of the days of the Reformation*.

11. Bodleian MS Ashmole 1406.

12. *Norfolk Archaeology or Miscellaneous Tracts Relating to the Antiquities of the County of Norfolk* (Norwich: 1847), vol. 1, pp. 57ff.

13. Bodleian MS e Mus 173 f 72 V-R.

14. T. Jackson, *A treatise concerning the originall of unbeliefe* (1625), pp. 178–9.

15. Somerset Record Office, Wells Diocesan Records, D/D/CA, Act Books 21 and 22; Richard Holworthy, *Discoveries in the Diocesan Registry* (Wells: 1927), p. 6.

16. George Lyman Kittredge, *Witchcraft in Old and New England* (New York: Russell & Russell, 1929), p. 146.

17. William Browne, *Britannia's Pastorals* (1695), pp. 146–7.

18. Richard Bovet, *Pandaemonium, or the Devil's Cloyster* (1684), pp. 208–9.

19. Carlo Ginzburg, *The Cheese and the Worms: the Cosmos of a Sixteenth-Century Miller*, trans. John and Anne Tedeschi (London and New York: Routledge, 1980).

20. *Spalding Club Miscellany*, ed. John Stuart (Aberdeen: 1841), vol. 1, pp. 119–25.

21. *The Examinacioun of John Walsh* (1566), reprinted in Barbara Rosen, ed., *Witchcraft in England 1558–1618* (Amherst: University of Massachusetts Press, 1991), p. 68. The original trial transcript is at the Exeter Record Office, MSS Chanter 855B, f. 310R. I am grateful to Marion Gibson for lending me her transcript of Walsh's trial.

22. Gail Kligman, *Calus: symbolic transformation in Romanian Ritual* (Chicago and London: University of Chicago Press, 1981).

23. Carlo Ginzburg, *Ecstasies: Deciphering the Witches' Sabbath*, pp. 104–8.

24. Gustav Henningsen, 'Ladies from Outside', p. 215.

25. Jacob Grimm, *Deutsche Mythologie* (1835), trans. by J. S. Stallybrass as *Teutonic Mythology*, 4 vols (London: Swan Sonnenschein & Allen, 1883–8), vol. 1, pp. 265–8.

26. *Dives and Pauper*, ed. Priscilla Heath Barnum (London: Early English Text Society, 1976), p. 158, lines 28–34.

27. James VI and I, *Daemonologie*, p. 132.

28. Bernardo Gui, *Interrogatoria ad sortilegos et divinos et invocatores demonum* (1315).

29. Henningsen, 'Ladies from Outside', pp. 191–215; Richard A. Horsley, 'Further Reflections on witchcraft and European folk religion', *History of Religions* 19 (1979), p. 89; Wolfgang Behringer, *Shaman of Oberstdorf*, p. 54.

30. Snorri Sturluson, *The Edda*, ed. Anthony Faulks (Oxford: Oxford World Classics, 1982), pp. 37–8.

31. Behringer, *Shaman of Oberstdorf*, p. 56.

32. Norman Cohn, *Europe's Inner Demons* (London: Macmillan, 1975), pp. 213–14; Horsley, 'Further Reflections', p. 89.

33. Vincent Crapanzano, 'Saints, *Jnun*, and dreams: an Essay in Moroccan Ethnopsychology', *Psychiatry* 38 (1975), pp. 145–59.

34. Éva Pócs, *Between the Living and the Dead*, trans. Szilvia Rédey and Michael Webb (Budapest: Central European University Press, 1999), p. 89.

35. Philip K. Dick, 'We Can Remember It For You Wholesale', in *We Can Remember It For You Wholesale* (London: Grafton, 1991), pp. 205–27.

36. J. Penry, *Three Treatises Concerning Wales*, ed. D. Williams (Cardiff: University of Wales Press, 1960).

37. *Strange and Wonderful News from the County of Wicklow in Ireland* (1678), p. 4.

38. *The Pinder of Wakefield*, ed. E. A. Horsman (Liverpool: Liverpool University Press, 1956), p. 70.

39. *Satirical Poems of the Time of the Reformation*, ed. J. Cranstoun (Scottish Text Society: 1891), vol. 1, p. 365, lines 370–79.

40. Bartholomaus Anhorn, *Magiologia* (1674), in Behringer, *Shaman of Oberstdorf*, p. 62.

41. Reginald Scot, *The Discoverie of Witchcraft* (1584), Book III, Chapter 2.

42. Purkiss, *The Witch in History*, pp. 163–6.

43. Richard Gough, *Antiquities and Memoirs of the Parish of Myddle* (Shrewsbury: 1875), pp. 37–8.

44. Kittredge, *Witchcraft in Old and New England*, p. 215.

45. Rosen, *Witchcraft in England*, p. 88.

46. Purkiss, *The Witch in History*, p. 138 and n. 92.

47. *The Strange Witch at Greenwich* (1650).

48. Purkiss, *The Witch in History*, p. 135.

49. Malcolm Gaskill, 'Witchcraft and Power in Early Modern England: the case of Margaret Moore', in *Women, Crime and the Courts in Early Modern England*, ed. Jenny Kermode and Garthine Walker (London: University College London Press, 1994), pp. 125–45.

50. Scot, *Discoverie*, Book V, Chapter 9.

51. Behringer, *Shaman of Oberstdorf*, p. 68; E. William Monter, *Witchcraft in France and Switzerland: The Borderlands during the Reformation* (Ithaca and London: Cornell University Press, 1976).

52. *Hertford (Hertfordshire) County Records*, vols 1–3, *Notes and Extracts from the Sessions Rolls, 1581 to . . . 1894*, compiled by W. J. Hardy (1905).

5. The Fairy Goes Literary: Puck and Others

1. William Tyndale, *The Exposition of the First Epistle of St John* (Antwerp: 1531), p. 139.

2. Thomas Harman, *A Caveat For Common Cursitors* (1568), p. 69.

3. Scot, *Discoverie*, Book VII, Chapter 15.

4. *Ibid.*, Book II, Chapter 19.

5. *Ibid.*, Book VII, Chapter 2.

6. *Ibid.*, Book IV, Chapter 10.

7. Thomas Nashe, *The Terrors of the Night* (1594), sig. B2V, in *The Works of Thomas Nashe*, ed. R. B. McKerrow, revised edition, F. P. Wilson, 5 vols (Oxford: Blackwell, 1966), vol. 1, p.347; William Baldwin, *Beware the Cat* (1584), p. 22.

8. Robert Burton, *The Anatomy of Melancholy*, ed. Nicolas K. Kiessling, Thomas C. Fulkner and Rhonda C. Blair, 3 vols (Oxford: Clarendon, 1986), vol. 1, pp. 186–7.

9. William Warner, *Albions England* (1612), Chapter 91; Samuel Rowlands, *More Knaves Yet?* (1613), in *The Complete Works of Samuel Rowlands*, 3 vols (Glasgow: 1880), vol. 2, p. 40; Samuel Harsnet, *Declaration of Egregious Popish Impostures* (1603), p. 134.

10. Richard Tarlton, *Tarlton's Newes out of Purgatory* (1630), sig. A3V.

11. *The Cobbler of Canterburie*, Appendix; *Tarlton's Newes*, p. 110.

12. *Robin Good-Fellow, his Mad Pranks and Merry Jests* (1628), sig. A4R.

13. *Tell-Truth's New-Year's Gift* (1593), sig. A2R.

14. *The Entertainment at Althorp*, in *Ben Jonson*, ed. C. H. Herford and Percy and Evelyn Simpson, 11 vols (Oxford: Clarendon, 1925–52), vol. 7, pp. 119–32, esp. p. 122, lines 58–9.

15. Robert Herrick, *Hesperides*, no. 557, in *Poetical Works*, ed. L. C. Martin (Oxford: Clarendon, 1956).

16. William Lilly, *Mr William Lilly's History of his Life and Times from the Year 1602 to 1681*, ed. Elias Ashmole (1715), p. 103.

17. Shakespeare, *Romeo and Juliet*, I.iv.

18. Seneca, *Phaedra*, ed. Michael Coffey and Roland Mayer (Cambridge: Cambridge University Press, 1990), lines 198–200.

19. *Carmina Anacreontea*, ed. Martin L. West (Leipzig: Teubner, 1984), nos 2, 15, 31; *Anakreontos Teiou mele*, ed. Henri Etienne (Lyons: 1554).

20. *The Poems of Lady Mary Wroth*, ed. Josephine A. Roberts (Baton Rouge and London: Louisiana State University Press, 1983).

21. 'The Merry Pranks of Robin-Goodfellow: very pleasant and witty', in J. O. Halliwell-Philips, *Illustrations of the Fairy Mythology of the Midsummer Night's Dream* (1845), pp. 155–65.

22. 'The Pranks of Puck', in *ibid.*, pp. 166–7.

23. *The Boke of Duke Huon of Burdeux*, trans. Sir John Bourchier, Lord Berners (1534), ed. S. L. Lee (London: Early English Text Society, 1882–7), pp. 63, 65, 73–7, 606.

24. Robert Greene, *The Scottish history of James the fourth* (1594), ed. Norman Sanders (London: Methuen, 1970), Induction, lines 12–18.

25. Arthur Golding, *Ovid's Metamorphoses* (1567), 8.178, 14.586; Gawin Douglas, *Aeneid* (1553).

26. Shakespeare, *A Midsummer Night's Dream*, II.i.

27. Edmund Spenser, *The Faerie Queene*, ed. Thomas P. Roche, jun. (Harmondsworth: Penguin, 1978), I.ix. 13.8–14.3.

28. Louis Montrose, ' "Shaping Fantasies": Figurations of Gender and Power in Elizabethan Culture', *Representations* 2 (1983), pp. 61–94; 'Why should he call her whore? Defamation and Desdemona's case', in Lisa Jardine, *Reading Shakespeare Historically* (London: Routledge, 1996), pp. 19–34.

29. Purkiss, *The Witch in History*, pp. 193–5.

30. Michael Drayton, *Nimphidia*, lines 41–8, in *The Works of Michael Drayton*, ed. J. William Hebel, 5 vols (Oxford: Blackwell, 1961), vol. 3, pp. 125–46.

31. Susan Stewart, *On Longing: Narratives of the Miniature, the Gigantic, the Souvenir, the Collection* (Durham, NC: Duke University Press, 1993).

32. Robert Herrick, 'The Fairie Temple, or Oberon's Chapel', lines 22–7.

33. John Selden, *Table Talk* (1689); John Aubrey, *The Natural History of Wiltshire*, ed. John Britton (London: 1847), p. 77; *The Midnight's Watch, or robin goodfellow his serious observation* (1643).

34. Kirk, *Secret Commonwealth*.

35. Ian Bostridge, 'Debates about witchcraft in England, 1650–1736' (Oxford D. Phil thesis, 1991), MS D. Phil c. 8703.

36. 'A Monstrous Shape', in Hyder E. Rollins, *A Pepysian Garland* (Cambridge: Cambridge University Press, 1922), p. 452.

37. *The Bridling, Saddling and Riding of a Rich Churl in Hampshire, by the subtle practice of one Judith Phillips, a professed cunning woman or fortune teller* (1595).

38. *The Several Notorious and Lewd Cozenages of John West and Alice West, falsely called the king and queen of fairies* (1613), p. 10.

39. Linda Levy Peck, *Court Patronage and Corruption in Early Stuart England* (London: Unwin Hyman, 1990).

40. Shakespeare, *Macbeth*, I.iii.

41. Lilly, *History of his Life*, pp. 102–3.

42. Sigmund Freud, 'Medusa's Head', pp. 273–4.

43. British Library, MS Add. 20006, f. 41v; J. Kent Clark, *Goodwin Wharton* (Oxford: Oxford University Press, 1984).

44. Patricia Parker, *Literary Fat Ladies* (London: Methuen, 1988).

45. Clark, *Goodwin Wharton*, p. 25.

46. MS Add. 20006, f. 37r.

47. Clark, *Goodwin Wharton*, p. 21.

48. MS Add. 20006, f. 32r; f. 100v.

49. Purkiss, *The Witch in History*, pp.161ff.

6. Into the Enlightenment

1. British Library N. Tab 2026/25, 19.

2. Leslie Fiedler, *Freaks: myths and images of the secret self* (New York: Simon & Schuster, 1978), p. 39.

3. *Ibid.*, pp. 51–3. Robert Bogdan, *Freak show: presenting human oddities for amusement and profit* (Chicago and London: University of Chicago Press, 1988), p. 157.

4. Fiedler, *Freaks*, p. 56; Thomas Fuller, *The History of the Worthies of England* (1662).

5. Lori Merrish, 'Cuteness and Commodity Aestheticism: Tom Thumb and Shirley Temple', in *Freakery: Cultural Spectacles of the Extraordinary Body*, ed. Rosemarie Garland Thomson (New York and London: New York University Press, 1996), pp. 185–203.

6. British Library MS Add. 32496; *A Discourse of Witchcraft as it was Acted in the family of Edward Fairfax*, ed. R. Monckton Milnes, Philobiblion Society (London: 1858–9), vol. 5, pp. 17–19.

7. Gough, *Antiquities and Memoirs*, pp. 37–8.

8. Bovet, *Pandaemonium*, pp. 284, 285.

9. John Milton, 'L'Allegro', 100–106, in *The Poems of John Milton*, ed. John Carey and Alastair Fowler (London: Longman, 1971).

10. Herford and Simpson, *Ben Jonson*, vol. 7, p. 122, esp. lines 53–63.

11. John Aubrey, *Remaines of Gentilisme and Judaisme*, in *Three Prose Works*, ed. John Buchanan-Brown (Fontwell: Centaur, 1972), Preface, p. 132.

12. Anthony Powell, *John Aubrey and his friends* (London: Heinemann, 1948), pp. 71–2.

13. British Library N. Tab 2026/25, 19.

14. Bogdan, *Freak Show*, pp. 47–8.

15. Geoffroi de Villehardouin, *The Conquest of Constantinople*, in *Chronicles of the Crusades*, trans. Margaret B. Shaw (Harmondsworth: Penguin, 1963), pp. 58–9.

16. Edward Said, *Orientalism* (Harmondsworth: Penguin, 1986).

17. Chrétien de Troyes, *Cligés*; *Huon of Bordeaux*, in three romances, *Auberon*, *Huon* and *Esclarmonde*, and in the sixteenth-century translation *The Boke of Duke Huon of Burdeux*, esp. pp. 40–41, 43, 50; Ariosto, *Orlando Furioso*, 6.59; Spenser, *The Faerie Queene*, I.x.58 and x.72.

18. Michael Camille, *Gothic Art* (London: Everyman Art Library, 1996), p. 37; Jarrett Packer, *Fairies in Legend and the Arts* (London: Cameron & Taylor, 1980), p. 16.

19. Kirk, *Secret Commonwealth*.

20. Herford and Simpson, *Ben Jonson*, vol. 7, pp. 337–56, lines 2–5.

21. William Browne, *Britannia's Pastorals* (Marston: Scolar Press, 1969), vol. 2, p. 132.

22. Spenser, *The Faerie Queene*, II.x.72.

23. Marco Polo, *Il libro di Marco Polo detto Milione*, trans. Guilio Einaudi (Turin: 1978), Chapter 71.

24. *The Book of Guy of Warwick*, ed. J. Zupitza (London: Early English Text Society, 1883–91), esp. p. 42.

25. Boiardo, *Orlando Innamorato* (1487), 1.25.5–7.

26. Spenser, *The Faerie Queene*, I.x.58; Isabel Rathborne, *The Meaning of Spenser's Fairyland* (New York: Scolar Press, 1937); Michael Murrin, 'Fairyland', in *The Spenser Encyclopedia*, ed. A. C. Hamilton (London: Routledge, 1990).

27. Spenser, *The Faerie Queene*, I.xi.7.

28. Bernal Díaz, *The Conquest of New Spain*, trans. J. M. Cohen (Harmondsworth: Penguin, 1963), p. 214.

29. Herford and Simpson, *Ben Jonson*, vol. 7, p. 346, lines 143–4.

30. Kirk, *Secret Commonwealth*, pp. 69, 73.

31. Diane Purkiss, *Women's Renaissance: Elizabeth Cary's Tragedie of Mariam and Edward II and Aemilia Lanyer's Salve Deus Rex Judaeorum* (London: William Pickering, 1994), p. xliv.

32. *A description of the King and Queen of Fairies, their Habit, Fare, their Abode, Pomp and State* (1635).

33. Sir Thomas Roe, in *The Embassy of Sir Thomas Roe to the Court of the Great Mogul*, ed. William Foster, 2 vols (London: Hakluyt Society, 1899), vol. 1, p. 412.

34. Hugh Thomas, *The Slave Trade* (London: HarperCollins, 1998).

35. Spells: British Library MS Sloane 3851 f. 129; British Library MS Sloane 1727 f. 18, 23; Bodleian Library MS Carte 79, 80, 81, 109, 233; Bodleian Library MS Rawlinson 49–54; Bodleian Library MS Ashmole 1406; Bodleian Library MS e. mus 173, f. 72v. Familiars: Diane Purkiss, *The Witch in History*.

36. *The Works of Thomas Nashe*, vol. 1, p. 317, line 29.

37. Kim Hall, *Things of Darkness: Economies of Race and Gender in Early Modern England* (Ithaca: Cornell University Press, 1995), p. 8.

38. *The Examinacioun of John Walsh*, in *Witchcraft in England*, p. 68.

39. *The Masque of Cole-Orton*, reprinted in R. Brotanek, *Die englischen Maskenspiele, Wiener Beiträge zur englischen Philologie*, vol. XV (Vienna and Leipzig: 1902).

40. 'The Queenes Majesties Entertainment at Woodstocke', ed. J. W. Cunliffe, *PMLA* 26 (1911), p. 98.

41. Thomas Randolph, *Poetical and Dramatic Works*, ed. W. C. Hazlitt, 2 vols (London: 1875).

42. Shakespeare, *The Tempest*, II.ii.

43. Thomas, *The Slave Trade*, p. 156.

44. *The Tempest*, I.ii.

45. Goethe, *The Collected Works*, ed. Christopher Middleton, 12 vols (Princeton, Princeton University Press, 1994), vol. 1, pp. 86–7.

46. John Keats, 'La Belle Dame sans Merci', in *Keats: The Complete Poems*, ed. Miriam Allott (London: Longmans, 1970), p. 500.

47. Samuel Taylor Coleridge, 'Songs of the Pixies', in *The Complete Poems*, ed. William Keach (London: Penguin, 1997), p. 62. For Coleridge's visit to the Pixies' Cave, see Richard Holmes, *Coleridge: Early Visions* (London: HarperCollins, 1989), pp. 50–51.

7. Victorian Fairies

1. George Cruikshank, *Cinderella* (1853); Anna Isabella Ritchie, 'Cinderella', first published in *Five Old Friends and a Young Prince* (1868), reprinted in Jack Zipes, *Victorian Fairy Tales: The Revolt of the Fairies and Elves* (London: Routledge, 1987), pp. 103–26.

2. Charles Dickens, 'The Magic Fishbone' (1868); reprinted in Zipes, *Victorian Fairy Tales*, pp. 89–100.

3. Sarah Trimmer Trimmer is cited in 'The Flowering of the Fairytale in Victorian England', in Jack Zipes, *When Dreams Came True: Classic Fairy Tales and their Tradition* (New York and London, 1999), p. 115.

4. M. A. C. [M. A. Cooke], *Better Than Fairies* (London: 1864).

5. Debra Mancuff, *The Return of King Arthur* (Auckland: David Bateman, 1995), p. 38.

6. John Ruskin, *Works*, 39 vols (1903–12), vol. 19, pp. 236–8.

7. On these kinds of theatrical events, see Michael Booth, *Victorian Spectacular Theatre 1850–1910* (London: Routledge & Kegan Paul, 1981).

8. Michael Booth, *English Plays of the Nineteenth Century*, vol. 5: *Pantomimes, Extravaganzas, and Burlesques* (London: Methuen, 1976).

9. Recent accounts of children on stage include Carolyn Steedman, *Strange Dislocations: Childhood and the Idea of Human Interiority 1780–1930* (Cambridge, Mass.: Harvard University Press, 1996), and Tracey Davis, 'The Employment of children in the Victorian theatre. Training, exploitation and the movement for reform', *New Theatre Quarterly* 2:60 (1986), pp. 117–35.

10. Charles Dickens, *Christmas Books* (Harmondsworth: Penguin, 1971), pp. 351–2. Dickens did however defend the chastity of the stage fairy in 'Gaslight Fairies', *Selected Journalism 1850–70*, ed. David Pascoe (Harmondsworth: Penguin, 1997), pp. 577–8.

11. Henry Mayhew, *London Labour and the London Poor* (1861).

12. 'The Fairies of the Stage', *Pall Mall Gazette* (9 February 1885), p. 4.

13. Millicent Garrett Fawcett, 'The Employment of Children in Theatres', *Contemporary Review* 56 (1889), p. 827.

14. Eileen Barlee, *Pantomime Waifs* (1884), pp. 16, 52–3.

15. *Ibid.*, p. 68.

16. Fawcett, 'The Employment of Children in Theatres', p. 828.

17. Barlee, *Pantomime Waifs*, pp. xiv–xv.

18. Mid-Victorian song, quoted in Lionel Lambourne, 'Fairies and the Stage', in Jeremy Maas et al., *Victorian Fairy Painting* (London: Royal Academy of Arts, 1997), catalogue of the 1997 RA exhibition, pp.47–53, epigraph.

19. *Fairy Phoebe; or Facing the Footlights* (London: 1887), pp. 14, 45, 36, 53, 56, 115, 132, 212.

20. Eliza Keating, *Beauty and the Beast* (1865), p. 9.

21. E. L. L. Blanchard, *Cherry and Fairstar; or the Pretty Green Bird and the Fairies of the Dancing Waters* (1861), p. 2.

22. *Theatrical Journal* 1 May 1841, in Trevor R. Griffiths, *A Midsummer Night's Dream* (Cambridge: Cambridge University Press, 1996), p. 23.

23. Douglas Jerrold, *Lloyds Weekly* (23 October 1853), p. 38.

24. Griffiths, *A Midsummer Night's Dream*, pp. 31–2.

25. Dutton Cook, *Nights at the Play* (1883), pp. 273–6.

26. Griffiths, *A Midsummer Night's Dream*, p. 33.

27. George Speaight, *The History of the English Toy Theatre* (London: Studio Vista, 1969), p. 176.

28. Christina Rossetti, 'Goblin Market' (1862), in *Poems and Prose*, ed. Jan Marsh (London: Dent, 1994), pp. 162–76.

29. Lorraine Janzen Kooistra, 'Modern Markets for *Goblin Market*', in *Victorian Poetry* 32 (1994), pp. 249–77, with sample illustrations by D. G. Rossetti, Laurence Housman, A. C. Michael, Arthur Rackham, Kinuko Craft (*Playboy*) and John Bolton (*Pacific Comics*).

30. Robert Jamieson, *Popular Ballads and Songs*, 2 vols (Edinburgh: Constable, 1806); H. W. Weber, R. Jamieson and Walter Scott, *Illustrations of Northern Antiquities* (Edinburgh: 1814).

31. Robert Browning, 'Childe Roland to the Dark Tower Came', in *Poetical Works*, ed. Ian Jack (London: Oxford University Press, 1970), p. 20, lines 121–4.

32. Archibald Maclaren, *The Fairy Family, a series of ballads and metrical tales, illustrating the fairy mythology of Europe* (London: 1857), pp. 59ff.

33. 'Cold Iron' (1909), in Rudyard Kipling, *Rewards and Fairies* (Harmondsworth: Penguin, 1991), pp. 53–67.

34. Charlotte Mew, 'The Changeling', in *Collected Poems and Prose* (London: Virago, 1982), pp. 13–14.

35. Walter de la Mare, 'Peak and Puke', in *Collected Rhymes and Verses* (London: Faber, 1989), p. 141.

36. J. W. Waterhouse, *La Belle Dame Sans Merci* (1893), oil on canvas, in the Hessisches Landesmuseum, Darmstadt.

37. *Art Journal* 16 (1864).

38. Edward Burne-Jones, *Morgan Le Fay* (1862), Leighton House, Kensington.

39. Hans Christian Andersen, 'The Little Mermaid', in *The Penguin Complete Fairy Tales and Stories of Hans Andersen*, trans. Erik Christian Haugaard (Harmondsworth: Penguin, 1985), pp. 57–76; Alison Prince, *Hans Christian Andersen: The Fan Dancer* (London: Allison & Busby, 1998).

40. Hans Christian Andersen, 'The Snow Queen', in *The Penguin Complete Fairy Tales and Stories of Hans Andersen*, pp. 234–62.

41. Alan Sinfield, *The Wilde Century* (London: Cassell, 1994).

42. Richard Dadd, *The Fairy Feller's Master-Stroke* (1855–64), Tate Britain; David Greysmith, *Richard Dadd. The Rock and the Castle of Seclusion* (London: Studio Vista, 1973).

43. John Millais, *Ferdinand Lured By Ariel* (1849), Makins Collection.

44. Gary Jay Williams, *Our Moonlight Revels: A Midsummer Night's Dream in the Theatre* (Iowa City: University of Iowa Press, 1997), p. 113.

45. John Anster Fitzgerald, *The Captive Robin* (n.d.), private collection; *The Chase of the White Mice* (c. 1864), Mrs Nicolette Wernick; *The Artist's Dream* (1857), private collection; *The Stuff That Dreams Are Made Of* (1858), private collection: all reproduced in Maas et al., *Victorian Fairy Painting*. Fitzgerald's paintings are also discussed by Carole G. Silver, *Strange and Secret Peoples: Fairies and Victorian Consciousness* (New York and Oxford: Oxford University Press, 1999), pp. 160, 162.

46. J. E. Taylor, *The Fairy Ring: a new collection of popular tales*, illustrated by Richard Doyle (London: Murray, 1846); Robert Huskisson, *The Mother's Blessing* (1848), private collection.

47. Lewis Carroll, 'Bruno's Revenge', first published 1867, in Jack Zipes, *Victorian Fairy Tales*, pp. 73–87, esp. 75; later revised as *Sylvie and Bruno*, in *The Works of Lewis Carroll* (London: Hamlyn, 1965), pp. 377–533.

48. Lewis Carroll, 'Acrostic', *The Works of Lewis* Carroll, p. 859.

49. J. A. Froude, *The Nemesis of Faith* (1904), p. 116.

50. Julia Briggs, *A Woman of Passion: The Life of E. Nesbit 1858–1924* (Harmondsworth: Penguin, 1987), p. 222; Compton Mackenzie, *Hunting the Fairies* (Harmondsworth: Penguin, 1959), p. 223.

51. Rose Fyleman, *Fairies and Chimneys* (Methuen: London, 1918), p. 8. This Fyleman poem was first published in *Punch*, 23 May 1917.

52. Helen Douglas Adams, *The Elfin Pedlar, and Tales Told by Pixy Pool* (New York and London: Putnam's, 1924), p. 45.

53. Archibald Maclaren, *The Fairy Family* (London: 1857), pp. 34ff.

54. Edith Howes, *The Cradle Ship* (London: Cassell, 1916).

55. Elizabeth Goudge, *The Fairies' Baby, and other stories* (London: W. & G. Foyle, 1919), pp. 3, 5.

56. M. Wallace-Dunlop and M. Rivett-Carnac, *Fairies, Elves and Flower Babies* (London: Duckworth, 1899), pp. 7, 11.

57. Goudge, *The Fairies' Baby*, p. 7.

58. Cecil Starr Johns, *The Fairies' Annual* (London and New York: John Lane, [1918]), p. 65.

59. T. Mullett Ellis, *The Fairies' Favourite; or, The Story of Queen Victoria told for children* (London: Ash Partners, 1897), pp. 33, 41, 42.

60. Algernon Charles Swinburne, 'The Triumph of Gloriana' (1881), ed. Edmund Gosse (London: privately printed, 1916).

61. Johns, *The Fairies' Annual*, p. 118.

62. *Fairy Tales. Published by command of . . . Gloriana, Queen of Fairyland. By a soldier of the Queen* (London and Edinburgh: 1879 [1878]), p. 12.

63. Wallace-Dunlop and Rivett-Carnac, *Fairies, Elves and Flower Babies*, p. 10.

64. Mark Lemon, *Tinykin's Transformation* (London: 1869).

65. *Jim Crow's Trip to Fairyland* (London: 1913).

66. Rudyard Kipling, 'Dymchurch Flit' (1906), in *Puck of Pook's Hill* (Harmondsworth: Penguin, 1990), pp. 182–93.

67. Rudyard Kipling, 'Baa Baa Black Sheep' (1888), in *Wee Willie Winkie* (Harmondsworth: Penguin, 1989), pp. 260–88.

8. Tinker Bell's Magic and the Fairies' Call to War

1. Sir Edward Seymour Hicks, *Bluebell in Fairyland* (London and New York: 1927), pp. 11, 13, 49, 32, 34.

2. On the manuscript and printed versions of *Peter Pan*, see Jacqueline Rose, *The Case of Peter Pan, or the impossibility of children's fiction* (London: Methuen, 1984), pp. 157–9, and Roger Lancelyn Green, *Fifty years of Peter Pan* (London: Peter Davies, 1954), pp. 140–42.

3. Lancelyn Green, *Fifty years of Peter Pan*, p. 69.

4. 'The Beautiful Mothers Scene', performed for part of the first run in 1904, Beinecke MS, cited in Lancelyn Green, *Fifty years of Peter Pan*, pp. 56–8.

5. Lancelyn Green, *Fifty years of Peter Pan*, p. 79.

6. Bruce K. Hanson, *The Peter Pan Chronicles* (New York: Birch Lane Press, 1993), pp. 102–3, Lancelyn Green, *Fifty years of Peter Pan*, pp. 121–3.

7. Quotations from the prose version of *Peter Pan* are taken from *Peter and Wendy*, ed. Peter Hollindale (Oxford: Oxford World's Classics, 1991), pp. 94, 88.

8. Catherine Haill and Nanette Newman, *Dear Peter Pan . . .* (London: Victoria & Albert Museum, 1983).

9. Andrew Birkin, *James Barrie and the Lost Boys* (London: Constable, 1979), p. 202.

10. Lancelyn Green, *Fifty years of Peter Pan*, p. 132–4.

11. Barrie's life: Andrew Birkin and Janet Dunbar, *J. M. Barrie: The Man behind the Image* (London: Collins, 1970); *The Little White Bird* (London: Hodder & Stoughton, 1902).

12. Rudyard Kipling, 'They', in *Traffics and Discoveries* (London: Macmillan, 1908), pp. 303–35; W. W. Jacobs, 'The Monkey's Paw, in *The Oxford Book of English Ghost Stories*, ed. Michael Cox and R. A. Gilbert (Oxford: Oxford University Press, 1989), pp. 180–89.

13. *Pinkie and the fairies* (London and New York, 1932), p.25.

14. *Fairy Star's Annual* (London: 1928).

15. Margaret Behrens, *Puck in Petticoats* (London: Jenkins, 1931).

16. Arthur Ransome, *Highways and Byways in Fairyland* (1906).

17. John Betjeman, *Summoned by Bells* (London: Murray, 1960), pp. 17–18.

18. *Britain's Defenders, or Peggy's peep into fairyland, a fairy play* (London and New York: Samuel French, 1917), p. 6.

19. Eleanor Gray, *The War Fairies* (1917), p. 2.

20. Robert Graves, *Fairies and Fusiliers* (London: William Heinemann: 1917).

21. *Broken Images: Selected Letters of Robert Graves 1914–1946*, ed. Paul O'Prey (London: Hutchinson, 1982), p. 86.

22. Graves, *Fairies and Fusiliers*, p. 37.

23. Paul Fussell, *The Great War and Modern Memory* (Oxford: Oxford University Press, 1977), pp. 135–7.

24. J. R. R. Tolkien, 'The Fall of Gondolin' and 'The Cottage of Lost Play', in *The Book of Lost Tales*, Part II (1984), pp. 144–220; Part I (1983), pp. 13–20; *Lord of the Rings* (1954–5); *The Silmarillion* (1977): all London: Allen & Unwin.

9. Photographing Fairies, and the Celtic Revival

1. Edward L. Gardner, *A Book of Real Fairies: the Cottingley photographs and their sequel* (London: Theosophical Publishing House, 1945); Arthur Conan Doyle, *The Coming of the Fairies* (London: Hodder, 1922), which reprints the articles from the *Strand Magazine* in more detail (*Strand*, December 1920, pp. 463–8; March 1921, pp. 199–201); Alex Owen in 'Doyle, Albion's Daughters, and the Politics of the Cottingley Fairies', *History Workshop Journal* 38 (1994), pp. 48–85; Joe Cooper, *The Case of the Cottingley Fairies* (London: Robert Hale, 1990).

2. Barbara Allen, 'The image on glass: technology, tradition, and the emergence of folklore', *Western Folklore* 41 (1982), pp. 85–103; Ronald Baker, 'The influence of mass culture on Modern legends', *Southern Folklore Quarterly* 40 (1976), pp. 367–76; Stewart Sanderson, 'The Cottingley Photographs: A Re-appraisal of the Evidence', *Folklore* 84 (1973), pp. 89–103.

3. Alex Owen, *The Darkened Room: Women, Power and Spiritualism in Late Victorian England* (London: Virago, 1989).

4. *Fairy Tales From Fairyland*, by 'Donald' and others, 1900, Preface.

5. Owen, *The Darkened Room*.

6. Doyle, *The Coming of the Fairies*, p. 468.

7. Edward Gardner, Letter to Conan Doyle, 25 June 1920, cited in *ibid.*, p. 17.

8. Cooper, *The Case of the Cottingley Fairies*, p. 192.

9. 'Do Fairies Exist?', *Westminster Gazette* (12 January 1921), p. 50.

10. Owen, 'Doyle, Albion's Daughters, and the Politics of the Cottingley Fairies', p. 67.

11. Geoffrey Hudson, *Fairies at Work and Play* (Theosophical Publishing House: London, 1925).

12. Cooper, *The Case of the Cottingley Fairies*, p. 137.

13. *Ibid.*, p. 175.

14. Owen, 'Doyle, Albion's Daughters, and the Politics of the Cottingley Fairies', p. 55.

15. *Fairy Tale: A True Story* (Paramount, 1997).

16. http://www.fairytalemovie.com.

17. This photograph is in the Brotherton Collection, Leeds University Library.

18. Janet Bord, *Fairies: Real Encounters with Little People* (New York: Carroll & Graf, 1997).

19. Micheál Coimin, *Laoi Oisin i dTir na nÓg* (1750), ed. and trans. Tomás O' Flannghaile (Dublin: 1907). In earlier versions of the Oisin story, Niamh is merely a mortal woman who elopes with Oisin.

20. Douglas Hyde, *Beside The Fire* (1890), pp. xvi–xvii.

21. W. B. Yeats, *The Celtic Twilight* (Gerrards Cross: Colin Smythe, 1994), p. 38.

22. W. B. Yeats, 'The Land of Heart's Desire' (1894), in *The Collected Plays of W. B. Yeats* (London: Macmillan, 1982), pp. 51–72.

23. Tim Pat Coogan, *Michael Collins* (London: Arrow Books, 1991), p. 37.

24. Padraic Pearse, *Collected Works*, 3 vols (Dublin and London: Maunsel, 1917–22), vol. 3, pp. 300–301.

25. *A Servant of the Queen: The Autobiography of Maud Gonne*, ed. Norman Jeffares and Anna McBride White (Chicago: University of Chicago Press, 1994; first published 1938), p. 134.

26. W. B. Yeats, *The Poems* (London: Dent, 1994): 'The Stolen Child', pp. 44–5; 'A Faery Song', pp. 58–9; 'The Host of the Air', pp. 74–5; 'The Man Who Dreamed of Faeryland', pp. 64–6; 'The Song of Wandering Aengus', pp. 76–7.

27. Brenda Maddox, *George's Ghosts: A New Life of W. B. Yeats* (London: Picador, 1999), pp. 145–6.

28. Lady Gregory, *Selected Writings* (Harmondsworth: Penguin, 1995). The bulk of Gregory's fairy folklore can be found in her *Visions and Beliefs in the West of Ireland* (Gerrards Cross: Colin Smythe, 1976)).

29. Appeared in print November 1893; indebted to William Allingham's 'The Dream'.

30. William Wilde, *Irish Popular Superstitions* (Dublin: 1852), p. 134.

31. William Allingham, *The Fairies. A child's song* (London: Hodder & Stoughton, 1912).

32. Yeats, 'The Host of the Air', lines 33–6.

33. Angela Bourke, 'Reading a Woman's Death: Colonial Texts and Oral

Tradition in Nineteenth-Century Ireland', *Feminist Studies* 21 (1995), pp. 553–86; and *The Burning of Bridget Cleary: A True Story* (London: Pimlico, 1999).

34. 'How the Shoemaker Saved His Wife', *Fairy Legends from Donegal*, collected by Sean O hEochaidh, trans. Máire Mac Neill (Dublin: University College Dublin Press, 1977), p. 59.

35. 'The Orphan and the Fairy Boy', in *Sceálta Chois Cladaigh, Stories of Sea and Shore*, pp. 15–18, and the haunting ballad in Seán Ó hEochaidh, Máire Ní Néill and Séamas Ó Catháin, *Síscéalta ó Thír Chonaill: Fairy Legends from Donegal* (Dublin: University College Dublin Press, 1977), pp. 67–9.

36. Gregory, *Visions and Beliefs*, p. 132.

37. Angela Bourke, 'Fairies and anorexia: Nuala Ni Dhomhnaill's "Amazing Grass"', p. 32.

38. Yeats, 'The Stolen Child', in *The Poems*, pp. 44–5, lines 13–27, 42–53.

10. Fairy Bubbles and Alien Abductions

1. Bord, *Fairies: Real Encounters with Little People*, p. 55.

2. Marion Zimmer Bradley, *The Mists of Avalon* (London: Fontana, 1988); T. H. White, *The Once and Future King* (London: Fontana, 1979), pp. 107–10.

3. *FernGully: The Last Rainforest* (Fox, 1992).

4. Alice Thomas Ellis, *Fairy Tale* (Harmondsworth: Penguin, 1997); Peter S. Beagle, *The Folk of the Air* (London: Headline, 1987); Alan Garner, *The Weirdstone of Brisingamen* (Harmondsworth: Penguin, 1963), and *The Moon of Gomrath* (Penguin, 1965).

5. Procter and Gamble, information sent upon request.

6. Antonia Forest, *Autumn Term* (Harmondsworth: Penguin, 1977).

7. Lawrence Schiller, *Perfect Murder, Perfect Town: JonBenet and the City of Boulder* (New York: HarperCollins, 1997). On JonBenet and child beauty pageants: Henry C. Giroux, 'Stealing Innocence: The Politics of Child Beauty Pageants', in *The Children's Culture Reader*, ed. Henry Jenkins (New York and London: New York University Press, 1998), pp. 265–82, esp. pp. 269–70.

8. Cicely Mary Barker, *The Complete Book of the Flower Fairies* (London: Warne, 1997), pp. 38, 24; James R. Kincaid, *Erotic Innocence: The Culture of Child Molesting* (Durham, NC, and London: Duke University Press, 1998).

9. *Flower Fairies Activity Book* (London: Warne, 1997).

10. *The Flower Fairies Fancy Dress Book* (London: Warne, 1999); Rosalind Coward, *Our Treacherous Hearts: Why Women Let Men Get Their Way* (London: Faber, 1992), pp. 77–9.

11. Susan Faludi, *Stiffed: Scenes from the Betrayal of Modern Man* (London: Chatto & Windus, 1999), p. 253.

12. Penny Dann, *The Secret Fairy Handbook, or How to be a Little Fairy* (London: Orchard, 1997).

13. Sigmund Freud, *The Interpretation of Dreams*. The Pelican Freud Library, 4 (Harmondsworth: Penguin, 1986), pp. 508–16; Rosemary Wells, 'The Making of an Icon: The Tooth Fairy in North American Folklore and Popular Culture', and Ted Tuleja, 'The Tooth Fairy: Perspectives on Money and Magic', in Narvaez, *The Good People: New Fairylore Essays*, pp. 406–25 and 426–54.

14. http://www.gossamer.x-philes.com, and see also http://www.ddeb.com; 'ddeb' stands for David Duchovny Estrogen Brigade; http://web.ukonline.co.uk/members/xfilesfanficarchive.d/contents.htm. This is the URL for The Gossamer Project, which tries to archive every X-Files fanfiction written and posted on the Net. There are many stories on fairies apart from those discussed here, and even an author whose penname (e-name?) is Queen Mab.

15. Kellie Matthews-Simons, 'Ancient Days', *http://spot.colorado.edu.matthewk/xfiles.htm*: author's permission to quote.

16. 'Fairy Story', in *The Collected Poems of Stevie Smith*, ed. James MacGibbon (Harmondsworth: Allen Lane, 1975), p. 487.

17. Ann Druffel, *How to Defend Yourself Against Alien Abduction* (London: Piatkus, 1998), pp. 99–100.

18. Gilbert Rodman, *Elvis after Elvis: The Posthumous Career of a Living Legend* (London: Routledge, 1997).

Index